Adobe® Illustrator® CS6
The Professional Portfolio

AGAINST THE CLOCK
mastering graphic technology

Managing Editor: Ellenn Behoriam
Cover & Interior Design: Erika Kendra
Copy Editor: Angelina Kendra
Printer: Prestige Printers

10   9   8   7   6   5   4   3   2   1

978-1-936201-13-6

AGAINST THE CLOCK

mastering graphic technology

4710 28th Street North, Saint Petersburg, FL 33714
800-256-4ATC • www.againsttheclock.com

Acknowledgements

ABOUT AGAINST THE CLOCK

Against The Clock, long recognized as one of the nation's leaders in courseware development, has been publishing high-quality educational materials for the graphic and computer arts industries since 1990. The company has developed a solid and widely-respected approach to teaching people how to effectively utilize graphics applications, while maintaining a disciplined approach to real-world problems.

Having developed the *Against The Clock* and the *Essentials for Design* series with Prentice Hall/Pearson Education, ATC drew from years of professional experience and instructor feedback to develop *The Professional Portfolio Series*, focusing on the Adobe Creative Suite. These books feature step-by-step explanations, detailed foundational information, and advice and tips from industry professionals that offer practical solutions to technical issues.

Against The Clock works closely with all major software developers to create learning solutions that fulfill both the requirements of instructors and the needs of students. Thousands of graphic arts professionals — designers, illustrators, imaging specialists, prepress experts, and production managers — began their educations with Against The Clock training books. These professionals studied at Baker College, Nossi College of Art, Virginia Tech, Appalachian State University, Keiser College, University of South Carolina, Gress Graphic Arts Institute, Hagerstown Community College, Kean University, Southern Polytechnic State University, Brenau University, and many other educational institutions.

ABOUT THE AUTHOR

Erika Kendra holds a BA in History and a BA in English Literature from the University of Pittsburgh. She began her career in the graphic communications industry as an editor at Graphic Arts Technical Foundation before moving to Los Angeles in 2000. Erika is the author or co-author of more than twenty books about Adobe graphic design software. She has also written several books about graphic design concepts such as color reproduction and preflighting, and dozens of articles for online and print journals in the graphics industry. Working with Against The Clock for more than ten years, Erika was a key partner in developing *The Professional Portfolio Series* of software training books.

CONTRIBUTING AUTHORS, ARTISTS, AND EDITORS

A big thank you to the people whose artwork, comments, and expertise contributed to the success of these books:

- **Bill Carberry,** Adobe Certified Instructor, ACI4Hire
- **Jorge Diaz,** International Academy of Design & Technology-Tampa
- **Pamela Harris,** Missouri Southern State University
- **Debbie Davidson,** Against The Clock, Inc.
- **Matthew Guanciale,** Against The Clock, Inc

Finally, thanks also to **Angelina Kendra**, editor, for making sure that we all said what we meant to say.

Project Goals

Each project begins with a clear description of the overall concepts that are explained in the project; these goals closely match the different "stages" of the project workflow.

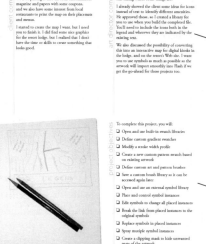

The Project Meeting

Each project includes the client's initial comments, which provide valuable information about the job. The Project Art Director, a vital part of any design workflow, also provides fundamental advice and production requirements.

Project Objectives

Each Project Meeting includes a summary of the specific skills required to complete the project.

Real-World Workflow

Projects are broken into logical lessons or "stages" of the workflow. Brief introductions at the beginning of each stage provide vital foundational material required to complete the task.

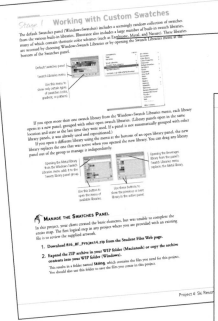

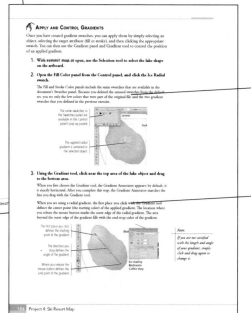

Step-By-Step Exercises

Every stage of the workflow is broken into multiple hands-on, step-by-step exercises.

Visual Explanations

Wherever possible, screen shots are annotated so you can quickly identify important information.

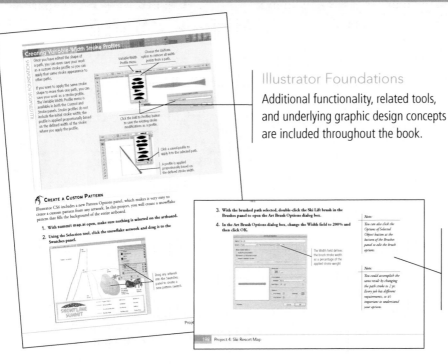

Illustrator Foundations

Additional functionality, related tools, and underlying graphic design concepts are included throughout the book.

Advice and Warnings

Where appropriate, sidebars provide shortcuts, warnings, or tips about the topic at hand.

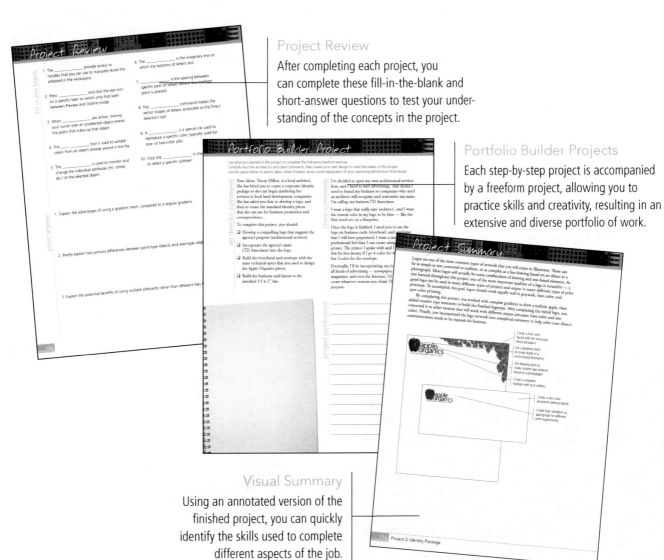

Project Review

After completing each project, you can complete these fill-in-the-blank and short-answer questions to test your understanding of the concepts in the project.

Portfolio Builder Projects

Each step-by-step project is accompanied by a freeform project, allowing you to practice skills and creativity, resulting in an extensive and diverse portfolio of work.

Visual Summary

Using an annotated version of the finished project, you can quickly identify the skills used to complete different aspects of the job.

The Against The Clock *Portfolio Series* teaches graphic design software tools and techniques entirely within the framework of real-world projects; we introduce and explain skills where they would naturally fall into a real project workflow.

The project-based approach in *The Professional Portfolio Series* allows you to get in depth with the software beginning in Project 1 — you don't have to read several chapters of introductory material before you can start creating finished artwork.

Our approach also prevents "topic tedium" — in other words, we don't require you to read pages and pages of information about text (for example); instead, we explain text tools and options as part of larger project (e.g., creating a logotype or building a folding brochure).

Clear, easy-to-read, step-by-step instructions walk you through every phase of each job, from creating a new file to saving the finished piece. Wherever logical, we also offer practical advice and tips about underlying concepts and graphic design practices that will benefit you as you enter the job market.

The projects in this book reflect a range of different types of Illustrator jobs, from creating a series of icons to designing a corporate identity to building a Web page. When you finish the eight projects in this book (and the accompanying Portfolio Builder exercises), you will have a substantial body of work that should impress any potential employer.

The eight Illustrator CS6 projects are described briefly here; more detail is provided in the full table of contents (beginning on Page viii).

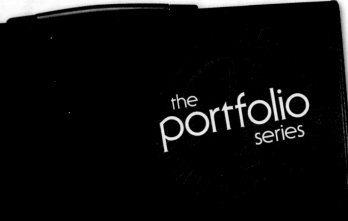

project 1

International Symbols

❏ Setting up the Workspace

❏ Drawing Basic Shapes

project 2

Balloon Festival Artwork

❏ Drawing Complex Artwork

❏ Coloring and Painting Artwork

❏ Exporting EPS and PDF Files

project 3

Identity Package

❏ Working with Gradient Meshes

❏ Working with Type

❏ Working with Multiple Artboards

❏ Combining Text and Graphics

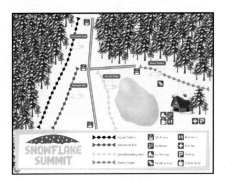

Our goal in this book is to familiarize you with the majority of the Illustrator tool set so you can be more productive and more marketable in your career as a graphic designer.

It is important to keep in mind that Illustrator is an extremely versatile and powerful application. The sheer volume of available tools, panels, and features can seem intimidating when you first look at the software interface. Most of these tools, however, are fairly simple to use with a bit of background information and a little practice.

Wherever necessary, we explain the underlying concepts and terms that are required for understanding the software. We're confident that these projects provide the practice you need to be able to create sophisticated artwork by the end of the very first project.

Contents

Contents

Contents

PREREQUISITES

The Professional Portfolio Series is based on the assumption that you have a basic understanding of how to use your computer. You should know how to use your mouse to point and click, as well as how to drag items around the screen. You should be able to resize and arrange windows on your desktop to maximize your available space. You should know how to access drop-down menus, and understand how check boxes and radio buttons work. It also doesn't hurt to have a good understanding of how your operating system organizes files and folders, and how to navigate your way around them. If you're familiar with these fundamental skills, then you know all that's necessary to use *The Professional Portfolio Series*.

RESOURCE FILES

All of the files you need to complete the projects in this book — except, of course, the Illustrator application files — are on the Student Files Web page at www.againsttheclock.com. See the inside back cover of this book for access information.

Each archive (ZIP) file is named according to the related project (e.g., **AI6_RF_Project1.zip**). At the beginning of each project, you must download the archive file for that project and expand that archive to access the resource files that you need to complete the exercises. Detailed instructions for this process are included in the Interface chapter.

Files required for the related Portfolio Builder exercises at the end of each project are also available on the Student Files page; these archives are also named by project (e.g., **AI6_PB_Project1.zip**).

ATC FONTS

You must download and install the ATC fonts from the Student Files Web page to ensure that your exercises and projects will work as described in the book. Specific instructions for installing fonts are provided in the documentation that came with your computer. You should replace older (pre-2004) ATC fonts with the ones on the Student Files Web page.

SYSTEM REQUIREMENTS

The Professional Portfolio Series was designed to work on both Macintosh or Windows computers; where differences exist from one platform to another, we include specific instructions relative to each platform. One issue that remains different from Macintosh to Windows is the use of different modifier keys (Control, Shift, etc.) to accomplish the same task. When we present key commands, we follow the Macintosh/Windows format — Macintosh keys are listed first, then a slash, followed by the Windows key commands.

Minimum System Requirements for Adobe Illustrator CS6:

Windows
- Intel® Pentium® 4 or AMD Athlon® 64 processor
- Microsoft® Windows® XP with Service Pack 3 or Windows 7 with Service Pack 1
- 1 GB of RAM (3 GB recommended) for 32 bit; 2 GB of RAM (8 GB recommended) for 64 bit
- 2GB of available hard-disk space for installation; additional free space required during installation (cannot install on removable flash storage devices)
- 1024×768 display (1280×800 recommended) with 16-bit video card
- DVD-ROM drive compatible with dual-layer DVDs

Mac OS
- Multicore Intel processor with 64-bit support
- Mac OS X v10.6.8 or v10.7
- 2 GB of RAM (8 GB recommended)
- 2 GB of available hard-disk space for installation; additional free space required during installation (cannot install on a volume that uses a case-sensitive file system or on removable flash storage devices)
- 1024×768 display (1280×800 recommended) with 16-bit video card
- DVD-ROM drive compatible with dual-layer DVDs

The software will not operate without activation. Broadband Internet connection and registration are required for software activation, validation of subscriptions, and access to online services. Phone activation is not available.

Adobe Illustrator is the industry-standard application for creating digital drawings or **vector images** (graphics composed of mathematically defined lines instead of pixels). Our goal in this book is to teach you how to use the available tools to create different types of work that you might encounter in your professional career. Some projects focus specifically on creating graphics and illustrations — which is the true heart of the application. And, although we do not advocate doing *all* page-layout work in Illustrator, we do recognize that many people use the application to create complete designs; Project 5: Letterfold Brochure, for example, uses Illustrator to combine different elements into a finished product.

Although not intended as a page-layout application, you can use the tools in Illustrator to combine type, graphics, and images into a cohesive design. Many people create flyers, posters, and other projects entirely within Illustrator. With the multiple-artboard capability that is explained in Project 3: Identity Package and Project 5: Letterfold Brochure, we will likely see more of this type of Illustrator work in the future.

The simple exercises in this introduction are designed to allow you to explore the Illustrator user interface. Whether you are new to the application or upgrading from a previous version, we highly recommend that you follow these steps to click around and become familiar with the basic workspace. When you work on Project 1, you will be better prepared to jump right in and start creating digital artwork.

Note:

Some people argue that Adobe Illustrator should not be used for page layout and that Adobe InDesign is the preferred page-layout application. However, the tools needed for basic page design are built into Illustrator CS6, so many people use Illustrator for that type of job, rather than buying a second application.

 ## EXPLORE THE ILLUSTRATOR INTERFACE

The first time you launch Illustrator, you will see the default user interface (UI) settings as defined by Adobe. When you relaunch after you or another user has quit, the workspace defaults to the last-used settings — including open panels and the position of those panels on your screen. We designed the following exercise so you can explore different ways of controlling panels in the Illustrator user interface.

1. **Create a new empty folder named WIP on any writable disk (where you plan to save your work).**

2. **Download the AI6_RF_Interface.zip archive from the Student Files Web page.**

3. **Macintosh users: Place the ZIP archive in your WIP folder, then double-click the file icon to expand it.**

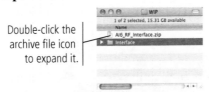

Double-click the archive file icon to expand it.

Windows users: Double-click the ZIP archive file to open it. Click the folder inside the archive and drag it into your primary WIP folder.

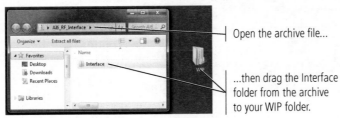

Open the archive file...

...then drag the Interface folder from the archive to your WIP folder.

The resulting **Interface** folder contains all the files you need to complete the exercises in this introduction.

4. **Macintosh users: While pressing Command-Option-Shift, launch Illustrator. Hold down the modifier keys until Illustrator opens.**

   Windows users: Launch Illustrator, then immediately press Control-Alt-Shift. Hold down the modifier keys until Illustrator opens.

   This step resets Illustrator to the preference settings that are defined by Adobe as the application defaults. This helps to ensure that your application functions in the same way as what we show in our screen shots.

5. **Open the Window>Workspace menu.**

   If you see a Reset Essentials option near the bottom, choose that option. If the Reset command has any other workspace name, choose Essentials near the top of the list, then choose Window>Workspace>Reset Essentials.

   Note:

   Saved workspaces (accessed in the Window>Workspaces menu, or in the Workspace switcher on the Application/Menu bar) provide one-click access to a defined group of tools.

   This step might or might not do anything, depending on what was done in Illustrator before you started this project. If you or someone else changed anything and then quit the application, those changes are remembered when Illustrator is relaunched. Because we can't be sure what your default settings show, by completing this step you are resetting the user interface to one of the built-in, default workspaces so your screen shots will match ours.

6. **Macintosh users: Open the Window menu and choose Application Frame to toggle that option on.**

   Many menu commands and options in Illustrator are **toggles**, which means they are either on or off; when an option is already checked, that option is toggled on (visible or active). You can toggle an active option off by choosing the checked menu command, or toggle an inactive option on by choosing the unchecked menu command.

This option should be checked.

On Macintosh systems, the Application bar includes a link to the Adobe Bridge application, a panel with different arrangements for tiling multiple open documents, a menu for accessing different saved workspaces, and a search option. On Windows systems, those options are available on the right side of the Menu bar.

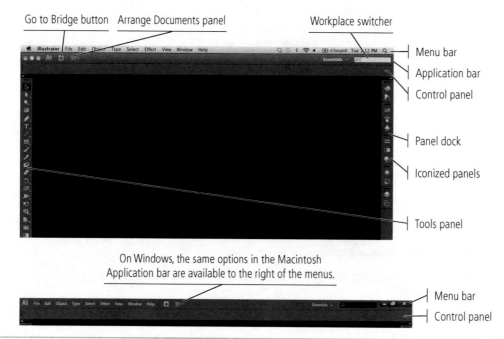

Go to Bridge button   Arrange Documents panel   Workplace switcher

Menu bar
Application bar
Control panel

Panel dock

Iconized panels

Tools panel

On Windows, the same options in the Macintosh Application bar are available to the right of the menus.

Menu bar
Control panel

In general, the Macintosh and Windows workspaces are very similar, but there are a few slight differences:

- On Macintosh, the application's title bar appears below the Menu bar; the Close, Minimize, and Restore buttons appear on the left side of the title bar, and the menu bar is not part of the Application frame.
- On Windows, the Close, Minimize, and Restore buttons appear at the right end of the Menu bar, which is part of the overall Application frame.

Also, Macintosh users have two extra menus (consistent with the Macintosh operating system structure). The Apple menu provides access to system-specific commands. The Illustrator menu follows the Macintosh system-standard format for all applications; this menu controls basic application operations such as About, Hide, Preferences, and Quit.

7. **Macintosh users: Choose Illustrator>Preferences>User Interface.**
   Windows users: Choose Edit>Preferences>User Interface.

Remember that on Macintosh systems, the Preferences dialog box is accessed in the Illustrator menu; Windows users access the Preferences dialog box in the Edit menu.

Preferences customize the way many of the program's tools and options function. When you open the Preferences dialog box, the active pane is the one you choose in the Preferences submenu. Once open, however, you can access any of the Preference categories by clicking a different option in the left pane; the right side of the dialog box displays options related to the active category.

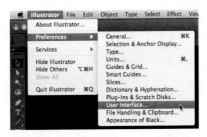

Note:

If a menu option is greyed out, it is not available for the active selection.

Understanding the Application Frame

ILLUSTRATOR FOUNDATIONS

On Windows, each running application is contained within its own frame; all elements of the application — including the Menu bar, panels, tools, and open documents — are contained within the Application frame.

Adobe also offers the Application frame to Macintosh users as an option for controlling your workspace. When the Application frame is active, the entire workspace exists in a

self-contained area that can be moved around the screen. All elements of the workspace (excluding the Menu bar) move when you move the Application frame.

The Application frame is inactive by default; you can toggle it on by choosing Window>Application Frame. If the menu option is checked, the Application frame is active; if the menu option is not checked, it is inactive.

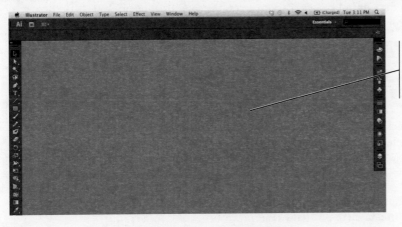

When the Application frame is not active, the desktop is visible behind the workspace elements.

8. In the Brightness section, choose any option that you prefer.

If you have used a previous version of Illustrator, you might have already noticed the rather dark appearance of the panels and interface background. In CS6, the application uses the medium-dark "theme" as the default. (We used the Light option throughout this book because text in the interface elements is easier to read in printed screen captures.)

9. Check the option to Auto-Collapse Iconic Panels, then click OK to close the Preferences dialog box.

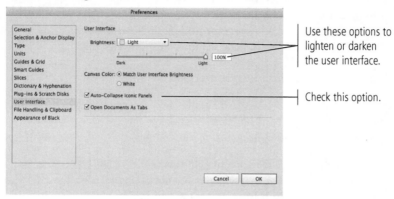

Use these options to lighten or darken the user interface.

Check this option.

10. Continue to the next exercise.

 EXPLORE THE ARRANGEMENT OF ILLUSTRATOR PANELS

As you gain experience and familiarity with Illustrator, you will develop personal artistic and working styles. Illustrator includes a number of options for arranging and managing the numerous panels so you can customize and personalize the workspace to suit your specific needs.

We designed the following exercise to give you an opportunity to explore different ways of controlling Illustrator panels. Because workspace preferences are largely a matter of personal taste, the projects in this book instruct you to use certain tools and panels, but where you place those elements within the interface is up to you.

1. With Illustrator open, Control/right-click the title bar above the column of docked panel icons. Make sure the Auto-Collapse Iconic Panels option is checked, then click away from the contextual menu to dismiss it.

As we explained in the Getting Started section, when commands are different for the Macintosh and Windows operating systems, we include the different commands in the Macintosh/Windows format. In this case, Macintosh users who do not have right-click mouse capability can press the Control key and click to access the contextual menu. You do not have to press Control *and* right-click to access the menus.

Dock title bar

This option should be checked (active).

Control/right-clicking a dock title bar opens the dock contextual menu, where you can change the default panel behavior. Many elements in Illustrator have contextual menus, which make it easy to access item-specific options.

Because you turned on the Auto-Collapse option in the User Interface preferences, this toggle is already checked. You can use either option — preference or contextual menu command — to toggle the option on or off at any time.

2. In the panel dock, click the third button from the top (Swatches).

Most Illustrator functionality is accessed in one of 34 panels. Virtually everything you do in Illustrator requires interacting with at least one panel; more often than not, you will use multiple panels to complete any given project.

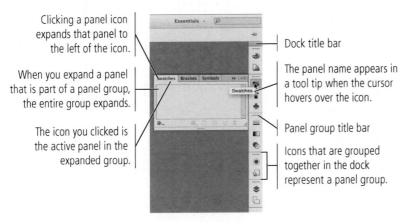

Clicking a panel icon expands that panel to the left of the icon.

When you expand a panel that is part of a panel group, the entire group expands.

The icon you clicked is the active panel in the expanded group.

Dock title bar

The panel name appears in a tool tip when the cursor hovers over the icon.

Panel group title bar

Icons that are grouped together in the dock represent a panel group.

3. Click away from the expanded panel, anywhere in the workspace.

Because the Auto-Collapse option is active, the expanded panel group collapses back to an icon when you click away from the panel.

4. Hover the mouse cursor over the left edge of the dock column until you see a two-facing arrow icon, then click the left edge of the docked panels (on the right side of the screen) and drag left.

When panels are iconized, you can expand the icons to show the panel names as well as the panel icons. This can be particularly useful until you become more familiar with the application and the icons used to symbolize the various panels.

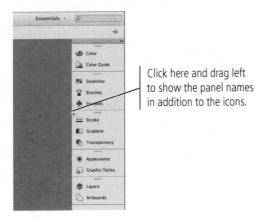

Click here and drag left to show the panel names in addition to the icons.

5. Double-click the dock title bar above the docked icons to expand the docked panels.

Double-clicking the dock title bar expands or collapses the entire dock column.

6. On the left side of the workspace, review the Tools panel. If you don't see all of the panel options, double-click the Tools panel title bar.

The Tools panel can be displayed as either one or two columns; double-clicking the Tools panel title bar toggles between these two modes.

Some monitors — especially laptops — are not high enough to display the large number of tools that are available in Illustrator's Tools panel. If this is the case, you should use the two-column mode.

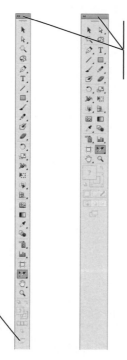

Double-click the Tools panel title bar to toggle between the one-column and two-column layouts.

If your monitor is not large enough to show all options, you should use the panel in two-column mode.

Note:

The Tools panel can also be floated by clicking its title bar and dragging away from the edge of the screen. To re-dock the floating Tools panel, simply click the title bar and drag back to the left edge of the screen.

ILLUSTRATOR FOUNDATIONS

The Illustrator Tools panel appears to contain 28 tools; however, many of the primary tools also have variations or similar tools nested under the primary tools.

Tool icons that show a small black arrow in the lower-right corner have **nested tools**. You can access nested tools by clicking the primary tool and holding down the mouse button until a pop-up menu shows the nested variations.

If you hover your mouse over a tool, a pop-up **tool tip** shows the name of the tool, as well as the associated keyboard shortcut for that tool if one exists. If a tool has a defined shortcut, pressing that key activates the associated tool. (If you don't see tool tips, check the Show Tool Tips option in the General pane of the Preferences dialog box.)

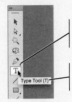

This arrow means the tool has other nested tools.

A tool tip shows the name of the tool.

If you drag the mouse cursor to the bar on the right of the nested-tool menu, the nested-tool options separate into their own floating toolboxes so you can more easily access the nested variations. (The primary tool is not removed from the main Tools panel.)

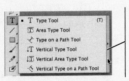

While holding down the mouse button, drag to here, then release the mouse button...

...to tear off a separate panel with all the related tools.

The chart to the right offers a quick reference of nested tools, as well as the keyboard shortcut for each tool (if any). Nested tools are shown indented and in italics.

- Selection tool (V)
- Direct Selection tool (A)
  - *Group Selection tool*
- Magic Wand tool (Y)
- Lasso tool (L)
- Pen tool (P)
  - *Add Anchor Point tool (+)*
  - *Delete Anchor Point tool (-)*
  - *Convert Anchor Point tool (Shift-C)*
- Type tool (T)
  - *Area Type tool*
  - *Type on a Path tool*
  - *Vertical Type tool*
  - *Vertical Area Type tool*
  - *Vertical Type on a Path tool*
- Line Segment tool (\)
  - *Arc tool*
  - *Spiral tool*
  - *Rectangular Grid tool*
  - *Polar Grid tool*
- Rectangle tool (M)
  - *Rounded Rectangle tool*
  - *Ellipse tool (L)*
  - *Polygon tool*
  - *Star tool*
  - *Flare tool*
- Paintbrush tool (B)
- Pencil tool (N)
  - *Smooth tool*
  - *Path Eraser tool*
- Blob Brush tool (Shift-B)
- Eraser tool (Shift-E)
  - *Scissors tool (C)*
  - *Knife tool*
- Rotate tool (R)
  - *Reflect tool (O)*
- Scale tool (S)
  - *Shear tool*
  - *Reshape tool*

- Width tool (Shift-W)
  - *Warp tool (Shift-R)*
  - *Twirl tool*
  - *Pucker tool*
  - *Bloat tool*
  - *Scallop tool*
  - *Crystallize tool*
  - *Wrinkle tool*
- Free Transform tool (E)
- Shape Builder tool (Shift-M)
  - *Live Paint Bucket tool (K)*
  - *Live Paint Selection tool (Shift-L)*
- Perspective Grid tool (Shift-P)
  - *Perspective Selection tool (Shift-V)*
- Mesh tool (U)
- Gradient tool (G)
- Eyedropper tool (I)
  - *Measure tool*
- Blend tool (W)
- Symbol Sprayer tool (Shift-S)
  - *Symbol Shifter tool*
  - *Symbol Scruncher tool*
  - *Symbol Sizer tool*
  - *Symbol Spinner tool*
  - *Symbol Stainer tool*
  - *Symbol Screener tool*
  - *Symbol Styler tool*
- Column Graph tool (J)
  - *Stacked Column Graph tool*
  - *Bar Graph tool*
  - *Stacked Bar Graph tool*
  - *Line Graph tool*
  - *Area Graph tool*
  - *Scatter Graph tool*
  - *Pie Graph tool*
  - *Radar Graph tool*
- Artboard tool (Shift-O)
- Slice tool (Shift-K)
  - *Slice Selection tool*
- Hand tool (H)
  - *Print Tiling tool*
- Zoom tool (Z)

7. With Illustrator open, choose Window>Symbols.

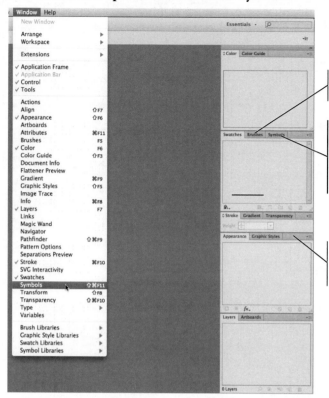

Each panel in the group is represented by a tab.

If you choose a panel that is already open in an expanded group, the selected panel comes to the front of the group.

The area behind the panel tabs is called the **drop zone**.

Note:

Individual panels can be toggled on and off using the Window menu.

If you choose a panel that is open but iconized, the panel expands to the left of its icon.

If you choose a panel that is open in an expanded group, that panel comes to the front of the group.

If you choose a panel that isn't currently open, it opens in the same position as when it was last closed.

8. Control/right-click the Symbols panel tab and choose Close from the contextual menu.

The panel's contextual menu is the only way to close a docked panel. You can also close an entire panel group by choosing Close Tab Group from the contextual menu.

Control/right-click the panel tab to access that panel's contextual menu.

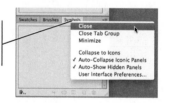

Note:

You can press the Tab key to temporarily hide all panels at one time. (Press the Tab key a second time to restore the same panels that were visible when you first pressed Tab.)

9. Click the drop zone in the panel group with the Swatches and Brushes panels, and drag away from the dock.

Panels and panel groups can be **floated** away from the dock by clicking a panel tab or the panel group's drop zone and dragging away from the dock.

This is the panel group drop zone.

When a group is expanded, click the group's drop zone to move the entire panel group.

When you release the mouse button, the panel group floats freely in the workspace.

Panel group title bar

10. Double-click the title bar of the floating panel group to iconize the group.

Floating panels (and panel groups) can be iconized just like panels in the dock.

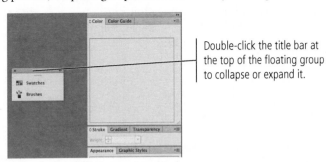

Double-click the title bar at the top of the floating group to collapse or expand it.

Note:

You can independently iconize or expand each floating panel (group) and each column of docked panels.

11. Click the Swatches panel icon (in the floating panel group) and drag the panel into the dock, below the first panel group. Release the mouse button.

Individual panels can be dragged to different locations (including into different groups) by dragging the panel's tab. The target location — where the panel will be located when you release the mouse button — is identified by the blue highlight.

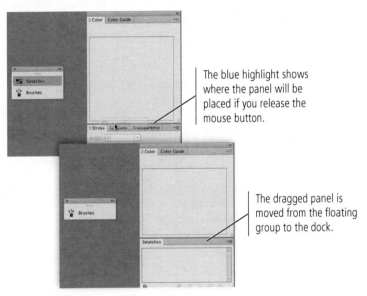

The blue highlight shows where the panel will be placed if you release the mouse button.

The dragged panel is moved from the floating group to the dock.

Note:

Most screen shots in this book show floating panels so we can focus on the most important issue in a particular image. In our production workflow, however, we make heavy use of docked and iconized panels and take full advantage of saved custom workspaces.

12. Click the Swatches panel tab, drag onto the drop zone area of the top panel group in the dock, then release the mouse button.

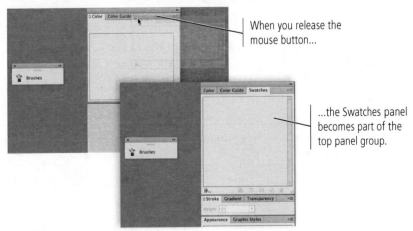

When you release the mouse button...

...the Swatches panel becomes part of the top panel group.

13. **Click the Appearance panel tab (in the dock), and drag the panel left until the blue highlight shows a second column added to the dock.**

You can create multiple columns of panels in the dock. This can be very useful if you need easy access to a large number of panels, and if you have a monitor with enough available screen space.

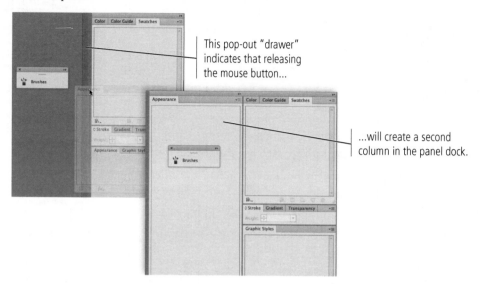

This pop-out "drawer" indicates that releasing the mouse button...

...will create a second column in the panel dock.

14. **Double-click the title bar above the left dock column to collapse the left column.**

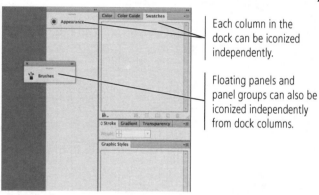

Each column in the dock can be iconized independently.

Floating panels and panel groups can also be iconized independently from dock columns.

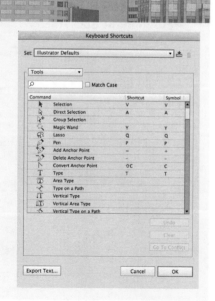

15. Hover the mouse cursor over the left edge of the dock column until you see a two-facing arrow icon, then click the left edge of the right dock column and drag left.

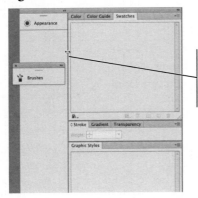

Dragging the left edge of a dock column changes the width of all panels in that column.

Note:

When you have more than one column in the dock, each column can be expanded or iconized independently of the other column(s).

16. Hover the mouse cursor over the bottom edge of the Swatches panel group (in the right column of the dock) until you see a two-facing arrow icon, then click and drag up.

When you drag the bottom edge of a docked group, other variable panels in the same column expand or contract to fit the available space. By "variable panels", we mean any panel that has an undefined number of options. Some panels, such as the Stroke panel that is visible here, have a fixed number of options so they do not expand or contract. The Layers panel, on the other hand, can list a variable number of items so it can be made larger or smaller.

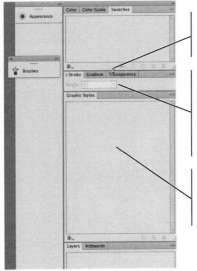

Dragging the bottom edge of a docked panel group changes the height of that group.

The Stroke panel has a defined number of options so it cannot be expanded; dragging this edge would expand or contract the variable panels above and below the Stroke panel group.

The Graphic Styles panel, which has an undefined number of options, expands or shrinks as necessary to fit the available vertical space.

17. Continue to the next exercise.

CREATE A SAVED WORKSPACE

By now you should understand that you have virtually unlimited control over the appearance of your Illustrator workspace — what panels are visible, where and how they appear, and even the size of individual panels and panel groups.

Over time you will develop personal preferences based on your work habits and project needs. Rather than re-establishing every workspace element each time you return to Illustrator, you can save your custom workspace settings so you can recall them with a single click.

1. **Click the Workspace switcher in the Application/Menu bar and choose New Workspace.**

   Again, keep in mind that we list differing commands in the Macintosh/Windows format. On Macintosh, the Workspace switcher is in the Application bar; on Windows, it's in the Menu bar.

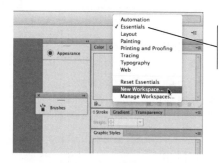

The Workspace switcher shows the name of the last-called workspace.

Note:

Because workspace preferences are largely a matter of personal taste, the projects in this book instruct you regarding which panels to use, but not where to place those elements within the interface.

2. **In the New Workspace dialog box, type Portfolio and click OK.**

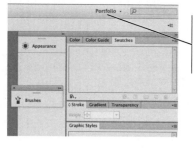

After saving the current workspace, the Workspace switcher shows the name of the new saved workspace.

3. **Click the Workspace switcher and choose Essentials from the list of available workspaces.**

   Calling a saved workspace restores the last-used state of the workspace. You made a number of changes since calling the Essentials workspace at the beginning of the previous exercise, so calling the Essentials workspace restores the last state of that workspace — in essence, nothing changes from the saved Portfolio workspace.

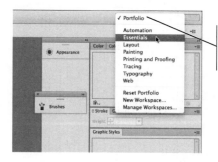

Custom workspaces are listed at the top of the Workspace switcher.

Note:

The Manage Workspaces option opens a dialog box where you can rename or delete user-defined custom workspaces. You can't alter the default workspaces that come with the application.

4. **Open the Workspace switcher and choose Reset Essentials (or choose Window>Workspace>Reset Essentials).**

Remember, saved workspaces remember the last-used state; calling a workspace again restores the panels exactly as they were the last time you used that workspace. For example, if you close a panel that is part of a saved workspace, the closed panel will not be reopened the next time you call the same workspace. To restore the saved state of the workspace, including opening closed panels or repositioning moved ones, you have to use the Reset option.

Note:

Saved workspaces can be accessed in the Window> Workspace submenu as well as the Workspace switcher on the Application/Menu bar.

5. **Continue to the next exercise.**

EXPLORE THE ILLUSTRATOR DOCUMENT WINDOW

There is much more to using Illustrator than simply arranging panels around the workspace. In this exercise, you open an Illustrator file and explore interface elements that will be important as you begin creating digital artwork.

Before completing this exericse, you should download and install the ATC fonts from the Student Files Web page.

1. **In Illustrator, choose File>Open.**

2. **Navigate to your WIP>Interface folder and select lion.ai in the list of available files.**

The Open dialog box is a system-standard navigation dialog box. This is one area of significant difference between Macintosh and Windows users.

Note:

Press Command/ Control-O to access the Open dialog box.

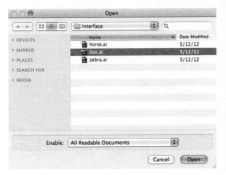

3. Click Open.

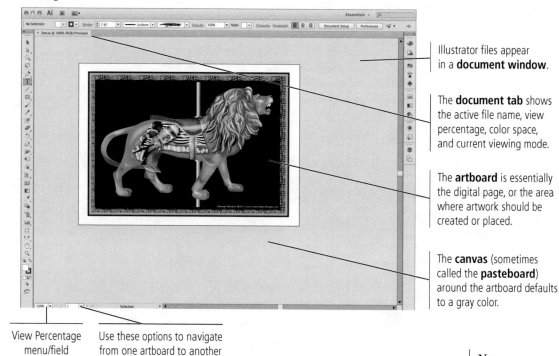

Illustrator files appear in a **document window**.

The **document tab** shows the active file name, view percentage, color space, and current viewing mode.

The **artboard** is essentially the digital page, or the area where artwork should be created or placed.

The **canvas** (sometimes called the **pasteboard**) around the artboard defaults to a gray color.

View Percentage menu/field

Use these options to navigate from one artboard to another within a single file.

4. Open the View Percentage menu in the bottom-left corner of the document window and choose 200%.

Different people prefer different view percentages, depending on a number of factors such as eyesight, monitor size, and so on. As you complete the projects in this book, you'll see our screen shots zoom in or out as necessary to show you the most relevant part of a particular file. In most cases we do not tell you what specific view percentage to use for a particular exercise, unless it is specifically required for the work being done.

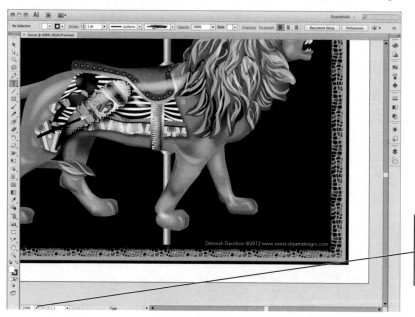

Type a specific percentage in the field or choose one of the predefined percentages from the attached menu.

Note:

Macintosh users: If you turn off the Application frame (Window>Application Frame), the new document will have its own title bar.

Note:

You can zoom an Illustrator document from 3.13% to 6400%.

5. **Choose View>Fit Artboard in Window.**

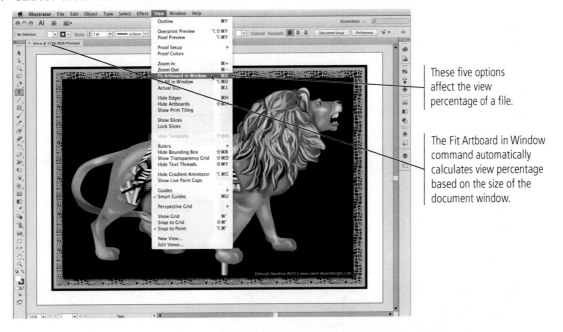

These five options affect the view percentage of a file.

The Fit Artboard in Window command automatically calculates view percentage based on the size of the document window.

6. **Review the options in the Control panel.**

We will not discuss all 34 Illustrator panels here, but the Control panel deserves special mention. This panel appears by default at the top of the workspace below the Menu bar (and the Application bar on Macintosh systems). It is context sensitive, which means it provides access to different options depending on which tool is active and what is selected in the document.

When nothing is selected in the file, the most important Control panel options open the Document Setup dialog box and the Preferences dialog box (more about these specific elements in the projects). Other options set the default stroke and fill attributes for the next object you create.

Note:

Many of the options available in the Control panel duplicate options in other panels or menu commands.

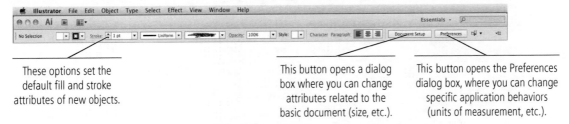

These options set the default fill and stroke attributes of new objects.

This button opens a dialog box where you can change attributes related to the basic document (size, etc.).

This button opens the Preferences dialog box, where you can change specific application behaviors (units of measurement, etc.).

7. **Click the Selection tool at the top of the Tools panel to make that tool active.**

The Selection tool (the solid arrow) is used to select entire objects in the file.

8. **Click the black area behind the lion to select that object in the file.**

9. Review the options in the Control panel.

When an object is selected in the file, the Control panel shows the attributes of the selected object.

Selection tool

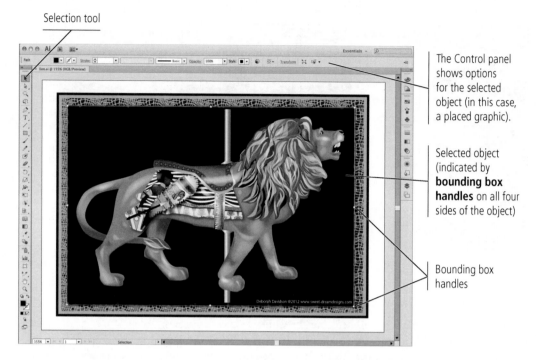

The Control panel shows options for the selected object (in this case, a placed graphic).

Selected object (indicated by **bounding box handles** on all four sides of the object)

Bounding box handles

10. Click the text near the bottom of the artwork to select the type object.

Again, the Control panel changes to show options related to type objects.

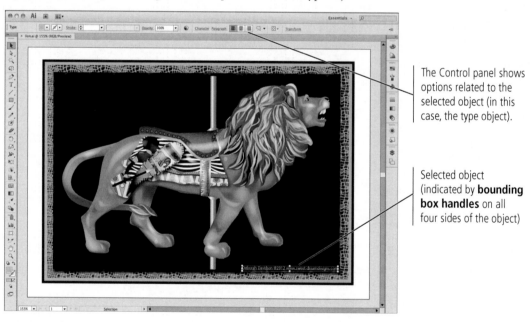

The Control panel shows options related to the selected object (in this case, the type object).

Selected object (indicated by **bounding box handles** on all four sides of the object)

11. Continue to the next exercise.

EXPLORE THE ARRANGEMENT OF MULTIPLE DOCUMENTS

Because designers frequently need to work with more than one Illustrator file at once, Illustrator CS6 incorporates a number of options for arranging multiple documents. We designed the following simple exercise to allow you to explore these options.

1. **With the lion.ai file open in Illustrator, choose File>Open.**

   The Open dialog box defaults to the last-used location, so you should not have to navigate back to the WIP>Interface folder.

2. **Click horse.ai in the list to select that file.**

3. **Press Command/Control, and click zebra.ai to add it to the active selection.**

   You can open more than one file at a time, as long as those files are in the same folder. Pressing Shift allows you select multiple contiguous (consecutive) files; pressing Command/Control allows you to select non-contiguous files.

4. **Click Open to open both selected files.**

When multiple files are open, each file is represented by a tab at the top of the document window.

5. **Click the horse.ai tab at the top of the document window.**

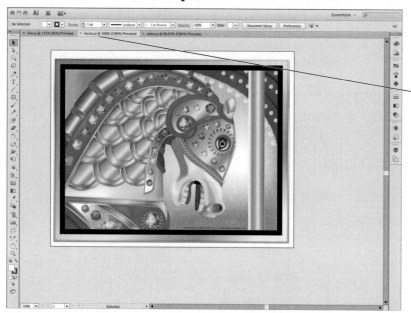

Clicking a specific tab makes that file active in the document window.

Note:

You can drag document tabs to rearrange their order. If you accidentally drag a tab out of the bar, it appears in a floating window; you can simply drag back to the document tab bar, or use the Consolidate All option to restore the floating document to a tabbed file.

6. **Choose Window>Arrange>Float in Window.**

Floating a document separates the file into its own document window.

The title bar of the separate document window shows the same information that was in the document tab.

7. **In the Application/Menu bar, click the Arrange Documents button to open the menu of defined arrangements.**

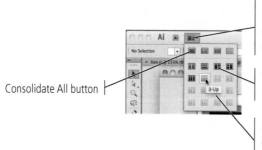

The Arrange Documents menu includes a number of tiling options for arranging multiple open files in the workspace.

Consolidate All button

The appearance of each icon suggests the result of each option.

Rolling your mouse cursor over an icon shows the arrangement name in a tool tip.

Note:

You can separate all open files by choosing Window>Arrange>Float All In Windows.

Note:

On Macintosh systems, the Application bar must be visible to access the Arrange Documents button.

8. Click the Consolidate All button (top-left) in the Arrange Documents panel.

The Consolidate All button consolidates all floating documents into a single tabbed document window (just like the default arrangement).

The remaining buttons in the top row separate all open files into individual document windows, and then arrange the different windows as indicated.

The lower options use a specific number of floating documents (2-Up, 3-Up, etc.); if more files are open than an option indicates, the extra files are consolidated as tabs in the first document window.

Note:

When multiple floating document windows are open, two options in the Window>Arrange menu allow you to cascade or tile the different document windows.

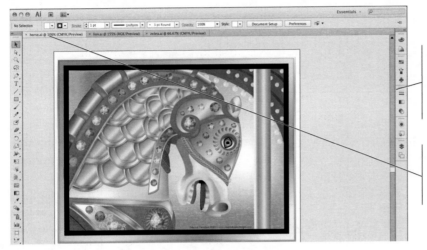

The consolidated document window snaps to fill the available monitor space (within the boundaries of docked panels).

The Consolidate All arrangement restores all open documents into a single document window.

9. Click the button at the bottom of the Tools panel to show the screen mode options.

Illustrator has three different **screen modes**, which change the way the document window displays on the screen. The default mode, which you saw when you opened these three files, is called Normal mode.

Note:

Press the F key to cycle though the screen modes.

> ✓ Normal Screen Mode
> Full Screen Mode with Menu Bar
> Full Screen Mode

10. Choose Full Screen Mode with Menu Bar from the Screen Mode menu.

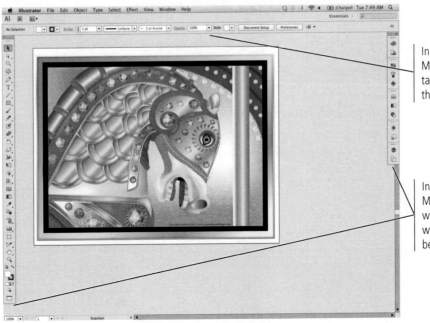

In Full Screen Mode with Menu Bar, the document tabs are hidden behind the Menu bar.

In Full Screen Mode with Menu Bar, the document window fills the entire workspace and extends behind the docked panels.

11. **Click the Screen Mode button at the bottom of the Tools panel and choose Full Screen Mode.**

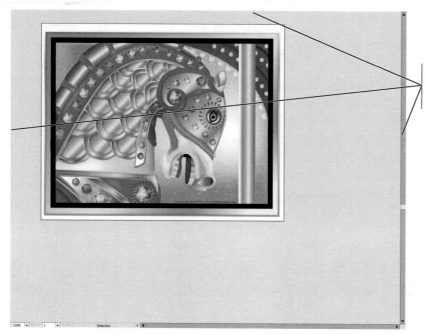

In Full Screen Mode, the Menu bar, title bar, and all panels are hidden.

Note:

All open files are listed at the bottom of the Window menu. You can use these menu options to navigate from one file to another, which is particularly useful if you're working in Full Screen Mode with Menu Bar because the document tabs are not visible in this mode.

12. **Press the Escape key to exit Full Screen Mode and return to Normal Screen Mode.**

13. **Click the Close button on the horse.ai tab.**

When multiple files are open, clicking the close button on a document tab closes only that file.

14. **Macintosh: Click the Close button in the top-left corner of the Application bar.**

Closing the Macintosh Application frame closes all open files, but does not quit the application.

On Macintosh, closing the Application frame closes all files open in that frame.

Windows: Click the Close button on each document tab to close the files.

Clicking the Close button on the Windows Menu bar closes all open files *and* quits the application. To close open files *without* quitting, you have to manually close each file using the document tabs.

Click the Close buttons on each document tab to close the open files.

Clicking the Menu bar Close button closes all open files, and also quits the application.

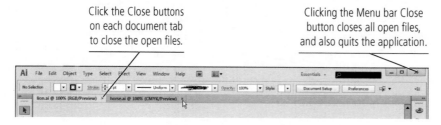

Most Illustrator projects require some amount of zooming in and out to various view percentages, as well as navigating around the document within its window. As we show you how to complete different stages of the workflow, we usually won't tell you when to change your view percentage because that's largely a matter of personal preference. But you should understand the different options for navigating around an Illustrator file so you can efficiently get to what you want.

To change the view percentage, you can type a specific percent in the **View Percentage field** of the document window or choose from the predefined options in the related menu.

You can also click with the **Zoom tool** to increase the view percentage in specific, predefined intervals (the same intervals you see in the View Percentage menu in the bottom-left corner of the document window). Pressing Option/Alt with the Zoom tool allows you to zoom out in the same defined percentages. If you drag a marquee with the Zoom tool, you can zoom into a specific location; the area surrounded by the marquee fills the available space in the document window.

The **View menu** also provides options for changing view percentage. (The Zoom In and Zoom Out options step through the same predefined view percentages as clicking with the Zoom tool.)

Zoom In	Command/Control-plus (+)
Zoom Out	Command/Control-minus (-)
Fit Artboard in Window	Command/Control-0 (zero)
Fit All in Window	Command-Option-0/ Control-Alt-0 (zero)
Actual Size (100%)	Command/Control-1

Whatever your view percentage, you can use the **Hand tool** to drag the file around in the document window. The Hand tool changes what is visible in the window; it has no effect on the actual content of the image.

The Navigator Panel

The **Navigator panel** (Window> Navigator) is another method of adjusting what you see, including the view percentage and the specific area that is visible in the document window. The Navigator panel shows a thumbnail of the active file; a red rectangle (called the Proxy Preview Area) represents exactly how much of the document shows in the document window.

The red rectangle shows the area of the file that is visible in the document window.

Drag the red rectangle to change the visible portion of the file.

Use the slider and field at the bottom of the panel to change the view percentage.

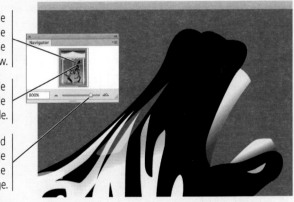

Saved Views

Named views can be helpful if you repeatedly return to the same area and view percentage. By choosing View>New View, you can save the current view with a specific name.

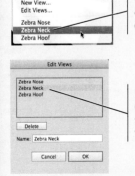

Saved views can be accessed at the bottom of the View menu.

Change view names or delete specific views by choosing View>Edit Views.

International Symbols

Biotech Services manages large-scale manufacturing facilities specializing in everything from digital photographic equipment to large earth-moving machines used to build new roads. The company builds plants all over the world that in many cases handle hazardous chemicals and undertake dangerous tasks — which means they must prominently display appropriate warnings. Biotech Services hired you to create a digital collection of universal symbols that they can use to create signs, print on the side of large machines, place as icons on their Web sites, and embroider onto employee uniforms.

This project incorporates the following skills:

❑ Placing raster images into an Illustrator file to use as drawing templates

❑ Creating and managing simple shapes and lines

❑ Using various tools and panels to transform objects' color, position, and shape

❑ Cloning objects to minimize repetitive tasks

❑ Using layers to organize and manage complex artwork

❑ Drawing complex shapes by combining simple shapes

client comments

We have a set of universal warning symbols on our Web site, but we need to use those same icons in other places as well. Our printer told us that the symbols on our Web site are "low res," so they can't be used for print projects. The printer also said he needs vector graphics that will scale larger and still look good. The printer suggested we hire a designer to create digital versions of the icons so we can use them for a wide variety of purposes, from large machinery signs to small plastic cards to anything else that might come up. We need you to help us figure out exactly what we need and then create the icons for us.

art director comments

Basically, we have the icons, but they're low-resolution raster images, so they only work for the Web, and they can't be enlarged. The good news is that you can use the existing icons as templates and more or less trace them to create the new icons.

The client needs files that can be printed cleanly and scaled from a couple of inches up to several feet. Illustrator vector files are perfect for this type of job. In fact, vector graphics get their resolution from the printer being used for a specific job, so you can scale them to any size you want without losing quality.

project objectives

To complete this project, you will:

❏ Create a grid that will eventually hold all icons in one document

❏ Control objects' stroke, fill, and transparency attributes

❏ Import and use the client's raster images as templates, which you can then trace

❏ Use layers to manage complex artwork

❏ Use the Line Segment tool to create a complex object from a set of straight lines

❏ Lock, unlock, hide, and show objects to navigate the objects' stacking order

❏ Rotate and reflect objects to create complex artwork from simple shapes

❏ Use the Pathfinder to combine simple shapes into a single complex object

Stage 1 Setting up the Workspace

There are two primary types of digital artwork: raster images and vector graphics. (**Line art**, sometimes categorized as a third type of image, is actually a type of raster image.)

Raster images are pixel-based, made up of a grid of individual **pixels** (**rasters** or **bits**) in rows and columns (called a **bitmap**). Raster files are **resolution dependent**; their resolution is determined when you scan, photograph, or create the file. As a professional graphic designer, you should have a basic understanding of the following terms and concepts:

- **Pixels per inch (ppi)** is the number of pixels in one horizontal or vertical inch of a digital raster file.

- **Lines per inch (lpi)** is the number of halftone dots produced in a linear inch by a high-resolution imagesetter, which simulates the appearance of continuous-tone color.

- **Dots per inch (dpi)** or **spots per inch (spi)** is the number of dots produced by an output device in a single line of output.

Drawing objects that you create in Illustrator are **vector graphics**, which are composed of mathematical descriptions of a series of lines and points. Vector graphics are **resolution independent**; they can be freely scaled and are output at the resolution of the output device.

✍ CREATE A NEW DOCUMENT

In this project, you work with the basics of creating vector graphics in Illustrator using a number of different drawing tools, adding color, and managing various aspects of your artwork. The first step is to create a new document for building your artwork.

1. **Download A16_RF_Project1.zip from the Student Files Web page.**

2. **Expand the ZIP archive in your WIP folder (Macintosh) or copy the archive contents into your WIP folder (Windows).**

    This results in a folder named **Symbols**, which contains all of the files you need for this project. You should also use this folder to save the files you create in this project.

3. **In Illustrator, choose File>New.**

4. **In the resulting New Document dialog box, type icons in the Name field.**

    The New Document dialog box defaults to the last-used settings.

5. **Choose Print in the New Document Profile menu, and make sure the Number of Artboards field is set to 1.**

    Illustrator CS6 includes the ability to create multiple **artboards** (basically, Illustrator's version of "pages"). You will work with multiple artboards in Project 3: Identity Package and Project 5: Letterfold Brochure.

6. **Choose Letter in the Size menu, choose Points in the Units menu, and choose the Portrait Orientation option.**

    The **point** is a standard unit of measurement for graphic designers. There are 72 points in an inch. As you complete this project, you will work with other units of measurement; you will convert the units later.

7. **Set all four bleed values to 0.**

    Bleed is the amount an object needs to extend past the edge of the artboard or page to meet the mechanical requirements of commercial printing.

Note:

If necessary, refer to Page 1 of the Interface chapter for specific information on expanding or accessing the required resource files.

Note:

To begin this project, we reset the built-in Essentials workspace. Feel free to work with whatever settings you are most comfortable using.

Note:

You learn more about bleeds in Project 3: Identity Package.

8. **If the Advanced options aren't visible, click the arrow button to the left of the word Advanced.**

9. **Make sure the Color Mode is set to CMYK and the Preview Mode is set to Default.**

   CMYK is the standard color mode for printing, and RGB is the standard color mode for digital distribution. You learn more about color and color modes in Project 2: Balloon Festival Artwork.

   Don't worry about the other Advanced options for now. You will learn about those in later projects when they are more relevant.

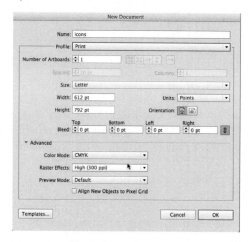

10. **Click OK to create the new file.**

   In the resulting document window, the letter-size "page" (or artboard) is represented by a dark black line. As we explained in the Interface chapter, the panels you see depend on what was done the last time you (or someone else) used the application. Because workspace arrangement is such a personal preference, we tell you what panels you need to use, but we don't tell you where to place them.

   In our screen shots, we typically float panels over the relevant area of the document so we can focus the images on the most important part of the file at any particular point. As you complete the projects in this book, feel free to dock the panels, grouped or ungrouped, iconized or expanded, however you prefer.

Note:

Our screen shots show the Macintosh operating system using the Application frame. If you're on a Macintosh system and your screen doesn't look like our screen shots, choose Window>Application Frame to toggle on that option.

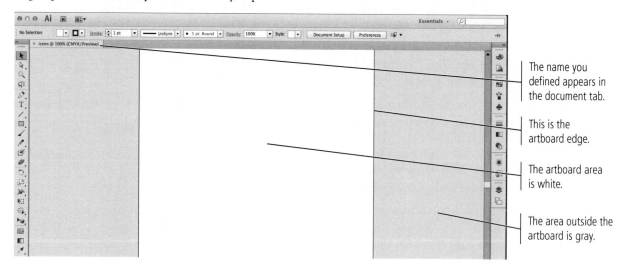

The name you defined appears in the document tab.

This is the artboard edge.

The artboard area is white.

The area outside the artboard is gray.

11. Choose File>Save As and navigate to your WIP>Symbols folder.

If you assign a name in the New Document dialog box (as you did in Step 4), that name becomes the default file name in the Save As dialog box.

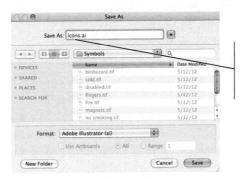

The file name defaults to the name you defined when you created the file, including the ".ai" extension.

Note:

Press Command/Control-S to save a document, or press Command/Control-Shift-S to open the Save As dialog box.

12. Click Save in the Save As dialog box. Review the options in the resulting Illustrator Options dialog box.

This dialog box determines what is stored in the resulting file. The default options are adequate for most files.

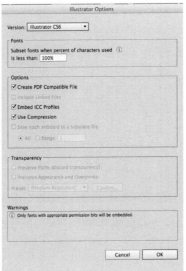

- Use the **Version** menu to save files to be compatible with earlier versions of the software. (Keep in mind that many features are not supported by earlier versions; if you save a file for an earlier version, some file information will probably be lost.)

- **Subset Fonts when Percent of Characters Used Is Less Than** determines when to embed an entire font instead of just the characters that are used in the file. Embedding the entire font can significantly increase file size.

- Make sure **Create PDF Compatible File** is checked if you want to use the file with other Adobe applications (such as placing it into an InDesign layout). This does not create a separate PDF file; it simply includes PDF preview data in the file.

- **Include Linked Files** embeds files that are linked to the artwork. You will learn about linked and embedded files in Project 5: Letterfold Brochure.

- **Embed ICC Profiles** stores color information inside the file for use in a color-managed workflow.

- **Use Compression** compresses PDF data in the Illustrator file.

- **Save Each Artboard to a Separate File** saves each artboard as a separate file; a separate master file with all artboards is also created.

- **Transparency** options determine what happens to transparent objects when you save a file for Illustrator 9.0 or earlier. Preserve Paths discards transparency effects and resets transparent artwork to 100% opacity and Normal blending mode. Preserve Appearance and Overprints preserves overprints that don't interact with transparent objects; overprints that interact with transparent objects are flattened.

13. Click OK to save the file, and then continue to the next exercise.

DEFINE SMART GUIDE PREFERENCES

Adobe Illustrator provides many tools to help you create precise lines and shapes. **Smart Guides** are temporary snap-to guides that help you create, align, and transform objects. Smart Guides also show you when the cursor is at a precise angle relative to the original position of the object or point you're moving. In this exercise, you will make sure the correct Smart Guides are active.

1. **With icons.ai open and nothing selected in the file, click the Preferences button in the Control panel.**

2. **Choose Smart Guides in the list of categories on the left.**

3. **Make sure the Alignment Guides, Object Highlighting, Anchor/Path Labels, and Measurement Labels options are selected and click OK.**

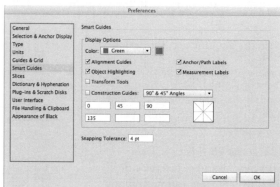

4. **Choose View>Smart Guides to make sure that option is toggled on (checked).**

   If the option is already checked, simply move your mouse away from the menu and click to dismiss the menu without changing the active option.

5. **Continue to the next exercise.**

Using Smart Guides

You can change the appearance and behavior of Smart Guides in the Preferences dialog box. The Display options determine what is visible when Smart Guides are active:

This anchor is being dragged with the Direct Selection tool.

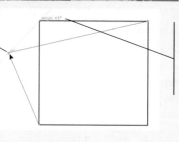

The Smart Guide shows that the anchor is being moved at a 45-degree angle from the original position.

- When **Alignment Guides** is active, Smart Guides show when a new or moved object aligns to the center or edge of a nearby object.

- When **Object Highlighting** is active, moving the mouse over any part of an unselected object shows the anchors and paths that make up that object.

- When **Transform Tools** is active, Smart Guides display when you scale, rotate, or shear objects.

- When **Anchor/Path Labels** is active, Smart Guides include labels that show the type of element (path or anchor) under the cursor.

- When **Measurement Labels** is active, Smart Guides show the distance and angle of movement.

- When **Construction Guides** is active, Smart Guides appear when you move objects in the file at or near defined angles (0°, 45°, 90°, and 135° are the default angles). A number of common angle options are built into the related menu, or you can type up to six specific angles in the available fields.

ILLUSTRATOR FOUNDATIONS

DRAW BASIC SHAPES

Now that you have a place to draw (the artboard), you're ready to start creating the icon artwork. The first step of this project requires a set of background shapes — simple rectangles with rounded corners — to contain each icon. Illustrator includes a number of shape tools that make it easy to create this kind of basic shape — rectangles (or squares), ellipses (or circles), and so on.

1. **With icons.ai open, click the Rectangle tool in the Tools panel and hold down the mouse button until the nested tools appear. Choose the Rounded Rectangle tool from the list of nested tools.**

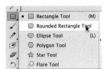

2. **Click the Default Fill and Stroke button at the bottom of the Tools panel.**

In Illustrator, the default fill is white and the default stroke is 1-pt black.

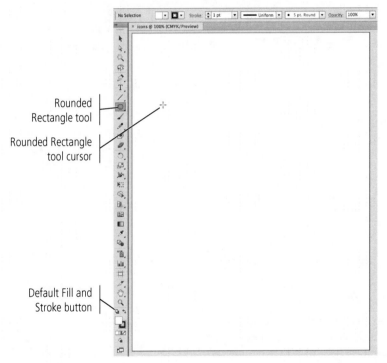

Rounded Rectangle tool

Rounded Rectangle tool cursor

Default Fill and Stroke button

Note:

You can also press D to restore the default fill and stroke colors.

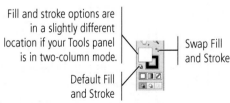

Fill and stroke options are in a slightly different location if your Tools panel is in two-column mode.

Default Fill and Stroke

Swap Fill and Stroke

3. **With the Rounded Rectangle tool active, click anywhere on the artboard.**

The resulting dialog box asks how big you want to make the new rectangle, defaulting to the last-used measurements. The default measurement system is points, as you defined when you created this file.

When the dialog box opens, the Width field is automatically highlighted. You can simply type to replace the existing value.

Note:

If you Option/Alt-click with any of the shape tools, the place where you click becomes the center of the new shape.

4. Type 1.5″ in the Width field and then press Tab to move to the Height field.

Regardless of what unit you see in the dialog box, you can enter values in whatever system you prefer, as long as you remember to type the correct unit in the dialog box fields (use ″ for inches, mm for millimeters, and pt for points; there are a few others, but they are rarely used). Illustrator automatically translates one unit of measurement to another.

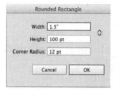

When you move to the next field, Illustrator calculates the conversion of 1.5 inches (the value you placed in the Width field) to 108 pt (the value that automatically appears in the Width field after you move to the Height field).

Pressing Tab automatically highlights the next field value.

5. Type 1.5″ in the Height field. Set the Corner Radius field to 12 pt, and then click OK.

A shape appears on the artboard with its top-left corner exactly where you clicked with the Rounded Rectangle tool.

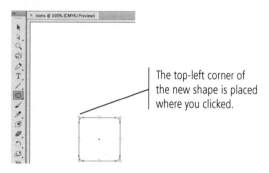

The top-left corner of the new shape is placed where you clicked.

Note:

A rounded-corner rectangle is simply a rectangle with the corners cut at a specific distance from the end (the corner radius). The two sides are connected with one-fourth of a circle, which has a radius equal to the amount of the rounding.

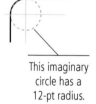

This imaginary circle has a 12-pt radius.

6. Click the Selection tool in the Tools panel and zoom in to 200%.

When the object is selected, the **bounding box** marks the outermost edges of the shape. **Bounding box handles** mark the corners and exact horizontal and vertical center of the shape. If you don't see the bounding box, choose View>Show Bounding Box.

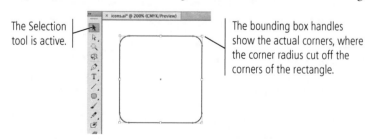

The Selection tool is active.

The bounding box handles show the actual corners, where the corner radius cut off the corners of the rectangle.

Note:

As a rule, we don't tell you what view percentage to use unless we want to highlight a specific issue. As you work through the projects in this book, we encourage you to zoom in and out as necessary to meet your specific needs.

7. **Select the Rounded Rectangle tool in the Tools panel.**

When you choose a nested tool, that variation becomes the default option in the Tools panel. You don't need to access the nested menu to select the Rounded Rectangle tool again as long as the application remains open. (If you quit and relaunch Illustrator, the regular Rectangle tool again becomes the default tool in that position.)

8. **Move the cursor to the right of the top edge of the existing shape.**

9. **When you see a green line connected to the top edge of the first shape, click, hold down the mouse button, and drag down and right to begin creating a second shape. Do not release the mouse button.**

The green line is a function of the Smart Guides feature, which provides instant feedback while you draw. As you drag, notice the cursor feedback showing the size of the new shape. Also notice that as you drag near the bottom edge of the first shape, a Smart Guide appears to indicate your position.

Note:

Cursor feedback and Smart Guides provide precise control over what you're creating — as individual objects and in relation to other objects on the artboard.

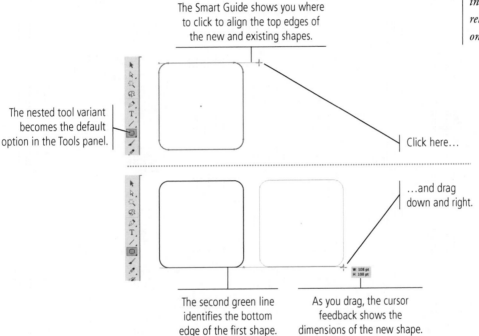

The Smart Guide shows you where to click to align the top edges of the new and existing shapes.

The nested tool variant becomes the default option in the Tools panel.

Click here...

...and drag down and right.

The second green line identifies the bottom edge of the first shape.

As you drag, the cursor feedback shows the dimensions of the new shape.

10. **While still holding down the mouse button, press the Shift key. When the cursor feedback shows both Width and Height values of 108 pt, release the mouse button to create the second shape.**

Pressing Shift **constrains** the shape to equal height and width. Although you can accomplish the same result by carefully monitoring the cursor feedback, pressing the Shift key makes the process faster and easier.

Note:

If you do something wrong, or aren't happy with your results, press Command/Control-Z to undo the last action you took.

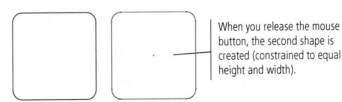

When you release the mouse button, the second shape is created (constrained to equal height and width).

Most Illustrator objects (including shapes like rounded-corner rectangles) contain two basic building blocks: anchor points and paths. These building blocks are the heart of vector graphics. Fortunately, you don't need to worry about the geometric specifics of vectors because Illustrator manages them for you — but you do need to understand the basic concept of how Illustrator works with anchor points and paths. You should also understand how to access those building blocks so you can do more than create basic shapes.

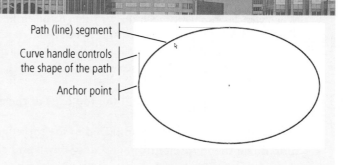

Path (line) segment

Curve handle controls the shape of the path

Anchor point

When you select an object with the **Selection tool** (the solid arrow), you can see the bounding box that identifies the outermost dimensions of the shape. Around the edges of the bounding box you see the bounding box handles, which you can use to resize the shape. (Press Command/Control-Shift-B to show or hide the bounding box of selected objects.)

When you select an object with the **Direct Selection tool** (the hollow arrow), you can see the anchor points and paths that make up the selected object rather than the object's bounding box. As you work with Illustrator, keep this distinction in mind: use the Selection tool to select an entire object; use the Direct Selection tool to edit the points and paths of an object.

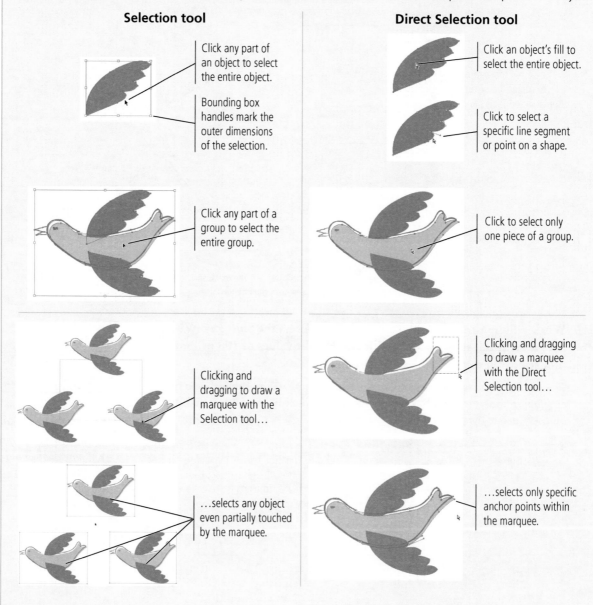

Selection tool

Click any part of an object to select the entire object.

Bounding box handles mark the outer dimensions of the selection.

Click any part of a group to select the entire group.

Clicking and dragging to draw a marquee with the Selection tool...

...selects any object even partially touched by the marquee.

Direct Selection tool

Click an object's fill to select the entire object.

Click to select a specific line segment or point on a shape.

Click to select only one piece of a group.

Clicking and dragging to draw a marquee with the Direct Selection tool...

...selects only specific anchor points within the marquee.

11. **Move the cursor to the right until a green line connects to the center of the second shape. Click, press Option/Alt-Shift, and drag down and right until a green line connects to the bottom of the second shape.**

Pressing the Option/Alt key allows you to create a shape from the center out; in other words, the point where you click will be the exact center of the resulting shape.

Pressing Shift as well constrains the new shape to equal height and width, growing out from the center point where you first clicked.

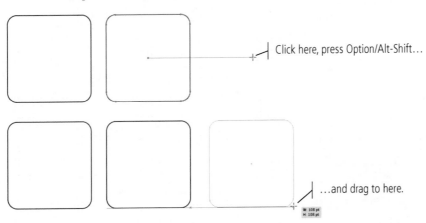

Click here, press Option/Alt-Shift...

...and drag to here.

W 108 pt
H 108 pt

Note:

Don't worry about the spaces between the objects. You'll adjust the object spacing in a later exercise.

12. **When the cursor feedback shows both Width and Height values of 108 pt, release the mouse button.**

13. **Save the file and continue to the next exercise.**

CONTROL FILL AND STROKE ATTRIBUTES

At the beginning of the previous exercise, you clicked the Default Fill and Stroke button in the Tools panel to apply a white fill and 1-pt black stroke to the objects you created. Obviously, most artwork requires more than these basic attributes. Illustrator gives you almost unlimited control over the fill and stroke attributes of objects on the artboard.

As you complete the projects in this book, you will learn about styles, patterns, gradients, effects, and other attributes that can take an illustration from flat to fabulous. In this exercise, you learn about a number of options for changing the basic fill, stroke, and color attributes for objects on the page.

1. **With icons.ai open, choose the Selection tool at the top of the Tools panel. Click the left rectangle on the artboard to select it.**

The Selection tool is used to select entire objects.

2. **Open the Swatches panel.**

The Swatches panel includes a number of predefined and saved colors, which you can use to change the color of the fill and stroke of an object. You can also save custom swatches, which you will learn about in Project 2: Balloon Festival Artwork.

Note:

Remember, panels can always be accessed in the Window menu.

3. **Near the bottom of the Tools panel, click the Stroke icon to bring it to the front of the stack.**

The Fill and Stroke icons in the Tools panel are used to change the color of the related attributes. Clicking one of these buttons brings it to the front of the stack (makes it active) so you can change the color of that attribute.

Use these pop-up panels to change the fill or stroke color of the selected object.

Selection tool

The object is selected with the Selection tool.

Clicking a swatch in the Swatches panel changes the color of the active attribute.

Clicking the Stroke icon brings it in front of the Fill icon.

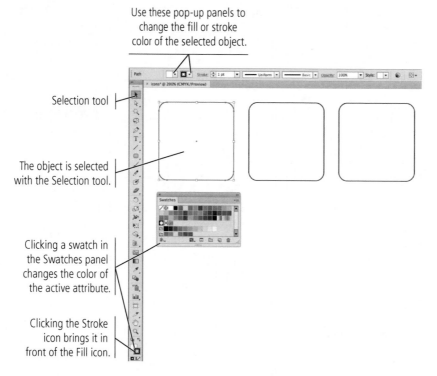

4. **In the Swatches panel, click the gold swatch at the end of the first row.**

Because the Stroke icon is active in the Tools panel, the color of the selected object's stroke (border) changes to gold.

5. **In the Tools panel, click the Fill icon to bring it to the front of the stack. In the Swatches panel, click the black swatch in the first row.**

Because the Fill icon is active in the Tools panel, clicking the black color swatch changes the fill color of the selected object.

These swatches reflect the colors that are applied to the selected object.

Use this swatch for the fill color.

Use this swatch for the stroke color.

Make sure the correct attribute is selected if you use the stand-alone Swatches panel to change attribute colors.

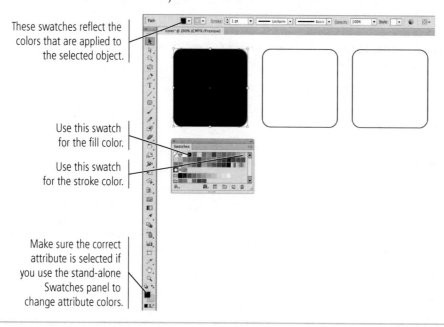

6. **Open the Stroke panel. With the rounded rectangle still selected on the artboard, change the Stroke Weight to 3 pt.**

The Stroke icon in the Tools panel does not need to be active to change the stroke weight. The Tools panel icons relate only to color changes made with the stand-alone Swatches or Color panels.

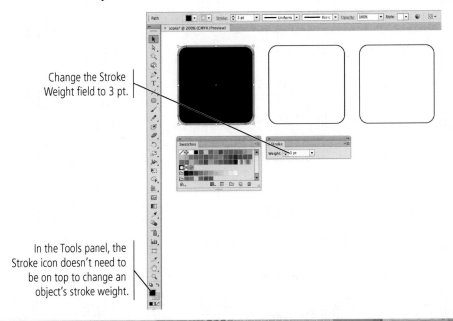

Change the Stroke Weight field to 3 pt.

In the Tools panel, the Stroke icon doesn't need to be on top to change an object's stroke weight.

Transforming Objects with the Bounding Box

Bounding box handles make it easy to transform an object on the artboard. You can resize an object by dragging any handle, and even rotate an object by placing the cursor directly outside a corner handle. (If Smart Guides are active, cursor feedback helps if you want to make specific transformations, or you can work freestyle and drag handles until you're satisfied with the results.)

Drag a side handle to change the height or width of an object.

Drag a corner handle to change both the height and shape of an object at once.

Shift-drag to maintain an object's original height-to-width aspect ratio.

Option/Alt-drag a corner handle to change the size around the object's center point.

Click directly outside an object's corner handle to rotate the object.

The Free Transform tool 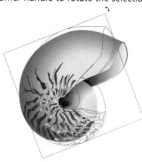 allows you to change the shape of selected objects by dragging the bounding box handles. Depending on where you click and whether you press a modifier key, you can use this tool to stretch, shrink, rotate, distort, or skew a selection.

Click a center handle to stretch or shrink the selection in one direction.

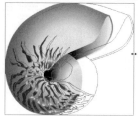

Click a corner handle to stretch or shrink the selection horizontally and vertically at the same time.

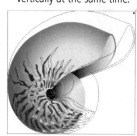

Click slightly outside a corner handle to rotate the selection.

Click a center handle, then press Command/Control to skew the selection.

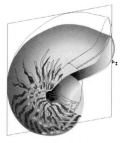

Click a corner handle, then press Command/Control to distort the selection.

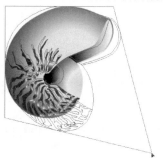

Click a corner handle, then press Command-Option-Shift/Control-Alt-Shift to alter the perspective of the selection.

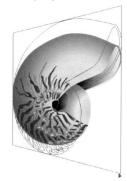

Press Option/Alt while making any free transformation to apply it equally on both sides of the selection center.

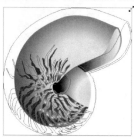

Press Shift and drag a handle to constrain the related transformation. For example, press Shift while dragging a corner handle to scale the selection at the same proportional height and width (below left) rather than scaling disproportionately (below right).

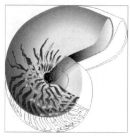

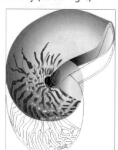

7. **With the rectangle still selected, click the Swap Fill and Stroke button in the Tools panel.**

   This button makes it easy to reverse the fill and stroke colors of an object; the stroke weight remains unaffected when you swap the colors.

   Click the Swap Fill and Stroke button to reverse the color attributes of the selected object.

   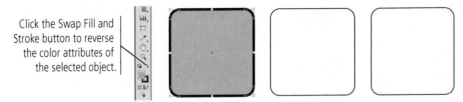

8. **Using the Selection tool, click the second rectangle on the artboard.**

   The Fill and Stroke icons change to reflect the colors of the selected objects.

9. **Click the Fill color swatch in the Control panel. Choose the gold swatch in the second row to change the fill color for the selected object.**

   When an object is selected with the Selection tool, the Control panel provides quick access to the stroke and fill attributes of the selected object.

   Clicking the Fill color swatch opens an attached Swatches panel so you can change the fill for the selected object without opening the separate Swatches panel.

   Click this color swatch to change the fill color of the selected object.

   Click this color swatch to change the stroke color of the selected object.

   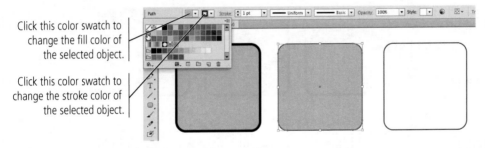

10. **In the Control panel, change the Stroke Weight value to 3 pt.**

    Again, the Control panel options allow you to change the attribute value without opening the Stroke panel. The Control panel can be a significant time-saver for common operations such as changing stroke and fill attributes.

    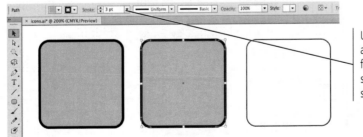

    Use the menu or type a value in the attached field to change the stroke weight of the selected object.

    Note:

    When you use the Control panel options, you don't need to worry about which icon is active in the Tools panel.

11. **Using the Selection tool, click the third rectangle on the artboard.**

    Again, the Fill and Stroke icons in the Tools panel change to reflect the colors of the selected object.

12. **Select the Eyedropper tool in the Tools panel, and then click the first or second rectangle on the artboard.**

The Eyedropper tool copies fill and stroke attributes from one object (the one you click) to another (the one you first selected).

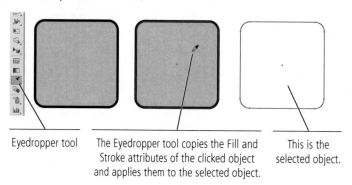

Eyedropper tool

The Eyedropper tool copies the Fill and Stroke attributes of the clicked object and applies them to the selected object.

This is the selected object.

Note:

You can double-click the Eyedropper tool in the Tools panel to define which attributes are picked up and applied by clicking with the tool.

13. **Press Command/Control and click anywhere on the artboard away from the three rectangles.**

Pressing Command/Control temporarily switches to the Selection tool. By clicking on the empty artboard area, you can quickly deselect the selected object(s). When you release the Command/Control key, the tool reverts to the one you last used.

The Eyedropper tool is still active.

Pressing Command/Control temporarily switches to the Selection tool.

The Fill and Stroke swatches remember the last-used options. The next object you create will have these same attributes.

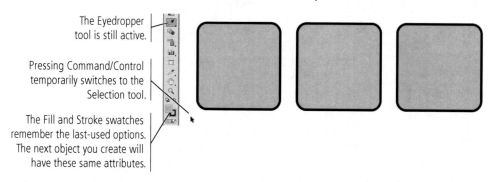

14. **Choose the Rounded Rectangle tool in the Tools panel.**

15. **To the right of the third shape on the artboard, use any method you learned in the previous exercise to draw a fourth rounded rectangle that is 108 pt square.**

The new rectangle has the same heavy black stroke and gold fill as the others. Don't worry if your shapes aren't entirely on the artboard; you will define their precise position in the next exercise.

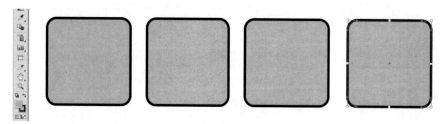

16. **Save the file (File>Save or Command/Control-S) and continue to the next exercise.**

CONTROL OBJECT POSITIONING

The ability to move objects around on the artboard is one of the advantages of digital drawing. On paper, you have to manually erase items and then redraw them in their new locations. Illustrator offers a number of tools that make it easy to move existing objects around the artboard, either as isolated objects or in relation to other elements on the page. In this exercise, you learn several techniques for moving objects on the artboard.

1. **With icons.ai open, change your zoom percentage so you can see all four shapes and the entire top of the artboard.**

2. **Choose View>Rulers>Show Rulers to show the rulers at the top and left edges of the document window.**

   Because you created this file using points as the default unit of measurement, the rulers — and fields in dialog boxes and panels — show measurements in points.

3. **Control/right-click the top ruler and choose Inches from the contextual menu.**

Rulers on the top and left edges show measurements in the default units of measurement.

4. **Choose the Selection tool from the top of the Tools panel. Click the left rectangle on the artboard to select it.**

5. **With the left rectangle selected, look at the right side of the Control panel. If you see the word "Transform", click it to open the pop-up Transform panel.**

   What you see in the Control panel depends on the size of your monitor (or the size of your Application Frame, if you've made it smaller than your monitor).

   If you have a wide monitor, the reference point proxy and the X, Y, W, and H fields of the Transform panel are available directly in the Control panel.

   If you have a smaller monitor that does not allow these fields to fit, the Control panel includes a hot-text link to the Transform panel. Clicking the link opens the Transform panel as a pop-up, directly below the Control panel; after you make a change in the pop-up panel, it collapses back into the Control panel.

Note:

The Change to Global Rulers option is only relevant when you work with multiple artboards. You will explore this in Project 3: Identity Package and Project 5: Letterfold Brochure.

Click these hot-text links to open the related pop-up panel.

Monitor width might limit the contents of your Control panel.

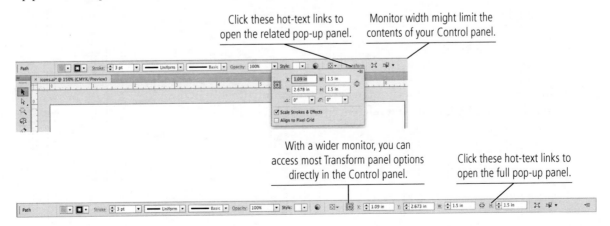

With a wider monitor, you can access most Transform panel options directly in the Control panel.

Click these hot-text links to open the full pop-up panel.

6. Review the Transform options.

The reference points correspond to the bounding box handles of the selected object. The selected square in this icon identifies which point of the object is being measured.

If you use the W or H fields to resize an object, you can constrain the object's height-to-width aspect ratio by clicking the chain icon (right of the W and H fields in the Transform panel, or between the W and H fields in the Control panel).

Note:

You could also use the stand-alone Transform panel (Window>Transform) to access these same options.

Reference point around which numeric transformations are based.

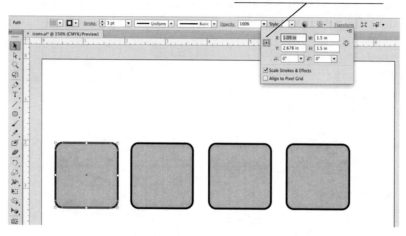

In Illustrator, the default **zero point** (the source of measurements) is the top-left corner of the artboard; the X and Y positions of an object are measured relative to that location. (The X axis is the horizontal value and the Y axis is the vertical value.)

Keep these ideas in mind when you move something in an Illustrator file:

- Moving something up requires subtracting from the Y value.
- Moving something down requires adding to the Y value.
- Moving something left requires subtracting from the X value.
- Moving something right requires adding to the X value.

You can change the zero point by clicking where the horizontal and vertical rulers meet and dragging to a new position. If you do reposition the zero point, you can double-click the intersection of the rulers to restore the default zero point.

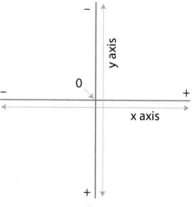

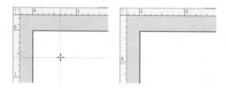

7. Using either the pop-up Transform panel or the option directly in the Control panel, click the top-left reference point to select it.

The X and Y fields now show the exact position of the top-left bounding box handle for the selected object.

Note:

The default zero point in Illustrator CS6 is the top-left corner of the artboard. This is a significant change if you have used CS4 or earlier versions.

8. Highlight the X field and type .5. Press Return/Enter to apply the change.

You don't need to type the measurement unit ("), or the preceding "0". Because the rulers are showing inches, Illustrator automatically applies inches as the unit of value.

If you used the pop-up Transform panel, the panel collapses as soon as you press Return/Enter to apply the change. You will have to click the Transform link again to complete the next step.

Note:

As with dialog boxes, you can enter values in a unit of measurement other than the default, as long as you remember to type the unit abbreviation.

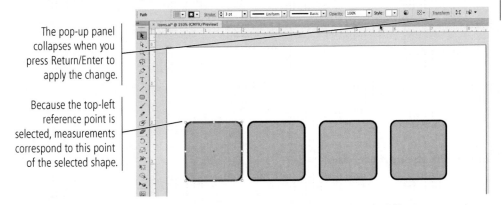

The pop-up panel collapses when you press Return/Enter to apply the change.

Because the top-left reference point is selected, measurements correspond to this point of the selected shape.

9. Highlight the Y field and type .5, then press Return/Enter to apply the change.

The top-left handle of the selected object is now 1/2" from the top and left edges. The numbers you typed correspond to the measurements you see on the rulers.

Note:

When a field value is highlighted in a panel or dialog box, you can use the Up Arrow and Down Arrow keys to increase or decrease (respectively) the highlighted value.

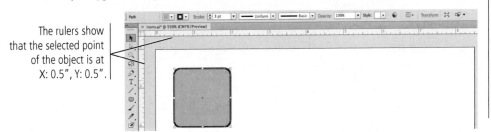

The rulers show that the selected point of the object is at X: 0.5", Y: 0.5".

10. Using the Selection tool, click the second rectangle on the artboard and drag until a green line appears, connecting the center points of the first and second shapes.

As you drag the cursor, feedback shows the relative position of the object. In other words, you can see the change (<u>diff</u>erence) in the object's position, both horizontally (<u>X</u>) and vertically (<u>Y</u>) — hence the "dX" and "dY" values.

In addition to providing cursor feedback, Smart Guides can be very useful for aligning objects on the artboard. As you drag, Illustrator identifies and highlights relative alignment, and snaps objects to those alignment points as you drag.

Note:

Remember, moving left decreases the X value and moving up decreases the Y value.

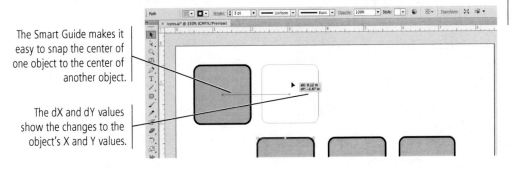

The Smart Guide makes it easy to snap the center of one object to the center of another object.

The dX and dY values show the changes to the object's X and Y values.

11. Release the mouse button while the center Smart Guide is visible.

If you don't see the alignment guides as you drag, make sure that option is checked in the Smart Guides preferences.

12. **Click the fourth shape on the page. In the Control or Transform panel, select the top-right reference point, type 8 in the X field, and type .5 in the Y field.**

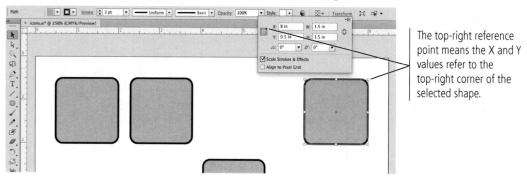

The top-right reference point means the X and Y values refer to the top-right corner of the selected shape.

Because you changed the reference point, you defined the X/Y position for the top-right bounding box handle of the fourth rectangle.

13. **Save the file and continue to the next exercise.**

 ALIGN AND DISTRIBUTE OBJECTS

In addition to dragging objects around the artboard, the Illustrator Align panel makes it very easy to align and distribute selected objects relative to one another, to a specific key object in the file, or to the overall artboard. In this exercise, you learn how to use the Align panel to align shapes.

1. **With icons.ai open, click and drag with the Selection tool to draw a marquee that touches some part of all four objects on the artboard.**

   The Selection tool selects objects, so the selection marquee only needs to touch the objects you want to select. The marquee doesn't need to surround the objects entirely.

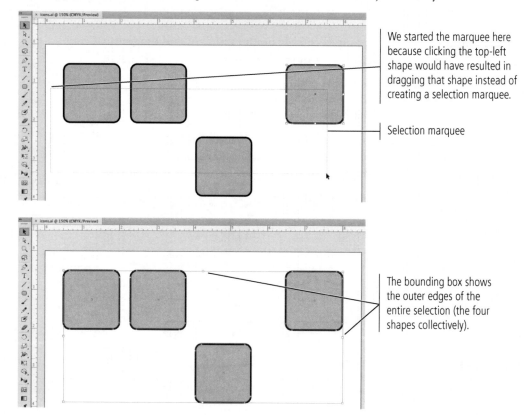

We started the marquee here because clicking the top-left shape would have resulted in dragging that shape instead of creating a selection marquee.

Selection marquee

The bounding box shows the outer edges of the entire selection (the four shapes collectively).

2. Open the Align panel (Window>Align) and click the Vertical Align Top button.

By default, alignment and distribution functions occur relative to the selected objects. In other words, when you click the Vertical Align Top button, Illustrator determines the topmost edge of the selected objects, and then moves the top edges of all other selected objects to that position.

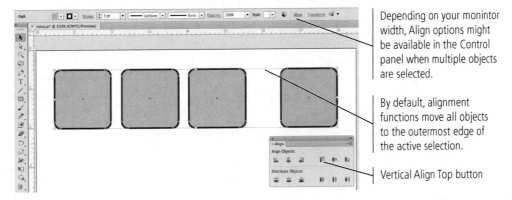

Depending on your moninter width, Align options might be available in the Control panel when multiple objects are selected.

By default, alignment functions move all objects to the outermost edge of the active selection.

Vertical Align Top button

3. With all four objects selected, click the Horizontal Distribute Center button.

By default, the distribution functions create equal distance between the selected point of the selected objects. In this case, Illustrator distributed the center points along the horizontal axis by determining the center positions of the outermost selected objects, and then moving the middle two objects to create equal distance between the centers of all four selected objects; the positions of the two outer objects remained unchanged.

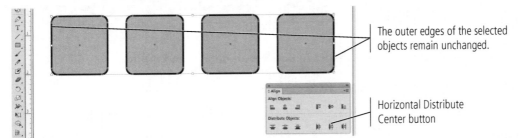

The outer edges of the selected objects remain unchanged.

Horizontal Distribute Center button

4. With all four objects selected, choose Object>Group.

When you group multiple objects, the group is essentially treated as a single object. A single bounding box surrounds all objects within the group.

5. Click inside any of the grouped objects; while still holding down the mouse button, press Option/Alt and drag down.

6. Use the Smart Guides and cursor feedback to drag exactly vertical (the dX value should be 0). When the dY value in the cursor feedback is 2 in, release the mouse button.

Pressing Option/Alt while you drag makes a copy of the original selection. This technique, called **cloning**, can save significant amounts of time when you build illustrations that contain numerous repetitive elements.

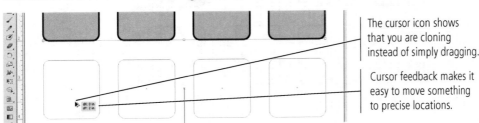

The cursor icon shows that you are cloning instead of simply dragging.

Cursor feedback makes it easy to move something to precise locations.

Note:

Press Command/ Control-G to group selected objects. Press Command/Control- Shift-G to ungroup grouped objects.

7. **With the second group of rectangles selected, choose Object>Transform> Transform Again.**

   This command repeats the last-used transformation. In this case, the last transformation was the cloning movement, so it creates the third row of rectangles.

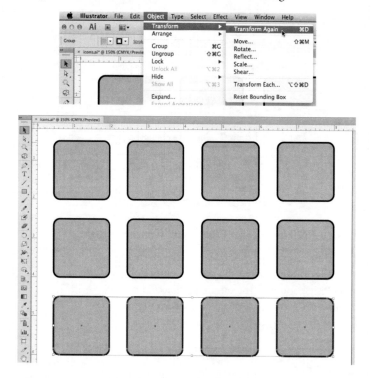

Note:

There is almost always more than one way to accomplish a specific task. The Align panel is useful for certain functions (especially distribution), but Smart Guides make object-to-object alignment very easy.

Note:

Press Command/ Control-D to repeat the last-used transformation.

8. **Click anywhere outside the rectangle shapes to deselect all objects and groups.**

9. **Save the file and continue to the next exercise.**

EDIT INDIVIDUAL GROUPED ELEMENTS

The client in this project requested only ten icons, so you don't need two of the rectangles in the third row. As you know, the Selection tool selects entire objects on the page. You also know that grouped objects are treated as a single object — which means you can't use the Selection tool to select part of a group. In this exercise, you use two techniques to work with component pieces of a group.

1. **With icons.ai open, use the Selection tool to click the fourth rectangle in the third row.**

   Because the four objects are grouped, the Selection tool selects the entire group. You need to use a different method to select certain elements within the group.

Selection tool

Because this object is part of a group, the Selection tool selects the entire group.

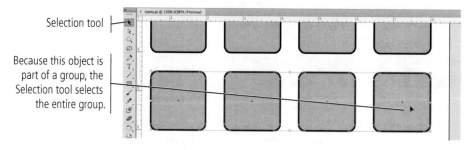

Note:

Think carefully about your ultimate goal when you group objects, especially for alignment purposes. If the objects in a group don't need to stay together, it's often a good idea to ungroup them.

2. **Click anywhere outside the rectangle shapes to deselect the group, then choose the Direct Selection tool in the Tools panel.**

The Direct Selection tool selects pieces of an object — specific paths, anchor points, or individual elements in a grouped object.

3. **Click the gold fill of the fourth rectangle in the third row.**

Because you clicked the fill, you selected the entire object. If you had clicked along the object's stroke, you would have selected that particular segment of the shape's edge.

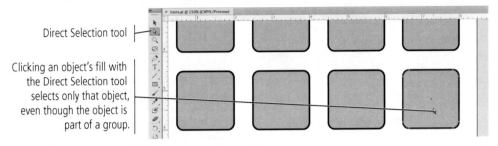

Direct Selection tool

Clicking an object's fill with the Direct Selection tool selects only that object, even though the object is part of a group.

4. **Press Delete to remove the selected object.**

Easy enough, especially because this is a very simple group of objects that don't overlap. When you start working with complex files that have multiple levels of grouping, however, it can be challenging to manipulate objects within a group using only the Direct Selection tool.

5. **Choose the Selection tool in the Tools panel, and then double-click the third rectangle in the third row.**

Double-clicking a group enters into Isolation mode, where only objects within the selected group are available. Basically, Isolation mode provides access to objects in the group without ungrouping the objects on the main artboard.

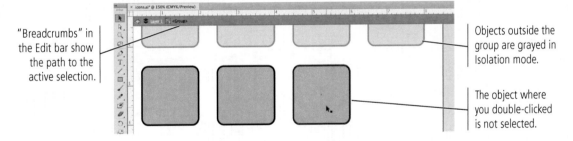

"Breadcrumbs" in the Edit bar show the path to the active selection.

Objects outside the group are grayed in Isolation mode.

The object where you double-clicked is not selected.

6. **Using the Selection tool, click the third rectangle in the third row to select it, and then press Delete.**

Because you created only a single level of grouping, you can now use the Selection tool to select individual objects.

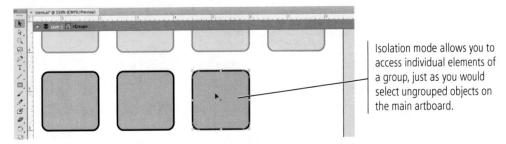

Isolation mode allows you to access individual elements of a group, just as you would select ungrouped objects on the main artboard.

7. **At the top of the document window, click the Arrow button twice to return to the main artboard.**

Click this button to exit Isolation mode.

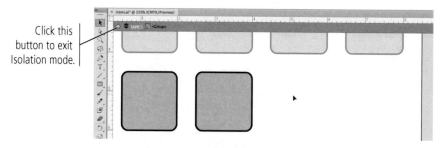

Note:

You can also press the ESC key to exit isolation mode.

The third row, now with two rectangles, is still a single group on the main artboard.

8. **Save the file and continue to the next exercise.**

Using the Group Selection Tool

You can create more than one level of group, called **nesting**, by selecting an existing group and grouping it with other objects or groups. You can use the **Group Selection tool** to help navigate complex levels of nested groups.

The first click with the Group Selection tool selects an individual object in a group. The second click selects that object's containing group. The third click adds the next containing group to the selection, and so on until the entire parent group is selected.

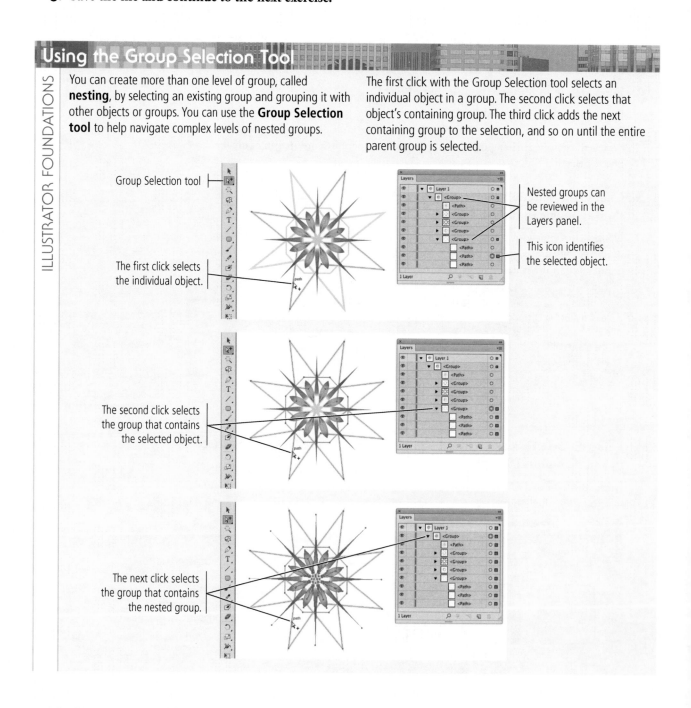

Group Selection tool

The first click selects the individual object.

Nested groups can be reviewed in the Layers panel.

This icon identifies the selected object.

The second click selects the group that contains the selected object.

The next click selects the group that contains the nested group.

IMPORT TEMPLATE IMAGES

Many Illustrator projects require you to start with something that has already been captured — a sketch, photograph, or low-resolution image (which is the case in this project). Illustrator makes it easy to place existing digital files to use as templates for your new artwork. You will use this feature in this exercise.

1. **With icons.ai open, choose File>Place. Navigate to your WIP>Symbols folder and click cold.tif to select that file.**

2. **At the bottom of the Place dialog box, check the Template option.**

   If you check the Link option, the placed file does not become a part of the actual file where you're working; for the file to output properly, Illustrator must be able to locate the linked file in the same location (hard drive, CD, etc.) as when you placed it. If the Link option is *not* checked, the placed file is **embedded** — it becomes part of the file where it's placed; the original external file is not necessary for the artwork to output properly. We will explore the details of placed files in later projects.

   In the case of this project, you are going to delete the template images after you create the artwork; it is not necessary to embed the template images.

   When you place an object as a template, it's added to the file on a separate, non-printing layer that is partially grayed, making it easier to work with.

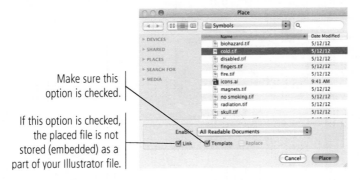

Make sure this option is checked.

If this option is checked, the placed file is not stored (embedded) as a part of your Illustrator file.

3. **Click Place.**

   When you place an object into Illustrator, it is automatically centered in the current document window.

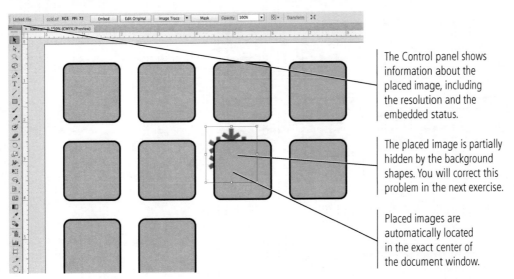

The Control panel shows information about the placed image, including the resolution and the embedded status.

The placed image is partially hidden by the background shapes. You will correct this problem in the next exercise.

Placed images are automatically located in the exact center of the document window.

4. **Choose File>Place a second time. Select `radiation.tif` in the list, check the Template option, and click Place.**

   The Place dialog box remembers the last-used location, so you don't have to re-navigate to the Symbols folder. The Link option also remembers the last-used settings. The Template option, however, always defaults to off, so you have to manually check this box for each template object.

   Make sure you remember to check the Template option.

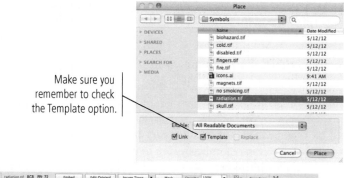

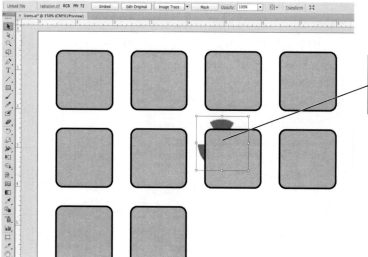

This image is also placed in the center of the document window, directly on top of the first placed image.

Note:

If you change the view percentage or scroll the document in the window before placing the second image, the second file will not be centered over the first. Instead, it will be centered in the docuemnt window based on the current view.

5. **Repeat Step 4 to place `fire.tif` into your file as a template image.**

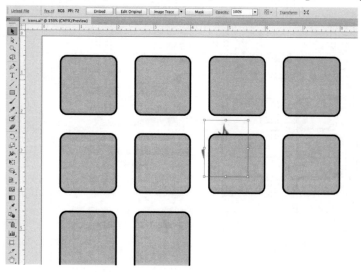

6. **Save the file and continue to the next exercise.**

MANAGE MULTIPLE LAYERS

When you create artwork in Illustrator, you almost always end up with more than one object on the artboard. In many cases, a completed file has dozens or hundreds of objects, arranged in specific order on top of one another. As files become more and more complex, it can be difficult to find and work with exactly the pieces you need. Illustrator layers are one of the most powerful tools available for solving this problem.

1. **In the open `icons.ai` file, open the Layers panel.**

   By default, all files have a single layer, named Layer 1. Your file has three additional layers — the template layers — below Layer 1. Template layers are locked by default, which means you can't select or modify objects on those layers.

   Click in this column to show or hide a layer.

   Click in this column to lock or unlock a layer.

   Double-click the layer thumbnail to open the Layer Options dialog box.

   Note:

   If you don't see all three locked template layers, you forgot to check the Template option when you placed one of the images. You can select and delete the placed file from the artboard, then replace the necessary image as a template.

2. **In the Layers panel, click the Layer 1 name and drag it below all three template layers in the stack.**

   The top-to-bottom position of objects or layers is called the **stacking order**. Objects and layers typically appear in the stack based on the order in which they are created — the first-created is at the bottom, the last-created is at the top, and so on in between.

   Placed template objects are the exception; these layers are placed *below* the currently selected layer (i.e., lower in the stacking order). In this case, the rectangle shapes are filled with a color, which obscures the template images on the underlying layers. To see the template images, you need to move the template object layers above the layer containing the background shapes. Rather than moving three layers above Layer 1, you can save a few clicks by moving Layer 1 below all of the template layers.

   Note:

   For a template layer, the Visibility icon is a small square instead of an eye.

   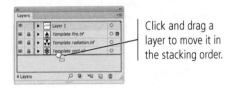

   Click and drag a layer to move it in the stacking order.

3. **Using the Selection tool, click the top-left rounded rectangle to select it.**

   Remember, this object is grouped with the other rectangles in the same row. You need to align the placed object to only the first rectangle, which means you need to be able to select only that object.

   As you saw in an earlier exercise, you can use Isolation mode to access a single element of a group. However, each rectangle shape is ultimately going to be a separate icon; you're simply creating them all in the same workspace. The best choice here is to simply ungroup the rectangles, returning them to individual objects.

4. **With the top-row group selected, choose Object>Ungroup.**

5. **Click away from the selected objects to deselect them, and then click the top-left rectangle to select that object only.**

   Note:

   Press Command/Control-Shift-G to ungroup objects in a group.

6. **In the Layers panel, click the Lock icon for the Template cold.tif layer.**

   Because you need to move the placed template object into the correct position, you first need to unlock the layer.

7. **With the Selection tool still active, press Shift and click anywhere inside the area where the template images are placed.**

   Pressing Shift allows you to add objects to the current selection. The first rectangle and the image should both be selected.

8. **With both objects selected, click the Align To button in the Control panel.**

Click this button to access the Align To options.

The placed template images are stacked on top of each other in the order you placed them.

Remember, the other two template object layers are still locked. Even though you can't see it, you can select the cold.tif image by clicking in the area where it is placed.

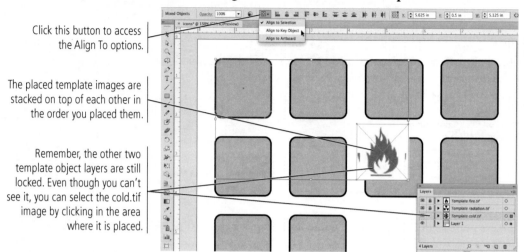

9. **Choose Align to Key Object in the menu.**

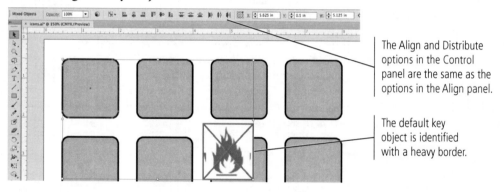

The Align and Distribute options in the Control panel are the same as the options in the Align panel.

The default key object is identified with a heavy border.

10. **Click the selected rounded rectangle on the artboard.**

   Key Object alignment allows you to define where you want other objects to align. By selecting the key object, you're telling Illustrator which object to use as the basis for alignment.

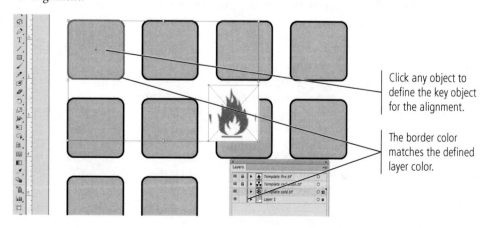

Click any object to define the key object for the alignment.

The border color matches the defined layer color.

11. **Click the Horizontal Align Center and Vertical Align Center buttons in the Control panel.**

Because you selected the rounded rectangle as the key object, the placed template image moves to the horizontal and vertical center of the rounded rectangle; the rectangle — the key object — remains in the same place.

12. **In the Layers panel, click the empty space to the left of the Template cold.tif layer to relock that layer.**

Now that the template object is in place, it's a good idea to lock it again so you don't accidentally move the object.

13. **Double-click the thumbnail of the Template cold.tif layer.**

Double-clicking a layer thumbnail opens the Layer Options dialog box for that layer, where you can change a number of attributes for the selected layer.

14. **Change the Dim Images To field to 30, and then click OK to close the Layer Options dialog box.**

Dimming the template image will make it easier to see your artwork when you start drawing.

15. Repeat Steps 6–14 to position the other two template images in the first-row rectangles (as shown in the following image).

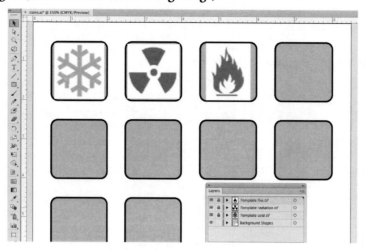

16. In the Layers panel, double-click the Layer 1 name to highlight the name. Type Background Shapes to change the layer name, then press Return/Enter.

Whenever you have more than one working layer, it's a good idea to use names that tell you what is on each layer. Doing so prevents confusion later when you or someone else needs to change a particular item.

Double-click the layer name to highlight it, so you can type a new name.

Press Return/Enter to finalize the new layer name.

17. In the Layers panel, click the empty space immediately left of the Background Shapes layer.

This step — locking the Background Shapes layer — is simply a safeguard to avoid accidentally changing the background rectangles while you're drawing the icon artwork.

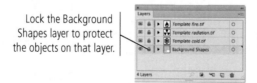

Lock the Background Shapes layer to protect the objects on that layer.

18. In the Layers panel, click the New Layer button at the bottom of the panel.

In the next stage of the project, you will start tracing the object in the template. The completed icon will be a black icon on top of the rounded rectangle with the gold background color.

At this point, most of the gold color in the background shapes is obscured by the placed images, because the template layers are above the layer containing the rectangles. If you tried to draw the icon shapes on the existing non-template layer, you would be drawing *behind* the template — in other words, you wouldn't be able to see what you were drawing. Instead, you need a layer above the template layers, where you can create the icon artwork.

New Layer button

19. In the Layers panel, drag Layer 5 to the top of the layer stack.

New layers are automatically placed immediately above the selected layer. You need this new layer to be above the template layers so you can see what you're drawing.

20. Double-click the Layer 5 thumbnail in the Layers panel. In the Layer Options dialog box, change the layer name to Icon Art and choose Magenta from the Color menu, then click OK.

The Color option has nothing to do with the stroke or fill colors used in the artwork on that layer; instead, it simply determines the color of bounding box handles and other visual indicators for objects on a layer. (The default for Layer 5, Yellow, can be very difficult to see. We chose Magenta because it shows better in our screen shots.)

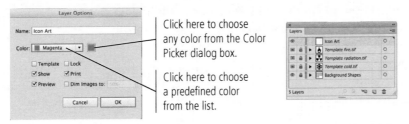

Click here to choose any color from the Color Picker dialog box.

Click here to choose a predefined color from the list.

21. Save the file and continue to the next stage of the project.

Stage 2 Drawing Basic Shapes

If you remember from the client meeting, the client's bitmap icons work fine on the Web, but they look terrible in print. After you redraw the icons in Illustrator, the client will be able to print them anywhere, with no loss in quality — which is the primary advantage of vector-based artwork vs. raster-based images. A number of tools and utilities can be used to create complex Illustrator artwork. Creating the icons in this project gives you an opportunity to experiment with some of these options. As you complete the other projects in this book, you will delve deeper into complex drawing techniques.

 CREATE ARTWORK WITH LINES

The snowflake icon is really nothing more than a series of straight lines — which makes it ideal for introducing the Line Segment tool. In this exercise, you create simple lines, and then use some basic modification techniques to create the final icon.

1. With icons.ai open, make sure the Icon Art layer is selected. Zoom in to the top-left rectangle (with the snowflake image).

2. **In the Tools panel, select the Line Segment tool, and then click the Default Fill and Stroke button.**

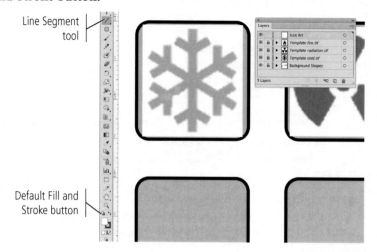

Line Segment tool

Default Fill and Stroke button

3. **Click at the bottom of the vertical line in the snowflake image, and then drag up to the top of the snowflake image. Release the mouse button while the cursor feedback shows the line at 90°.**

As you drag, the cursor feedback shows the length and — more importantly in this case — the angle of the line you're drawing. If you don't see the cursor feedback, choose View>Smart Guides to toggle on that option.

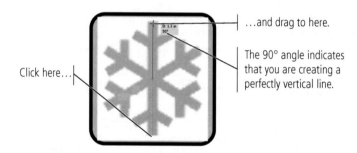

Click here...

...and drag to here.

The 90° angle indicates that you are creating a perfectly vertical line.

Note:

You can also press Shift to constrain a line to increments of 45°.

4. **With the Line Segment tool still active, click the cursor on the top of the left flake branch in the template image; while holding down the mouse button, drag down and right until you see the word "path" appear near the cursor, then release the mouse button.**

The word "path" is another function of Illustrator's Smart Guides; when you drag near an existing path, Illustrator identifies the path so you can place a point exactly on top of the existing path.

Click here and hold down the mouse button...

...drag to here, and then release the mouse button.

The word "path" is a function of Smart Guides.

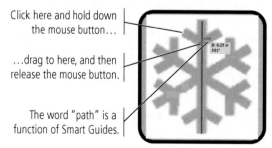

5. **Move the cursor to the top of the right flake branch until you see a green line connecting to the top of the left branch that you drew in Step 4.**

6. **Click and hold the mouse button, drag down and left until the word "anchor" appears next to the cursor, and then release the mouse button.**

   The "anchor" label indicates that you have dragged to the position of an existing anchor point (in this case, the endpoint of the left flake branch). As you can see, Illustrator makes it easy to create precise lines and shapes in relation to other objects on the page.

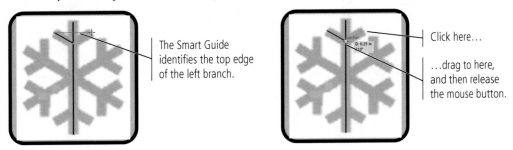

The Smart Guide identifies the top edge of the left branch.

Click here…

…drag to here, and then release the mouse button.

7. **Choose the Selection tool from the Tools panel, and then click the vertical line that you drew in Step 3. Choose Object>Lock>Selection.**

   When an object is locked, you can't select or change it — just as locking a template layer protects the template object from being moved. In the next few steps, you select and join the endpoints of the two angled lines, which is much easier if the vertical line can't be selected (you want the vertical line to remain unchanged).

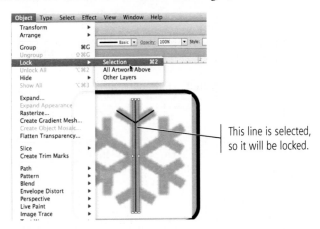

This line is selected, so it will be locked.

8. **Using the Direct Selection tool, drag a marquee around the bottom points of both angled lines.**

   You want to join the lines' endpoints, so you need to select only those specific points (instead of the entire lines). As mentioned earlier, you need the Direct Selection tool to select specific points on a path.

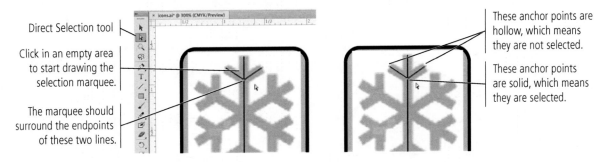

Direct Selection tool

Click in an empty area to start drawing the selection marquee.

The marquee should surround the endpoints of these two lines.

These anchor points are hollow, which means they are not selected.

These anchor points are solid, which means they are selected.

9. **Choose Object>Path>Join.**

   This command connects any two selected open endpoints. If the selected points overlap, as in this exercise, the two points are simply combined into a single corner endpoint. If the two selected points do not overlap, Illustrator automatically connects them with a straight line segment.

10. **Choose the Selection tool to reveal the bounding box for the selected object.**

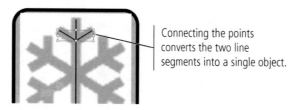

Connecting the points converts the two line segments into a single object.

11. **Save the file and continue to the next exercise.**

 REFLECT DRAWING OBJECTS

Illustrator includes four important transformation tools — Rotate, Reflect, Scale, and Shear. Each of these transformations can be applied by hand using the related tool in the Tools panel, as well as numerically using the appropriate dialog box from the Object>Transform menu.

   Much of the work you do in Illustrator requires changing objects that already exist. In this exercise, you use reflection to create additional sections of the snowflake icon.

1. **With icons.ai open, choose the Selection tool in the Tools panel. Make sure the angled-branch object is selected on the artboard.**

   Because the Selection tool is active, you can now see the bounding box of the selected object — both angled lines, which have been joined into a single object.

2. **Choose Object>Transform>Reflect.**

   You can reflect objects around the vertical or horizontal axis at specific degrees. In this case, you want to make the branches at the bottom of the snowflake, so you need to reflect the object around the horizontal axis.

3. **In the Reflect dialog box, make sure the Preview check box is active.**

   The Preview option, which is available in all of the Illustrator transformation dialog boxes, allows you to see the effects of your changes before you commit them.

4. **Choose the Horizontal option and click Copy.**

   If you click OK in any of the transformation dialog boxes, the transformation directly affects the selected object. Because you want another branch for the bottom of the flake, you are using the Copy function instead of simply clicking OK.

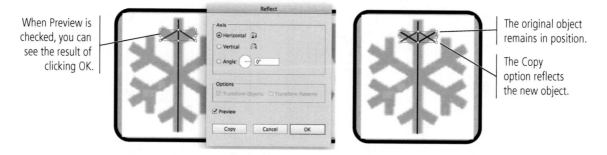

When Preview is checked, you can see the result of clicking OK.

The original object remains in position.

The Copy option reflects the new object.

5. **With the Selection tool still active, click the reflected branches and drag them to the bottom of the flake. Place the object appropriately, using the template image as a guide.**

   Again, the Smart Guides help you place the object; the green line and cursor feedback show the angle at which you're moving the selected object, so you can more easily maintain the same horizontal position.

Note:

Reflecting on the horizontal axis flips the object top over bottom. Reflecting around the vertical axis flips the object left to right.

Use cursor feedback to move the shape to the exact horizontal position (dX = 0).

6. **Choose Object>Unlock All.**

   Remember, you locked the original vertical line to protect it while you worked with the endpoints of the angled branches. Now that you have one complete set of branches, you can use the existing objects to create the remaining icon elements — which means you need to unlock the vertical line so you can access and copy it.

Note:

The Unlock All command affects individually locked objects on unlocked layers. It does not affect objects on locked layers.

7. **Choose Select>All.**

   All three objects — the vertical line and the two branch objects — are now selected.

8. **In the Control panel, change the stroke width to 7 pt.**

9. **Choose Object>Group.**

   Because these three objects are basically a single entity in the icon, it's a good idea to treat them as a single object.

10. **Save the file and continue to the next exercise.**

ROTATE DRAWING OBJECTS

Very few projects are entirely horizontal, making rotating objects a foundational Illustrator skill. In this exercise, you use several rotation techniques to create the rest of the snowflake artwork.

1. **With icons.ai open, make sure the grouped object is selected.**

2. **Activate the Rotate tool in the Tools panel.**

   When you select the Rotate tool, an **origin point** appears by default at the center of the selected object. This origin point is the point around which rotation occurs. If you want to rotate an object around some other point, you can single-click anywhere to define a different origin point.

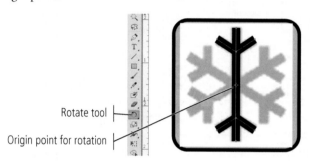

Rotate tool

Origin point for rotation

Note:

The Illustrator transformation tools all use this same origin point concept as the basis for transformations. You can click without dragging to reposition the origin point before applying the transformation.

3. **Click near the top of the vertical line, hold down the mouse button, and then drag left and down until the line appears over the next branch in the snowflake. Note the angle in the cursor feedback, and then release the mouse button.**

   As you can see, the rotation moved the selected objects around the origin point. Unfortunately, the vertical line is no longer there because you just rotated it.

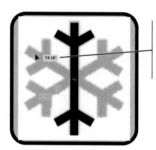

When you drag with the Rotate tool, the cursor feedback shows the angle of rotation.

When you release the mouse button, the original object rotates.

4. **Press Command/Control-Z to undo the rotation.**

5. **With the group still selected, double-click the Rotate tool to open the Rotate dialog box.**

   This dialog box is the same one you would see by choosing Object>Transform>Rotate. Transformation dialog boxes, which default to the last-used settings for that transformation, make it easy to apply very specific numeric transformations to selected objects.

Note:

You can Option/Alt-click and drag to clone an object while you transform it. In other words, if you press Option/Alt while dragging with the Rotate tool, you can create a rotated copy.

6. **Type 60 in the Rotate field, and then click Copy.**

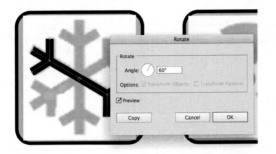

Note:

The Transform Again command applies the last-used transformation of any type to a selected object without opening a dialog box. This command might result in movement, rotation, reflection, shear, or scale, depending on the last transformation you applied.

7. **Choose Object>Transform>Transform Again to create the third branch of the snowflake icon.**

As before, the Transform Again command repeats the last-used transformation — in this case, the copy-rotate transformation from Step 6.

8. **Choose Select>All. Using the Align or Control panel, click the Vertical Align Center and Horizontal Align Center buttons.**

Because each "branch" is a group, the three sets of branches are now exactly centered in both directions. This step might not cause a noticeable change, depending on how precisely you placed the lines, but it's a good idea to be certain that the groups align properly.

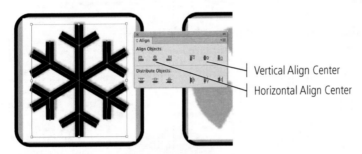

Vertical Align Center
Horizontal Align Center

9. **With all snowflake objects selected, choose Object>Lock>Selection.**

10. **In the Layers panel, select the Template cold.tif layer and click the Delete Selection button at the bottom of the panel. Click Yes in the confirmation message.**

Since the snowflake drawing is complete, you no longer need the template image.

Click here to delete the selected layer.

Adobe Illustrator

"Template cold.tif" contains artwork. Do you want to delete this layer?

No   Yes

11. **Save the file and continue to the next exercise.**

DIVIDE BASIC SHAPES INTO COMPONENT PIECES

Using the Illustrator Pathfinder panel, you can combine multiple shapes in a variety of ways, or you can use one object as a "cookie cutter" to remove or separate one shape from another. As you work with more complicated artwork in Illustrator, you will find many different ways to use the Pathfinder functions, either alone or in combination.

1. **With icons.ai open, make sure the Icon Art layer is selected in the Layers panel. Zoom into the second rectangle in the first row of background shapes.**

2. **Select the Ellipse tool (nested under the Rounded Rectangle tool) in the Tools panel. Set the fill color to black and the stroke color to None.**

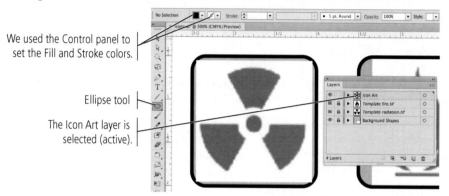

We used the Control panel to set the Fill and Stroke colors.

Ellipse tool

The Icon Art layer is selected (active).

3. **Click in the center of the radiation icon, press Option/Alt-Shift, and then drag to create a circle that covers the entire template icon.**

Remember, pressing Option/Alt allows you to draw a shape from the center out. Pressing Shift constrains the shape to equal height and width.

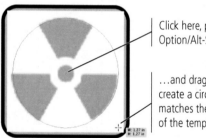

Click here, press Option/Alt-Shift…

…and drag out to create a circle that matches the outer edge of the template image.

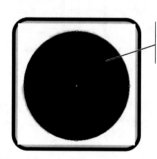

The fill color appears when you release the mouse button.

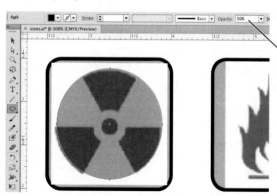

Note:

The fill color does not appear until you release the mouse button.

4. **With the new circle selected, change the Opacity field in the Control panel to 50.**

Opacity defines the transparency of the selected object. In this case, you're reducing the opacity from 100% (entirely solid or opaque) so you can see the template image behind the circle you just drew.

Change the shape's Opacity value so you can see the underlying template image.

Note:

You can also use the Transparency panel to change an object's opacity.

Note:

You'll work with opacity as a design element in Project 6: Cereal Box.

5. **Using the Ellipse tool, click again in the center of the template image, press Option/Alt-Shift, and drag to create the smaller circle in the center of the shape.**

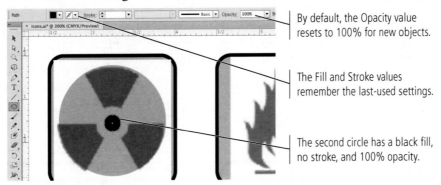

By default, the Opacity value resets to 100% for new objects.

The Fill and Stroke values remember the last-used settings.

The second circle has a black fill, no stroke, and 100% opacity.

6. **With the smaller circle selected, change the fill color to None and the stroke color to white. Change the stroke weight to 5 pt.**

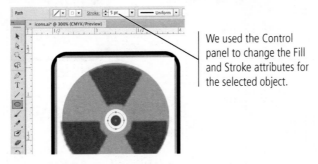

We used the Control panel to change the Fill and Stroke attributes for the selected object.

7. **Open the Stroke panel (Window>Stroke). If you only see the Stroke Weight field, open the panel's Options menu and choose Show Options.**

Because you used the template image to draw the small circle shape, the default position of the path does not accomplish the goal of creating the white ring. You can use the Stroke panel options to change the position of the stroke relative to the path, which better meets your needs in this artwork.

Click here to open the panel Options menu.

8. **With the small circle selected, click the Align Stroke to Outside button in the Stroke panel.**

All 5 pt of the stroke weight moves outside the object path.

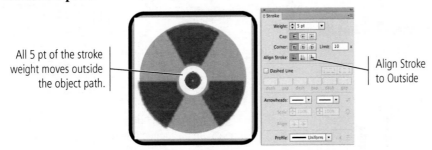

Align Stroke to Outside

9. **Press and hold Command/Control to temporarily access the Selection tool, and click away from the existing shapes to deselect them.**

If you don't deselect the circle, changing the Fill and Stroke attributes in the next step will change the attributes of the selected shape.

10. **Choose the Line Segment tool in the Tools panel, and then click the Default Fill and Stroke button at the bottom of the Tools panel.**

11. **Move the cursor below the circles you created until you see the Smart Guide connecting to the existing shapes' center points. Click and drag up to create a vertical line that extends past the top edge of the outer circle.**

Although none of the icon wedges have a vertical line, it's easier to start at vertical and rotate the objects as necessary.

Note:

To create the vertical line, use the cursor feedback to drag a 90° line, or press Shift to automatically constrain the line to 90°.

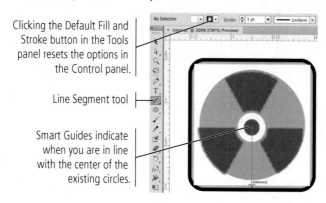

Clicking the Default Fill and Stroke button in the Tools panel resets the options in the Control panel.

Line Segment tool

Smart Guides indicate when you are in line with the center of the existing circles.

Extend the line past the top of the outer circle.

The Stroke Panel in Depth

The **Cap** options define the appearance of a stroke beyond the endpoint of the line.

None end cap style

Round end cap style

Square end cap style

The **Corner** options define the appearance of corners where two lines meet. When Miter Join is selected, you can define a miter limit in the Limit field. A miter limit controls when the corner switches from a pointed joint to a beveled joint, as a factor of the stroke weight. If you define a miter limit of 2 for a 2-point line, the corner is beveled if the pointed corner extends beyond 4 points (2 × 2).

Miter join   Rounded join   Beveled join

The **Align Stroke** options determine where the stroke is placed relative to the actual path.

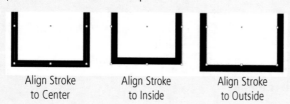

Align Stroke to Center   Align Stroke to Inside   Align Stroke to Outside

When the **Dashed Line** option is checked, you can define a specific pattern of dashes and gaps in the related fields. The two buttons to the right of the check box determine how a dash pattern is stretched (or not) so that line ends or object corners have the same appearance.

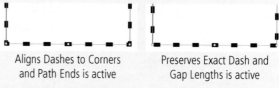

Aligns Dashes to Corners and Path Ends is active   Preserves Exact Dash and Gap Lengths is active

The **Arrowheads** options can be used to control end treatments on each end of a line. You can choose an arrowhead shape from the menus, and change the scale of applied arrowheads (relative to the applied stroke weight).

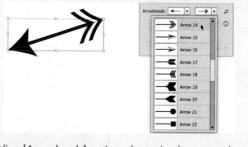

The Align [Arrowheads] options determine how arrowhead treatments are positioned relative to the path endpoint.

Place Arrow Tip at End of Path   Extend Arrow Tip Beyond End of Path

12. Using the Selection tool, draw a marquee around the three objects that you have created to select them all. Use the options in the Align or Control panel to align the selected objects horizontally and vertically.

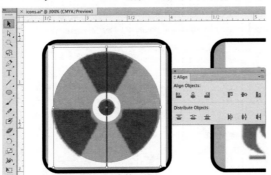

13. Click away from the selected objects, and then select only the vertical line.

The icon has six wedges, which means each half of the circle needs to be divided into three pieces. To accomplish this, you use precise rotation to slice the larger circle into the necessary parts.

14. With the vertical line selected, choose Object>Transform>Rotate. Type **60** in the Angle field and click Copy.

This menu command has the same result as double-clicking the Rotate tool, but you don't have to switch tools.

A full circle has 360 degrees. You're cutting the circle into six equal pieces; one sixth of 360° is 60°, so this is the exact angle that you need to create the correct number of pieces.

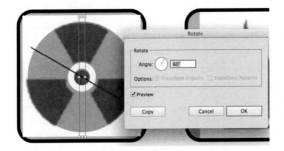

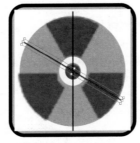

15. Choose Object>Transform>Transform Again to make a third line.

The Transform Again command applies the last-used transformation of any type to a selected object without opening a dialog box. Because you used the Rotate dialog box with the Copy button in the previous step, the Transform Again command copies the current selection and rotates it by the same angle you used in Step 14.

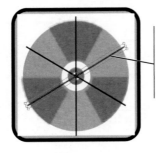

You now have all the pieces you need. The next step is to use these basic elements to create the final icon.

16. Using the Selection tool, select the smaller circle only and choose Object>Path>Outline Stroke.

This command changes the object stroke to a filled object. You drew the white circle to "cut out" the smaller black circle from the wedges. The Pathfinder functions recognize strokes for cutting apart shapes, but the stroke weight is not considered when the new paths are generated. To create the thick white space in the actual icon, you need to convert the heavy stroke to a filled shape.

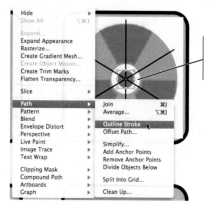

The original object had a 5-pt stroke weight.

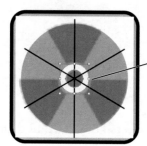

The Outline Stroke command changes the selected object to a filled shape with no visible stroke attributes.

17. Select all the objects in the icon, and then open the Pathfinder panel (Window>Pathfinder).

You can drag a marquee with the Selection tool, or choose Select>All. Because you locked the snowflake artwork in the first icon, those objects are not selected.

Note:

Press Command/ Control-A to select all unlocked objects on the artboard.

18. In the Pathfinder panel, click the Divide button.

Options in the Pathfinder panel allow you to cut shapes out of other shapes and merge multiple shapes into a single shape.

It's important to realize that many Pathfinder options can be applied in more than one way. We're using the Divide and Unite options in this exercise to give you an idea of what you can accomplish with the Pathfinder.

Divide button

The Divide function slices apart all possible shapes of the selected objects. Everywhere two objects overlap, a new shape is created.

Because the straight lines are open shapes, they divide the circles into sixths, but the open ends of the lines (outside the area of the larger circle) are removed.

19. Save the file and continue to the next exercise.

In the Pathfinder panel, the top row of buttons — the Shape Modes — create complex shapes by combining the originally selected shapes. (You can press Option/Alt and click a Shape Mode to maintain the paths from the original objects.)

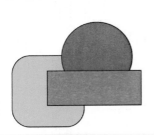

Original objects

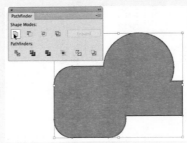

Unite combines all selected objects into a single shape. By default, the Shape options result in a single new object.

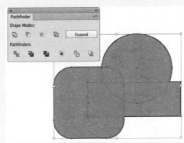

If you Option/Alt-click a shape mode button, the result maintains the original paths unless you manually expand it.

Minus Front removes overlapping areas from the backmost shape in the selection.

Intersect creates a shape of only areas where all selected objects overlap.

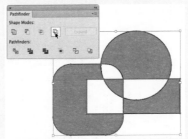

Exclude removes any areas where two objects overlap.

The second row of options — the Pathfinders — do exactly that. The resulting shapes are some combination of the paths that made up the originally selected objects.

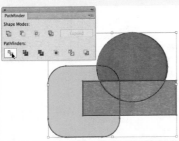

Divide creates separate shapes from all overlapping areas of selected objects.

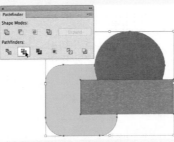

Trim removes underlying areas of overlapping objects. Objects of the same fill color are not combined.

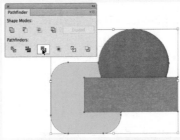

Merge removes underlying areas of overlapping objects. Objects of the same fill color are combined.

Crop returns the areas of underlying objects that are within the boundary of the topmost object.

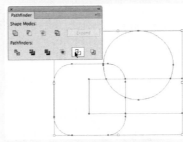

Outline divides the selected objects, then returns unfilled, open paths.

Minus Back removes the area of underlying objects from the front object.

WORK IN ISOLATION MODE

Groups can be invaluable when you need to treat multiple items as a single object. When items are grouped, it is easy to move and manipulate the entire group as a single object. In many cases, however, you will need to make changes to only part of a group. Depending on the complexity of the file, this can be very difficult without first breaking apart the group ("ungrouping"). Illustrator's Isolation mode offers a convenient workspace, where you can work with grouped objects as if they were stand-alone objects.

1. **With icons.ai open, use the Selection tool to double-click any of the shapes in the radiation icon to enter Isolation mode.**

   When you use the Pathfinder panel, the resulting shapes are automatically grouped. Because all of these shapes make up the icon artwork, it's a good idea to leave them grouped. Isolation mode allows you to work with the constituent objects without ungrouping.

2. **Using the Selection tool, click the wedge shape in the top-left area of the icon, and then press Delete.**

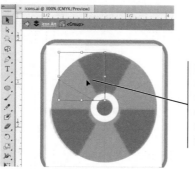 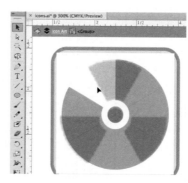

Because you're working in Isolation mode, you can use the Selection tool to select one object, even though the object is part of a group on the main artboard.

3. **Select and delete every other wedge in the outside area of the group.**

4. **Choose View>Outline.**

   Outline mode allows you to see and work with the basic shapes only. This way, object fills don't obscure the shapes that you need to see clearly.

5. **Click in the center set of wedges and drag a marquee that encompasses the center points of all six center wedges.**

   If you tried to do this in Preview mode, clicking one of the filled shapes and dragging would actually move the shape you clicked. Because the fills are not technically present in Outline mode, you can use the click-drag method to select all six shapes instead of Shift-clicking each one individually.

   Be sure you don't click on any actual line when you begin to draw the selection marquee. If necessary, zoom in so you can clearly see the empty spaces in the small wedge shapes.

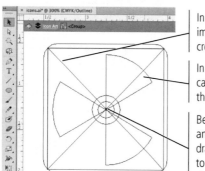 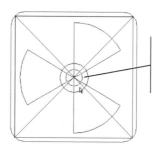

In Outline mode, linked images appear with crossed diagonal lines.

In Outline mode, you can't see or interact with the objects' Fill attributes.

Because you can't select an object's fill, you can drag a selection marquee to select only the six small shapes in the icon center.

Note:

Don't be confused by the crossed diagonal lines that identify the linked template image.

When you release the mouse button, you can see that all six objects are selected.

6. **In the Pathfinder panel, click the Unite button.**

   This function merges the selected shapes into a single object.

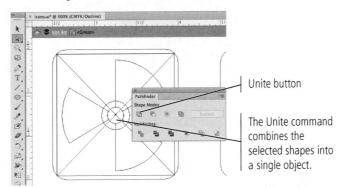

Unite button

The Unite command combines the selected shapes into a single object.

7. **Choose View>Preview to exit Outline mode and display the normal artwork.**

8. **Using the Selection tool, click to select any one of the black (partially transparent) objects.**

9. **Choose Select>Same>Opacity.**

   The options in this menu are very useful for finding objects that share specific attributes.

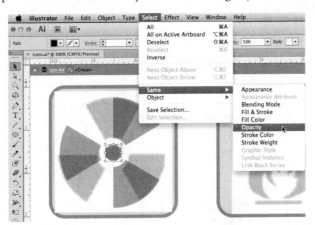

Note:

You can also use the Select Similar Objects menu in the Control panel to select objects with like attributes.

10. **Change the Opacity value (in the Control panel) to 100 for the selected objects.**

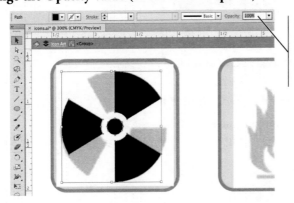

Because you no longer need to see the underlying template image, you can restore your artwork to 100% opacity.

11. **At the top of the document window, click the arrow button twice to return to the main artboard.**

    Your icon is almost complete; you only need to rotate the shape to match the image.

12. **Save the file and continue to the next exercise.**

USE MEASUREMENTS TO ADJUST YOUR ARTWORK

Depending on the type of work you do, Illustrator drawings can be entirely freeform, precisely measured, or a combination of the two (as in this case). The Measure tool evaluates different dimensional attributes of objects on the page. As you might expect from the name, the Measure tool acts like a digital tape measure. In addition to sizes and positions, the tool also measures angles — an important feature for technical drawing that requires precise detail.

1. **With icons.ai open, choose the Measure tool in the Tools panel (nested under the Eyedropper tool).**

2. **Click at the outside corner of the left wedge, and then drag down and right along the shape edge (as shown in the following image).**

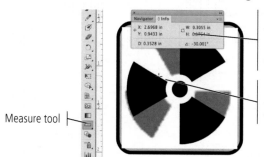

Measure tool

When you use the Measure tool, measurements appear in the Info panel (which opens automatically).

Click and drag along this line (down and right) to find the angle of the line.

Note:

If you drag from the inside out, the Info panel shows an angle of 150°. This provides the same information, because 180° — your goal — minus 150° equals 30°.

The Measure tool tells you that the angle of this line is –30°. You need it to be 180° (horizontal), which means you need to rotate the shape by 30°.

3. **Select the group with the Selection tool, and then choose Object>Transform>Rotate.**

4. **Change the Angle field to 30 and click OK.**

5. **In the Layers panel, select and delete the Template radiation.tif layer.**

After you remove the template image, you can see the remaining problem — the Divide Pathfinder function left a white ring in the shape. You need to remove these white objects.

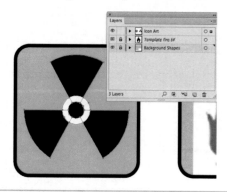

6. **Click away from all objects to deselect the icon artwork.**

7. **Using the Direct Selection tool, click the fill of one of the white shapes to select it.**

   Remember, all of the constituent shapes are part of a group — the result of the Pathfinder Divide function — so you can't use the Selection tool. The irregular position of these small shapes also makes it difficult to individually select the six objects with the Direct Selection tool.

8. **With the white-filled shape selected, choose Select>Same>Fill Color.**

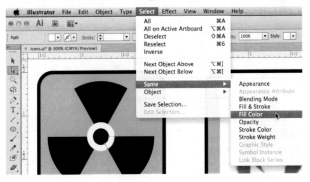
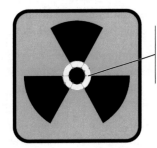

All six white-filled objects are selected because the original selection had a white fill.

9. **With all six white shapes in the icon selected, press Delete.**

Note:

Be careful when you use the Select Similar functions. They select all similar unlocked objects on the entire artboard. If the art for another unlocked icon had a white fill, for example, it would also be selected.

10. **Select all objects in the radiation icon art and choose Object>Lock>Selection.**

    This step protects the completed icon artwork from inadvertently being changed while you work on the rest of this project.

11. **Save the file and continue to the next exercise.**

 DRAW WITH THE PENCIL TOOL

At this point, you have used a number of basic shapes to create finished icon artwork. As you might already realize, however, not all artwork can be created from basic shapes and lines. Illustrator includes everything you need to create artwork in any form, from a basic square to irregular shapes without a single visible straight edge. The Pencil tool is one method for creating custom shapes. Like a regular pencil on a piece of paper, the Pencil tool creates lines that follow the path of your cursor. (If you have a digital drawing tablet, the Pencil tool can be particularly useful for drawing custom artwork.)

Note:

In Project 2: Balloon Festival Artwork, you will learn how to use the Pen tool to control every point and path of your Illustrator drawings.

1. **With icons.ai open, make sure the Icon Art layer is selected in the Layers panel. Zoom in to the third rectangle in the first row of background shapes.**

2. **Choose the Pencil tool and click the Default Fill and Stroke button in the Tools panel.**

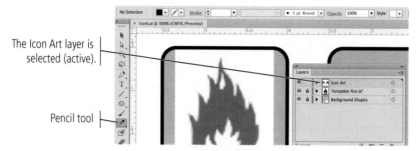

The Icon Art layer is selected (active).

Pencil tool

3. **Double-click the Pencil tool in the Tools panel.**

Double-clicking certain tools in the Tools panel opens an Options dialog box, where you can control the default behavior for the selected tool. The Pencil tool options include:

- **Fidelity.** This option determines how far apart anchor points are added as you drag. Higher values result in fewer points and smoother lines; lower values result in more anchor points, which can make the lines appear choppy.

- **Smoothness.** This option determines how closely a path follows the path of your cursor. Lower values result in more anchor points, especially if your cursor movement is choppy.

- **Fill New Pencil Strokes.** By default, pencil paths are not filled regardless of the fill color defined in the Tools panel.

- **Keep Selected.** If this option is checked, the line you draw is automatically selected when you release the mouse button.

- **Edit Selected Paths.** If this option is checked, drawing near a selected path can change the existing path. This is an important distinction (especially when Keep Selected is checked) because you can accidentally edit the first path instead of creating a second shape.

4. **Set the Fidelity value to 2.5 pixels and Smoothness to 0%.**

To draw this icon, you must make many fine movements and change direction often. Even though this icon artwork doesn't have to be exact to communicate the necessary message ("fire"), you should try to match the template as closely as possible.

5. **Make sure the Fill New Pencil Strokes and Edit Selected Paths options are unchecked, and then click OK.**

6. **Click at the bottom-left point of the fire icon, hold down the mouse button, and begin dragging around the shape of the fire. When you get near your original starting point, press Option/Alt and release the mouse button.**

As you drag, a colored line indicates the path you're drawing. Don't worry if the path isn't perfect; when you release the mouse button, Illustrator automatically smoothes the path.

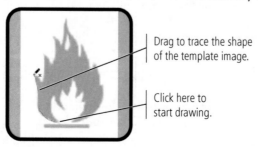

Drag to trace the shape of the template image.

Click here to start drawing.

The Pencil tool creates open-ended lines. To create a closed shape with your path, press Option/Alt before releasing the mouse button at your original starting point.

The hollow circle in the cursor icon indicates that releasing the mouse button will create a closed shape.

When you release the mouse button, the shape shows the defined stroke color but not the fill color.

7. **Click near the top point of the white flame area (inside the first path) and drag to create the white inner shape in the fire icon. Press Option/Alt before releasing the mouse button so you end up with a closed shape.**

Use the Pencil tool to draw this shape. Press Option/Alt before releasing the mouse button to create a closed shape.

8. **Using the Rectangle tool, draw the shape below the fire in the template image.**

9. **In the Layers panel, delete the Template fire.tif layer.**

10. **Use the Selection tool to select all three shapes of the icon art. Change the fill color to black and the stroke color to None.**

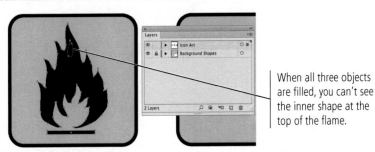

When all three objects are filled, you can't see the inner shape at the top of the flame.

11. **Choose Object>Compound Path>Make.**

    This option combines all three selected shapes into a single shape; the area of the smaller shape is removed from the larger shape behind it.

As a compound path, the inner shape is removed from the outer shape.

Note:

*A **compound path** is a single shape made up of more than one path. Compound paths usually have inner "empty" areas, such as the letter O or Q.*

12. **Save the file and close it.**

1. _____ are composed of mathematical descriptions of a series of lines and points; they are resolution independent, can be freely scaled, and are automatically output at the resolution of the output device.

2. _____ are pixel-based, made up of a grid of individual pixels (rasters or bits) in rows and columns.

3. The _____ is a rectangle that marks the outermost edges of an object, regardless of the actual object shape.

4. _____ is the relative top-to-botom order of objects on the artboard, or of layers in the Layers panel.

5. The _____ is used to select entire objects or groups.

6. The _____ is used to select individual paths and points of a shape, or to select component pieces within a group.

7. The _____ is used to draw freeform paths defined by dragging the mouse cursor.

8. Press _____ to temporarily access the Selection tool; releasing the modifier key restores the previously selected tool.

9. The _____ is used to create complex shapes by combining multiple selected objects.

10. A(n) _____ is a single object that is made up of more than one shape.

1. Briefly explain the difference between vector graphics and raster images.

2. Briefly explain the difference between the Selection tool and the Direct Selection tool.

3. Briefly explain the difference between Shape Mode and Pathfinder operations in the Pathfinder panel.

Use what you learned in this project to complete the following freeform exercise.
Carefully read the art director and client comments, then create your own design to meet the needs of the project.
Use the space below to sketch ideas; when finished, write a brief explanation of your reasoning behind your final design.

art director comments

The client is pleased with the first three icons, and they want you to complete the rest of the warning icons. They also want you to create an additional set of icons for travel and outdoor activities that they offer as benefits during their international corporate conferences.

To complete this project, you should:

❏ Complete the remaining international warning icons. The bitmap versions are in your WIP>Symbols folder.

❏ Carefully consider the best approach for each icon and use whichever tool (or tools) you feel is most appropriate.

❏ Create a second Illustrator file for the six new recreation icons.

client comments

We host a number of large, international conventions and conferences every year, and many attendees bring their families along for a working vacation. To keep everyone happy, we have started offering different outdoor activities for the families while their spouses are attending sessions, but the international crowd means that many people need visual help getting to the right place.

Since you did such a good job on the first three icons, we would like you to finish those. But first, we want you to create icons for horseback riding, sailing, swimming, hiking, rock climbing, and nature walks.

We don't have the images for these ones, so we would like you to come up with something. Remember, icons need to be easily recognizable, so they should very clearly convey visually what each one is for.

project justification

_____

_____

_____

_____

_____

_____

_____

_____

_____

_____

_____

_____

_____

_____

Project Summary

The skills that you learned in this project will serve as the foundation for most work you create in Illustrator. You learned how to place raster images as templates, from which you created scalable vector graphics that will work in virtually any printed application. You learned a number of techniques for selecting objects and component pieces of objects, as well as various options for aligning objects relative to one another and to the artboard.

You learned how to draw primitive geometric shapes, and how to control the color of objects' fill and stroke attributes. You used a number of transformation options, including cloning methods to copy existing objects. Finally, you learned how to draw freeform shapes to suit more complex needs. As you move forward in this book, you will build on the basic skills you learned in this project to create increasingly complex artwork.

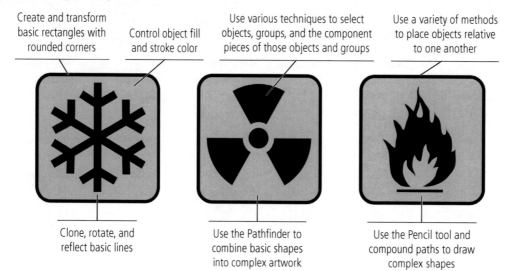

Create and transform basic rectangles with rounded corners

Control object fill and stroke color

Use various techniques to select objects, groups, and the component pieces of those objects and groups

Use a variety of methods to place objects relative to one another

Clone, rotate, and reflect basic lines

Use the Pathfinder to combine basic shapes into complex artwork

Use the Pencil tool and compound paths to draw complex shapes

Balloon Festival Artwork

Your client is the marketing director for the Temecula Hot Air Balloon Festival, which attracts thousands of tourists to the desert community throughout the three-day event. You have been hired to create the primary artwork for this year's event, which will be used in a variety of different products (ads, souvenirs, etc.).

This project incorporates the following skills:

❏ Drawing complex custom shapes with the Pen tool

❏ Editing anchor points and handles to control the precise position of vector paths

❏ Drawing irregular shape outlines by painting with the Blob Brush tool

❏ Creating a custom color scheme using saved swatches

❏ Adding interest and depth with color gradients

❏ Adjusting color, both globally and in specific selections

❏ Saving multiple file versions for various print applications

client comments

Although the festival is popular, it's an aging crowd; we hope to bring in more families so we can get more younger people interested in ballooning as a hobby. This year is the 25th anniversary of the festival, and we've added a range of entertainment and educational options for younger children.

We want this year's artwork to be very bright and colorful; we also want a "cartoon-y" look that might appeal to young kids. It will be used on everything from festival programs to glassware — we're even planning on a teddy bear who is wearing a t-shirt with the artwork silk-screened on the back.

art director comments

I sketched a mock-up of a hot air balloon that you can use as the basis for the artwork. You should use the Pen tool to draw the balloon because simple shapes won't work and the Pencil tool doesn't provide fine enough control to efficiently achieve what you need.

Temecula is on the edge of the desert in southern California, so I'm going to have your partner create a desert panorama scene to put behind the balloons.

Rather than just one balloon floating over the desert, the finished piece should create the effect of a whole fleet of balloons. You can just clone the first balloon a couple of times, but make sure you change the color scheme in each one so they are all a bit different.

This is going to be a complex piece of artwork, so I recommend using layers to organize the various pieces. That will make it far easier to edit specific components as necessary if the client decides to make changes.

project objectives

To complete this project, you will:

❏ Use the Pen tool to draw precise curves

❏ Adjust anchor points and handles to precisely control the shape of vector objects

❏ Use the Blob Brush tool to "paint" the area of vector shapes

❏ Define custom color swatches to allow easy universal changes

❏ Create color gradients to blend multiple colors in a single object

❏ Adjust gradients in context on the artboard

❏ Change colors in specific selected objects

❏ Save multiple file versions for use in various design applications

Stage 1 Drawing Complex Artwork

In Project 1: International Symbols, you used a number of techniques to create finished artwork from basic shapes. Of course, much of the artwork you create will require far more complexity than simple lines and geometric shapes. When you need to produce custom artwork — whether from scratch or by tracing a hand-drawn sketch or photo — Illustrator includes a powerful set of tools to create and manipulate every point and path in the illustration. In the first stage of this project, you begin exploring the Pen tool, as well as other options for building and controlling custom shapes.

 ## PREPARE THE DRAWING WORKSPACE

As with any project, setting up the workspace is an important first step. This project requires a single artboard to contain the entire illustration.

1. **Download A16_RF_Project2.zip from the Student Files Web page.**

2. **Expand the ZIP archive in your WIP folder (Macintosh) or copy the archive contents into your WIP folder (Windows).**

   This results in a folder named **Festival**, which contains the files you need for this project. You should also use this folder to save the files you create in this project.

3. **In Illustrator, choose File>New. Type balloons in the Name field, choose Letter in the Size menu, and choose Inches in the Units menu.**

4. **If the Advanced options are not visible, click the right-arrow button to show those options. Choose CMYK in the Color Mode menu and choose High (300 PPI) in the Raster Effects menu.**

   This illustration will be printed in various documents, so you should design the job in the CMYK color mode. Some Illustrator functions, such as effects and gradient meshes, will be rasterized for commercial output; the High (300 PPI) raster effects setting results in sufficient resolution for those elements.

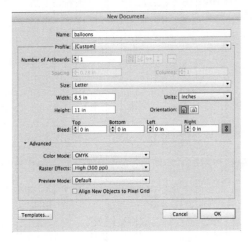

5. **Click OK to create the file.**

6. **Choose File>Place. Navigate to the file sketch.jpg in your WIP>Festival folder. Make sure the Link option is not checked and the Template option is checked, and then click Place.**

    You will use this client-supplied sketch to create the primary artwork for this illustration.

    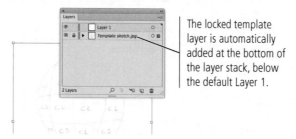

    The locked template layer is automatically added at the bottom of the layer stack, below the default Layer 1.

7. **Double-click the template layer icon in the Layers panel to open the Layer Options dialog box. Uncheck the Dim Images option and click OK.**

    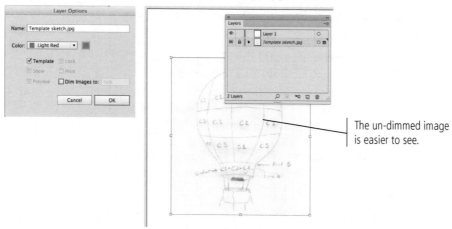

    The un-dimmed image is easier to see.

8. **Double-click the Layer 1 name in the Layers panel to highlight it. Rename the layer Balloon 1, then press Return/Enter to finalize the new name.**

9. **Click away from the placed sketch image to deselect it.**

10. **Save the file as an Illustrator file named balloons.ai in your WIP>Festival folder, and then continue to the next exercise.**

USE THE PEN TOOL TO TRACE THE SKETCH

As you discovered in Project 1: International Symbols, many objects can be drawn with the basic shape tools. The true power of Illustrator, however, comes from being able to draw just as you would on a piece of paper — including freeform objects that have no basis in geometric shapes. You used the Pencil tool in Project 1 to begin working with custom artwork. In this project, you use the Pen tool, which provides far more power to control the precise position of every line in a drawing. In fact, many believe the Pen tool is the most powerful and important tool in the Illustrator Tools panel.

Note:

*The lines you create by connecting anchor points and pulling handles are called **Bézier curves**.*

When you draw with the Pen tool, an anchor point marks the end of a line segment, and the point handles determine the shape of that segment. That's the basic definition of a geometric vector. Fortunately, you don't need to be a mathematician to master the Pen tool because Illustrator handles the underlying geometry for you.

Each segment in a path has two anchoring end points and two associated handles. In the image shown to the right, we first clicked to create Point A and dragged to the right (without releasing the mouse button) to create Handle A1. We then clicked and dragged to create Point B and Handle B1; Handle B2 was automatically created as a reflection of B1 (Point B is a smooth symmetrical point).

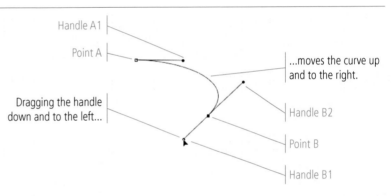

The image to the right shows the result of dragging Handle B1 to the left instead of to the right. Notice the difference in the curve, as compared to the curve above. When you drag the handle, the segment arcs away from the direction of the handle.

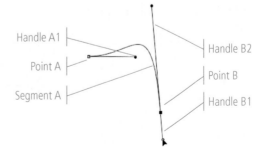

It's important to understand that every curved segment is connected to two handles. In this image, dragging the handle to the right pulls out the arc of the connected segment. You could change the shape of Segment A by dragging either Handle A1 or B2.

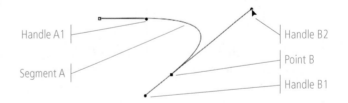

The final concept you should understand about anchors and handles (for now, at least) is that clicking and dragging to create a point creates a smooth symmetrical point. Dragging one handle of a smooth point also changes the other handle of that point. In the image shown below, dragging Handle B1 also moves Handle B2, which affects the shape of Segment A.

You can create corner points by simply clicking with the Pen tool instead of clicking and dragging. Corner points do not have their own handles; the connected segments are controlled by the handles of the other associated anchor points.

Handle of other connected point controls the segment shape

Corner point has no handles.

You can convert a smooth point into a corner point by clicking the point with the Convert Anchor Point tool (nested under the Pen tool), or click and drag a corner point to convert it to a smooth point. If you click and drag a specific handle with the Convert Anchor Point tool, you can move one handle without affecting the opposing handle of the same point.

1. **With balloons.ai open, choose the Pen tool in the Tools panel.**

2. **Using the Control panel, set the stroke to 1-pt black and the fill to None.**

3. **Click with the Pen tool to place the first anchor point on the left side of the balloon where the round part meets the flat base.**

   We typically find it easier to start drawing at a corner (if one exists).

Note:

As you draw, zoom in as necessary to view different parts of the sketch.

You should have a fill of None and a 1-pt black stroke.

Pen tool

Click here to create the first anchor point.

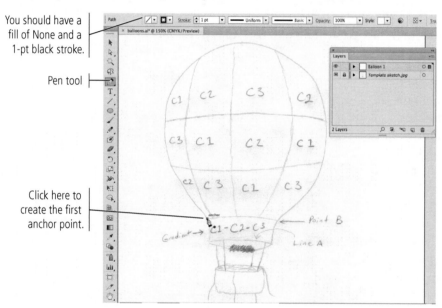

4. **Click the right side of the balloon (at Point B in the sketch) and immediately drag right and slightly down to create handles for the second point. When the segment between the two points matches the line in the sketch, release the mouse button.**

   When you click and drag without releasing the mouse button, you create handles, which determine the shape of the segment that connects the two points.

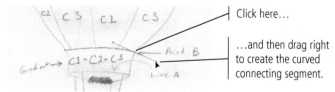

   Click here…

   …and then drag right to create the curved connecting segment.

5. **Click again on the second anchor point and release the mouse button without dragging.**

Clicking a smooth point as you draw converts it to a corner point, removing the outside handle from the point; the inside handle that defines the shape of the connecting segment remains in place. This allows you to change direction as you draw.

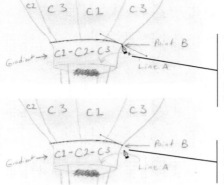

The inverted "v" in the cursor icon indicates that clicking will create a corner point, which will enable you to change direction.

After clicking, the right handle of the point is gone.

6. **Option/Alt-click the second anchor point, hold down the mouse button, and pull slightly up and right to generate a new handle for the right side of the anchor point.**

Pulling the new handle determines the direction of the next segment you create. The curve will bend in the direction of the new handle.

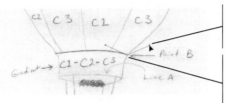

The handle you drag will define the next segment shape.

Option/Alt-click and drag from this point to add a handle on the right side of the point.

Note:

If you're editing an existing path, you can click a point with the Convert Anchor Point tool (nested under the Pen tool) to change a smooth point to a corner point. You can also click and drag to change an existing corner point to a smooth point.

7. **Click and drag to create a new point (with handles) on the outside edge of the balloon where the C3 section meets the C1 section.**

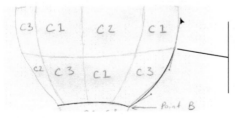

Click here and immediately drag up and right until the connecting segment matches the shape of the sketched line.

Note:

When we say "click and drag", you should hold down the mouse button until the end of the step.

8. **Continue adding points and handles to outline the entire outside edge of the balloon.**

   As a general rule, use as few points as necessary to create a shape with the Pen tool. We used a total of seven points to create this shape; those points are highlighted in the image following the next step.

9. **Click the original point without dragging to close the shape.**

   When you return to the original point, the cursor shows a small hollow circle. This indicates that clicking the existing point will close the shape.

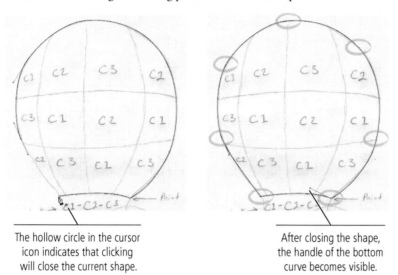

The hollow circle in the cursor icon indicates that clicking will close the current shape.

After closing the shape, the handle of the bottom curve becomes visible.

10. **Using the Direct Selection tool, click Point B to select that anchor point.**

    Depending on your precision when you dragged the handles, some curves might not match the sketch. When tracing a hand-drawn sketch, your shape doesn't need to be exact — but it should be close. You can use the Direct Selection tool to edit any specific anchor point or segment.

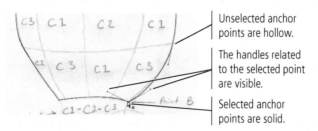

Unselected anchor points are hollow.

The handles related to the selected point are visible.

Selected anchor points are solid.

11. **Use the Direct Selection tool to make any adjustments you feel necessary. You can move specific anchor points by dragging them to a new position, and/or drag handles to adjust curve segments that connect two anchor points.**

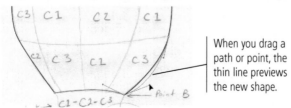

When you drag a path or point, the thin line previews the new shape.

12. **Save the file and continue to the next exercise.**

SELECT AND EDIT COMPLEX PATHS

In Illustrator, you can manipulate and change your drawings until they precisely match your vision for the artwork. You can use numerous options to select and modify shapes — or parts of shapes — so you can create exactly what you need, regardless of what is already on the artboard.

1. **With balloons.ai open, choose the Direct Selection tool.**

2. **With nothing selected, click the horizontal segment that represents the bottom of the balloon shape.**

3. **Choose Edit>Copy to copy the selected segment.**

4. **Choose Object>Hide>Selection.**

   The Hide command affects only the selected object(s). The object is still on the artboard but not visible, and the layer is still visible.

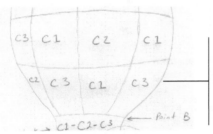

Even though you selected only the bottom segment of the balloon shape, the entire balloon shape is now hidden; you can't hide a single segment of a shape.

5. **Choose Edit>Paste in Front.**

   The segment you copied is pasted in exactly the same place as the original. Because you selected the segment with the Direct Selection tool, only that segment (not the entire object) was copied and pasted.

6. **Choose the Pen tool in the Tools panel and move the cursor over the right open endpoint.**

   The diagonal line in the cursor indicates that clicking will connect to the existing opening endpoint.

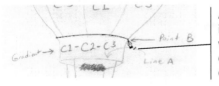

A diagonal line in the cursor icon indicates that clicking will connect to the open endpoint so you can continue drawing the shape.

> **Note:**
>
> *If you turn on Smart Guides (View>Smart Guides), the cursor shows the word "anchor" when the cursor is over an existing anchor point. This can be helpful if you are trying to connect to an open endpoint of an existing line (as in Step 6).*

7. **Click to resume working from the open endpoint.**

8. **Click and drag to create the bottom-right point of the balloon shape. Drag the handle down and right until the connecting curve matches the shape of the line in the sketch.**

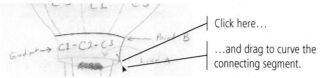

Click here…

…and drag to curve the connecting segment.

9. **Click the point from Step 8 to remove the handle from the outside of the point, and then click and drag again to create the bottom-left point.**

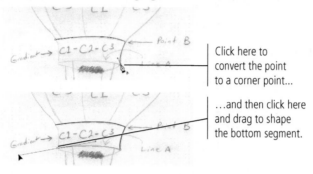

Click here to convert the point to a corner point...

…and then click here and drag to shape the bottom segment.

10. **Move the cursor over the open left endpoint of the top segment and click to close the shape.**

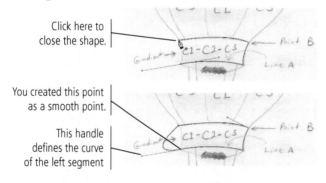

Click here to close the shape.

You created this point as a smooth point.

This handle defines the curve of the left segment

11. **Choose the Direct Selection tool in the Tools panel. Press Option/Alt, and then click and drag the outside handle of the bottom-left point. Drag the handle right until the left segment matches the shape of the line in the sketch.**

Remember, the Direct Selection tool allows you to adjust individual anchor points and handles. Option/Alt-dragging one handle of a smooth point converts the point to a corner point, but leaves both handles in place. This method allows you to change the direction of an existing point, but leave the opposite curve intact.

Option/Alt-dragging a handle converts the connected anchor point to a corner point.

12. **Save the file and continue to the next exercise.**

BUILD SHAPES FROM OVERLAPPING PATHS

The Shape Builder tool makes it very easy to break apart overlapping objects into component pieces. This tool offers similar functionality as the Pathfinder, but on a piece-by-piece basis rather than for entire selected shapes. In this exercise, you will use the Shape Builder tool to break up the balloon into the individual patches that are shown on the sketch.

1. **With balloons.ai open, choose Object>Show All.**

    Although the Hide command affects only selected objects, the Show All command is not selective; all hidden objects become visible.

2. **Using either the Selection or Direct Selection tool, select only the bottom shape and choose Object>Lock>Selection.**

    Because the lower shape is now locked, you can't select it.

    You can't lock only part of an object, so the entire object is locked even if you only select one of the segments or anchor points using the Direct Selection tool.

3. **Using the sketch as a guide, use the Pen tool to create the leftmost vertical line in the balloon, starting and stopping past the edges of the balloon shape (as shown in the following image).**

    You are going to use the Shape Builder tool to divide the balloon into the necessary shapes. For this process to work properly, the dividing lines need to be at least on top of the outside shape; to be sure, you should extend the lines farther than they need to be.

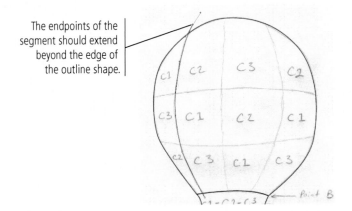

4. **While the Pen tool is still active, press Command/Control to temporarily access the Selection tool and click away from the line to deselect it.**

    When you release the mouse button, you return to the Pen tool. This technique allows you to easily deselect the current path and then continue to draw the next, unconnected path.

    Remember, simply click away from an object with the Selection or Direct Selection tool to deselect it. You can also press Command/Control-Shift-A to deselect the current selection.

5. **Repeat Steps 3–4 to create the remaining vertical and horizontal lines of the balloon.**

If you don't deselect the path from Step 3 before clicking to draw the next line, the third click would create a segment that is connected to the last place you clicked (on the first line). In the context of this exercise, a single line with multiple anchor points is much more difficult to control than two separate lines with open endpoints.

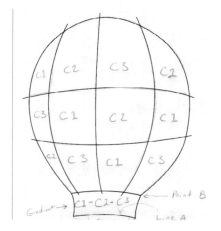

Note:

If necessary, use the Direct Selection tool to adjust the anchor points and handles of the line until they match the sketch.

6. **Choose the Selection tool in the Tools panel, and then choose Select>All.**

Because the bottom shape is locked, it is not included in the selection.

7. **Choose the Shape Builder tool in the Tools panel, and then reset the default fill and stroke colors.**

Note:

Press Command/ Control-A to select everything in the drawing space that is not locked.

8. **Move the cursor over the top-left section of the balloon (C1 in the sketch).**

The Shape Builder tool identifies overlapping areas of selected objects, which is why you had to select the pieces in Step 6.

Shape Builder tool

The highlight previews the shape that will be created by clicking.

The defined fill and stroke colors will apply to the resulting shape.

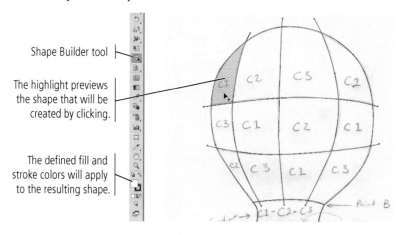

9. **Click the highlighted area to create the new shape.**

Because you set the Fill color to white, the resulting shape obscures the sketch behind it. This helps to identify which pieces you have already created.

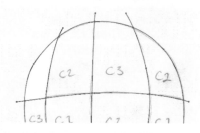

10. **Repeat Steps 8–9 for the remaining 11 pieces of the balloon.**

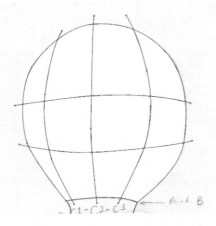

11. **Press Option/Alt, and move the cursor over the first line segment outside the right balloon edge. When the line segment is highlighted and the cursor shows a minus sign in the icon, click the segment to remove it.**

    The Shape Builder tool can be used to both create and remove shapes. Pressing Option/Alt switches the tool into Erase mode so you can remove paths or shapes.

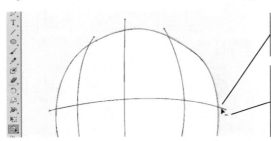

The area or path that will be affected by clicking is highlighted.

Pressing Option/Alt with the Shape Builder tool allows you to remove areas or paths, as indicated by the "–" in the cursor icon.

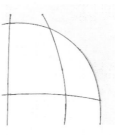

12. **Repeat Step 11 to remove the remaining extraneous line segments.**

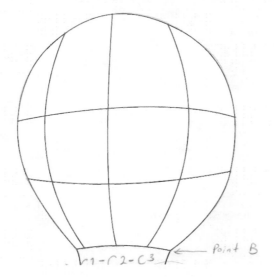

13. **Save the file and continue to the next exercise.**

More on the Shape Builder Tool

As you just saw, the Shape Builder tool makes it very easy to cut apart overlapping objects into pieces. The tool offers a number of options that can significantly enhance your ability to create complex, sophisticated artwork.

If a small opening exists in a path, you can activate **Gap Detection** settings to overlook small, medium, large, or custom-sized gaps in the open paths. This option is especially useful if the Consider Open Filled Paths as Closed option is not checked.

The **Pick Color From** menu determines whether the tool recognizes all swatches in the file or only colors that are actually used in the artwork.

You can also use the **Highlight** options to determine what, if anything, is highlighted when you move the tool cursor over a shape.

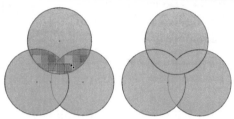

Click and drag with the Shape Builder tool to combine multiple pieces into a single shape.

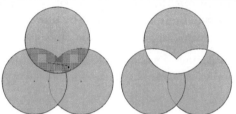

Option/Alt-click and drag with the Shape Builder tool to remove multiple pieces at the same time.

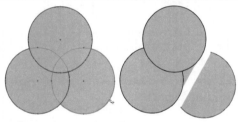

When In Merge Mode, Clicking Stroke Splits the Path is checked in the tool options dialog box, click a path to cut apart the path at the nearest anchor points.

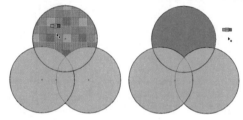

When Cursor Swatch Preview is checked in the tool options dialog box, three swatches appear above the tool cursor. You can use the Left and Right Arrow keys to move through the available color swatches.

ADJUST ANCHOR POINTS AND HANDLES

Practice is the best way to master Bézier curves. In this exercise, you use the techniques you have already learned to adjust and fine-tune the filled shapes created in the previous exercise.

1. **With balloons.ai open, choose the Direct Selection tool.**

2. **Deselect all objects by clicking away from the current selection, then click the top-left segment of the balloon's outer edge (labeled C1 in the sketch).**

   Remember, clicking a segment with the Direct Selection tool reveals the handles that define the shape of the segment.

3. **If your segment includes an extra anchor point, place the Pen tool cursor over the point and click to delete it.**

Your original points might have been in different places, depending on where you clicked to create the initial outline shape. When the Shape Builder tool divides the objects into separate shapes, it creates anchor points as necessary at the intersections, but also maintains the original points — which are not always necessary.

Delete unnecessary points from the outside of your balloon shape.

Place the Pen tool over an existing point to temporarily access the Delete Anchor Point tool.

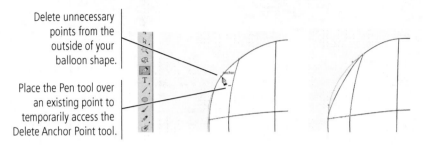

4. **Using the Direct Selection tool, click the top handle of the selected segment and drag up and left.**

By adjusting the segment, you can create the "pillow" appearance of the panels of a hot air balloon. The point where the two shapes meet is unaffected by dragging the point handle.

5. **Repeat Steps 2–4 to adjust the top edges of the other three top shapes to remove unnecessary anchor points and create a similar "pillow" effect on the four top pieces of the balloon.**

6. **Choose Object>Unlock All.**

As with the Show All command, the Unlock All command affects all individually locked objects, regardless of when the Lock command was applied. It does not affect objects on layers that have been locked in the Layers panel.

7. **Select the now-unlocked shape that makes up the band around the bottom of the balloon and change its fill to white.**

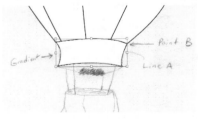

8. **Save the file and continue to the next exercise.**

Keep the following points in mind as you work with the Pen tool (and its four nested variations) and Bézier curves.

Using the Direct Selection tool...

Click a specific anchor point to select it and show all handles that relate to that point.

Click a specific segment to select it and show all handles that relate to that segment.

Option/Alt drag a handle of a smooth point to convert it to a corner point.

Using the Pen tool...

Place the cursor over an existing point to temporarily access the Delete Anchor Point tool.

Place the cursor over an existing segment to temporarily access the Add Anchor Point tool.

Press Option/Alt and place the cursor over an existing point to temporarily access the Convert Anchor Point tool.

 ADD DETAIL WITH THE PENCIL AND LINE SEGMENT TOOLS

Drawing with the Pencil tool is similar to sketching with a pencil and paper. The Pencil tool is a good choice if you want to create an object that appears sketchy or hand-drawn. Illustrator adds anchor points and handles as necessary to create the path you draw; you don't have control over where the anchor points are placed, but you can edit the path however you prefer.

1. **With balloons.ai open, select the Pencil tool in the Tools panel. Set the fill to none and the stroke to 1-pt black.**

2. **Double-click the Pencil tool in the Tools panel to open the Pencil Tool Options dialog box.**

3. **Set the Fidelity value to 2 pixels and Smoothness to 1%. Make sure Keep Selected is checked and Edit Selected Paths is not checked, and then click OK.**

   Low Fidelity and Smoothness settings result in fewer anchor points, which makes it easier to edit later (especially when working with small shapes).

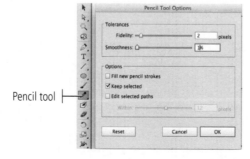

Pencil tool

4. **Starting at the top-right corner, carefully trace the outline of the basket. As you approach the starting point, press Option/Alt and release the mouse button to close the basket shape.**

As you drag the Pencil tool, a dotted line shows the path you traced (and thus, the shape you created). Don't worry if the shape isn't perfect; you will clean up the path in the next step.

5. **Adjust the anchor points and handles of the resulting shape until you are satisfied with the result.**

6. **Deselect the basket shape. Activate the Pencil tool, change the fill color to None, and change the stroke weight to 2 pt.**

7. **Trace the rope lines hanging from the basket. Select the two lines that appear to be behind the basket and choose Object>Arrange>Send to Back.**

8. **Use the Line Segment tool with a 2-pt stroke weight to draw the lines that connect the basket shapes to the balloon shapes.**

Using the Line Segment tool, you don't need to deselect after each line. The Line Segment tool also makes it much easier to create straight lines.

These lines don't need to be perfect, because the ends will be covered by the shapes you will create in the next exercise.

9. **Change the Line Segment tool stroke weight to 1 pt, and then draw crossing diagonal lines to represent a "basket weave" texture (using the following image as a guide).**

10. **Select the basket shape and change its fill color to white.**

11. **Save the file and continue to the next exercise.**

Editing Anchor Points with the Control Panel

When you are working with Bézier paths, the Control panel provides a number of options for editing selected anchor points.

A Convert Selected Anchor Points to Corner. This button removes the direction handles from both sides of the selected point(s).

B Convert Selected Anchor Points to Smooth. This button adds symmetrical direction handles to both sides of the selected point(s).

C Show Handles for Multiple Selected Anchor Points. If this option is toggled on, direction handles display for all selected points.

D Hide Handles for Multiple Selected Anchor Points. If this option is toggled on, direction handles are not visible when more than one point is selected.

E Remove Selected Anchor Points. This button removes the selected point from the path. If the removed point was between two other points, the connecting segment is not removed.

F Connect Selected End Points. This button has the same effect as the Object>Path>Join command.

G Cut Path at Selected Anchor Points. This button results in two overlapping, open endpoints where the selected point was previously a single point.

H Isolate Selected Object. This button enters isolation mode with the object containing the selected anchor point(s). If points are selected on more than one object, this button is not available.

I Point Position. Use the X and Y fields to define a specific position for the selected point. You can also use mathematical operations to move a point relative to its current position (e.g., move it left by typing "-1" after the current X value).

CREATE SHAPES WITH THE BLOB BRUSH TOOL

The Blob Brush tool is used to paint filled shapes, which you can manipulate just as you would any other shape made up of anchor points and handles. In this exercise, you use the Blob Brush tool to quickly create the inside areas of the balloon and basket.

1. **With balloons.ai open, select everything on the artboard (Select>All), and lock the selection (Object>Lock>Selection).**

   Note:

   Press Command/ Control-A to select all objects in the file.

2. **Double-click the Blob Brush tool in the Tools panel to open the Blob Brush Tool Options dialog box.**

3. **Make sure Keep Selected is checked. Set the Fidelity value to 4 pixels and Smoothness value to 9%. In the Default Brush Options area, define a 10-pt brush size with a 0° angle and 100% Roundness. Click OK to apply the settings.**

   Like the Pencil tool, the Blob Brush tool Tolerance options determine the accuracy of the resulting shape. Higher Fidelity and Smoothness values result in finer precision, but also more anchor points on the shape. The lower half of the dialog box defines the size, angle, and roundness of the brush cursor.

Blob Brush tool ⊢

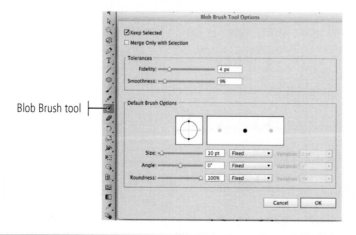

Note:

Press the right bracket key ( ]) to increase the brush size by 1 point. Press the left bracket key ([ ) to reduce the brush size by 1 point.

4. **Set the stroke color to Black and the fill to None.**

5. **At the bottom of the Tools panel, choose the Draw Behind option.**

   If your Tools panel is in one-column mode, the Drawing Mode options are available in a pop-up menu.

   If your Tools panel is in two-column mode, the Drawing Mode options are presented as three buttons (from left to right: Draw Normal, Draw Behind, and Draw Inside).

   When you use the Draw Behind mode, new objects are automatically placed behind the selected object(s), or at the bottom of the stacking order if nothing is selected.

6. **Click at the right side of the balloon base and drag an arc that flows down and to the left, as shown in the following illustration.**

   When you release the mouse button, the result is a single shape that fills the entire area where you drew; overlapping areas of the shape you paint combine to make one shape.

   As you paint, the path might look a bit sketchy; however, the resulting path is smoothed based on the Smoothness option defined in the Blob Brush Tool Options dialog box.

When you draw with the Blob Brush tool, the cursor shows the size and shape of the defined brush.

Click and drag left, following this line in the sketch.

When you release the mouse button, the result is a filled shape based on where you dragged the brush cursor.

Anchor points are automatically created to define the outside edge of the shape.

It is important to note that the resulting path is filled with the *stroke* color you defined in Step 4. When you "paint" with the Blob Brush tool, the defined fill color has no effect on the resulting shape. You are essentially painting a shape that matches the brush stroke you see while you drag; once created, you can then select the shape and change its fill and stroke attributes just as you would for any other object.

7. **With the new shape still selected, click again near the left edge and drag right to fill in the entire area inside the balloon. Continue dragging until the entire area is painted, and then release the mouse button**

Start here...

...and drag to here to fill in the entire area.

The new shape is automatically merged with the selected shape.

Because you are using the Draw Behind mode, areas behind the existing shapes are not visible.

If the Merge Only with Selection option is checked in the Blob Brush Tool Options dialog box, Blob Brush shapes only automatically merge with existing, selected brush strokes. To create separate shapes from the blob paths, deselect any previously drawn shapes.

8. **Repeat this process to create a shape that represents the inside of the balloon basket, as shown below.**

9. **If necessary, adjust the anchor points of the two new shapes until you are satisfied with the results.**

10. **In the Tools panel, click the Drawing Mode button and choose Draw Normal.**

The drawing mode remains at the last-used setting. Although it isn't exactly necessary to do this right now, it is very easy to forget and later accidentally draw in the wrong mode — which means you would have to undo your work in one way or another.

11. **Save the file and continue to the next stage of the project.**

ILLUSTRATOR FOUNDATIONS

Using the Draw Inside Mode

The Draw Inside mode, which is only available when an existing object is already selected, is an easy way to create new objects inside a **clipping path** (a shape that defines areas of other objects that will be visible; anything outside the area of the clipping path is not visible).

If you select the clipped object with the Selection tool, you can use the Edit Clipping Path and Edit Contents buttons in the Control panel to edit either shape without ungrouping and without entering isolation mode.

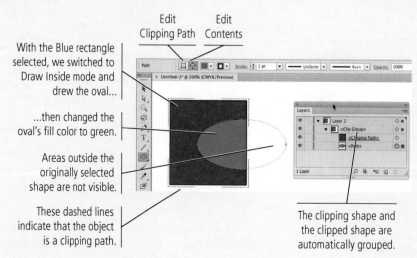

Edit Clipping Path

Edit Contents

With the Blue rectangle selected, we switched to Draw Inside mode and drew the oval...

...then changed the oval's fill color to green.

Areas outside the originally selected shape are not visible.

These dashed lines indicate that the object is a clipping path.

The clipping shape and the clipped shape are automatically grouped.

Stage 2 Coloring and Painting Artwork

The CMYK color model, also called "process color," recreates the range of printable colors by overlapping layers of cyan, magenta, yellow, and black inks in varying percentages from 0–100.

Using theoretically pure pigments, a mixture of equal parts of cyan, magenta, and yellow would produce black. Real pigments, however, are not pure; the actual result of mixing these three colors usually appears as a muddy brown. The fourth color, black (K), is added to cyan, magenta, and yellow to extend the range of printable colors and allow much purer blacks to be printed. (Black is abbreviated as "K" because it is the "key" color to which others are aligned on the printing press. Using K for black also avoids confusion with blue in the RGB color model, which is used for digitally distributed files.)

In process-color printing, each of the four process colors — cyan, magenta, yellow, and black — is imaged, or separated, onto an individual printing plate. Each color separation is printed on a separate unit of a printing press. When printed on top of each other in varying percentages, the semi-transparent inks produce the range of colors in the CMYK **gamut**. Other special colors (called spot colors) are printed using specifically formulated inks as additional color separations.

 +  + 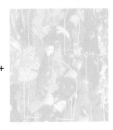 +  =

Different color models have different ranges or gamuts of possible colors. A normal human visual system is capable of distinguishing approximately 16.7 million different colors; color reproduction systems, however, are far more limited. The RGB model has the largest gamut of the output models. The CMYK gamut is much more limited; many of the brightest and most saturated colors that can be reproduced using light (in the RGB model) cannot be reproduced using CMYK inks.

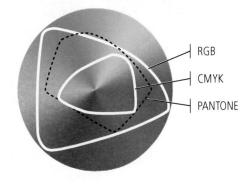

RGB

CMYK

PANTONE

USE THE COLOR PANEL TO DEFINE CUSTOM SWATCHES

As you saw in the original sketch, the balloon in this project will be filled using three different colors (indicated as C1, C2, and C3). In the next two exercises, you will use the Color panel to create the colors you need, and then save those colors as custom swatches.

1. With balloons.ai open, choose Object>Unlock All.

You need to be able to select an object before you can change its color attributes. Remember, the Unlock All command unlocks all locked objects on the artboard; it does not, however, affect layers that have been locked in the Layers panel.

2. **Deselect everything, then open the Color and Swatches panels.**

Because you defined CMYK as the color mode for this document, the Color panel shows ink value sliders for those four primary colors.

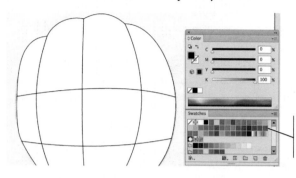

The default Swatches panel includes a number of default swatches.

Note:

We dragged both panels out of the panel dock so we could work with both panels at once.

Note:

The default swatches appear in every new file you create, even if you delete them from a specific file.

If you don't see four color fields/sliders in the Color panel, open the panel options menu and choose Show Options.

Click here to open the panel Options menu.

3. **Using the Selection tool, select only the basket shape. In the Color panel, make sure the Fill icon is on top of the Stroke icon.**

Like the options in the Tools panel, the Fill and Stroke icons determine which attribute you are currently changing. Whichever icon is on top will be affected by changes to the color values.

4. **Highlight the C (cyan) field and type 15. Press Tab to highlight the M (magenta) field and type 25. Press Tab again and change the Y (yellow) field to 45. Press Tab again and change the K (black) field to 0.**

The selected object dynamically reflects the new color as you change the color values.

The Fill and Stroke icons serve the same purpose here as they do in the Tools panel.

Type directly in these fields to enter specific values.

You can also drag these sliders to adjust the component color percentages.

Or you can click in the spectrum to select a color.

Note:

Press Shift while dragging any of the sliders in the Color panel to drag all four sliders at once. Their relative relationship to each other remains the same while you drag.

5. **With the basket shape still selected, make sure the Fill icon is active in the Color panel, and then click the New Swatch button at the bottom of the Swatches panel.**

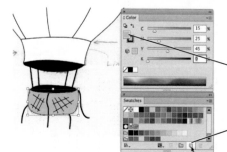

Because the Fill icon is active, the fill color is the one that will be stored in the new swatch.

Click this button to make a new swatch from the currently active color.

6. **Click OK to accept the default options in the New Swatch dialog box.**

The color is automatically named based on the color percentages. You should avoid changing a swatch name unless absolutely necessary.

There's the new swatch.

7. **Open the Swatches panel Options menu and choose Select All Unused.**

The default Swatches panel includes a number of basic swatches that provide a good starting point for some artwork; however, because you are creating your own swatches for this project, the built-in ones are unnecessary. When you build custom swatches, it's a good idea to delete any default swatches that you don't need.

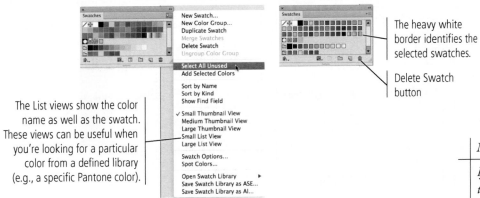

The List views show the color name as well as the swatch. These views can be useful when you're looking for a particular color from a defined library (e.g., a specific Pantone color).

The heavy white border identifies the selected swatches.

Delete Swatch button

Note:

If you delete a swatch that you applied to objects in a project, there is no effect on the existing objects; you simply can't apply that color to any new objects in the project.

8. **Click the Swatches panel Delete button, and then click Yes in the resulting warning dialog box.**

9. **Save the file and continue to the next exercise.**

CREATE GLOBAL SWATCHES

The basket shape is now filled with a custom swatch, which is stored in the Swatches panel for the open document. You also need three more colors to fill the various sections of the balloon. You are going to use a different method to create these colors, and then save them as swatches that can be changed at any time to dynamically modify the colors in the artwork.

1. **With balloons.ai open, select all of the white-filled objects and change their fill to 50% opacity.**

You can either draw a marquee to select the white-filled objects, or use the Select Similar Objects options. Changing the objects' opacity allows you to see the color indicators on the original sketch.

2. **Deselect everything, and then select only the top-left section of the balloon (labeled C1 in the sketch).**

3. **Press Shift and click the other three C1 shapes to add them to the selection.**

   By pressing Shift, you can click to add other objects to the current selection. Shift-clicking an object that is already selected removes it from the active selection.

4. **In the Color panel, click a green area in the color spectrum bar.**

   All four selected objects fill with the green color you clicked. They seem lighter because they are still semi-transparent.

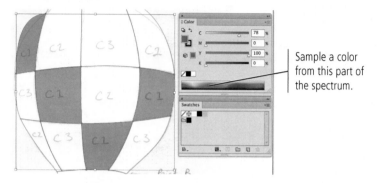

Sample a color from this part of the spectrum.

5. **With the Fill icon still active, click the New Swatch button in the Swatches panel.**

6. **Check the Global option in the New Swatch dialog box and click OK.**

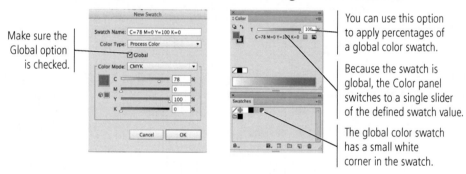

Make sure the Global option is checked.

You can use this option to apply percentages of a global color swatch.

Because the swatch is global, the Color panel switches to a single slider of the defined swatch value.

The global color swatch has a small white corner in the swatch.

7. **Select the four shapes marked C2 in the sketch.**

8. **Repeat the process from Steps 4–6 to fill the C2 shapes with a blue color and then create a global swatch from the color.**

9. **Select the four shapes marked C3 in the sketch, fill them with a purple color, and then create a third global swatch from the color.**

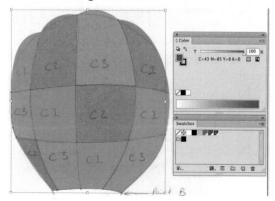

Note:

When an object is colored with a global swatch, you can click the process button under the percentage field to convert the applied swatch to the component color percentages (i.e., breaking the link to the global swatch).

10. **With the purple shapes still selected, choose Select>Same>Opacity. Return the selected objects' opacity to 100%.**

You no longer need to see the color markers on the sketch, so you can return these objects to full opacity.

11. **Deselect all objects in the file, then save the file and continue to the next exercise.**

ADD A COLOR GRADIENT

The original sketch shows that the bottom of the balloon needs to be a gradient of the three colors in the balloon sections. Illustrator's Gradient tool makes it easy to create this gradient based on the three custom swatches you defined in the previous exercise.

1. **With balloons.ai open, select the shape that represents the bottom edge of the balloon by clicking the path with the Selection tool.**

2. **Open the Gradient panel (Window>Gradient). If you see only a gradient sample in the panel, open the panel Options menu and choose Show Options.**

If you don't see the gradient stops under the ramp, click the ramp once to show the stops.

3. **Click the swatch in the top-left corner.**

Clicking the swatch applies the linear gradient to the selected object.

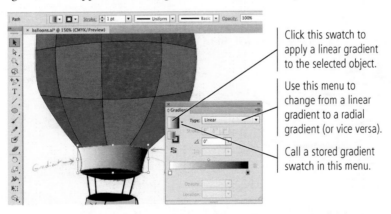

Click this swatch to apply a linear gradient to the selected object.

Use this menu to change from a linear gradient to a radial gradient (or vice versa).

Call a stored gradient swatch in this menu.

4. **In the Gradient panel, double-click the left gradient stop on the gradient ramp.**

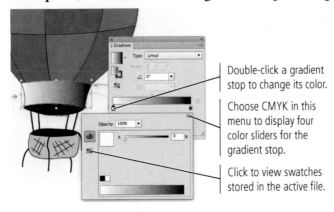

Double-click a gradient stop to change its color.

Choose CMYK in this menu to display four color sliders for the gradient stop.

Click to view swatches stored in the active file.

5. **In the pop-up panel, click the Swatches button to display the swatches stored in the current document.**

6. **Click the blue global swatch you created in the previous exercise, and then press Return/Enter to close the pop-up panel.**

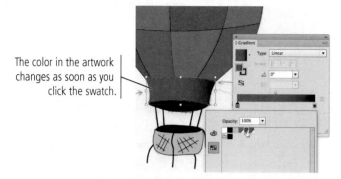

The color in the artwork changes as soon as you click the swatch.

7. **Double-click the right gradient stop to open the pop-up panel. Apply the purple custom swatch to this stop.**

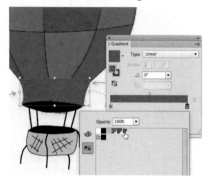

Note:

You can also drag a swatch from the Swatches panel onto a particular gradient stop to change the color of that stop.

Note:

You can remove a stop by dragging it down and off the gradient ramp.

8. **Click once below the gradient ramp to add another stop to the gradient. With the new stop selected, type 50 in the Location field.**

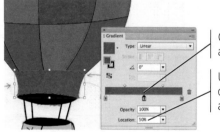

Click below the ramp to add stops to the gradient.

Use the Location field to define a precise position along the ramp.

9. **Double-click the middle stop and apply the green swatch.**

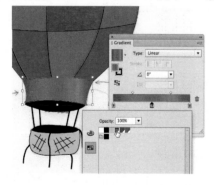

10. Click the left gradient stop and drag right until the Location field shows approximately 10%.

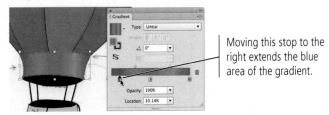

Moving this stop to the right extends the blue area of the gradient.

11. Click the right gradient stop and drag left until the Location field shows approximately 90%.

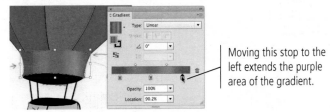

Moving this stop to the left extends the purple area of the gradient.

12. Click the marker above the gradient ramp between the left and middle stops. Drag left until the Location field shows approximately 40%.

This point indicates where the colors of the two surrounding stops are equally mixed. Dragging the point extends the gradient on one side of the point and compresses the gradient on the other side. (You can also simply select the midpoint icon and then type a specific position in the Location field.)

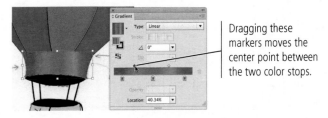

Dragging these markers moves the center point between the two color stops.

13. Click the marker above the gradient ramp between the middle and right stops. Drag right until the Location field shows approximately 60%.

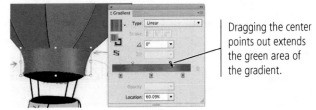

Dragging the center points out extends the green area of the gradient.

14. Save the file and continue to the next exercise.

EDIT GLOBAL COLOR SWATCHES

Global swatches offer a particular advantage when you need to change the colors used in your artwork. In the case of this project, the client requested a red-orange-yellow scheme for the balloon, so you need to change the custom swatches you created earlier.

1. With **balloons.ai** open, deselect all objects on the artboard.

2. In the Swatches panel, double-click the blue custom swatch.

3. In the resulting Swatch Options dialog box, make sure the Preview option is checked.

4. **Change the color values to C=0 M=100 Y=100 K=0, and then click OK to change the swatch definition.**

Because this is a global color swatch, any objects that use the color — including the gradient — reflect the new swatch definition. Locked objects are also affected by the change.

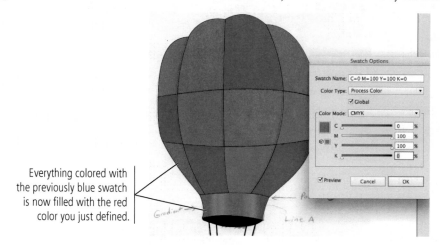

Everything colored with the previously blue swatch is now filled with the red color you just defined.

5. **Repeat Steps 2–4 to change the green swatch definition to C=0 M=10 Y=100 K=0.**

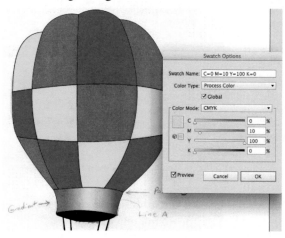

6. **Repeat Steps 2–4 to change the purple swatch definition to C=0 M=60 Y=100 K=0.**

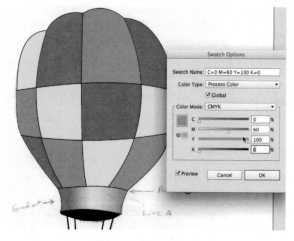

7. **Select all the objects on the Balloon layer and group them (Object>Group).**

8. **Save the file and continue to the next exercise.**

USE THE GRADIENT TOOL

In addition to simply applying a gradient with the Gradient panel, you can also use the Gradient tool to define the gradient directly in the context of the artwork.

1. **Open the file desert.ai from your WIP>Festival folder.**

2. **Select the front dune shape, then fill it with the default black-to-white linear gradient in the Gradient panel.**

3. **Choose the Gradient tool in the Tools panel.**

   When a selected object is filled with a gradient, choosing the Gradient tool reveals the Gradient Annotator for that shape. The Gradient Annotator is simply a visual tool for applying most of the same options that are available in the Gradient panel.

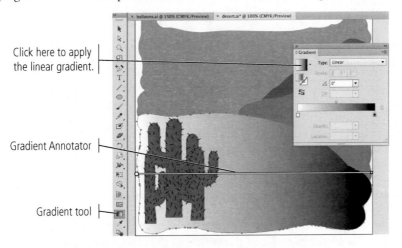

Click here to apply the linear gradient.

Gradient Annotator

Gradient tool

Note:

You can turn off the Gradient Annotator in the View menu (View>Hide Gradient Annotator).

4. **Move your cursor over the Gradient Annotator to show the associated stops.**

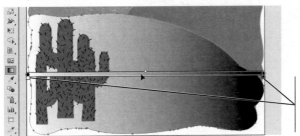

Moving the cursor near the Gradient Annotator reveals the gradient stops.

Note:

If the current selection is part of a group, selecting the Gradient tool does not reveal the Gradient Annotator. You have to first deselect the active group, and then click a specific object with the Gradient tool to show the Gradient Annotator for the object.

5. **On the Gradient Annotator, click the white stop and drag to about the halfway point of the gradient.**

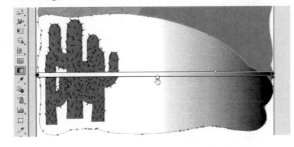

6. **Place the cursor directly below the left end of the Gradient Annotator. When you see a plus sign (+) in the cursor, click to add a new stop to the gradient.**

Click below the
Gradient Annotator
to add a new stop.

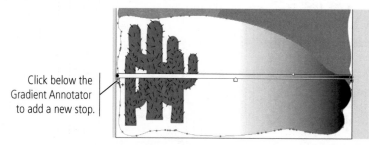

7. **Double-click the new stop to open the pop-up panel. Change the stop color to the available orange swatch.**

Double-click a stop to
change the stop's color.

Click this button to
show color sliders in
the pop-up panel.

Click this button to
show existing swatches
in the pop-up panel.

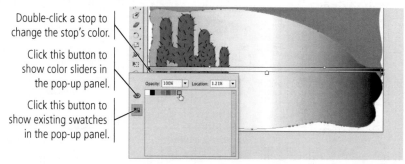

8. **Repeat Step 7 to apply the same orange swatch to the right gradient stop.**

9. **Click the right end of the annotator and drag left (toward the center of the artboard), until the Annotator is about two-thirds the width of the selected object.**

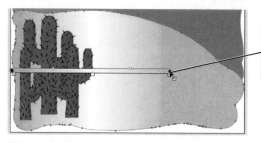

Drag the right end of
the annotator to shorten
or lengthen the gradient
within the shape.

10. **Place the cursor near the right end of the Gradient Annotator. When the cursor changes to a rotation symbol, click and drag down to rotate the gradient clockwise.**

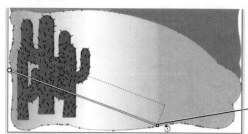

Rotate the gradient
by clicking directly
outside the right end
of the gradient.

Note:

After you rotate the Gradient Annotator, it snaps back to the center of the object.

11. **Select the second dune shape, and then click the gradient swatch in the Gradient panel.**

The Gradient panel remembers the last-used gradient, so you can simply click the sample to apply the gradient to the new object.

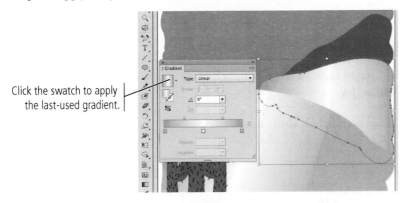

Click the swatch to apply the last-used gradient.

12. **Using the Gradient tool, click near the left edge of the selected shape and drag close to the right edge of the selected shape.**

Rather than dragging the Annotator bar, you can also click and drag with the Gradient tool to define the direction and position of the gradient within a selected object.

Dragging with the Gradient tool defines the direction and position of the gradient. When working with a linear gradient, the first place you click with the Gradient tool defines the location for the starting color of the gradient; where you release the mouse button marks the location for the ending color of the gradient. Any areas beyond the two ends fill with the end-stop colors of the gradient.

Note:

If you have multiple objects selected when you drag with the Gradient tool, the single gradient will extend across all selected objects.

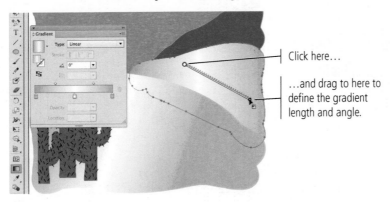

Click here…

…and drag to here to define the gradient length and angle.

13. **Use the same method from Steps 11–12 to apply the gradient to the third dune shape. Drag this gradient from the bottom-left area to the top-right area of the selected shape.**

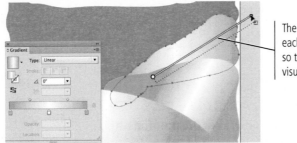

The gradient angle on each dune is different, so the three dunes remain visually distinct.

14. **Save the file as `poster.ai` in your WIP>Festival folder and continue to the next exercise.**

The next step in the process is to place your finished balloon in the background illustration; you can then duplicate the balloon artwork to create a small fleet of different-colored balloons floating over the desert.

You created the entire balloon artwork on a single layer. In this exercise, you add multiple layers so you can organize and manage the additional balloon objects.

1. **With `poster.ai` open, click the Cactus layer in the Layers panel. Press Shift, then click the Sky layer to select all three layers.**

2. **Choose Merge Selected in the Layers panel Options menu.**

3. **Double-click the new layer name in the layers panel. Type `Desert`, then press Return/Enter to finalize the new layer name.**

4. **Activate (or open, if necessary) the `balloons.ai` file.**

5. **Select the sketch layer in the Layers panel and drag it to the panel's Delete button.**

Drag the template (sketch) layer to the Delete button to remove that layer.

Note:

If you delete a non-template layer that contains artwork, Illustrator asks you to confirm that you want to delete the layer (and all artwork on the layer).

6. **Select everything on the artboard, choose Edit>Copy, save the `balloons.ai` file, and then close it.**

7. **With `poster.ai` active, click the New Layer button in the Layers panel. Change the new layer name to `Balloon 1`.**

8. **Make sure the Balloon 1 layer is active in the Layers panel and choose Edit>Paste. Drag the pasted artwork to the approximate center of the artboard.**

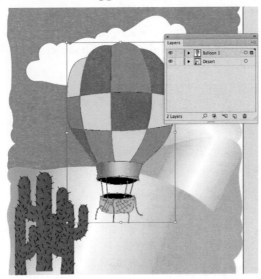

9. **Click the Balloon 1 layer and drag it to the New Layer button at the bottom of the Layers panel.**

   You now have a copy of the layer you dragged. You see no difference on the artboard because the copy is in the same position as the original layer.

   Drag an existing layer to the New Layer button to make an exact copy of the layer.

   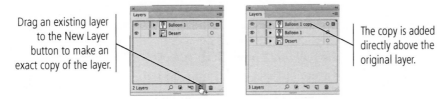

   The copy is added directly above the original layer.

10. **Rename the Balloon 1 copy layer as Balloon 2.**

11. **Drag the Balloon 2 layer to the New Layer button. Rename this layer Balloon 3.**

12. **Lock all but the Balloon 3 layer, and then choose Select>All.**

    Because all the other layers are locked, you selected only the artwork on the Balloon 3 layer. The difference between locking objects and locking layers depends on what you need to accomplish. In this case, it's best to place each piece of artwork on its own layer, so you can lock the layers you want to protect from change.

    Click this column to show or hide a layer.

    Click this column to lock or unlock a layer.

    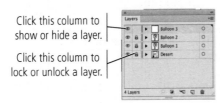

Note:

You can also select all objects on a specific layer by clicking the space at the right edge of the Layers panel (to the right of the round Target icon).

13. **Choose Object>Transform>Scale. In the Scale dialog box, type 75% in the Uniform Scale field. Make sure the Scale Strokes & Effects option is checked, and then click OK.**

   If Scale Strokes & Effects is not checked, a 2-pt stroke will remain a 2-pt stroke, even if you reduce the selected object to 10% of its original size. With the Scale Strokes & Effects option checked, a 2-pt stroke scaled to 75% becomes a 1.5-pt stroke.

14. **Drag the scaled artwork left.**

15. **Lock the Balloon 3 layer and unlock the Balloon 2 layer.**

16. **Repeat Steps 12–14 for the artwork on the Balloon 2 layer. Scale it to 50%, and then move it right and up to make it seem farthest back in the fleet.**

   The different scaling, position, and stacking order of the three balloons creates the illusion of depth within the illustration.

17. **Unlock all three Balloon layers. In the Layers panel, click the Balloon 1 layer and drag it to the top of the layer stack.**

18. **Adjust the position and scale of each balloon until you are satisfied with the overall result.**

19. **Save the file and continue to the next exercise.**

ILLUSTRATOR FOUNDATIONS

Many vague and technical-sounding terms are mentioned when discussing color. Is hue the same as color? The same as value? As tone? What's the difference between lightness and brightness? What is chroma? And where does saturation fit in?

This problem has resulted in several attempts to normalize color communication. A number of systems have been developed to define color according to specific criteria, including Hue, Saturation, and Brightness (HSB); Hue, Saturation, and Lightness (HSL); Hue, Saturation, and Value (HSV); and Lightness, Chroma, and Hue (LCH). Each of these models or systems plots color on a three-dimensional diagram, based on the elements of human color perception — hue, colorfulness, and brightness.

Hue is what most people think of as color — red, green, purple, and so on. Hue is defined according to a color's position on a color wheel, beginning from red (0°) and traveling counterclockwise around the wheel.

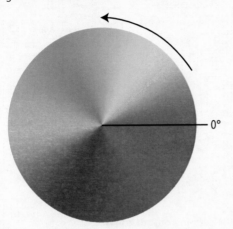

Saturation (also called "intensity") refers to the color's difference from neutral gray. Highly saturated colors are more vivid than those with low saturation. Saturation is plotted from the center of the color wheel. Color at the center is neutral gray and has a saturation value of 0; color at the edge of the wheel is the most intense value of the corresponding hue and has a saturation value of 100.

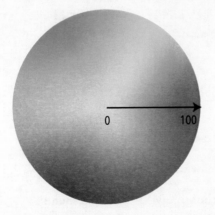

If you bisect the color wheel with a straight line, the line creates a saturation axis for two complementary colors. A color is dulled by the introduction of its complement. Red, for example, is neutralized by the addition of cyan (blue and green). Near the center of the axis, the result is neutral gray.

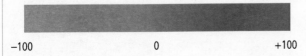

-100   0   +100

Chroma is similar to saturation, but chroma factors in a reference white. In any viewing situation, colors appear less vivid as the light source dims. The process of chromatic adaptation, however, allows the human visual system to adjust to changes in light and still differentiate colors according to the relative saturation.

Brightness is the amount of light reflected off an object. As an element of color reproduction, brightness is typically judged by comparing the color to the lightest nearby object (such as an unprinted area of white paper).

Lightness is the amount of white or black added to the pure color. Lightness (also called "luminance" or "value") is the relative brightness based purely on the black-white value of a color. A lightness value of 0 means there is no addition of white or black. Lightness of +100 is pure white; lightness of −100 is pure black.

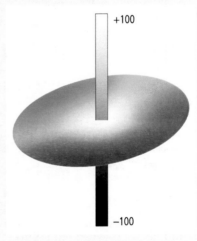

All hues are affected equally by changes in lightness.

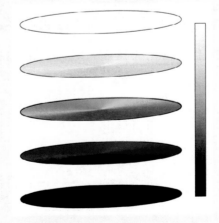

RECOLOR ARTWORK

Your illustration is nearly complete. The only work left to do is to change the colors of the two new balloons. Although you could manually select the shapes and apply different ink percentages, Illustrator includes a sophisticated tool that makes it easy to experiment with and change all colors in a selection.

1. **With poster.ai open, click the empty space to the right of the Balloon 3 layer name to select all objects on that layer.**

2. **Click the Recolor Artwork button in the Control panel.**

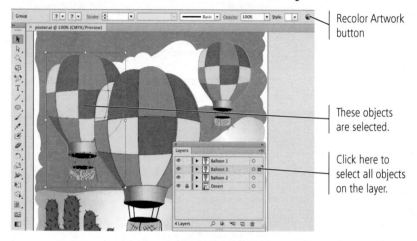

Recolor Artwork button

These objects are selected.

Click here to select all objects on the layer.

Note:

You can also choose Edit>Edit Colors>Recolor Artwork to open the dialog box.

The Recolor Artwork dialog box shows all colors used in the selection. You can edit or replace individual colors, or you can apply global changes that affect the entire selection.

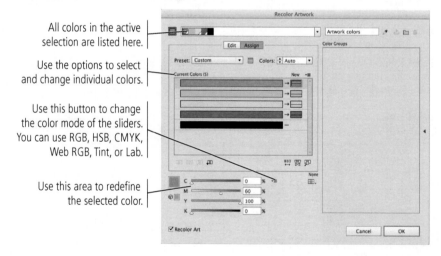

All colors in the active selection are listed here.

Use the options to select and change individual colors.

Use this button to change the color mode of the sliders. You can use RGB, HSB, CMYK, Web RGB, Tint, or Lab.

Use this area to redefine the selected color.

3. **Click the Edit button to show the active colors on a color wheel.**

4. **Click the button to the right of the color sliders and choose CMYK from the menu.**

5. **Make sure the Recolor Art option is checked, and then click the Display Segmented Color Wheel button.**

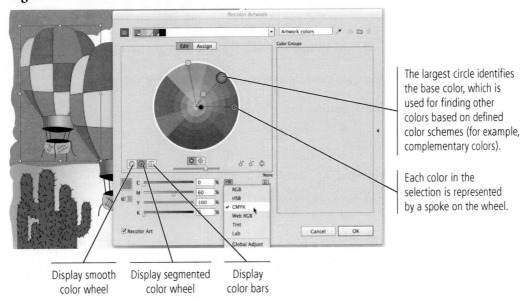

The largest circle identifies the base color, which is used for finding other colors based on defined color schemes (for example, complementary colors).

Each color in the selection is represented by a spoke on the wheel.

Display smooth color wheel   Display segmented color wheel   Display color bars

6. **Click the orange circle and drag it to a middle-blue area on the color wheel.**

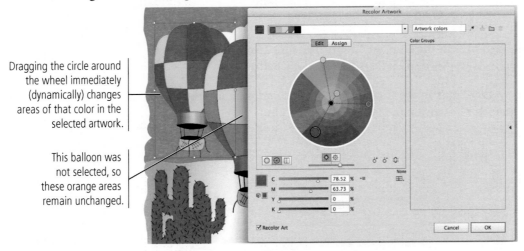

Dragging the circle around the wheel immediately (dynamically) changes areas of that color in the selected artwork.

This balloon was not selected, so these orange areas remain unchanged.

7. **Click the yellow circle and drag it to a medium-dark green.**

8. **Click the red circle and drag it to a medium-dark purple.**

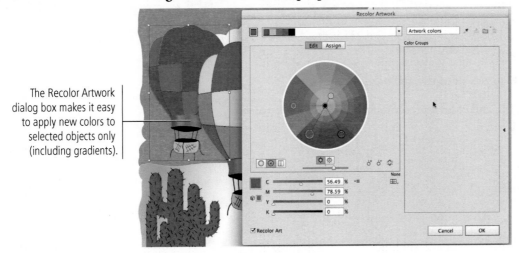

The Recolor Artwork dialog box makes it easy to apply new colors to selected objects only (including gradients).

9. Click OK to return to the artboard.

10. Select everything on the Balloon 2 layer, and then click the Recolor Artwork button in the Control panel.

11. With the dialog box in Assign mode, make sure the first color is selected in the list.

12. Click the button to the right of the color sliders and choose CMYK from the menu.

13. Use the sliders to change the color definition to C=0 M=100 Y=0 K=0.

Because Recolor Art is checked, the selected artwork immediately reflects the change.

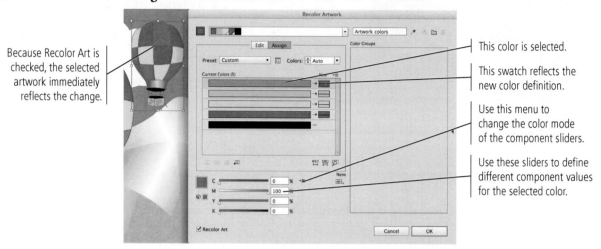

This color is selected.

This swatch reflects the new color definition.

Use this menu to change the color mode of the component sliders.

Use these sliders to define different component values for the selected color.

14. Click the red color in the Current Colors list, and then use the sliders to change the color definition to C=100 M=0 Y=15 K=0.

15. Click the yellow color in the Current Colors list, and then use the sliders to change the color definition to C=0 M=0 Y=60 K=0.

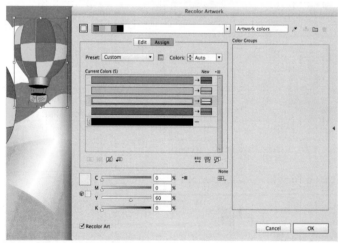

Note:

If you are working with global color swatches, you can also use the Tint slider you saw earlier when you worked with the global color swatches.

16. Click OK to return to the artboard.

17. Save the file and continue to the final stage of the project.

ILLUSTRATOR FOUNDATIONS

The Recolor Artwork dialog box has dozens of options for changing colors, and the sheer number of choices can be intimidating. However, you already used two of the most important options in this dialog box, so you should feel confident in your ability to use it — especially when experimenting with colors to use in a particular piece of artwork. In addition to the functions you already used, the Recolor Artwork dialog box also enables global color changes.

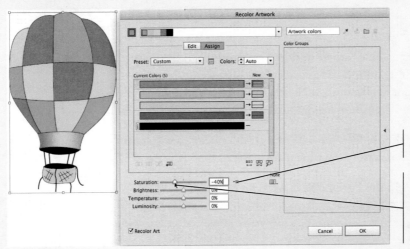

Choose Global Adjust in the menu…

…then use the sliders to adjust the overall saturation, brightness, temperature, or luminosity of the selected artwork.

You should also understand that you aren't required to do a 1-to-1 replacement. You can replace multiple colors with the same new color by simply dragging one current color onto another. (This is especially useful if you are converting four-color artwork to a two-color or one-color job.)

Drag one current color onto another to replace both colors with the same new color.

When you release the mouse button, both colors appear in the same row.

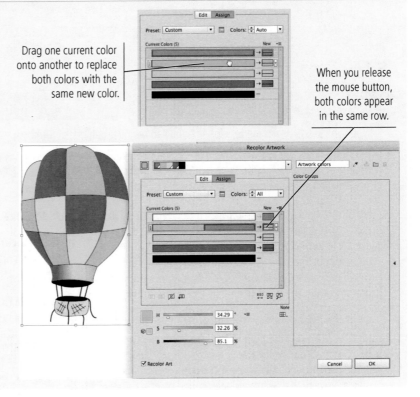

Although most current versions of page-layout software can manage the native Illustrator file format, some older applications that are still in common use can't interpret Illustrator files. For those applications, you need to save files in formats that can be used — namely, EPS and PDF.

 SAVE AN EPS FILE

The EPS (Encapsulated PostScript) file format was designed for high-quality print applications. The format can store both raster and vector elements, and it supports transparency. Before page-layout applications were able to support native Illustrator files (or PDF), EPS was the most common format used for files created in Illustrator.

1. **With poster.ai open, choose File>Save As and (if necessary) navigate to your WIP>Festival folder as the target location.**

2. **Choose Illustrator EPS in the Format/Save As Type menu.**

The file name automatically changes to show the correct extension (.eps).

3. **Click Save.**

EPS Options

When you save a file in the EPS format, you can define a number of format-specific options.

Version allows you to save a file to be compatible with earlier versions of Illustrator. Be aware that features not available in earlier versions will be lost in the saved file.

Format defines the type of preview that will be saved in the file (these previews are used for applications that can't directly read the EPS file format). Be aware that Windows users cannot access Macintosh-format previews; if you're working in a Windows-based or cross-platform environment, use one of the TIFF preview options.

Another advantage of the TIFF preview is the ability to save the preview with a transparent background or opaque background. When you choose TIFF (8-bit Color) in the Preview menu, you can choose the **Transparent** option to save a preview that will show background objects through the empty areas of the artwork; the **Opaque** option creates the preview with a solid white background.

Transparency options control the output settings for transparent and semi-transparent objects, including drop shadows and other effects. (These options will be explained in depth in Project 6: Cereal Box.)

Embed Fonts (for other applications) embeds used fonts into the EPS file. This ensures that the type appears properly when the file is placed into another application.

Include Linked Files embeds linked files.

Include Document Thumbnails creates a thumbnail image of the artwork that displays in the Illustrator Open and Place dialog boxes.

Include CMYK PostScript in RGB Files allows RGB color documents to be printed from applications that do not support RGB output. When the EPS file is reopened in Illustrator, the RGB colors are preserved.

Compatible Gradient and Gradient Mesh Printing is necessary for older printers and PostScript devices to print gradients and gradient meshes; those elements (explained in Project 3: Identity Package) are converted to the JPEG format.

Adobe PostScript® determines what level of PostScript is used to save the artwork. PostScript Level 2 represents color as well as grayscale vector and bitmap images. PostScript Level 3 includes the ability to print mesh objects when printing to a PostScript 3 printer.

4. **In the resulting EPS Options dialog box, choose TIFF (8-bit Color) in the Format menu and click the Transparent radio button. Make sure Embed Fonts is checked.**

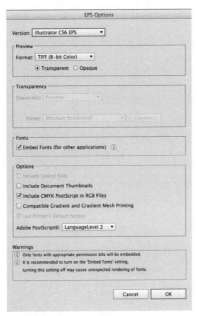

5. **Click OK to create the EPS file.**

6. **Close the EPS file and continue to the next exercise.**

 ## SAVE A FILE AS PDF

Adobe PDF (or simply PDF, for Portable Document Format) has become a universal method of moving files to virtually any digital destination. One of the most important uses for the PDF format is the ability to create perfectly formatted digital documents, exactly as they would appear if printed on paper. You can embed fonts, images, drawings, and other elements into the file so all the required bits are available on any computer. The PDF format can be used to move your artwork to the Web as a low-resolution RGB file or to a commercial printer as a high-resolution CMYK file.

1. **Open poster.ai from your WIP>Festival folder, then choose File>Save As. If necessary, navigate to your WIP>Festival folder as the target location.**

2. **Choose Adobe PDF in the Format/Save As Type menu and click Save.**

Again, the extension automatically changes to reflect the selected format (.pdf).

3. Review the options in the General pane.

Read the description area to see what Adobe has to say about these options.

Choose another category from this menu to see the related options.

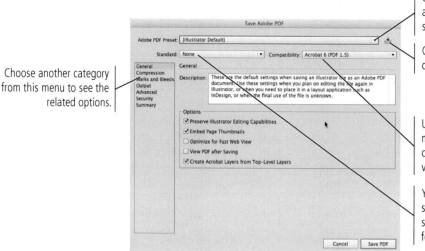

Use this menu to access an existing group of saved settings (called a preset).

Click this button to save your current options as a preset.

Use the Compatibility menu to save the file to be compatible with older versions of Acrobat Reader.

You can save PDFs using several different technical standards (PDF/X formats) for printing applications.

4. Choose Illustrator Default in the Adobe PDF Preset menu.

5. Click Compression in the list of categories on the left and review the options.

These options allow you to reduce the resulting file size by compressing color, grayscale, and/or monochrome bitmap (raster) images. You can also compress text and line art by clicking the check box at the bottom.

Note:

The other categories of options are explained in later projects that discuss transparency and color management.

6. Review the Marks and Bleeds options.

These options add different marks to the output page:

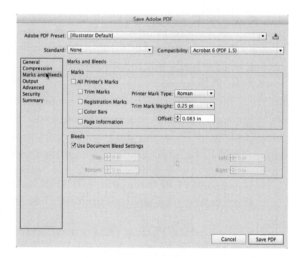

- **Trim marks** indicate the edge of the page, where a page printed on a larger sheet will be cut down to its final size. You can also define the thickness (weight) of the trim marks, as well as how far from the page edge the lines should appear (offset).

- **Registration marks** resemble a small crosshair. These marks are added to each ink unit on a printing press to make sure the different inks are properly aligned to one another.

- **Color bars** are rows of small squares across the sheet, used to verify press settings for accurate color reproduction.

- **Page information** adds the file name, date, and time of output.

- **Bleeds** define how much of elements outside the page boundaries will be included in the final output. Most printers require at least a 0.125″ bleed on each side, but you should always ask before you create the final file.

7. Click Save PDF.

8. Close the Illustrator file.

Note:

Most printers require trim marks to be created outside the bleed area. Always check with your service provider when saving a PDF for commercial output.

Project Review

fill in the blank

1. The _____ tool is used to place anchor points that are connected by line segments.

2. The _____ tool is used to change a smooth anchor point to a corner anchor point (and vice versa).

3. The _____ tool is used to edit individual anchor points (and their related handles) on a vector path.

4. _____ is the range of possible colors within a specific color model.

5. _____ are the four component colors in process-color output.

6. The _____ panel includes value sliders for each component in the defined color model.

7. The _____ is used to paint shapes of solid color based on the defined brush size and the area you drag with a single mouse click.

8. The _____ appears over a gradient-filled object when selected with the Gradient tool; you can use it to control the position and direction of color in the gradient-filled object.

9. Changes made to a _____ color swatch are reflected in all elements where that color is applied.

10. The _____ dialog box can be used to change individual colors in an entire file, or to make global changes to all colors in the file.

short answer

1. Describe three ways to deselect the current selection on the artboard.

2. Briefly explain the significance of "process color" related to Illustrator artwork.

3. Briefly explain the advantage of using the PDF format for creating printable files.

Use what you learned in this project to complete the following freeform exercise.
Carefully read the art director and client comments, then create your own design to meet the needs of the project.
Use the space below to sketch ideas; when finished, write a brief explanation of your reasoning behind your final design.

art director comments

The former marketing director for the Temecula Balloon Festival recently moved to Florida to be the director of the annual Miami Jazzfest. She was pleased with your work on the balloon festival project, and would like to hire you to create the advertising for next year's jazz festival event.

To complete this project, you should:

❑ Develop artwork that will be the primary image for posters and print advertisements, as well as shirts and other souvenirs.

❑ Create the primary artwork to fit onto the festival program cover, which is 8×10″.

client comments

Jazzfest is one of the longest running and well-known music festivals in the southeastern United States. In addition to the music, the festival also features food from prominent restaurants; the food is almost as big an attraction as the music — maybe even moreso for some people.

We want artwork that appeals to a 40-something, middle- and upper-class audience; tickets to this event are fairly expensive, but we always have some very well-known acts that make it worth the price.

Finally, we want the artwork to be an appealing aspect of our ad campaign, but we want it to be artwork in its own right as well. The artwork gets printed as posters that are hung in some very exclusive establishments around the Miami area, and they weren't happy with the cartoon style of art used in previous years.

project justification

_____
_____
_____
_____
_____
_____
_____
_____
_____
_____
_____
_____
_____

Project Summary

This project built on the skills you learned in Project 1: International Symbols, incorporating more advanced drawing techniques that allow you to exercise precise control over every point and path in a file. The Pen tool is arguably one of the most important tools you will use throughout your career as an illustrator; although it can be challenging at first, practice is the best way to master this skill.

The second half of this project explored color in Illustrator: applying color, saving global color swatches to make changes more efficiently, using gradients to add visual interest, and making changes to specific colors throughout a selection.

Finally, you created files in two different formats that are commonly used to share Illustrator artwork with other applications. EPS and PDF formats are invaluable parts of design workflows using software applications that can't import native Illustrator files.

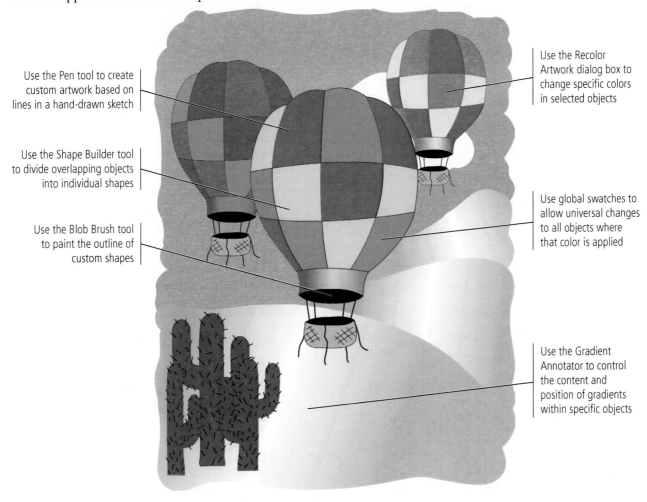

Use the Pen tool to create custom artwork based on lines in a hand-drawn sketch

Use the Shape Builder tool to divide overlapping objects into individual shapes

Use the Blob Brush tool to paint the outline of custom shapes

Use the Recolor Artwork dialog box to change specific colors in selected objects

Use global swatches to allow universal changes to all objects where that color is applied

Use the Gradient Annotator to control the content and position of gradients within specific objects

Identity Package

Your client, Graham Apple, owns an organic orchard in Central Florida. He hired you to create a corporate identity package so he can begin branding his products to reach a larger consumer base in gourmet groceries throughout the Southeast. He asked you to develop a logo, and then create the standard identity pieces (letterhead and envelope) that he will use for business promotion and correspondence.

This project incorporates the following skills:

❏ Developing custom logo artwork based on an object in a photograph

❏ Using a gradient mesh to create realistic color blends

❏ Converting type to outlines and manipulating letter shapes to create a finished logotype

❏ Using layers to easily manage complex artwork

❏ Creating multiple artboards to contain specific projects and layouts

❏ Building various logo versions to meet specific output requirements

❏ Saving EPS files for maximum flexibility

❏ Printing desktop proofs of individual artboards

client comments

It's just a coincidence that my last name is Apple and I own an organic orchard, but I might as well take advantage where I can. I want my logo to be — surprise! — an apple, with some creative type treatment for the name of the farm (Apple Organics).

Once the logo is complete, I want you to use it to create letterhead and envelopes that I will have preprinted; I want a more professional feel than I can create using my laser printer. The printer I spoke with said I could do this for less money if I go "four-color" for the letterhead, but "two-color" for the envelope; I really don't know what that means — I'm hoping you do.

art director comments

The logo is the first part of this project because you will use it on the other two pieces. The client told you exactly what he wants, so that part is taken care of. I had our photographer take a good apple picture; use that as the basis for the one you draw in the logo art.

The client wants to print the letterhead in four-color and the envelope in two-color, so you will have to create two different versions of the logo. Since logos are used on far more than just these two jobs in this one application, you should also create a one-color version because the client will inevitably ask for it at some point.

project objectives

To complete this project, you will:

- ❏ Use the Pen tool to trace the outline of a photograph
- ❏ Create a gradient mesh
- ❏ Use Smart Guides to manage a gradient mesh
- ❏ Use effects to add object highlights
- ❏ Create and control point-type objects
- ❏ Convert text to outlines so you can manipulate the letter shapes
- ❏ Use the Appearance panel to revert gradient mesh objects back to regular paths
- ❏ Apply spot-color inks for special printing applications
- ❏ Create versions of the final logo for one-color, two-color, and four-color printing
- ❏ Print desktop proofs of the completed identity pieces

Stage 1 Working with Gradient Meshes

There are several important points to keep in mind when you design a logo. First, logos need to be scalable. A company might place its logo on the head of a golf tee or on the side of a building. This is a strong argument for using the simpler line-art approach instead of photography. Vector graphics — the kind you typically create in Illustrator — can be scaled as large or small as necessary without losing quality; photographs are raster images, and they can't be greatly enlarged or reduced without losing quality. That's why you're converting a photograph (a raster image) into a vector graphic in this project.

Second, you almost always need more than one version of any given logo — very often in more than one file format. Different kinds of output require different formats (specifically, one set of files for print and one for the Web), and some types of jobs require special options saved in the files — such as the four-color, two-color, and one-color versions of the logo that you will create in this project.

SET UP THE WORKSPACE

Your client needs several versions of a new logo, including one with realistic color. Illustrator includes a number of tools ideally suited for creating lifelike illustrations. In this project, you will work from a photograph to create a vector-based apple graphic that will be part of your client's logo. You will start with the full-color version, and then work from there to create the other variations that are part of a typical logo package.

1. **Download AI6_RF_Project3.zip from the Student Files Web page.**

2. **Expand the ZIP archive in your WIP folder (Macintosh) or copy the archive contents into your WIP folder (Windows).**

   This results in a folder named **Organics**, which contains the files you need for this project. You should also use this folder to save the files you create in this project.

3. **In Illustrator, choose File>New.**

4. **Type apple in the Name field, choose Letter as the page size, and choose Inches as the unit of measurement.**

   At this point, you are simply using the artboard as a drawing space, so you only need to make it large enough to draw. Later, you will adjust the artboard to meet the specific needs of the finished logo.

5. **Make sure the Number of Artboards field is set to 1.**

   Later in this project, you will add multiple artboards to hold various versions of the logo. For now, you only need one artboard, which will serve as a drawing board.

6. **In the Advanced options, choose CMYK in the Color Mode menu and choose High (300 ppi) in the Raster Effects menu.**

   Because the CMYK gamut is smaller than the RGB gamut, you are starting with the smaller gamut to avoid the color shift that could occur if you started with RGB and converted the colors to CMYK. You are also creating the file to meet the high-resolution requirements of commercial printing. While not part of this project, you can easily use the Save For Web utility to export low-resolution RGB versions of the file for digital media.

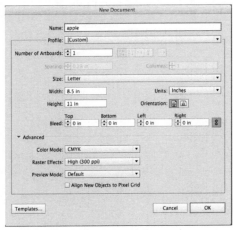

7. **Click OK to create the new file.**

8. **Choose File>Place. Navigate to `apple.jpg` in your WIP>Organics folder. Make sure the Link and Template options are not checked, and click Place.**

Choosing the Template option places an image onto a template layer that is automatically dimmed. That's not what you want to do here; you want the photograph to remain at full visibility so you can extract colors from the photo.

Make sure neither of these options is checked.

9. **Center the photo to the horizontal and vertical center of the artboard.**

10. **Rename Layer 1 Apple Photo, and then lock the layer.**

For most of the drawing process, you will use the Apple Photo layer as the basis of your artwork. You will draw on other layers, and then delete the photo layer when your apple graphic is complete.

Lock the Apple Photo layer to protect it.

You're starting with a letter-size artboard. After you finish the logo graphic, you will resize the artboard to fit the artwork.

11. **Save the file as a native Illustrator file named `apple.ai` in your WIP>Organics folder, and then continue to the next exercise.**

DRAW THE APPLE SHAPES

In Project 2: Balloon Festival Artwork, you used the Pen tool to create custom shapes using a hand-drawn sketch as your template. The apple shape in this logo is another example of a custom shape composed of lines and paths. In this project you use a photo as your guide. The first step is to determine what shapes you need to create.

1. **With apple.ai open, create a new layer at the top of the layer stack. Double-click the layer thumbnail to open the Layer Options dialog box. Change the layer name to Apple Front and change the layer color to Yellow, then click OK.**

   Because the apple you are tracing is red, the red layer color can make it difficult to distinguish the layer's objects. Using a high-contrast color such as yellow makes the paths, handles, etc., easier to see.

2. **Using the Pen tool with a 1-pt black stroke and no fill, draw the outline of the front part of the apple. Follow the shape of the apple as it curves in front of the stem.**

   We started our contour line at the bottom part of the apple where there is a sharp corner because starting a contour line on a curve often creates less than perfect results. Use our image as a rough guide for where to place the anchor points; yours doesn't have to match exactly, but it should come close.

Note:

Refer back to Project 2: Balloon Festival Artwork for details about drawing and editing Bézier curves.

Pen tool

Skip over the area that wraps behind the stem.

We started drawing here (at a corner).

3. **If necessary, use the Direct Selection tool to adjust the anchor points and handles until the outline matches the shape of the apple.**

4. **Create another new layer and rename it Apple Back. In the Layers panel, drag this layer below the Apple Front layer.**

5. **On the Apple Back layer, use the Pen tool to draw the shape of the back part of the apple (where the apple curves behind the stem).**

   Be sure to overlap this shape with the Apple Front shape so no blank space will show between the two elements later.

Overlap this line to ensure complete coverage when you start adding color.

6. **Create a new layer and rename it Stem.**

Since you were just working on the Apple Back layer, the new Stem layer should automatically reside between the Apple Front and Apple Back layers in the Layers panel (which is where you want it to reside). If not, drag the Stem layer to the correct position before continuing.

7. **Draw the outline of the stem on the active Stem layer. Again, overlap the bottom of the Stem shape with the Apple Front shape.**

You now have all the outlines for the apple, with each outline on its own layer. When you start adding gradient meshes in the next exercises, you will see how important it is to use a different layer for each element.

The Stem shape overlaps the Apple Front shape.

8. **Save the file and continue to the next exercise.**

CREATE A GRADIENT MESH

A gradient mesh is basically a special type of fill. Each point in the mesh can have a different color value; the colors of adjacent mesh points determine the colors along the gradient between the two points. When you paint objects with a mesh, it's similar to painting with ink or watercolor. It takes considerable practice to become proficient with gradient meshes.

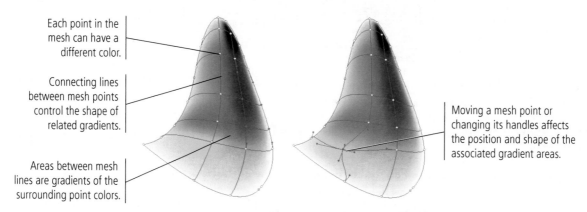

Each point in the mesh can have a different color.

Connecting lines between mesh points control the shape of related gradients.

Areas between mesh lines are gradients of the surrounding point colors.

Moving a mesh point or changing its handles affects the position and shape of the associated gradient areas.

One of the techniques you will explore in this project is Illustrator's Outline mode. Outline mode allows you to see the points and paths of an object without the colors and fills. This viewing mode can be very useful when you need to adjust anchor points of one shape while viewing the underlying objects.

1. **With apple.ai open, click the eye icons in the Layers panel to hide the Apple Back and Stem layers, and then select the Apple Front layer.**

2. **Using the Selection tool, select the outline shape on the Apple Front layer.**

3. **Using the Eyedropper tool, click a medium-red color in the apple image to fill the selected apple shape with the sampled color.**

   You can add a gradient mesh to a path without filling it with color first, but if you don't choose a color, the mesh will automatically fill with white. It's easier to create a good mesh if you start with a fill that colors most of the object.

Eyedropper tool cursor

Eyedropper tool

4. **Choose Object>Create Gradient Mesh and make sure the Preview option is checked.**

5. **In the Create Gradient Mesh dialog box, set the Rows value to 8 and the Columns value to 9, and make sure the Appearance menu is set to Flat.**

The Rows and Columns settings determine how many lines will make up the resulting mesh.

Note:

When you convert a path to a mesh, the shape is no longer a path. You cannot apply a stroke attribute to a gradient mesh object.

6. **Click OK to create the mesh.**

7. **Choose View>Outline.**

   In Outline mode, you see only the edges or **wireframes** of the objects in the file. (Your mesh might appear different than ours, based on where you placed your anchor points on the shape edges. Don't worry — you will still be able to achieve the same overall effect as what you see in our examples.)

Note:

In our screen shots, we have the bounding box turned off to better show only the mesh points. You can turn off the bounding box by choosing View>Hide Bounding Box.

8. Command/Control-click the eye icon next to the Apple Photo layer to return it to Preview viewing mode.

You can now see the mesh wireframe and the actual pixels of the apple image, enabling you to sample colors directly from the apple image, and then use those colors to paint the mesh points.

The iris in the icon is missing when a layer displays in Outline mode.

Note:

When working in Outline mode, Command/Control-clicking a layer's visibility icon (the eye icon) returns only that layer to Preview mode.

9. Using the Direct Selection tool, click the top-left point on the inside of the mesh object to select only that mesh point.

Don't select one of the mesh points on the outside edge of the shape.

Gradient Mesh Options

When creating a gradient mesh, the number of rows and columns you create depends on the size and shape of the object you want to shade. You might want to experiment with these settings before you click OK and create the mesh. If you add too many mesh points, the colors blend incorrectly and take a long time to paint; if you add too few mesh lines, it can be difficult — if not impossible — to add enough depth to the illustration. (Even though you can use the Mesh tool to add and delete mesh lines later, it's more efficient to create a mesh as close as possible to what you need as the final result.)

The Appearance option in the Create Gradient Mesh dialog box determines how colors affect the mesh you create:

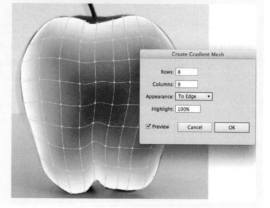

- The **Flat** option, which you used in this exercise, spreads a single color to all points in the mesh. If you don't fill the shape with a color before creating the mesh, the mesh object will fill with solid white.

- The **To Center** option (upper right) creates a white highlight at the center of the mesh and gradually spreads the highlight color outward toward the object edges. The Highlight (%) field controls the strength of the white in the resulting mesh.

- The **To Edge** option (lower right) is essentially the opposite of the To Center option; the white highlight appears around the edges of the mesh, blending to the solid color in the center of the mesh object.

10. **With the mesh point selected, choose the Eyedropper tool in the Tools panel, and then click next to the selected mesh point to sample the color from the apple photo.**

Because the mesh object is still displayed in Outline mode, you can't see the effect of the color sampling.

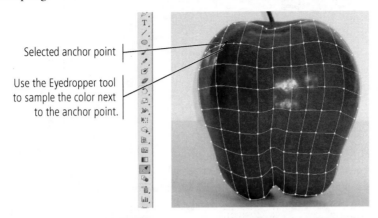

Selected anchor point

Use the Eyedropper tool
to sample the color next
to the anchor point.

11. **Press and hold the Command/Control key to temporarily access the Direct Selection tool, and then click the next mesh point on the same vertical mesh line.**

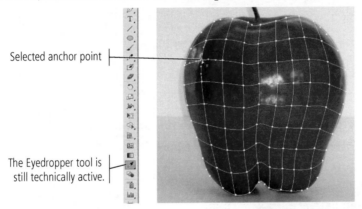

Selected anchor point

The Eyedropper tool is
still technically active.

Note:

You can use the Opacity field in the Control panel to define a different opacity for every point in a gradient mesh.

12. **Release the Command/Control key to return to the Eyedropper tool, and then click to sample the color next to the selected mesh point.**

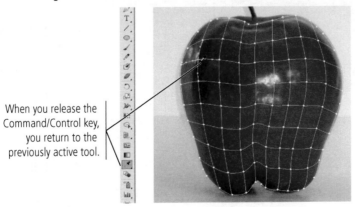

When you release the
Command/Control key,
you return to the
previously active tool.

13. **Continue this process to change the color of the mesh points in the first three columns of the mesh.**

14. **Choose View>Preview to see the actual content of the visible layers.**

15. **Deselect everything on the page and review your progress.**

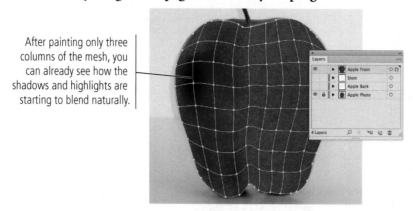

After painting only three columns of the mesh, you can already see how the shadows and highlights are starting to blend naturally.

16. **Command/Control-click the eye icon for the Apple Front layer to change only that layer back to Outline mode.**

17. **Using the same technique from the previous steps, finish painting all the mesh points in the mesh object.**

    Ignore the bright highlights for now; you will add the proper highlights later.

    This task might seem tedious because there are so many points in the mesh, but with this process, you can create realistic depth in a flat vector object in a matter of minutes. To accomplish the same result using manual techniques would require many hours of time and a high degree of artistic skill.

18. **Command/Control-click the Apple Front layer eye icon to return the layer to Preview mode, and then deselect the mesh object and review your results.**

19. **Save the file and continue to the next exercise.**

WORK WITH A MESH USING SMART GUIDES

It can be difficult to select and manipulate points in a mesh in Preview mode because you can't see the actual mesh lines and points until the mesh object is selected. You could move your cursor around until you locate the exact mesh point you want to work with; or you could continue switching back and forth between Preview and Outline modes. Both methods, however, can be time consuming (and frustrating).

Fortunately, Smart Guides solve this problem. Using Smart Guides, you can see the entire mesh wireframe as soon as your cursor touches any part of the object — providing a temporary outline/preview combination.

1. **With apple.ai open, choose View>Smart Guides to make sure that option is turned on.**

2. **Make sure the Snap to Point option is toggled off in the View menu.**

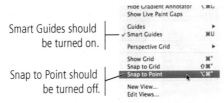

Smart Guides should be turned on.

Snap to Point should be turned off.

Note:

When using Smart Guides, make sure the Snap to Point option is toggled off. If Snap to Point is active, Smart Guides will not work (even if you have the command selected in the menu).

3. **Make sure everything in the file is deselected, and then roll the Direct Selection tool over the apple shape.**

   You can now see the mesh points and lines, as well as the precise location of the Direct Selection tool.

With Smart Guides turned on, you can easily view and select specific anchors in the mesh.

4. **Command/Control-click the visibility icon for the Apple Front layer so you can see the photo behind the mesh object.**

5. **Using the Eyedropper tool, sample the highlight color on the top-left side of the apple shape.**

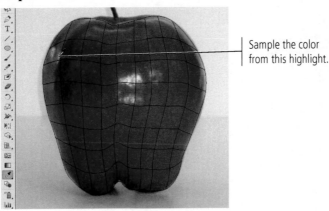

Sample the color from this highlight.

6. **Command/Control-click the visibility icon for the Apple Front layer to restore that layer to Preview mode.**

7. **Choose the Mesh tool from the Tools panel.**

   The Mesh tool adds new gridlines to an existing mesh, or it creates a mesh if you click inside a basic shape that doesn't currently have a mesh.

8. **Click the third horizontal mesh line, between the first and second vertical mesh lines, to create a new vertical mesh line (as shown in the following image).**

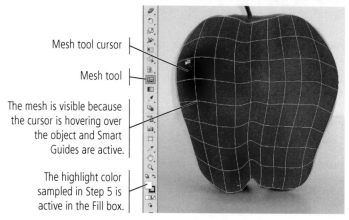

Mesh tool cursor

Mesh tool

The mesh is visible because the cursor is hovering over the object and Smart Guides are active.

The highlight color sampled in Step 5 is active in the Fill box.

Clicking this horizontal mesh line adds a new vertical mesh line, colored with the highlight color you sampled in the previous step.

9. **Press Command/Control and click away from the mesh object to deselect it.**

10. **Change the Apple Front layer to Outline mode.**

11. **Select the Mesh tool. Click twice along the vertical mesh line directly below the stem to add two horizontal mesh lines between the first two rows of the existing mesh.**

   It isn't necessary to return the layer to Preview mode before adding lines to the mesh.

Click this vertical mesh line twice to add two horizontal mesh lines.

Note:

Clicking a horizontal mesh line with the Mesh tool creates a new vertical mesh line. To add a horizontal mesh line, click the Mesh tool on a vertical mesh line.

12. **Using the Direct Selection tool, select the point on the (now) second horizontal mesh line, directly below the stem.**

   This is one of the mesh lines you created with the Mesh tool in the previous step.

Note:

It might be helpful to deselect the mesh after adding the first new mesh line, and then click again to add the second mesh line.

13. **With the mesh point selected, use the Eyedropper tool to sample the light red of the apple's highlight to change the color of the point.**

When you change the color of a mesh point, you change the way surrounding colors blend into that point's color. By changing this point to a medium red, you reduce the distance over which the highlight color (in the lower point) can blend — effectively shortening the highlight area.

Changing this anchor point to a lighter red adds a highlight to the apple graphic, more closely matching the highlight in the original image.

Note:

Remember, pressing Command/Control with another tool selected temporarily accesses the Direct Selection tool.

14. **Command/Control-click to select the mesh point to the immediate left of the point where you placed the highlight.**

15. **Release the mouse button to return to the Eyedropper tool, and then sample the highlight color again to spread the highlight horizontally across the apple.**

16. **Repeat Steps 14–15 for the point to the right of the one you changed in Step 13.**

By filling these two anchors with the highlight color, you extend the highlight horizontally along the mesh line.

17. **Deselect the mesh object, return the Apple Front layer to Preview mode, and review your work.**

The highlight adds depth, but it spreads a bit too far down (compared to the original image).

18. **Using the Direct Selection tool, drag up the three mesh points immediately below the highlight points.**

Reducing the distance between the points shortens the distance of the blended highlight-colored area.

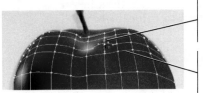

Moving the anchors below the highlight shortens the height of the blended highlight.

As soon as you move the cursor over the object, the mesh lines become visible.

19. **Continue adjusting the positions and colors of the mesh points until you are satisfied with the result.**

20. **Choose View>Smart Guides to toggle off the Smart Guides.**

21. **Save the file and continue to the next exercise.**

 COLOR THE REMAINING OBJECTS

Building and coloring the shape for the apple's front should have given you a good idea of how mesh points control color blending from one point to another. Because you set up the file using layers for the individual shapes that make up the apple, it will be fairly easy to create additional meshes for the remaining pieces of the apple.

1. **With apple.ai open, hide the Apple Front layer and show the Apple Back layer.**

2. **Using the Selection tool, select the shape on the Apple Back layer.**

3. **Using the Eyedropper tool, click a darker part of the apple to fill the selected shape with the sampled color.**

4. **Choose Object>Create Gradient Mesh and add a 3-row, 5-column mesh with the Appearance menu set to Flat.**

5. **Use the same method you learned in the previous exercise to color the mesh points for the Apple Back shape.**

   Switch the Apple Back layer to Outline mode, and then use the Eyedropper tool to sample colors from the photo for each point in the mesh.

6. **Show the Apple Front layer and review your work.**

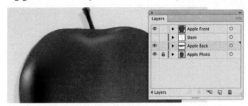

7. **Lock the Apple Back layer, and then show the Stem layer.**

8. **Select the stem shape and fill it with a color sampled from the lightest color near the top of the stem.**

9. **Change the Stem layer to Outline mode.**

10. **Deselect all objects, and then use the Eyedropper tool to sample the dark color of the stem.**

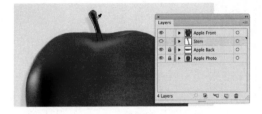

11. **Return the Stem layer to Preview mode.**

12. **Using the Mesh tool, click in the middle of the stem shape to create a mesh.**

   The stem shape is converted to a mesh, and a new mesh point (with the color you sampled in Step 10) is added where you click.

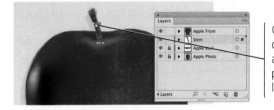

Clicking with the Mesh tool converts the stem shape to a mesh object and adds a point (and the associated lines) where you click.

13. **Deselect everything, and then hide the Apple Photo layer to review your work.**

14. **Show the Apple Photo layer again, save the file, and then continue to the next exercise.**

USE FILTERS TO ADD OBJECT HIGHLIGHTS

As with any illustration, painting, or drawing, the details separate good work from great work. In this exercise, you add the highlights on the front and left sides of the apple to finish the illustration.

1. **With `apple.ai` open, hide the Apple Front, Apple Back, and Stem layers.**

2. **Create a new layer named `Highlights` and move this layer to the top of the stack in the Layers panel.**

3. **Using the Pen tool with a 1-pt black stroke and no fill, create the shapes of the highlights on the front of the apple.**

4. **Select all the highlight shapes you drew in Step 3 and fill them with a color sampled from the highlights in the photo.**

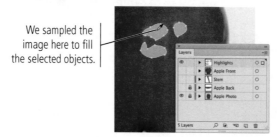

We sampled the image here to fill the selected objects.

5. **Deselect all objects. Select one of the larger highlight shapes and choose Effect>Stylize>Feather.**

Make sure you choose from the Illustrator Effects list (at the top of the menu) and not the Photoshop Effects list. (You will learn more about these effects, including the difference between the two sets, in Project 6: Cereal Box.)

6. **Activate the Preview option in the Feather dialog box, and then set the Feather Radius to 0.2".**

The Feather effect softens the edges of the shape, blending from fully opaque to fully transparent. A higher Feather Radius value extends the distance from opaque to transparent color in the effect.

It is difficult to evaluate the actual results while the Apple Front layer is hidden.

7. **Click OK, and then show the Apple Front layer.**

With the Apple Front layer showing, the large feather radius appears weak.

8. **With the feathered object selected, open the Appearance panel.**

   Effects in Illustrator are non-destructive attributes, which means they do not permanently change the object being styled. Because these effects are stored as object attributes, you can change the settings for any effect at any time.

9. **In the Appearance panel, click the Feather hot text to open the dialog box for that appearance attribute.**

Note:

"Hot text" is any text in the user interface that appears blue and underlined. Clicking these hot-text links opens a panel or dialog box where you can change related settings.

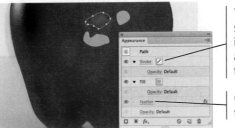

The Appearance panel shows the attributes — including stroke, fill, and applied effects — defined for the selected object.

Click the Feather hot text to open that dialog box.

10. **Make sure the Preview option is checked, and then experiment with the Feather Radius setting until you are satisfied with the highlight.**

11. **Apply the Feather effect to all highlight areas, changing the Feather Radius value as appropriate for each object.**

12. **Delete the Apple Photo layer, and then show and unlock all remaining layers.**

13. **Select everything on the artboard. Use the Control or Transform panel to position the top-left corner of the selection at X: 0.1″, Y: 0.1″.**

14. **Lock all layers, save the file, and continue to the next stage of the project.**

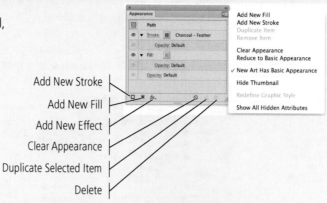

The Appearance panel allows you to review and change the appearance attributes of objects, including stroke, fill, transparency, and applied effects.

As you know, the last-used settings for fill color, stroke color, and stroke weight are applied to new objects. Other attributes, such as the applied brush or effects, are not automatically applied to new objects. If you need to create a series of objects with the same overall appearance, you can turn off the **New Art Has Basic Appearance** option in the Appearance panel Options menu.

Clicking the **Clear Appearance** button reduces the selected object to a fill and stroke of None. Choosing **Reduce to Basic Appearance** in the panel Options menu resets an object to only basic fill and stroke attributes; fill color and stroke weight and color are maintained, but all other attributes are removed.

Add New Stroke
Add New Fill
Add New Effect
Clear Appearance
Duplicate Selected Item
Delete

You can use the **Duplicate Selected Item** button to create multiple versions of the same attribute for an object, such as two stroke weights/colors — allowing you to compound the effect without layering multiple objects. If you want to remove a specific attribute, simply select that item and click the panel's **Delete** button.

Stage 2 Working with Type

To create a complete logo, you pair logo artwork with text that makes up the corporate brand (the company name and tagline, if there is one). Illustrator includes sophisticated tools for controlling type — from changing the font and size to controlling the appearance of quotes and using styles to format long blocks of text.

In this stage of the project, you will use some of the basic type formatting options to set your client's company name. You will also use illustration techniques to manipulate the individual letter shapes in the company name to create the finished logotype.

Type Terminology

Before you begin the exercises in the second stage of this project, you should understand the terms that are commonly used when people talk about type. Keep the following terms in mind as you work through the next exercises.

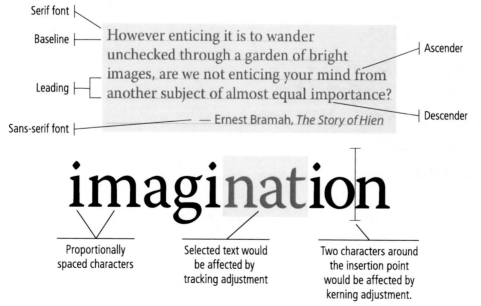

Type is typically divided into two basic categories: serif and sans serif. **Serif type** has small flourishes on the ends of the letterforms; **sans-serif** has no such decorations (sans is French for "without"). There are other categories of special or decorative fonts, including script, symbol, dingbat, decorative, and image fonts.

The actual shape of letters is determined by the specific **font** you use; each character in a font is referred to as a **glyph**. Fonts can be monospaced or proportionally spaced. In a monospace font, each character takes up the same amount of space on a line; in other words, a lowercase i and m occupy the same horizontal space. In a proportionally spaced font, different characters occupy different amounts of horizontal space as necessary.

The **x-height** of type is the height of the lowercase letter x. Elements that extend below the baseline are called **descenders** (as in g, j, and p); elements that extend above the x-height are called **ascenders** (as in b, d, and k).

The size of type is usually measured in **points** (there are approximately 72 points in an inch). When you define a type size, you determine the distance from the bottom of the descenders to the top of the ascenders (plus a small extra space above the ascenders called the **body clearance**).

When you set type, it rests on a non-printing line called the **baseline**. If a type element has more than one line in a single paragraph, the distance from one baseline to the next is called **leading** (pronounced "ledding"). Most applications set the default leading as 120% of the type size.

Serif
Sans-serif

CREATE POINT-TYPE OBJECTS

Creating type in Illustrator is fairly simple; simply click with the Type tool and begin typing. Many advanced options are also available, such as importing type from an external file, using type areas to control long blocks of text, and so on. In this project, you concentrate on the basic type formatting controls.

1. **With apple.ai open (from your WIP>Organics folder), create a new layer named Logotype at the top of the layer stack.**

2. **Choose the Type tool in the Tools panel, and then click the empty area of the artboard to the right of the apple graphic.**

   You can create two basic kinds of type (or text) objects in Illustrator: **point-type objects** (also called **path type**), where the text usually resides on a single line or path; and **area-type objects,** where the text fills a specific shape (usually a rectangle).

   When you single-click with the Type tool, you create **point type**. You will see a flashing **insertion point** where text will appear when you begin typing.

3. **With the insertion point flashing, type apple.**

   When you add a new type object (either point type or area type) without changing anything in Illustrator, the type is automatically set in the last-used font and type settings, which will probably be different from one computer to the next.

Note:

We used Magenta as the layer color so it would be more visible in our screen captures.

When you click the Type tool, Illustrator automatically switches to a black fill and no stroke (unless you define different defaults).

Wherever you click with the Type tool, you'll see this flashing insertion point.

When working with text, the Control panel includes some common text formatting options.

Type tool

apple

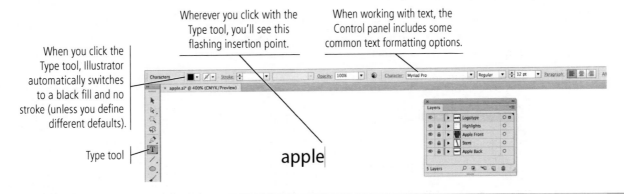

4. **Choose the Direct Selection tool in the Tools panel.**

When selected with the Direct Selection tool, you can see the point and path that make up the type object.

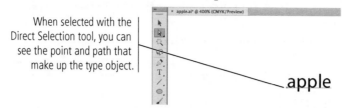

5. **With the type object selected, click the Paragraph Align Center button in the Control panel.**

Remember, different options are available in the Control panel, depending on the width of your monitor. If the Paragraph Align buttons are not available in the Control panel, you can click the Paragraph hot-text link, or open the stand-alone Paragraph panel (Window>Type>Paragraph).

Individual characters do not need to be selected to change text formatting. Changes made while a type *object* is selected apply to all text in that type object.

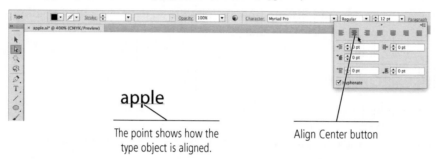

The point shows how the type object is aligned.

Align Center button

6. **Click the arrow to the right of the Font menu in the Control or Character panel. Scroll through the list of fonts and choose ATC Oak Normal.**

If your Control panel does not include the Font menu, click the Character hot-text link to open the Character panel, and then apply the ATC Oak Normal font.

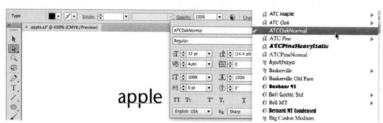

You can simply type in the Font field to find a specific font. As you type in the field, Illustrator skips to the first available font with the characters you type (for example, typing "Aar" would automatically find an installed font named Aardvark).

7. **Click the Selection tool in the Tools panel.**

When the Selection tool is active, you can see the bounding box of the type object. Like any other object, you can use the bounding box handles to stretch, scale, or rotate the type object (including the characters in the type object).

If you don't see the bounding box, choose View>Show Bounding Box to toggle it on.

> *Note:*
>
> *You can also open the regular Character panel by choosing Window>Type> Character.*

> *Note:*
>
> *In the Character Panel, the Font menu shows a preview sample of each font. This preview is not available in the Type>Font menu.*

8. **Click any of the type object's corner handles and drag out to make the type larger. When the cursor feedback shows the object's height of approximately 0.5 in, release the mouse button.**

When you resize a type object with the Selection tool, you'll probably notice that the baseline of the letters moves when you drag the bottom-right handle. You might need to reposition the type object and resize it a couple of times to achieve the desired result.

Note:

You can press Shift after you begin dragging to constrain the object's original proportions.

Note:

We turned Smart Guides on (View>Smart Guides) to show the cursor feedback in our screen shots.

9. **In the Control panel, click the Character hot text to open the Character panel directly below the hot text.**

In addition to the font and size values in the main Control panel, the Character panel provides access to all character formatting options that can be applied in Illustrator.

The Size menu shows the new size that results from resizing the object by dragging its bounding box handles.

If you do not constrain the resizing process, you might have a horizontal or vertical scale other than 100% of the font size.

Some argue that you should never artificially scale type horizontally or vertically (as you did in Step 8) because it distorts the spacing and shape of characters, and requires more processing time for an output device to accurately output the non-standard type sizes.

However, in this case the type will eventually be converted to vector outlines, so artificially scaling the type will cause no problems.

10. **In the Character panel, change the Size field to 72. Make sure both the horizontal and vertical scale values are set to 100%.**

Pressing Tab moves through the panel fields; as soon as you move to a new field, your changes in the previous field are reflected in the document. You can also press Return/Enter to apply a change and collapse the Character panel back into the Control panel.

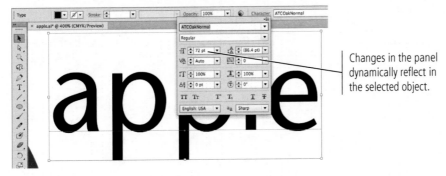

Changes in the panel dynamically reflect in the selected object.

11. Using the Type tool, double-click the word "apple" to select all the letters in the word, and then open the stand-alone Character panel (Window>Type>Character).

Tracking and kerning are two terms related to the horizontal spacing between characters in a line of text. **Kerning** is the spacing between two specific characters; **tracking** refers to the spacing between all characters in a selection.

Most industrial-quality font families come with built-in kern and track values. Smaller type does not usually pose tracking and kerning problems; when type is very large, however, spacing often becomes an issue. To fix spacing problems, you need to adjust the kerning and/or tracking values.

Note:

Kerning and tracking are largely matters of personal preference. Some people prefer much tighter spacing than others.

The Character Panel in Depth

ILLUSTRATOR FOUNDATIONS

The Character panel, accessed either from the Control panel hot text or as an independent panel by choosing Window>Type>Character, includes all the options you can use to change the appearance of selected text characters.

If these options are not visible, choose Show Options in the panel Options menu.

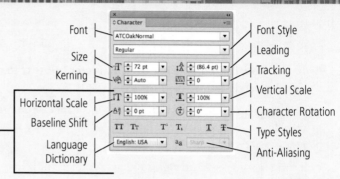

Font · Font Style · Size · Leading · Kerning · Tracking · Horizontal Scale · Vertical Scale · Baseline Shift · Character Rotation · Language Dictionary · Type Styles · Anti-Aliasing

- **Leading** is the distance from one baseline to the next. Adobe applications treat leading as a character attribute, even though leading controls the space between lines of an individual paragraph. (Space between paragraphs is controlled using the Space Before option in the Paragraph panel.) To change leading for an entire paragraph, you must first select the entire paragraph. This approach means you can change the leading for a single line of a paragraph by selecting any character(s) in that line; however, changing the leading for any character in a line applies the same change to the entire line that contains those characters.

- **Kerning** increases or decreases the space between pairs of letters. Kerning is used in cases where particular letters in specific fonts need to be manually spread apart or brought together to eliminate a too-tight or too-spread-out appearance. Manual kerning is usually necessary in headlines or other large type elements. (Many commercial fonts have built-in kerning pairs, so you won't need to apply much hands-on intervention with kerning. Adobe applications default to the kerning values stored in the **font metrics**.)

- **Tracking**, also known as "range kerning," refers to the overall tightness or looseness across a range of characters. Tracking and kerning are applied in thousandths of an **em** (or the amount of space occupied by an uppercase "M," which is usually the widest character in a typeface).

- **Vertical Scale** and **Horizontal Scale** artificially stretch or contract the selected characters. This scaling is a quick way of achieving condensed or expanded type if those variations of a font don't exist. (Type that has been artificially condensed or expanded too much looks bad because the scaling destroys the type's metrics; if possible, use a condensed or expanded version of a font before resorting to horizontal or vertical scaling.)

- **Baseline Shift** moves the selected type above or below the baseline by a specific number of points. Positive numbers move the characters up; negative values move the characters down.

- **Character Rotation** rotates only selected letters, rather than rotating the entire type object.

- Type Styles — **All Caps, Small Caps, Superscript, Subscript, Underline**, and **Strikethrough** — change the appearance of selected characters.

- **Language Dictionary** defines the language that is used to check spelling in the story.

- **Anti-Aliasing** can be used to help smooth the apparent edges of type that is exported to a bitmap format that does not support vector information.

12. Change the Tracking field to –25 to tighten the space between all selected letters.

You can change the field manually, choose a pre-defined value from the Tracking menu, or click the up- or down-arrow button to change the tracking by 1 unit with each click.

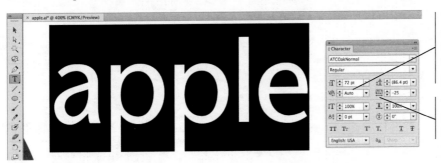

The Kern (Pair) value remains set to "Auto," which is the default setting built into this particular typeface.

The Tracking field icon has an arrow below the two letters.

13. Click with the Type tool to place the insertion point between the "a" and the "p".

This is a good example of a **kern pair** that needs adjustment. The Auto setting built into the font leaves a little too much space between the two characters — even after you have tightened the tracking considerably.

14. Change the Kerning value to –20.

Like tracking, you can change this value manually, choose a value from the pop-up menu, or use the Kerning field buttons to change kerning by 1 unit.

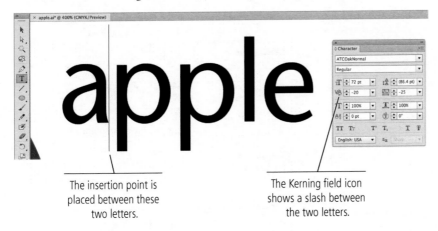

The insertion point is placed between these two letters.

The Kerning field icon shows a slash between the two letters.

Note:

When the insertion point is flashing in a type object, you can't use the keyboard shortcuts to access tools; instead, pressing a key adds that letter to the current type object, at the location of the insertion point.

These slight modifications to tracking and kerning improve the overall appearance and readability of the logo. Later in the project, you will use a different technique to adjust letter spacing. For now, however, you should become familiar with making this type of manual adjustment.

15. Save the file and continue to the next exercise.

Point Type vs. Area Type

Clicking with the Type tool creates a point-type object. Clicking and dragging with the Type tool creates an area-type object. **Point type** (or path type) starts at a single point and extends along or follows a single path. **Area type** fills up an area (normally a rectangle). The following images show point type on the left and area type on the right.

The difference between the two kinds of type becomes obvious when you try to resize them or otherwise modify their shapes using the Selection tool. Area type is contained within an area. If you resize that area, the type doesn't resize; it remains within the area but simply flows (or wraps) differently. If you scale or resize point type by dragging a bounding box handle, the type within the object resizes accordingly.

This point-type object is selected with the Direct Selection tool. You can see the paths that make up the single type object.

This is a point type object, which is created by clicking once with the Type tool.

This is an area type object, which is created by clicking and dragging with the Type tool.

This area-type object is selected with the Direct Selection tool. You can see the edges of the type object, but no bounding box handles appear.

The object is selected with the Selection tool. You can now see the object's bounding box handles.

This is a point type object, which is created by clicking once with the Type tool.

This is an area type object, which is created by clicking and dragging with the Type tool.

The object is selected with the Selection tool. You can see the edges of the type object, as well as the object's bounding box handles.

Resizing the bounding box with the Selection tool resizes the text in the point-type object.

This is a point type object, which is created by clicking once with the Type tool.

This is an area type object, which is created by clicking and dragging with the Type tool. dragging with the Type tool.

Resizing the bounding box with the Selection tool resizes the object; the text rewraps inside the new object dimensions.

Another consideration is where the "point" sits on the type path. When you change the paragraph alignment of point type, the point remains in the same position; the text on the point moves to the appropriate position, relative to the fixed point.

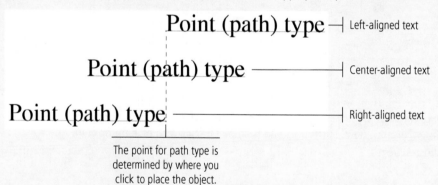

Point (path) type — Left-aligned text

Point (path) type — Center-aligned text

Point (path) type — Right-aligned text

The point for path type is determined by where you click to place the object.

When you're working with type, it can be easier — at least at first — to work with bounding boxes turned off. You can turn off the bounding boxes for all objects — including type objects — by choosing View>Hide Bounding Box.

MANIPULATE TYPE OBJECTS

When you work with type in Illustrator, you need to be aware of a few special issues that can affect the way you interact with the application. This exercise explores some common problems that can arise when you work with type, as well as some tricks you can use to work around them.

1. **With apple.ai open, select the Type tool in the Tools panel. Click at the end of the existing type object to place the insertion point.**

2. **Move the Type tool cursor below the existing type object and click.**

   When the insertion point is already flashing, you can't click with the Type tool to create a new point-type object.

   Clicking moves the insertion point in the existing type object, but does not create a new type object.

3. **With the insertion point flashing, press Command/Control.**

   As you know, this modifier key temporarily switches the active tool to the Selection tool. The bounding box of the type object remains visible as long as you hold down the Command/Control key.

4. **While still holding down the Command/Control key, click within the bounding box of the type object.**

   When you click, you select the actual type object. The point and path become active, and the insertion point no longer flashes. You can use this method to move or modify a type object without switching away from the Type tool.

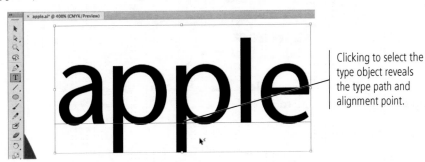

   Clicking to select the type object reveals the type path and alignment point.

Note:

If you want to add another type object, you have to first deselect the one where the insertion point is flashing. To accomplish this, you can Command/Control-click away from the currently active type object.

Remember, pressing Command/Control temporarily switches to the Selection or Direct Selection tool (whichever was last used); when you release the Command/ Control key, you return to the previously active tool — in this case, the Type tool.

You can also choose Select>Deselect, and then click again with the Type tool to create a new type object.

5. **Release the Command/Control key to return to the Type tool.**

6. **Click below the existing type object to create a new type object.**

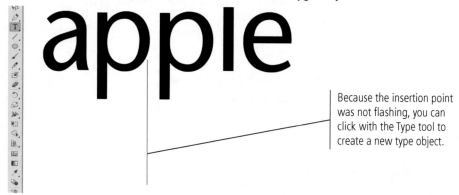

Because the insertion point was not flashing, you can click with the Type tool to create a new type object.

7. **Type organics.**

When you add a new type object, the type is automatically set using the last-used formatting options.

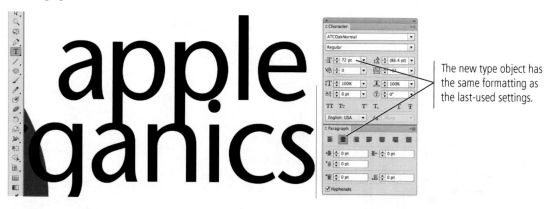

The new type object has the same formatting as the last-used settings.

8. **Press Command/Control. Click the new type object and drag it up until the descender of the second "p" in apple aligns with the stem of the "g" in the word "organics."**

Leave approximately 0.125″ between the baseline of "apple" and the x-height of the letters in "organic."

The layer color shows the new position of the type object.

9. **Release the mouse button to reposition the type object, and then release the Command/Control key to return to the Type tool.**

10. **Save the file and continue to the next exercise.**

CONVERT TYPE TO OUTLINES

In Illustrator, fonts — and the characters that compose them — are like any other vector objects. They are made up of anchors and paths, which you can modify just as you would any other vector object. To access the anchor points, however, you must first convert the text to outlines.

1. **With apple.ai open, use the Selection tool to select both type objects in the file.**

2. **Choose Type>Create Outlines.**

   When you convert the type to outlines, the anchor points and paths that make up the letter shapes appear. Each type object (in this case, one for "apple" and one for "organics") is a separate group of letter shapes.

3. **Click away from the objects to deselect them, and then click the word "apple."**

4. **In the Layers panel, click the arrow to the left of the Logotype layer name to expand the layer.**

   In addition to arranging layers, you can use the expanded lists in the Layers panel to review and manage the individual objects on each layer (called **sublayers**).

Click this arrow to expand the layer.

The square identifies the location of the selected object(s).

This icon indicates the target object.

5. **In the Layers panel, expand the apple group.**

6. **Click the Target icon for the first (lowest) "p" to select only that object.**

   By expanding the individual layers, you can use the Layers panel to access and work with individual objects in a group, without ungrouping the objects.

Click the Target icon to select or deselect a specific object within a group.

7. **Press the Right Arrow key to nudge the selected object right (narrowing the space between the letter shapes).**

   You could have fine-tuned the letter spacing with the tracking and kerning controls before you converted the letters to outlines. Since you're working with these letters as graphics, however, you are accessing and nudging individual pieces of a group to adjust the spacing in the overall logotype.

8. **Repeat Step 7 to move the "a" shape right, and again to move the "l" and "e" shapes left.**

   As mentioned previously, letter spacing is largely a matter of personal preference. You might prefer more or less space between the letters than what you see in our images.

Note:

*Open the General pane of the Preferences dialog box to change the distance an object moves when you press the arrow keys (called the **keyboard increment**).*

Press Shift and an arrow key to move an object 10 times the default keyboard increment.

9. **In the Layers panel, collapse the apple group and expand the organics group.**

10. **Click the Target icon for the "s" shape, and then Shift-click the Target icons for the "c", "i", "n", and "a" shapes.**

    Just as Shift-clicking objects selects multiple objects, Shift-clicking the Target icons allows you to easily select multiple objects within a group.

11. **Press the Left Arrow key to nudge the selected shapes left.**

12. **In the Layers panel, shift-click the Target icon for the selected "a" letter shape.**

    Shift-clicking a selected object (Target icon) deselects that object only.

13. **Press the Left Arrow key to nudge the remaining selection left.**

14. **Continue selecting and nudging the letter shapes to reduce the spacing between all letters in the word "organics." Use the following image as a guide.**

    Don't worry about the overlap between the two lines of text at this point; you will fix those issues in the next exercise.

15. **Save the file and continue to the next exercise.**

Because you converted the letter shapes to outlines, the logo text no longer behaves as type. You can now apply your drawing skills to adjust the vector shapes and create a unique appearance for your client's logotype. Remember, you can use the Add Anchor Point tool to add points to a vector path, use the Delete Anchor Point tool to remove points from a vector path, and use the Convert Anchor Point tool to convert smooth points to corner points (and vice versa). All three of these tools are nested below the Pen tool in the Tools panel.

1. **With apple.ai open, use the Direct Selection tool to adjust the anchor points at the bottom of the "p" to follow the same arch as the lowercase "r".**

   Remember, click directly on an anchor point to select and move only that point. The selected point appears solid, while unselected points appear hollow.

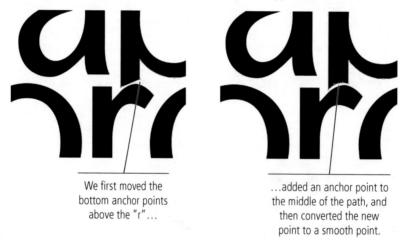

We first moved the bottom anchor points above the "r"...

...added an anchor point to the middle of the path, and then converted the new point to a smooth point.

Note:

It is helpful to zoom in very close to complete this part of the project.

2. **Using the Direct Selection tool, click the second "p" in the word "apple". Press Shift, and then click the "g" in the word "organics".**

3. **Using the Shape Builder tool, click and drag to merge the two shapes that make up the "p" and "g".**

Shape Builder tool

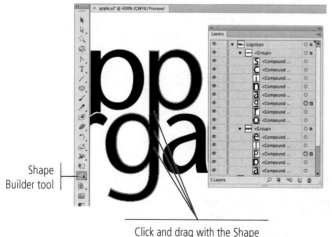

Click and drag with the Shape Builder tool to merge the selected areas into a single shape.

The merged object moves into the group with the object where you first clicked.

4. **Using the Direct Selection tool, click the edge of the dot (above the letter "i") to show the anchor points of that shape. Use what you know about points and handles to change the dot to a leaf shape.**

5. **In the Layers panel, click the Target icon for the "i" shape to select the entire compound path. Change the fill color of the selected object to a medium green from the built-in swatches.**

6. **Select both groups of type shapes and group them.**

The Layers panel shows nested levels of groups.

7. **Zoom out so you can see the apple artwork and the logotype graphics.**

8. **In the Control panel, click the Transform hot text to open the Transform panel. Make sure the W and H fields are linked, and type 250% in the W field.**

Remember: The appearance of the Transform hot text depends on the width of your Application frame; if you have enough horizontal screen space, the Transform hot text is replaced by individual X, Y, W, and H fields. In that case, you can click any of those field names to open the Transform panel.

When you press Return/Enter (or simply click away from the Transform panel), the logotype group is scaled proportionally to 250% of its original size.

Click the hot-text link in the Control panel to access the related panel.

You can resize this group just as you would any other object.

9. **Drag the logotype group so the "a" and "o" closely align with the outer contour of the apple shape. Use the following image as a guide.**

10. **Save the file and continue to the next stage of the project.**

Stage 3   Working with Multiple Artboards

For all intents and purposes, the Apple Organics logo is now complete. However, you still need to create the alternate versions that can be used in other applications. You need a two-color version for jobs that will be printed with spot colors, and you need a one-color version for jobs that will be printed with black ink only.

In older workflows, creating multiple variations of a logo meant generating multiple files, with each variation residing in a separate file. In Illustrator CS6, you can streamline the process by creating a single file that includes multiple artboards, with each artboard containing one variation of the logo.

In this stage of the project, you adjust the artboard to fit the completed logo. You then duplicate the artwork on additional artboards, and adjust the colors in each version to meet the specific needs of different color applications.

 ## ADJUST THE DEFAULT ARTBOARD

When you place an Illustrator file into another file (for example, a page-layout file in InDesign or even another Illustrator file) you can decide how to place that file — based on the artwork boundaries (the outermost bounding box), on the artboard boundaries, or on other specific dimensions. To make the logo artwork more placement-friendly, you should adjust the Illustrator artboard to fit the completed logo artwork.

1. **With apple.ai open, unlock all layers in the file. Select everything on the artboard, then review the W and H values in the Control or Transform panel.**

   You created this file with a letter-size artboard. As you can see, the size is both too narrow and too high for the finished artwork.

Note:

Your W and H values might be slightly different than what you see in our screen shots, but they should be in the same general ballpark.

When the Artboard tool is active, the Control panel presents a number of options for adjusting the active artboard.

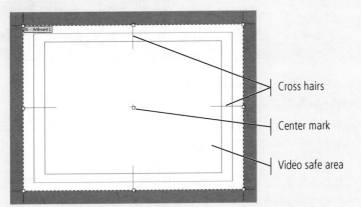

A   Use this menu to change the artboard to a predefined size (letter, tabloid, etc.)

B   Click to change the artboard to portrait orientation

C   Click to change the artboard to landscape orientation

D   Click to add a new artboard at the currently defined size. The cursor is "loaded" with the new artboard; you can click to place the new artboard in the workspace.

E   Click to delete the active artboard

F   Type here to define a name for the active artboard

G   Click to toggle the Move/Copy Artwork with Artboard option. When active, objects on the artboard move along with the artboard being moved (or cloned).

H   Click **Show Center Mark** displays a point in the center of the crop area.

I   Click **Show Cross Hairs** displays lines that extend into the artwork from the center of each edge.

J   Click **Show Video Safe Areas** displays guides that represent the areas inside the viewable area of video.

K   Click to open the Artboard Options dialog box

L   Choose a registration point for changes in size or position

M   Use these fields to define the position of the artboard. (The first artboard always begins at X: 0, Y: 0.)

N   Use these fields to change the size of the artboard. If the link icon is active, the height and width will be constrained.

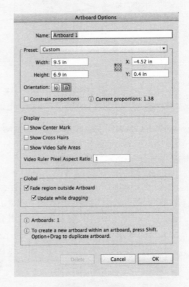

Clicking the Artboard Options button opens a dialog box where you can further manage and control the selected artboard. Most of these options (Preset, Width, Height, Orientation, and Position) are the same as those available in the Control panel. The remaining choices are explained here:

- **Constrain Proportions** maintains a consistent aspect ratio (height to width) if you resize the artboard.
- **Video Ruler Pixel Aspect Ratio** specifies the pixel aspect ratio used for artboard rulers.
- **Fade Region Outside Artboard** displays the area outside the artboard darker than the area inside the artboard.
- **Update While Dragging** keeps the area outside the artboard darker as you move or resize the artboard.

2. Select the Artboard tool in the Tools panel.

When the Artboard tool is active, the artboard edge is surrounded by marching ants; you can drag the side and corner handles to manually resize the artboard in the workspace.

Artboard center point

Artboard tool

Drag the handles to manually resize the artboard.

3. In the Control panel, select the top-left reference point and then change the artboard width to 11.9" and the height to 5.4".

If your Control panel does not show the W and H fields, click the Artboard Options button in the Control panel and use the Artboard Options dialog box to change the artboard width and height.

These dimensions are large enough to entirely encompass the logo artwork. If your dimensions are different than ours, use whatever values you need to fit your artwork and leave a bit of white space on all four sides.

4. Click the Selection tool to exit the Artboard-editing mode.

5. Save the file and continue to the next exercise.

Your goal is to create three separate versions of the logo — the four-color version that's already done, a two-color version for spot-color applications, and a one-color version that will be used in jobs that are printed black-only.

As you created the artwork, you used five layers to manage the arrangement and stacking order of the various elements. The Apple Back layer is behind the Stem layer, which is behind the Apple Front layer, which is behind the Apple Highlights layer. This precise order produces the effect you need to create a realistic illustration.

Now that the drawing is complete, however, you will use layers for a different purpose — to create, isolate, and manage multiple versions of the logo in a single file.

1. **With apple.ai open, make sure all layers are unlocked in the Layers panel.**

2. **Click the Target icon of the Stem layer to select the objects on that layer.**

3. **Click the Selected Art icon to the right of the Target icon and drag down to the Apple Back layer.**

   Dragging the Selected Art icon is an easy way to move objects from one layer to another without manually cutting and pasting.

Target icon

The Selected Art icon indicates what is selected in the file.

Drag the Selected Art icon to a different layer to move selected objects without affecting their position on the artboard.

4. **Expand the Apple Back layer.**

The mesh object that was on the Stem layer is now on the Apple Back layer, at the top of the sublayer stack.

The stem object guides now show the color of the Apple Back layer instead of the color of the Stem layer.

5. **Repeat Steps 2–3 for the Apple Front, Highlights, and Logotype layers.**

6. **Shift-click to select the four empty layers in the Layers panel, and then click the panel's Delete button.**

7. **Rename the Apple Back layer** `Four Color`.

You can access the sublayers, so you can still use the panel to select, arrange, and manage individual objects.

8. **Collapse the Four Color layer to hide the sublayers.**

9. **Save the file and continue to the next exercise.**

 COPY THE ARTBOARD AND ARTWORK

Now that all the logo artwork resides on a single layer, the final step is to create the two alternate versions of the logo. This process is largely a matter of cloning the existing artboard and artwork — but you need to complete a few extra steps to convert the mesh objects to standard filled paths.

1. **With apple.ai open, choose the Artboard tool in the Tools panel.**

2. **With the only artboard currently active, highlight the contents of the Name field in the Control panel and type** `Four Color Apple`.

3. **Make sure the Move/Copy Artwork with Artboard option is toggled on.**

4. **Place the cursor inside the artboard area. Press Option/Alt-Shift and then click and drag down to clone the existing artboard.**

Note:

You might want to zoom out so you can see the entire original artboard and the empty space below it.

The Artboard name appears in the Name field and in the artboard tag.

The Move/Copy Artwork with Artboard option should be toggled on.

Pressing Option/Alt clones the existing artboard, just as you would clone a regular drawing object.

Because Move/Copy Artwork with Artboard is toggled on, the logo artwork and the artboard are cloned at the same time.

5. **When the new artboard/artwork is entirely outside the boundaries of the first artboard, release the mouse button.**

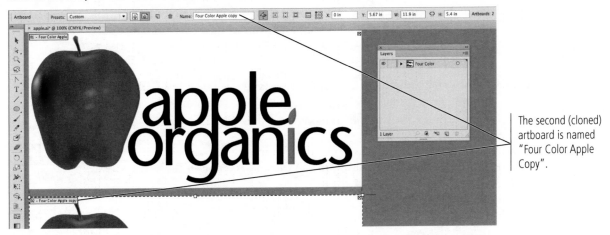

The second (cloned) artboard is named "Four Color Apple Copy".

6. **With the second artboard active, change the Name field to Two Color Apple.**

7. **Add a new layer to the file. Change the new layer's name to Two Color.**

8. **Using the Selection tool, drag a marquee to select all the objects on the second artboard.**

9. **In the Layers panel, drag the Selected Art icon from the Four Color layer to the Two Color layer.**

The second version of the artwork should now be on the Two Color layer.

10. **Save the file and continue to the next exercise.**

CONVERT MESH OBJECTS TO REGULAR PATHS

When you created the gradient meshes in the first stage of this project, you saw that adding the mesh removed the original path you drew. When you worked on the mesh, you might have noticed that the Control panel showed that the selected object was transformed from a path object to a mesh object.

To create the flat two-color version of the logo, however, you need to access the original paths you drew to create the mesh objects. There is no one-step process to convert the mesh object back to a flat path object, so you need to take a few extra steps to create the flat version of the logo.

1. **With apple.ai open, deselect everything in the file and then open the Artboards panel (Window>Artboards).**

   The Artboards panel can be used to access and arrange the various artboards in a file.

2. **Double-click Two Color Apple in the panel.**

   This forces the selected artboard to fill the space available in the document window.

Note:

Because the black-only version of the logo is also flat, you are going to create the flat two-color version first, and then clone it. Doing so avoids unnecessary repetition of the process presented in this exercise.

3. **Expand the Two Color layer in the Layers panel.**

4. **Use the Layers panel to select the mesh object that represents the Front Apple shape, and then open the Appearance panel.**

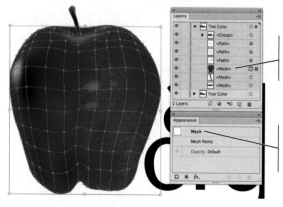

Remember, you can use the sublayers to access individual objects on the same layer.

The Appearance panel shows that the selected object is a mesh.

Note:

When working with a mesh object, it can be helpful to turn off object bounding boxes (View>Hide Bounding Box).

5. With the mesh object selected, click the Add New Stroke button at the bottom of the Appearance panel.

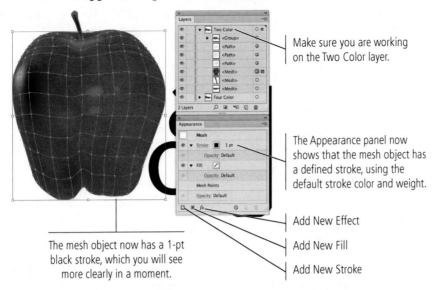

Make sure you are working on the Two Color layer.

The Appearance panel now shows that the mesh object has a defined stroke, using the default stroke color and weight.

Add New Effect

Add New Fill

Add New Stroke

The mesh object now has a 1-pt black stroke, which you will see more clearly in a moment.

Note:

In addition to changing the existing attributes of an object, you can also use the Appearance panel to compound effects and attributes. In other words, you can add a new stroke to any object, including an object that already has a defined stroke.

6. With the mesh object still selected, choose Object>Expand Appearance.

This command converts the selected object into separate constituent objects — one path for the shape's stroke attribute and one for the object's mesh fill — which are automatically grouped together.

7. In the Layers panel, expand the new group.

8. Use the Layers panel to select only the mesh object in the group.

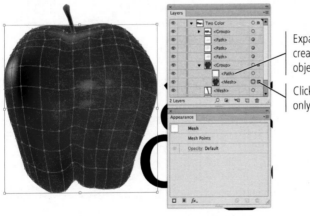

Expanding the appearance creates separate (grouped) objects for each attribute.

Click here to select only the mesh object.

Note:

New appearance attributes are created on top of the currently selected appearance. You can drag the appearance names in the panel to change their stacking sequence, which can have a significant impact on the end result.

9. **Press Delete/Backspace to remove the selected mesh object.**

You now have a simple path object that is essentially the Apple Front shape. However, you need to complete one more step because the path is still part of the group that was created by the Expand Appearance command.

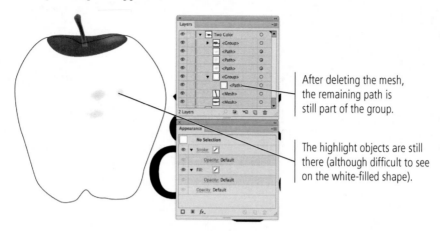

After deleting the mesh, the remaining path is still part of the group.

The highlight objects are still there (although difficult to see on the white-filled shape).

10. **Use the Layers panel to select the path in the group, and then choose Object>Ungroup.**

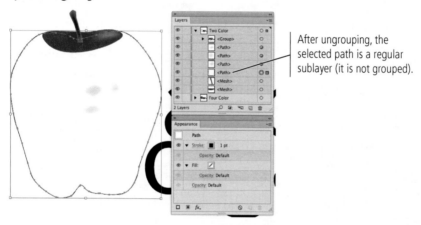

After ungrouping, the selected path is a regular sublayer (it is not grouped).

11. **Repeat this process to convert the other two mesh objects (the Stem shape and the Apple Back shape) back into standard paths with the default stroke attributes.**

12. **Select and delete the three highlight shapes.**

In a flat logo, the highlight shapes are unnecessary. In fact, the technical aspects involved in reproducing the feather effect applied to those shapes can cause output problems.

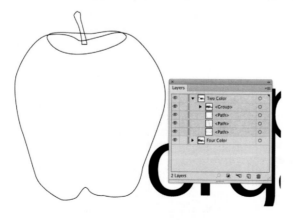

13. **Save the file and continue to the next exercise.**

ADD SPOT COLOR TO THE TWO-COLOR LOGO

Spot colors are created with special premixed inks that produce a certain color with one ink layer; spot colors are not built from the standard process inks used in CMYK printing. When you output a job with spot colors, each spot color appears on its own separation. Spot inks are commonly used to reproduce colors you can't get from a CMYK build, in two- and three-color documents, and as additional separations in a process color job when an exact color (such as a corporate color) is needed.

You can choose a spot color directly from the library on your screen, but you should look at a printed swatch book to verify that you're using the color you intend. Special inks exist because many of the colors can't be reproduced with process inks, nor can they be accurately represented on a monitor. If you specify spot colors and then convert them to process colors later, your job probably won't look exactly as you expect.

Note:

In the United States, the most popular collections of spot colors are the Pantone Matching System (PMS) libraries. TruMatch and Focoltone are also used in the United States. Toyo and DICColor (Dainippon Ink & Chemicals) are used primarily in Japan.

1. **With apple.ai open, choose Window>Swatch Libraries>Color Books>Pantone+ Solid Coated.**

   Illustrator includes swatch libraries of all the common spot-color libraries. You can open any of these libraries to access the various colors available in each collection.

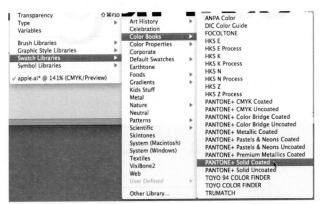

2. **In the Pantone+ Solid Coated library Options menu, choose Small List View to show the color names for each swatch.**

   It is often easier to view swatches with their names and samples, especially when you need to find a specific swatch (as in this exercise).

3. **On the Two Color artboard/layer, select the shape that represents the apple front.**

4. **In the Find field of the color library panel, type 188.**

   You could simply scroll through the panel to find the color you want, but typing a number in the Find field automatically scrolls the panel to that color.

Note:

The View options in the panel Options menu are available for all swatch panels, including colors, patterns, and brushes. You will use many types of swatches in Project 4: Ski Resort Map.

5. **Make sure the Fill icon is active in the Tools panel, and then click Pantone 188 C in the swatch Library panel.**

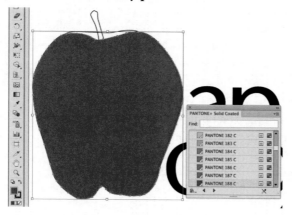

6. **Review the Swatches panel (Window>Swatches).**

   When you apply a color from a swatch library, that swatch is added to the Swatches panel for the open file.

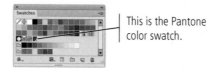

   This is the Pantone color swatch.

7. **Using whichever method you prefer, change the stroke color of the selected object to None.**

8. **Select the Apple Back shape. Apply Pantone 188 C as the fill color and None as the stroke color.**

9. **Select the Stem shape. Swap the current stroke and fill colors so the shape is filled with black and has no stroke.**

10. **Select the shape that comprises the "p" and "g" in the logotype and change the fill color to Pantone 188 C.**

    Because this shape is part of a group, you must use the Direct Selection tool or the sublayers in the Layers panel to select only this shape.

11. **Select the "i" shape. Change the fill color to white (not None) and change the stroke to 2-pt Pantone 188 C.**

    Because our leaf slightly overlaps the "e", we used white as the fill color instead of None.

12. **Choose the Artboard tool. With the Move/Copy Artwork with Artboard option still active, press Option/Alt-Shift and then click and drag down to clone the flat version. Rename the new artboard** One Color Apple.

13. **Move the artwork on the third artboard to a new layer named** One Color. **Change all Pantone 188 C elements in the third version to black.**

Change all Pantone 188 C elements in this version to black.

14. **Save the file, close it, and then continue to the next exercise.**

 ## EXPORT EPS LOGO FILES

Although the current versions of most graphic-design software can work with native Illustrator files, many older applications — especially page-layout software — require EPS (Encapsulated PostScript) files for vector-based files created in Illustrator. Because logos need to be versatile, you are going to save EPS files in this exercise so the necessary pieces are in place if and when they are needed.

1. **With** apple.ai **open, choose File>Save As. If necessary, navigate to your WIP>Organics folder as the target location.**

2. **Choose Illustrator EPS in the Format/Save As Type menu. Activate the Use Artboards option and make sure the All radio button is selected.**

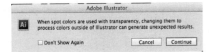

3. **Click Save. Read the resulting warning and then click Continue.**

   Because your file uses a spot-color swatch, the application warns you about potential output problems if you use transparency with gradients. Because you did not use spot colors in any of the transparent elements (this is why you deleted the feathered highlights), you can dismiss this message.

4. **In the resulting EPS Options dialog box, choose High Resolution in the Transparency Preset menu.**

Both gradient meshes and feather effects require rasterization at some point to properly output the subtle changes in color. The High Resolution option creates high enough resolution for most print applications. (You'll learn more about this issue in Project 6: Cereal Box.)

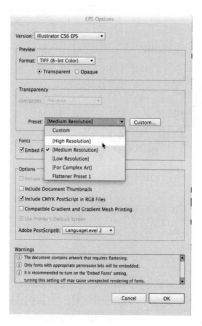

5. **Check the Compatible Gradient and Gradient Mesh Printing option.**

This option helps older output devices to print gradient meshes.

6. **Click OK to generate the EPS files. When the Parsing process is complete, close the open file.**

7. **On your desktop, open your WIP>Organics folder.**

Because you checked the Use Artboards option, Illustrator generated four separate EPS files: one that contains all three logos with no consideration of the artboard concept, and separate files for each of the three defined artboards.

8. **Continue to the next stage of the project.**

Stage 4 **Combining Text and Graphics**

The final stage of this project requires two additional layouts: a letterhead and a business envelope. Rather than adding more artboards to the logo file, you are going to create a new file that will contain both pieces of stationery. This means you must place the logos from the original apple.ai file, and understand how to work with objects that are placed from external files.

WORK WITH PLACED GRAPHICS

Some production-related concerns dictate how you design a letterhead. In general, there are two ways to print a letterhead: commercially in large quantities or one-offs on your desktop laser or inkjet printer. (The second method includes a letterhead template, which you can use to write and print your letters from directly within a page-layout program. While this method is quite common among designers, it is rarely done using Illustrator.)

If your letterhead is being printed commercially, it's probably being printed with multiple copies on a large press sheet, from which the individual letterhead sheets will be cut. (In fact, most commercial printing happens this way.) This type of printing typically means that design elements can run right off the edge of the sheet, called **bleeding**. If you're using a commercial printer, always ask the output provider whether it's safe (and cost-effective) to design with bleeds, and find out how much bleed allowance to include.

If you're designing for a printer that can only run letter-size paper, you need to allow enough of a margin area for your printer to hold the paper as it moves through the device (called the **gripper margin**); in this case, you can't design with bleeds.

1. **Open the New Document dialog box (File>New). Name the new file stationery, with 1 artboard that is letter-size in portrait orientation. Define 0.125" bleeds on all four sides, CMYK color mode, and 300 PPI raster effects.**

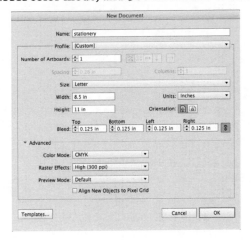

2. **Click OK to create the new file.**

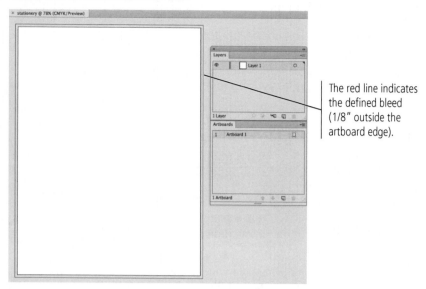

The red line indicates the defined bleed (1/8″ outside the artboard edge).

3. **Choose File>Place. Navigate to the file `apple.ai` in your WIP>Organics folder, make sure Link and Template are both unchecked, and then click Place.**

Until now, you have placed raster images in the JPEG format. Different types of files, however, have different options that determine what is imported into your Illustrator file.

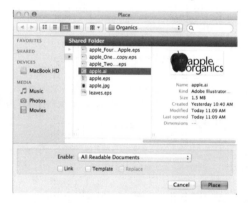

Understanding Placed-Image Bounding Boxes

The **Crop To** option determines exactly what is placed into an Illustrator file. (If you are placing an Illustrator file, many of these options produce the same result.)

- The **Bounding Box** setting places the file's bounding box, or the minimum area that encloses the objects on the page or artboard.

- The **Art** setting crops incoming files relative to the size and position of any objects selected at the time of the cropping. For example, you can create a frame and use it to crop an incoming piece of artwork.

- Use the **Crop** setting when you want the position of the placed file to be determined by the location of a crop region drawn on the page (when placing an Illustrator file, this refers to the defined artboard).

- The **Trim** setting identifies where the page will be physically cut in the production process, if trim marks are present.

- The **Bleed** setting places only the area within bleed margins (if a bleed area is defined). This is useful if the page is being output in a production environment. (The printed page might include page marks that fall outside the bleed area.)

- The **Media** setting places the area that represents the physical paper size of the original PDF document (for example, the dimensions of an A4 sheet of paper), including printers' marks.

4. **Review the options in the Place PDF dialog box.**

   Although you're placing a native Illustrator (.ai) file, the dialog box shows options for placing PDF files. Illustrator files use PDF as the underlying structure (which is what enables multiple artboard capability), so the options are the same as the ones you would see if you were placing a PDF file.

5. **Choose Art in the Crop To menu, and then click OK to place the four-color logo.**

6. **If you get a warning about an unknown image construct, click OK to dismiss it.**

   For some reason, gradient mesh objects *created in Illustrator* are unrecognized *by Illustrator*, which is the case with this logo file. Gradient meshes are imported into the new file as "non-native art" objects that can't be edited in the new file unless you use the Flatten Transparency command to turn them into embedded raster objects.

7. **Open the General pane of the Preferences dialog box. Make sure the Scale Strokes & Effects option is checked, and then click OK.**

   If this option is checked, scaling an object also scales the applied strokes and effects (including the Feather effect you used to create the front highlight objects) proportionally to the new object size. For example, reducing an object by 50% changes a 1-pt stroke to a 0.5-pt stroke. If this option is unchecked, a 1-pt stroke remains a 1-pt stroke, regardless of how much you reduce or enlarge the object.

   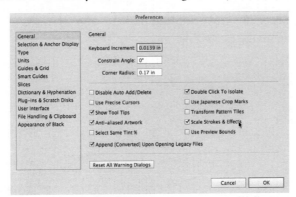

Note:

On Macintosh, open the Preferences dialog box in the Illustrator menu. On Windows, open the Preferences dialog box in the Edit menu.

8. **With the placed artwork selected, use the Transform panel to scale the artwork to 3″ wide (constrained). Using the top-left reference point, position the artwork 1/8″ from the top and left edges (as shown in the following image).**

   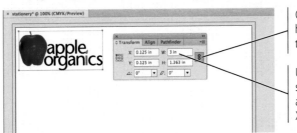

   Constrain the width and height before changing the object size.

   Use the Transform panel to scale the image to 3″ wide and position the group at X: 0.125″, Y: 0.125″.

Note:

Remember, your original artwork might be a slightly different size than ours, so your resized height might also be slightly different than what is shown here.

9. Using the Type tool, click to create a new point-type object. Type 564 Orchard Way. Format the type as 10-pt ATC Oak Normal with right paragraph alignment. Apply a medium-red swatch as the type fill color and define no stroke color.

10. Using the Selection tool, position the type object directly to the left of the "g" descender (use the following image as a guide).

11. Option/Alt-click-drag the type object to clone it to the right. Press the Shift key after you begin dragging to constrain the clone's movement to exactly horizontal. Move the clone immediately to the right of the "g" descender, and then release the mouse button.

12. Change the cloned object to left paragraph alignment, and then change the type to Orange, FL 35682.

13. Activate the Selection tool, then choose File>Place. Navigate to the file **leaves.eps** in your WIP>Organics folder and click Place.

This format, which you used to create alternate versions of the apple logos in the previous exercise, is commonly used for vector-based images — especially when saving files for older page-layout applications that do not support the native Illustrator format. When you place an EPS file into Illustrator, you do not have additional options; it is **parsed** (processed) and placed onto the Illustrator artboard.

14. Drag the placed graphic so the edges of the artwork bleed past the edge of the artboard area. Use the following image as a guide.

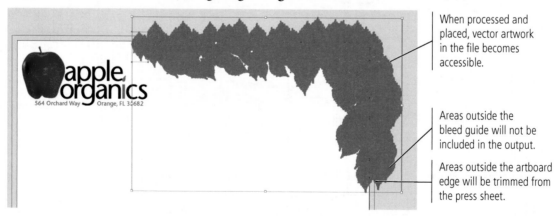

When processed and placed, vector artwork in the file becomes accessible.

Areas outside the bleed guide will not be included in the output.

Areas outside the artboard edge will be trimmed from the press sheet.

15. Save the file as an Illustrator file named **stationery.ai** in your WIP>Organics folder, and then continue to the next exercise.

CREATE THE ENVELOPE LAYOUT

In general, printed envelopes can be created in two ways. You can create and print the design on a flat sheet, which will be specially **die cut** (stamped out of the press sheet), and then folded and glued into the shape of the finished envelope. Alternatively (and usually at less expense), you can print on pre-folded and -glued envelopes.

Both of these methods for envelope design have special printing requirements, such as ensuring no ink is placed where glue will be applied (if you're printing on flat sheets), or printing far enough away from the edge (if you're printing on pre-formed envelopes). Whenever you design an envelope, consult with the output provider that will print the job before you get too far into the project.

In this case, the design will be output on pre-folded #10 business-size envelopes (4-1/8″ by 9-1/2″). The printer requires a 1/4″ gripper margin around the edge of the envelope where you cannot include any ink coverage.

Note:

*The **live area** is the "safe" area inside the page edge, where important design elements should remain. Because printing and trimming are mechanical processes, there will always be some variation, however slight. Elements too close to the page edge run the risk of being accidentally trimmed off.*

1. **With stationery.ai open, zoom out until you can see the entire artboard and an equal amount of space to the right.**

2. **Choose the Artboard tool. With the current artboard active, type Letterhead in the Name field of the Control panel.**

3. **Place the cursor to the right of the existing artboard, click, and drag to create a new artboard.**

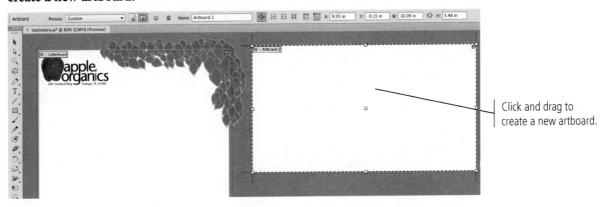

Click and drag to create a new artboard.

4. **With the second artboard active, use the fields in the Control panel to change the artboard dimensions to W: 9.5″, H: 4.13″.**

   If the W and H fields are not visible in your Control panel, click the Artboard Options button in the Control panel and use the resulting dialog box to change the artboard size.

5. **With the second artboard active, type Envelope in the Name field of the Control panel.**

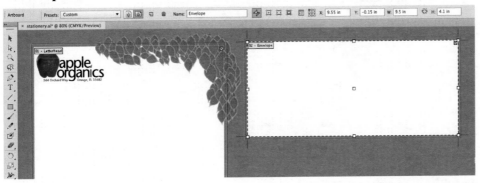

6. Choose File>Place. Navigate to the file **apple.ai** in your WIP>Organics folder and click Place.

7. In the Place PDF dialog box, click the right-arrow button to show 2 of 3, then click OK.

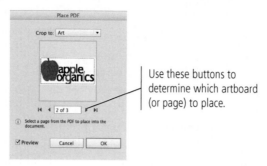

Use these buttons to determine which artboard (or page) to place.

8. Make the Selection tool active. If rulers are not visible in your document window, choose View>Show Rulers.

9. Choose View>Rulers and make sure the menu option reads "Change to Global Rulers".

When Artboard rulers are active — which you want for this exercise — the menu command reads to "Change to Global Rulers".

Artboard rulers show all measurements from the zero-point of the active artboard. Global rulers show all measurements from the zero-point of Artboard 1 (unless you reset the zero-point when a different artboard is active).

Note:

You can't switch between Artboard and Global rulers while the Artboard tool is active.

10. Select the placed object with the Selection tool. Scale it to 2.5″ wide (constrained) and place it 0.25″ from the top and left edges of the envelope artboard.

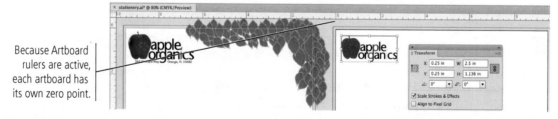

Because Artboard rulers are active, each artboard has its own zero point.

11. Copy the type objects from the letterhead and paste them onto the envelope layout. Change the size of the type in the pasted objects to 8 pt and change the fill to Pantone 188 C (the same color you used in the two-color logo artwork).

12. Save the file and continue to the next exercise.

PRINT DESKTOP PROOFS OF MULTIPLE ARTBOARDS

Before you send a file to a commercial output provider, it's a good idea to print a sample to see how the artwork looks on paper. Illustrator provides a large number of options for outputting files, including the ability to define the area of the actual artwork.

There are two important points to remember about using inkjet and laser proofs. First, inkjet printers are usually not PostScript driven; because the commercial output process revolves around the PostScript language, proofs should be created using a PostScript-compatible printer if possible (if not, the proofs might not accurately represent what will appear in final output). Second, inkjet and laser printers typically do not accurately represent color.

1. **With stationery.ai open, choose File>Print.**

   The Print dialog box is divided into eight sections or categories, which display in the window on the left side of the dialog box. Clicking one of the categories in the list shows the associated options in the right side of the dialog box.

2. **In the Printer menu, choose the printer you want to use, and then choose the PPD for that printer in the PPD menu (if possible).**

   If you are using a non-PostScript printer, complete as much of the rest of this exercise as possible based on the limitations of your output device.

3. **With the General options showing, choose the Range radio button and type 1 in the field.**

   By default, all artboards in the file are output when you click Print.

   If your printer can only print letter-size paper, you need to tile the letterhead artboard to multiple sheets so you can output a full-size proof. Tiling is unavailable when printing multiple artboards, so in this exercise you are printing each artboard separately.

4. **In the Options section, make sure the Do Not Scale option is selected.**

   As a general rule, proofs — especially final proofs that would be sent to a printer with the job files — should be output at 100%.

5a. **If your printer is capable of printing oversize sheets, choose Tabloid/A3/11×17 in the Media menu. Choose the Portrait orientation option.**

Note:

The most important options you'll select are the Printer and PPD (PostScript printer description) settings, located at the top of the dialog box. Illustrator reads the information in the PPD to determine which of the specific print options are available for the current output.

Note:

You can purchase a software RIP (such as the one we use from Birmy Graphics) that allows you to print PostScript information to some inkjet printers. Consult the documentation that came with your printer to see if this option is available.

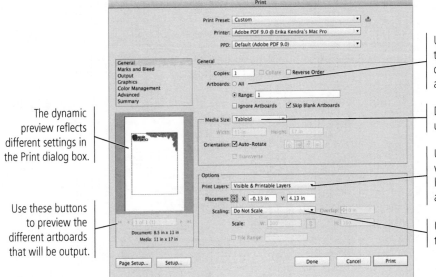

The dynamic preview reflects different settings in the Print dialog box.

Use these buttons to preview the different artboards that will be output.

Use these options to print more than one copy and reverse the output order of the multiple artboards (last to first).

Define the paper size used for the output.

Use this menu to output visible and printable layers, visible layers, or all layers.

Use these options to scale the output (if necessary).

5b. **If you can only print to letter-size paper, turn off the Auto-Rotate option and choose the Landscape orientation option. Choose Tile Full Pages in the Scaling menu and define a 1″ Overlap.**

To output a letter-size page at 100% on letter-size paper, you have to tile to multiple sheets of paper; using the landscape paper orientation allows you to tile to 2 sheets instead of 4 (as shown in the preview area).

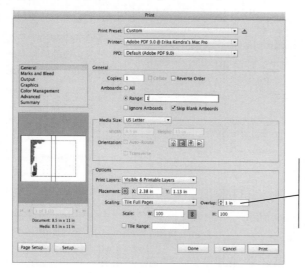

When tiling a page to multiple sheets, you can define a specific amount of space that will be included on both sheets.

6. **Click the Marks and Bleed option in the list of categories on the left. Activate the All Printer's Marks option, and then change the Offset value to 0.125″.**

If you type the value in the Offset field, Illustrator automatically rounds up to the nearest two-decimal value. Since 0.13″ is larger than the 0.125″ bleed, this offset position is fine.

7. **In the Bleeds section, check the Use Document Bleed Settings option.**

When you created the stationery file, you defined 1/8″ bleeds on all four sides of the artboard. Checking this box in the Print dialog box includes that same 1/8″ extra on all four sides of the output.

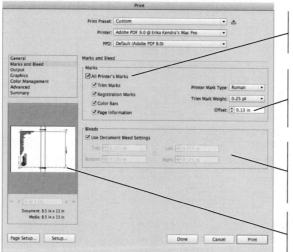

Use these options to select individual printer's marks or print all marks.

The Offset value determines how far from the page edge the printer's marks will be placed.

Use these fields to include a specific amount of space beyond the defined crop area in the output.

The preview now includes all selected printer's marks and the defined bleed area.

8. **Click the Output option in the list of categories on the left. Choose Composite in the Mode menu.**

   You can print all colors to a single sheet by choosing Composite, or you can print each color to an individual sheet by choosing Separations (Host-based). The third option — In-RIP Separation — allows the file data to be separated by the output device instead of by the software.

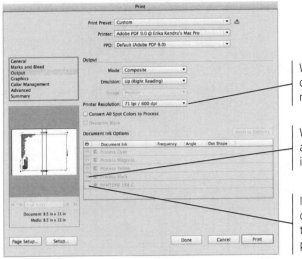

Note:

The other options in this dialog box (Emulsion and Image) are reserved for high-end commercial output to a filmsetter or imagesetter.

When printing separations, choose the line screen and resolution for the output.

When printing separations, click any of these icons to stop that ink separation from outputting.

If a job includes spot colors, click the icon in this column to convert the spot color to process color for the output.

9. **Click Print to output the artwork.**

10. **Choose File>Print again. Choose the Range radio button and type 2 in the field to print the envelope layout.**

11. **Choose Letter/US Letter in the Size menu and choose the Landscape orientation option. Choose Do Not Scale in the Scaling menu.**

   In this case, a letter-size sheet is large enough to print the envelope artboard without scaling. (Some of the printer's marks might be cut off by the printer's gripper margin, but that is fine for the purpose of a desktop proof.)

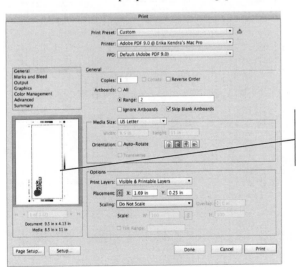

The preview area shows that the envelope artboard will fit on a letter-size page at 100% if you use landscape orientation.

12. **Click Print to output the envelope proof.**

13. **When the document comes back into focus, save and close it.**

fill in the blank

1. The _____ provide access to handles that you can use to manually resize the artboard in the workspace.

2. Press _____ and click the eye icon on a specific layer to switch only that layer between Preview and Outline mode.

3. When _____ are active, moving your cursor over an unselected object reveals the paths that make up that object.

4. The _____ tool is used to sample colors from an object already placed in the file.

5. The _____ is used to monitor and change the individual attributes (fill, stroke, etc.) of the selected object.

6. The _____ is the imaginary line on which the bottoms of letters rest.

7. _____ is the spacing between specific pairs of letters (where the insertion point is placed).

8. The _____ command makes the vector shapes of letters accessible to the Direct Selection tool.

9. A _____ is a special ink used to reproduce a specific color, typically used for one- or two-color jobs.

10. Click the _____ in the Layers panel to select a specific sublayer.

short answer

1. Explain the advantages of using a gradient mesh, compared to a regular gradient.

2. Briefly explain two primary differences between point-type objects and area-type objects.

3. Explain the potential benefits of using multiple artboards rather than different files for different pieces.

Use what you learned in this project to complete the following freeform exercise.
Carefully read the art director and client comments, then create your own design to meet the needs of the project.
Use the space below to sketch ideas; when finished, write a brief explanation of your reasoning behind your final design.

art director comments

Your client, Tracey Dillon, is a local architect. She has hired you to create a corporate identity package so she can begin marketing her services to local land development companies. She has asked you first to develop a logo, and then to create the standard identity pieces that she can use for business promotion and correspondence.

To complete this project, you should:

❏ Develop a compelling logo that suggests the agency's purpose (architectural services).

❏ Incorporate the agency's name (TD Associates) into the logo.

❏ Build the letterhead and envelope with the same technical specs that you used to design the Apple Organics pieces.

❏ Build the business card layout to the standard 3.5 × 2″ size.

client comments

I've decided to open my own architectural services firm, and I need to start advertising. That means I need to brand my business so companies who need an architect will recognize and remember my name. I'm calling my business TD Associates.

I want a logo that really says 'architect', and I want the central color in my logo to be blue — like the blue you'd see on a blueprint.

Once the logo is finished, I need you to use the logo on business cards, letterhead, and envelopes that I will have preprinted; I want a more professional feel than I can create using my laser printer. The printer I spoke with said I could do this for less money if I go 4-color for the letterhead, but 2-color for the envelope.

Eventually, I'll be incorporating my logo into all kinds of advertising — newspaper, local magazines, and even the Internet; I'd like you to create whatever versions you think I'll need for any purpose.

project justification

_____

_____

_____

_____

_____

_____

_____

_____

_____

_____

_____

_____

_____

Logos are one of the most common types of artwork that you will create in Illustrator. These can be as simple as text converted to outlines, or as complex as a line drawing based on an object in a photograph. Most logos will actually be some combination of drawing and text-based elements. As you learned throughout this project, one of the most important qualities of a logo is versatility — a good logo can be used in many different types of projects and output in many different types of print processes. To accomplish this goal, logos should work equally well in grayscale, four-color, and spot-color printing.

By completing this project, you worked with complex gradients to draw a realistic apple, then added creative type treatment to build the finished logotype. After completing the initial logo, you converted it to other variants that will work with different output processes (two-color and one-color). Finally, you incorporated the logo artwork into completed stationery to help solve your client's communication needs as he expands his business.

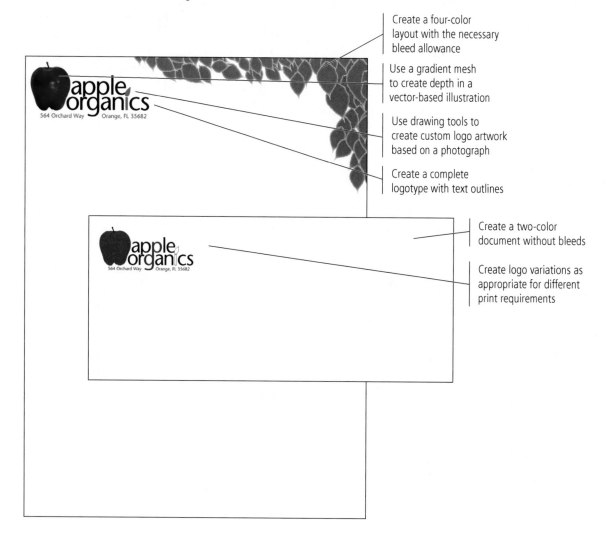

Create a four-color layout with the necessary bleed allowance

Use a gradient mesh to create depth in a vector-based illustration

Use drawing tools to create custom logo artwork based on a photograph

Create a complete logotype with text outlines

Create a two-color document without bleeds

Create logo variations as appropriate for different print requirements

Ski Resort Map

Your client manages a ski resort. He wants to create a basic map of the resort to show the locations of various resort features and amenities. The map will be printed independently, but also placed into other projects, such as the local entertainment magazine and local restaurant menus.

This project incorporates the following skills:

❑ Accessing and managing built-in libraries of swatches, brushes, and symbols

❑ Defining custom art and pattern brushes for specific applications

❑ Applying and controlling brush strokes in relation to paths

❑ Saving user-defined libraries of custom assets

❑ Opening and using symbol libraries created by other users

❑ Understanding and creating symbols and symbol instances

❑ Transforming symbol instances and editing symbol artwork

❑ Replacing symbols in placed instances

❑ Creating a clipping mask

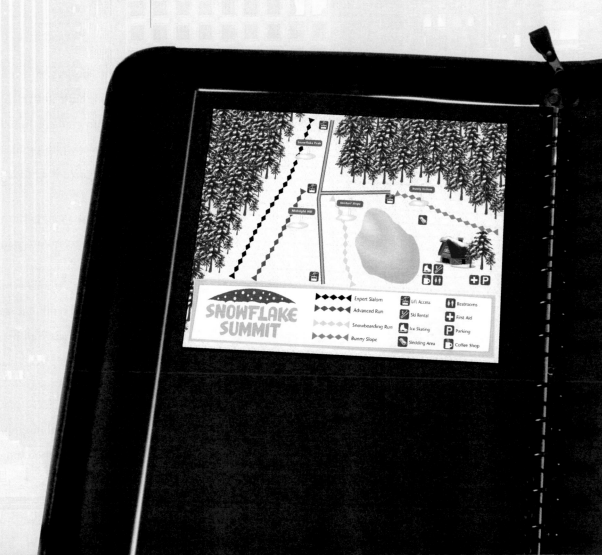

client comments

This map will be available on kiosks around the resort, but it is also going to be used in advertising and cross-promotional marketing. We'll be placing it into the local entertainment magazine and papers with some coupons, and we also have some interest from local restaurants to print the map on their placemats and menus.

I started to create the map I want, but I need you to finish it. I did find some nice graphics for the resort lodge, but I realized that I don't have the time or skills to create something that looks good.

art director comments

When you see what he gave us, you can see what needs to be done. He didn't get any farther than different colored lines and some text telling where some things are.

I already showed the client some ideas for icons instead of text to identify different amenities. He approved those, so I created a library for you to use when you build the completed file. You'll need to include the icons both in the legend and wherever they are indicated by the existing text.

We also discussed the possibility of converting this into an interactive map for digital kiosks in the lodge, and on the resort's Web site. I want you to use symbols as much as possible so the artwork will import smoothly into Flash if we get the go-ahead for those projects too.

project objectives

To complete this project, you will:

- ❏ Open and use built-in swatch libraries
- ❏ Define custom gradient swatches
- ❏ Modify a stroke width profile
- ❏ Create a new custom pattern swatch based on existing artwork
- ❏ Define custom art and pattern brushes
- ❏ Save a custom brush library so it can be accessed again later
- ❏ Open and use an external symbol library
- ❏ Place and control symbol instances
- ❏ Edit symbols to change all placed instances
- ❏ Break the link from placed instances to the original symbols
- ❏ Replace symbols in placed instances
- ❏ Spray mutiple symbol instances
- ❏ Create a clipping mask to hide unwanted parts of the artwork

Stage 1 Working with Custom Swatches

The default Swatches panel (Window>Swatches) includes a seemingly random collection of swatches from the various built-in libraries. Illustrator also includes a large number of built-in swatch libraries, many of which contain thematic color schemes (such as Earthtone, Metal, and Nature). These libraries are accessed by choosing Window>Swatch Libraries or by opening the Swatch Libraries menu at the bottom of the Swatches panel.

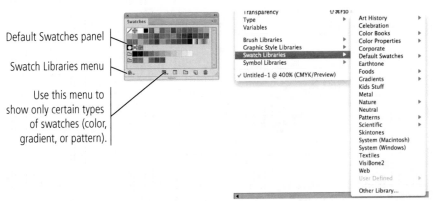

Default Swatches panel

Swatch Libraries menu

Use this menu to show only certain types of swatches (color, gradient, or pattern).

If you open more than one swatch library from the Window>Swatch Libraries menu, each library opens as a new panel, grouped with other open swatch libraries. (Library panels open in the same location and state as the last time they were used. If a panel is not automatically grouped with other library panels, it was already used and repositioned.)

If you open a different library using the menu at the bottom of an open library panel, the new library replaces the one that was active when you opened the new library. You can drag any library panel out of the group to manage it independently.

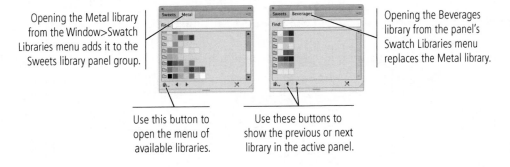

Opening the Metal library from the Window>Swatch Libraries menu adds it to the Sweets library panel group.

Opening the Beverages library from the panel's Swatch Libraries menu replaces the Metal library.

Use this button to open the menu of available libraries.

Use these buttons to show the previous or next library in the active panel.

MANAGE THE SWATCHES PANEL

In this project, your client created the basic elements, but was unable to complete the entire map. The first logical step in any project where you are provided with an existing file is to review the supplied artwork.

1. Download **AI6_RF_Project4.zip** from the Student Files Web page.

2. Expand the ZIP archive in your WIP folder (Macintosh) or copy the archive contents into your WIP folder (Windows).

   This results in a folder named **Skiing**, which contains the files you need for this project. You should also use this folder to save the files you create in this project.

3. Open the file summit map.ai from your WIP>Skiing folder.

The file includes a very basic map, with mostly plain text and basic solid lines, and a few graphics that have been placed by the client. Your job is to add visual interest using a variety of methods, including custom gradients, patterns, brush strokes, and symbols.

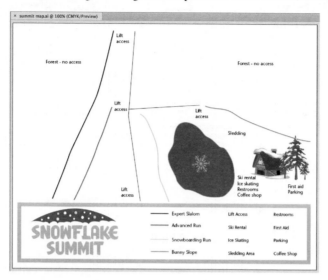

4. Open the Swatches panel (Window>Swatches).

The default Swatches panel (Window>Swatches) includes a seemingly random collection of swatches from the various built-in libraries. Every new file includes these swatches, plus any custom swatches that have been created in the file.

The file you were provided for this project also includes four custom global swatches.

5. Open the Swatches panel Options menu and choose Select All Unused.

Note:

When a library displays in Thumbnail mode, you can roll the mouse over a specific swatch to see the swatch name in a tool tip. The same option is available for brush libraries, graphic style libraries, and symbol libraries.

6. Click the panel's Delete button. When asked, click Yes to confirm the deletion.

Selected swatches are highlighted in the panel.

Delete button

7. **Open the panel Options menu and choose Small List View. Click the bottom-right corner of the panel and drag until you see the entire list of swatches.**

The Swatches panels appear by default in Thumbnail mode. If you choose one of the List View options, you see the name of the color, as well as an icon that indicates the type of the color. Viewing swatches by name can be useful because the swatch name indicates the components of the associated color.

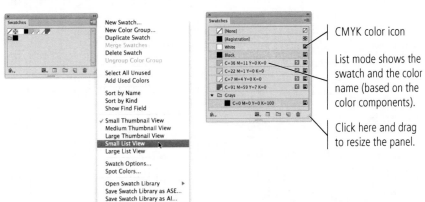

CMYK color icon

List mode shows the swatch and the color name (based on the color components).

Click here and drag to resize the panel.

Note:

The Registration swatch, which can't be deleted, is a special color that outputs at 100% of all inks. It is typically used for file information on a printing plate, outside the trim area; you should never use the registration color inside the artboard boundaries.

8. **Click the Grays folder in the panel and drag to the panel's Delete button.**

The only swatch in this color group is 100% Black — the same as the basic Black swatch that is not in the group; there is no reason to maintain two swatches with the same color make-up, so you are deleting the extra black swatch to keep the panel more manageable.

Drag the folder to the Delete button.

If you drag only the swatch, you would leave the empty color group folder.

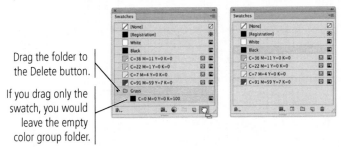

Note:

Deleting a used swatch does not affect objects where the color is applied.

9. **Save the file and continue to the next exercise.**

DEFINE GRADIENT SWATCHES

As you learned in Project 2: Balloon Festival Artwork, a gradient smoothly merges one color into another color. Illustrator supports both linear gradients, which move in a line from one color to another; and radial gradients, which move from one color at the center of a circle to another color at the outer edges.

Illustrator also includes a number of built-in pattern and gradient swatches, which can be accessed in the Window>Swatch Libraries>Gradients or >Patterns submenus. (Several of these swatches are also available in the default Swatches panel.) You can even use the panel to display only swatches of a specific kind.

The built-in swatch libraries are stored in separate panels. If you use a gradient or pattern swatch from one of the library collections, it is automatically added to the file's Swatches panel.

You can also create your own gradient and pattern swatches, which are stored in the file's Swatches panel. In this exercise, you will create two custom gradient swatches that you can apply to any object in the file.

Note:

Gradient and pattern libraries, as with any other kind of swatch library, open in their own panels.

1. With **summit map.ai** open, open the Gradient panel (Window>Gradient).

2. Choose Radial in the Type menu.

3. Drag the **C=7 M=4 Y=0 K=0 swatch** from the Swatches panel onto the left stop of the gradient ramp (in the Gradient panel).

   The stop color changes from black to blue, and the sample swatch now shows the effect of the new stop color.

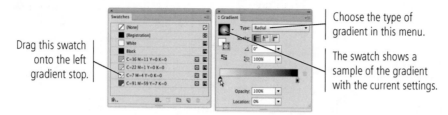

Drag this swatch onto the left gradient stop.

Choose the type of gradient in this menu.

The swatch shows a sample of the gradient with the current settings.

4. Drag the **C=36 M=11 Y=0 K=0 swatch** from the Swatches panel onto the right stop of the gradient ramp.

Drag this swatch onto the right gradient stop.

5. Drag the **C=22 M=1 Y=0 K=0 swatch** from the Swatches panel to the middle of the gradient ramp.

6. Click the new stop and drag right until the Location field shows 67%.

Drag this swatch to the midpoint of the gradient ramp to add a new stop...

...then drag the stop until the Location is 67%.

Note:

Delete specific stops from the gradient by dragging the stops down and away from the gradient ramp.

7. Drag the **C=36 M=11 Y=0 K=0 swatch** in the Swatches panel to the 33% location on the gradient ramp.

8. Double-click the new stop to open the options for that stop. Change the tint slider to 72%.

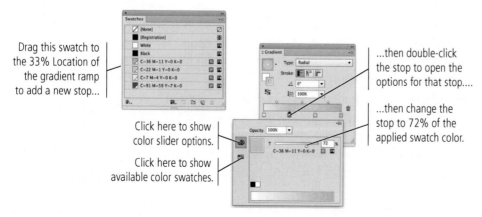

Drag this swatch to the 33% Location of the gradient ramp to add a new stop...

...then double-click the stop to open the options for that stop....

...then change the stop to 72% of the applied swatch color.

Click here to show color slider options.

Click here to show available color swatches.

9. **Click the sample swatch in the Gradient panel and drag it into the main Swatches panel.**

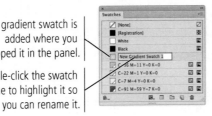

Drag this sample into the Swatches panel.

10. **Double-click the new swatch name in the Swatches panel. Type Ice Radial to rename then swatch, then press Return/Enter to finalize the new name.**

The gradient swatch is added where you dropped it in the panel.

Duble-click the swatch name to highlight it so you can rename it.

Note:

You can also double-click the swatch thumbnail to open the Swatch Options dialog box, where you can rename the swatch.

11. **In the Gradient panel, choose Linear in the Type menu.**

   Changing the type of gradient does not change the color-stop settings.

12. **Repeat Steps 9–10 to create a new gradient swatch named Ice Linear.**

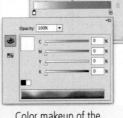

13. **Save the file and continue to the next exercise.**

Using Spot Colors in Gradients

If you create a gradient that blends a spot color into a process-color build, the results will be unpredictable at best and disastrous at worst. In short, we strongly discourage this practice. It is possible, however, to create a gradient that blends from a spot color to white; doing so simply requires a simple trick to avoid output problems.

The images to the right show the components of a basic linear gradient that blends from white to Pantone Green. By default, the White stop is actually a CMYK build, with all four ink components set to zero.

When a Pantone color blends into the CMYK white, the intermediate steps of the gradient will actually be created with CMYK builds instead of shades of the Pantone color — resulting in extra separations for a job that might not allow for them.

To solve the problem, you can apply the same spot color to both stops, and use the Color panel to define the white color as 0% of the spot color. When both stops in the gradient are colored with a Pantone color (regardless of the defined tint for the stop), the intermediate shades of the gradient will be created as shades of the Pantone color instead of CMYK percentages.

Color makeup of the first gradient stop

Color makeup of the second gradient stop

Once you have created gradient swatches, you can apply them by simply selecting an object, selecting the target attribute (fill or stroke), and then clicking the appropriate swatch. You can then use the Gradient panel and Gradient tool to control the position of an applied gradient.

1. **With summit map.ai open, use the Selection tool to select the lake shape on the artboard.**

2. **Open the Fill Color panel from the Control panel, and click the Ice Radial swatch.**

   The Fill and Stroke Color panels include the same swatches that are available in the document's Swatches panel. Because you deleted the unused swatches from the default set, you see only the few colors that were part of the original file and the two gradient swatches that you defined in the previous exercise.

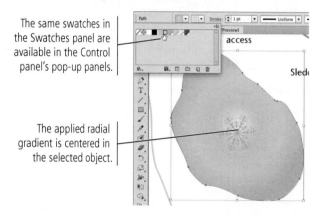

The same swatches in the Swatches panel are available in the Control panel's pop-up panels.

The applied radial gradient is centered in the selected object.

3. **Using the Gradient tool, click near the top area of the lake object and drag to the bottom area.**

   When you first choose the Gradient tool, the Gradient Annotator appears; by default, it is exactly horizontal. After you complete this step, the Gradient Annotator matches the line you drag with the Gradient tool.

   When you are using a radial gradient, the first place you click with the Gradient tool defines the center point (the starting color) of the applied gradient. The location where you release the mouse button marks the outer edge of the radial gradient. The area beyond the outer edge of the gradient fills with the end-stop color of the gradient.

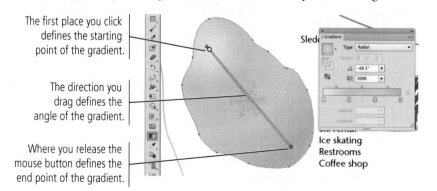

The first place you click defines the starting point of the gradient.

The direction you drag defines the angle of the gradient.

Where you release the mouse button defines the end point of the gradient.

Ice skating
Restrooms
Coffee shop

Note:

If you are not satisfied with the length and angle of your gradient, simply click and drag again to change it.

4. **In the Gradient panel, change the Aspect Ratio field to 50%.**

   Changing the aspect ratio of a radial gradient converts the gradient shape to an ellipse instead of a circle. A 50% aspect ratio means the gradient's height is half (50%) its width.

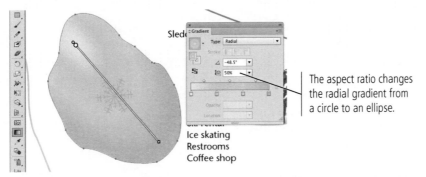

The aspect ratio changes the radial gradient from a circle to an ellipse.

5. **Using the Selection tool, select the rectangle shape around the logo.**

6. **Open the Stroke Color panel from the Control panel, and click the Ice Linear swatch.**

   When you apply a gradient to a stroke, the default option (Apply Gradient within Stroke) basically "fills" the stroke with the gradient.

By default, gradients are applied within the stroke.

7. **In the Gradient panel, bring the Stroke attribute to the front of the stack.**

8. **Click the Apply Gradient Along Stroke button.**

   Using the Apply Gradient Along Stroke option, the gradient is applied in a linear fashion. Depending on the shape of the path, this option might not make a noticeable difference. For this rectangle, however, you can see that the starting point of the gradient is located at the bottom-right corner of the stroke; the gradient then travels around the shape, until the ending point of the gradient meets the same corner.

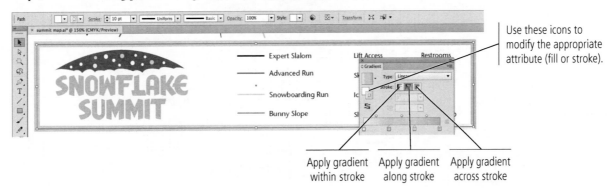

Use these icons to modify the appropriate attribute (fill or stroke).

Apply gradient within stroke

Apply gradient along stroke

Apply gradient across stroke

9. **Click the Apply Gradient Across Stroke button.**

   Using the Apply Gradient Across Stroke option, the gradient begins at the outside edge of the path and ends on the inside edge.

10. **Save the file and then continue to the next exercise.**

 ## Edit a Path Profile

In addition to simply applying stroke attributes to a path, you can use the Width tool to adjust the shape of a stroke at any point along a specific path. This moves beyond the ability to manipulate the points and segments that make up a shape. In this exercise, you will modify the path that surrounds the legend.

1. **With summit map.ai open, choose the Width tool in the Tools panel.**

2. **Move the cursor over the top-left corner of the legend box.**

3. **When you see the word "anchor" in the cursor feedback, click and drag out from the point. When the overall width is approximately 0.28″, release the mouse button.**

   When a path is selected, clicking the path with the Width tool adds a width point. You can drag out from the width point to add symmetrical width handles, which change the stroke width at that point along the path. If you click and drag an existing width handle, the opposite handle is also affected.

   When the Width tool cursor is over an existing stroke, the cursor feedback shows the overall width of the stroke at that point, as well as the width of each side of the stroke.

Note:

It might help to zoom in so you can more clearly see the acnhor points that make up the shape.

Cursor feedback shows the width of the stroke, and each side of the stroke.

Width tool

Note:

You are changing the path's width at the corner, so you're using the corner anchor point as a guide.

   Clicking and dragging with the Width tool adds symmetrical handles on both sides of the path.

Click and drag to add symmetrical width handles on both sides of the path.

4. **Move the cursor until the feedback shows an intersection with the center of the placed logo.**

The path is still just a path, even though you edited its width.

5. **Press Option/Alt, then click and drag down until cursor feedback shows that Side 2 is approximately 0.08".**

If you press Option/Alt while dragging from a width point, you add non-symmetrical width handles. You can also Option/Alt-click an existing width handle and drag to adjust it independently of the opposing handle.

Option/Alt-click and drag to create non-symmetrical handles.

Note:

In this step, don't worry if the measurements are not exact; you will learn how to define precise side widths in the next few steps.

6. **About half-way across the stroke, click and drag down slightly to initiate the width points, then drag up until the overall width of the point is approximately 0.1".**

In this case, the two sides of the stroke are already different because you created non-symmetrical handles on the previous point. Dragging the handles of this point maintains the proportional relationship between the two sides.

Note:

To remove a width point from a stroke, click with the Width tool to select a particular point, then press Delete/Backspace.

7. **Double-click the new point from Step 6. In the resulting Width Point Edit dialog box, activate the link icon to force the Side 1 and Side 2 fields to symmetrically proportional lengths.**

You can numerically manipulate the length of width handles by double-clicking a particular width point. When the link icon is active, changing one side has a proportional effect on the other side.

8. **Change the Side 1 field to 0.04", then press Tab to highlight the Side 2 field.**

Because you linked the two fields, the width of Side 2 is also changed proportionally (from 0.039 to 0.026 in our example).

Note:

If multiple points are selected when you double-click, this dialog box will include fields for each point.

9. **Click OK to close the Width Point Edit dialog box.**

10. **Click the point you added in Step 6 (the one in the middle of the top edge) and drag right until that point is aproximately two-thirds of the way across the frame edge.**

Note:

If you Shift-click and drag a width point, other points on the path adjust proportionally.

You can move a specific width point by clicking and dragging; other width points are not affected.

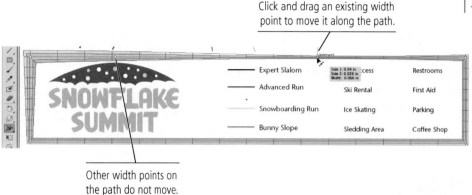

Click and drag an existing width point to move it along the path.

Other width points on the path do not move.

When you release the mouse button, you can see the effect of moving one width point on the overall path shape. The lower edge of the path is very close to the logo, so you should edit the path width at that point to provide a slightly larger gap between the logo and the path.

11. **Double-click the width point above the logo on the top of the frame edge. Change the Side 2 field to 0.07″ and then click OK.**

Because you did not link the two Side fields, changing one does not affect the other; in this case, you are modifying the width on only Side 2 — the side nearest the logo.

12. **Add and adjust width points along the bottom path of the shape until you are satisfied with the overall result.**

13. **Save the file and continue to the next exercise.**

ILLUSTRATOR FOUNDATIONS

Once you have edited the shape of a path, you can even save your work as a custom stroke profile so you can apply that same stroke appearance to other paths.

If you want to apply the same stroke shape to more than one path, you can save your work as a stroke profile. The Variable Width Profile menu is available in both the Control and Stroke panels. Stroke profiles do not include the initial stroke width; the profile is applied proportionally based on the defined width of the stroke where you apply the profile.

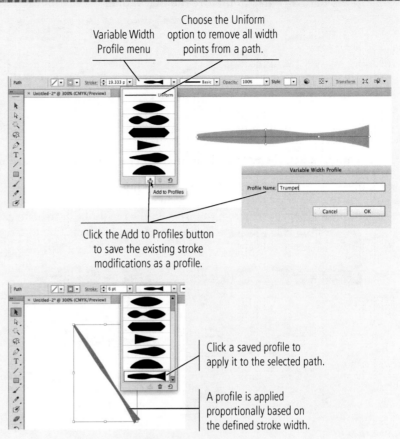

Variable Width Profile menu

Choose the Uniform option to remove all width points from a path.

Click the Add to Profiles button to save the existing stroke modifications as a profile.

Click a saved profile to apply it to the selected path.

A profile is applied proportionally based on the defined stroke width.

CREATE A CUSTOM PATTERN

Illustrator CS6 includes a new Pattern Options panel, which makes it very easy to create a custom pattern from any artwork. In this project, you will create a snowflake pattern that fills the background of the entire artboard.

1. **With summit map.ai open, make sure nothing is selected on the artboard.**

2. **Using the Selection tool, click the snowflake artwork and drag it to the Swatches panel.**

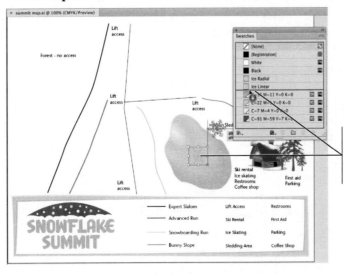

Drag any artwork into the Swatches panel to create a new pattern swatch.

3. **Double-click the new swatch name in the panel. Type** Snowflakes, **then press Return/Enter to finalize the new name.**

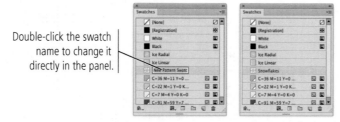

Double-click the swatch name to change it directly in the panel.

4. **Double-click the swatch thumbnail to enter into Edit Pattern mode.**

Edit Pattern mode is a special interface where you can define specific parameters of the pattern. The Pattern Options panel includes a number of options that make it easy to define a custom pattern from any artwork. You can define the repeating area (the "tile") and the manner in which the tile is repeated, and see an instant on-screen preview of each change you define.

Note:

You can also click the Edit Pattern button at the bottom of the Swatches panel.

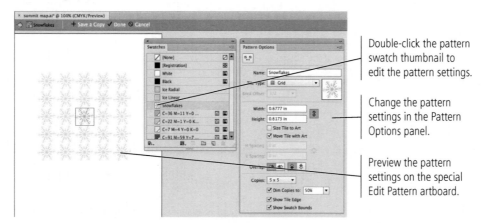

Double-click the pattern swatch thumbnail to edit the pattern settings.

Change the pattern settings in the Pattern Options panel.

Preview the pattern settings on the special Edit Pattern artboard.

5. **Zoom in so you can more clearly see the pattern.**

6. **At the bottom of the Pattern Options panel, uncheck the Show Swatch Bounds option (if necessary).**

The Copies menu defines how many copies of the pattern artwork appear in the pattern preview. The Dim Copies To field reduces the opacity of the copies so you can more easily distinguish the actual pattern artwork.

The Tile Edge, which appears as a solid black line on the artboard, is the area that is repeated when you apply the pattern. The Swatch Bounds is simply the storage space surrounding the pattern artwork; if you change the tile size, the swatch boundary grows or shrinks to accommodate the new tile size.

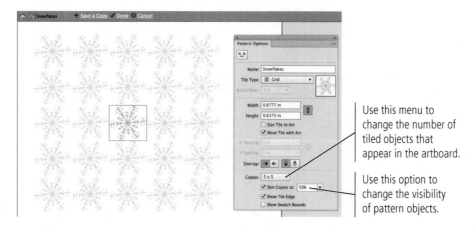

Use this menu to change the number of tiled objects that appear in the artboard.

Use this option to change the visibility of pattern objects.

When you first create a pattern, the tile size matches the size of the pattern artwork. You can use the Width and Height fields in the Pattern Options panel to change the tile size, or click the Pattern Tile tool at the top of the panel to manually resize the tile on the artboard.

Click the Pattern Tile tool to access the tile handles on the artboard.

Click and drag the handles to change the tile size.

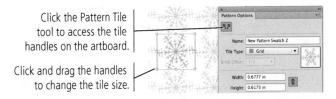

7. **Activate the link icon to link the Width and Height fields. Change the Width field to 0.5″, then press Return/Enter.**

If you use the fields in the panel to change the tile size, you can activate the link icon to maintain the original aspect ratio of the tile; changing one field applies a proportional change to the other field.

Changing the tile size changes the way individual objects interact when the pattern is repeated. Artwork outside the tile area is still included in the pattern, overlapping the other repeating objects.

Note:

Don't confuse changing the tile size with changing the artwork size.

If you change the size of the artwork, you can check the Size Tile to Art option to force the tile to match the resized artwork. When this option is active, you can use the H Spacing and V Spacing fields to add or remove a specific amount of space around the artwork when it is repeated in the panel. You can also use the Overlap options to determine how individual objects affect others in the repeated pattern, which is useful if pattern artwork has applied effects or transparency.

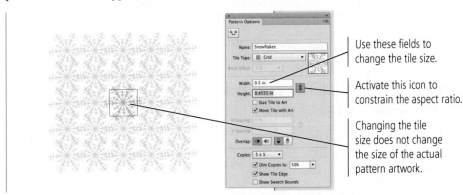

Use these fields to change the tile size.

Activate this icon to constrain the aspect ratio.

Changing the tile size does not change the size of the actual pattern artwork.

8. **In the Tile Type menu, choose Brick by Row. In the Brick Offset menu, choose 1/3.**

The Tile Type menu determines how the pattern artwork repeats. When you choose one of the Brick options, you can use the Brick Offset menu to determine how the "bricks" are stacked in the repeating pattern.

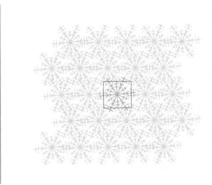

9. **Click the Done option at the top of the document window.**

   Clicking Done saves the changes to the existing pattern. If you had already applied the pattern anywhere in the file, those objects would reflect the new pattern.

   You can also click Save a Copy to save your changes as a new pattern; in this case, the changes would not be reflected in any objects where the original pattern had been applied.

   If you click Cancel, the changes are not saved and the existing pattern is not affected.

10. **Select and delete the snowflake from the middle of the lake.**

11. **Using the Rectangle tool, create a shape that fills the entire artboard. Apply a 6-pt. black stroke, then apply the Snowflakes pattern as the shape's fill.**

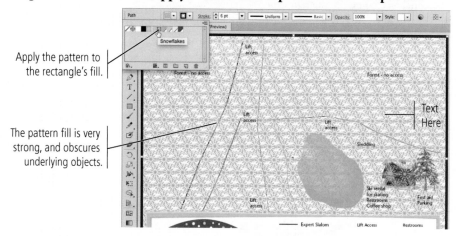

Apply the pattern to the rectangle's fill.

The pattern fill is very strong, and obscures underlying objects.

12. **Create a new layer named `Background`, and move it to the bottom of the layer stack.**

13. **Expand Layer 1 and locate the pattern-filled rectangle ("path"). Click the Selected Art icon and drag to the Background layer.**

Note:

You can double-click a specific object in the layers panel to name it, just as you name specific layers. For example, you could rename the "path" item as "Background filled rectangle".

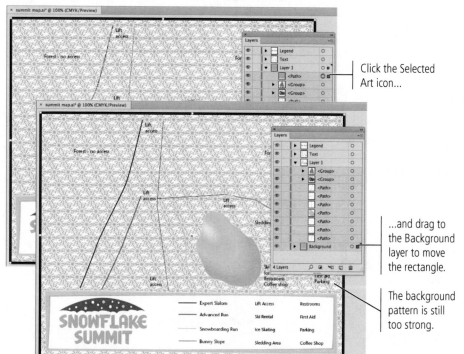

Click the Selected Art icon...

...and drag to the Background layer to move the rectangle.

The background pattern is still too strong.

14. **Deselect everything on the artboard.**

15. **In the Swatches panel, double-click the Snowflakes pattern swatch to re-enter Edit Pattern mode. At the bottom of the Pattern Options panel, change the Dim Copies menu to 100%.**

Changing the Dim Copies option allows you to better see the actual pattern that will result from your changes.

16. **Using the Selection tool, click to select the snowflake artwork in the pattern tile. Using the Color panel, change the fill tint to 20%.**

Pattern artwork is still artwork, which means you can modify it just as you would any other artwork.

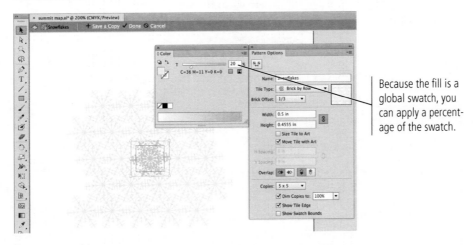

Because the fill is a global swatch, you can apply a percentage of the swatch.

17. **Click the Done link at the top of the document window.**

When you click Done, the changes are reflected anywhere the pattern has been applied. As you can see, lightening the color in the pattern artwork makes the overall background pattern much more subtle.

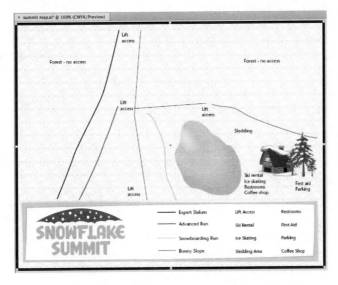

18. **Save the file and then continue to the next stage of the project.**

Stage 2 Working with Brushes

Brushes enhance or (as Adobe puts it) decorate paths. The default Brushes panel (Window>Brushes) includes several basic brushes of different types. You can use the Brushes panel Options menu to change the panel display, manage brushes, and load different brush libraries.

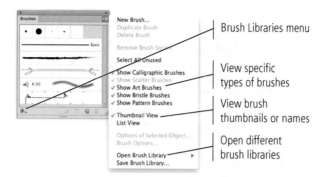

Illustrator includes a number of different types of brushes, divided into five categories:

- **Calligraphic brushes** create strokes that resemble what you would draw with the angled tip of a calligraphic pen.

- **Scatter brushes** scatter copies of an object along a path.

- **Art brushes** apply a brush stroke or object shape across the length of a path.

- **Bristle brushes** create strokes that mimic the behavior of real artist's brushes.

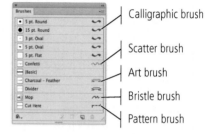

- **Pattern brushes** paint a pattern of defined tiles along the length of a path. You can define different tiles for straight edges, inner and outer corners, and the beginning and end of a path.

The Brushes panel appears by default in Thumbnail mode. If you choose List View in the panel Options menu, you see the name of the brush, as well as an icon that indicates the type of the brush. Viewing brushes by name can be useful — especially when working with the built-in brushes — because the brush names indicate what each brush creates.

Beyond the few brushes in the default Brushes panel, you can also open a number of built-in brush libraries using the Brush Libraries menu at the bottom of the Brushes panel or at the bottom of the Window menu.

Brush libraries open in the same position as when they were last used. If you open more than one brush library, the new library opens as a separate tab in the existing panel group unless it has already been moved into a different panel group.

Note:

In the above image, we added the Confetti brush to the default panel so we could show you the icon for a scatter brush. This brush is not included in the default Brushes panel.

CREATE A NEW ART BRUSH

To complete this project, you need to create two custom brushes: one to define the ski lifts, and one to define the ski runs. As we mentioned above, an art brush applies an object along the length of a path. You will use this type of brush to create the ski lift paths. To create an art brush, you must first create the object you want to use as the brush stroke.

1. **With summit map.ai open, create a new layer named Ski Lift immediately above Layer 1.**

2. **Select the two ski-lift paths on the artboard. In the Layers panel, click the Selected Art icon for Layer 1, then drag to the Ski Lift layer.**

If you dragged the Selected Art icon for any specific path, only that path would be moved to the new layer. Because you dragged the Selected Art icon for the active layer that contained both paths, both are moved to the new layer.

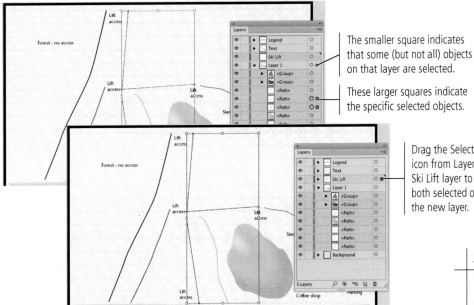

The smaller square indicates that some (but not all) objects on that layer are selected.

These larger squares indicate the specific selected objects.

Drag the Selected Art icon from Layer 1 to the Ski Lift layer to move both selected objects to the new layer.

Note:

We changed the layer color of the Ski Lift layer from the default yellow to a color that is more visible in our screen shots.

3. **Hide all but the Ski Lift layer, then click away from the two paths to deselect everything.**

4. **Anywhere on the artboard, create a 5-pt black line that is 1″ long. Change the stroke color to 75% black.**

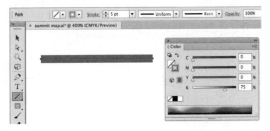

5. **With the line selected, choose Edit>Copy.**

6. **Choose Edit>Paste in Front to paste a copy of the line directly on top of the original.**

The Paste options are very useful for positioning copied objects.

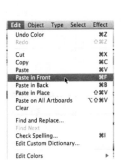

- **Paste** puts the copy in the center of the document window.
- **Paste in Front** puts the copy in the same place as the copied object, one level higher in the object stacking order than the current selection.
- **Paste in Back** puts the copy in the same place as the copied object, one level lower in the object stacking order than the current selection.
- **Paste in Place** puts the copy on the selected artboard in the same position as it was on the original artboard.
- **Paste on All Artboards** puts a copy on all artboards in the document, in the same position as the original artboard. (A copy is also placed on the original artboard, so you might want to remove the duplicate copy from the original active artboard.)

7. **With the pasted line still selected, change the stroke weight to 2.5 pt and change the stroke color to 40%.**

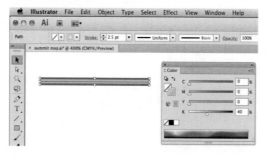

8. **Select both lines, then choose Object>Path>Outline Stroke.**

This command converts a stroked path to a filled object. The original stroke color becomes the fill color of the resulting shape.

After outlining the strokes, the two objects are now filled shapes. The original paths are no longer available.

9. **Select both rectangles and group them (Object>Group or Command/Control-G).**

10. **Make sure the basic Brushes panel is open (Window>Brushes), and then drag the grouped rectangles into the Brushes panel.**

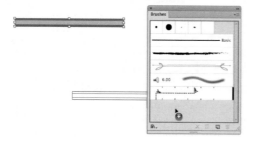

Note:

Depending on what you (or other users) did before beginning this project, your Brushes panel might have fewer or more default brushes than what you see in our screen shots. It doesn't matter in this case, because you will only use the brushes that you create.

11. **In the resulting New Brush dialog box, choose the Art Brush radio button and then click OK.**

12. Type **Ski Lift** in the Name field of the resulting dialog box, and then click OK.

After you click OK in the dialog box, the new brush appears in the Brushes panel.

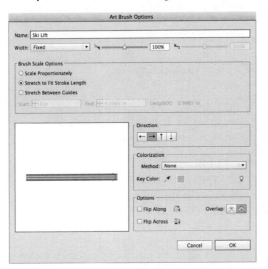

There's the new art brush.

Note:

You can't create an art brush from objects that use gradients, meshes, bitmap elements, masks, or type.

13. Delete the grouped lines from the artboard, then save your work and continue to the next exercise.

Understanding Art Brush Options

ILLUSTRATOR FOUNDATIONS

Art brush options control how the object is applied as a brush stroke. This dialog box opens automatically when you create a new art brush. You can also double-click an existing art brush to change the options for that brush.

The **Width** field defines the width of the brush stroke relative to the applied stroke weight. For example, a 200% Width value would result in a 2-pt-wide apparent stroke if the path has a 1-pt defined stroke weight.

The **Fixed** menu can be used to allow a variable stroke width based on a number of factors, including pressure and tilt from drawing tablet hardware.

The Brush Scale Options determine how the artwork is applied across the length of a stroke.

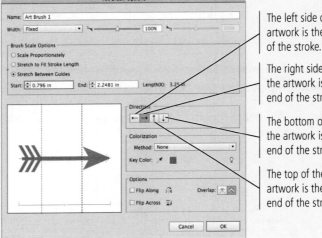

The left side of the artwork is the end of the stroke.

The right side of the artwork is the end of the stroke.

The bottom of the artwork is the end of the stroke.

The top of the artwork is the end of the stroke.

- **Scale Proportionally** stretches the artwork both horizontally and vertically to match the stroke length.

- **Stretch to Fit Stroke Length** which stretches the brush artwork horizontally across the entire length of the stroke (in only the direction of the stroke).

- **Stretch Between Guides** can be used to determine certain areas of the brush artwork that do not stretch. Areas between the defined Start and End guides (dashed lines in the Preview area) will stretch across the stroke length.

The **Direction** options control the direction of brush artwork relative to the path. The active button matches the direction of the arrow in the preview; both of these indicate which side of the original artwork will be the end of the stroke.

The **Colorization** determine how colors in the paths are affected by colors in the brush stroke artwork.

Flip Along and **Flip Across** reverse the orientation of the art in relation to the path.

The **Overlap** options control how the artwork is treated on corners.

CONTROL AN ART BRUSH STROKE

Applying a brush stroke is simple — draw a path (or select an object) and click the brush you want to apply (either in the Brushes panel or in the Control panel menu). Once a brush stroke is applied, however, you should also understand how to control it.

1. **With summit map.ai open, select the two paths that represent the ski lifts.**

2. **Click the Ski Lift brush in the Brushes panel.**

   The paths immediately take on the appearance of the brush you created earlier. You created the original darker-line stroke as 5 pt; when you created a brush from the grouped rectangles, you left the Width field (in the Art Brush Options dialog box) at 100%.

   The width of the path stroke is important when using brushes. When you apply artistic brush strokes, the width of the path's stroke actually defines the percentage of the brush width that will be applied. In this case, the width of the path stroke is 1 pt, so the applied brush stroke is 100% of the brush size. In other words, applying the brush to a 1-pt path results in a brush stroke with a 5-pt width.

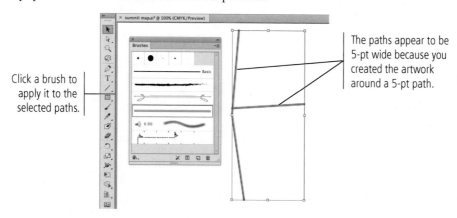

Click a brush to apply it to the selected paths.

The paths appear to be 5-pt wide because you created the artwork around a 5-pt path.

3. **With the brushed path selected, double-click the Ski Lift brush in the Brushes panel to open the Art Brush Options dialog box.**

4. **In the Art Brush Options dialog box, change the Width field to 200% and then click OK.**

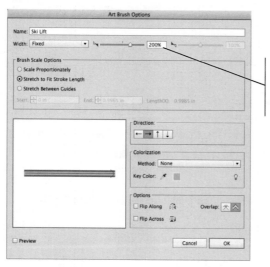

The Width field defines the brush stroke width as a percentage of the applied stroke weight.

Note:

You can also click the Options of Selected Object button at the bottom of the Brushes panel to edit the brush options.

Note:

You could accomplish the same result by changing the path stroke to 2 pt. Every job has different requirements, so it's important to understand your options.

5. **In the resulting dialog box, click Apply to Strokes.**

When you change the options for a specific brush, you can determine what to do for strokes where the brush has already been applied.

- If you click Apply to Strokes, the changes will be applied to any path where the brush has been applied.
- If you click Leave Strokes, existing paths are unaffected; a copy of the changed brush is added to the Brushes panel.
- If you click Cancel, the Brush Options dialog box closes without applying the new brush options.

6. **Save the file and continue to the next exercise.**

 EXPAND BRUSH STROKES INTO OBJECTS

If you look at the map as it is now, you might notice a problem where the ski lift paths connect — the dark gray of the horizontal path overlaps the light gray of the vertical path. To more accurately reflect the appearance of a single path that branches off in a different direction, you need to convert the path strokes to regular objects so you can manipulate selected parts of the paths (i.e., where the lines intersect).

1. **With summit map.ai open, zoom in so you can more clearly see where the two paths meet.**

2. **Select both paths, then choose View>Hide Bounding Box.**

When the bounding box is hidden, you can better see the selected paths without the bounding box that marks the outer bounds of the active selection.

3. **Open the Appearance panel (Window>Appearance).**

The Appearance panel shows the properties of the selected objects, including the applied stroke and fill attributes. You can see here that the stroke attribute is Ski Lift.

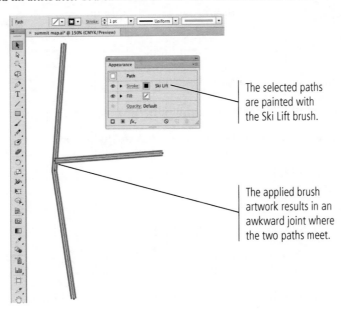

The selected paths are painted with the Ski Lift brush.

The applied brush artwork results in an awkward joint where the two paths meet.

Note:

If you try to delete a brush that has been used in the open file, you must decide what to do with the strokes where the brush has already been applied.

If you click Expand Strokes, the applied brush strokes are converted to filled objects.

If you click Remove Strokes, objects that include the deleted brush strokes are reduced to their basic appearance (fill color, stroke color, and weight).

If you click Cancel, your artwork is unaffected and the brush remains in the Brushes panel.

4. **With the paths still selected, choose Object>Expand Appearance.**

In the Appearance panel, you now see that the selection is a group. When you expand the appearance of a selection, Illustrator simplifies the selection (as much as possible) into basic filled and stroked shapes; the resulting shapes are grouped.

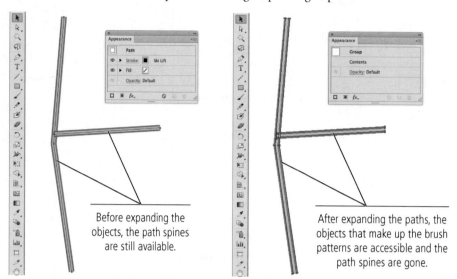

Before expanding the objects, the path spines are still available.

After expanding the paths, the objects that make up the brush patterns are accessible and the path spines are gone.

5. **In the Layers panel, expand the Ski Lift layer.**

As a result of expanding the strokes, each path is now a group.

6. **Click the arrows to expand each group.**

Each group contains the two paths in the artwork that made up the brush stroke.

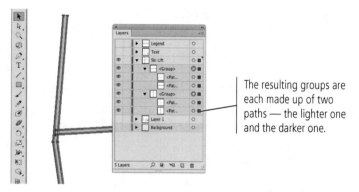

The resulting groups are each made up of two paths — the lighter one and the darker one.

7. **With the expanded path still selected, choose Object>Ungroup.**

8. **Deselect everything, and then select the lighter path of the horizontal ski lift.**

9. **Choose Select>Same>Fill Color to select the other object that has the lighter fill.**

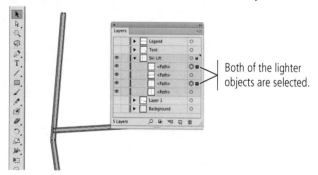

Both of the lighter objects are selected.

10. **In the Pathfinder panel (Window>Pathfinder), click the Unite button.**

   All the selected shapes are now a single object. When you use the Pathfinder, the merged objects move to the stacking-order position of the highest object in the original selection, as you can see in the Layers panel. This is unlike the Shape Builder tool, which moves the merged object to the stacking-order position of the first object you click.

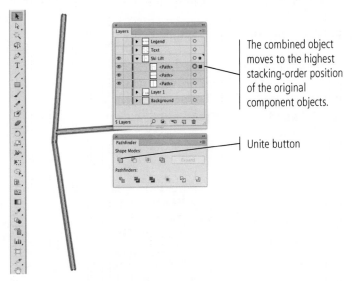

The combined object moves to the highest stacking-order position of the original component objects.

Unite button

11. **Repeat Steps 8–10 to unite the darker objects into a single shape.**

   You don't need to send the combined object to the back of the stacking order because it is already behind the lighter object.

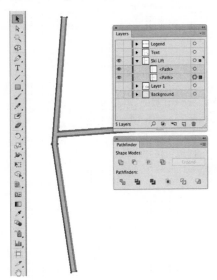

12. **Save the file and continue to the next exercise.**

CREATE PATTERN BRUSH TILES

While an art brush stretches a specific piece of artwork along a path, a pattern brush repeats specific artwork along the path. You can even define different artwork to use for sides, corners, and endpoints of a specific path. In this exercise, you will use an art brush to define the four different ski runs at the resort.

1. **With summit map.ai open, hide the Ski Lift layer and show Layer 1.**

2. **Create a new layer named Ski Runs immediately above Layer 1.**

3. **Select the four ski-lift paths on the artboard. In the Layers panel, click the Selected Art icon for Layer 1, then drag to the Ski Runs layer.**

4. **Hide Layer 1, then deselect everything on the artboard.**

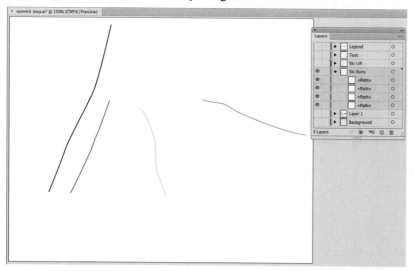

5. **Choose the Rectangle tool, then click and drag anywhere on the page to create a rectangle that is 0.4″ square. Fill the new rectangle with black and apply a stroke of None.**

6. **Rotate the rectangle 45°. If you don't see all eight bounding box handles on the shape, choose View>Show Bounding Box.**

When you rotate the object, the bounding box remains attached to the original object dimensions.

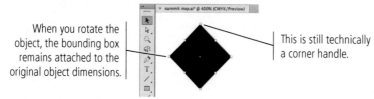

This is still technically a corner handle.

7. **Choose Object>Transform>Reset Bounding Box.**

When you rotated the shape in Step 6, the bounding box rotated along with the shape; the corners are still the corners. If you drag what appears to be the top handle, you would change the height and width of the shape.

The Reset Bounding Box command restores the bounding box to a horizontal rectangle. If you drag the top-center handle, you will affect only the height of the shape.

Resetting the bounding box restores it to a horizontal rectangle.

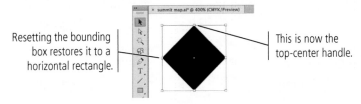

This is now the top-center handle.

8. **Using the Selection tool, click the top bounding box handle and drag down until the cursor feedback shows the object's height as 0.35".**

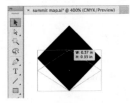

9. **Press Option/Alt, then drag the shape to the right to clone it.**

10. **Using the Line Segment tool, draw a line that vertically bisects the diamond.**

Smart guides make it easy to create a path that exactly aligns to the center of the diamond.

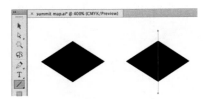

11. **Choose the Selection tool, then press Shift and click the diamond shape to add it to the selection.**

12. **In the Pathfinder panel, click the Divide button.**

13. **In the Layers panel, expand the Ski Runs layer, then expand the group at the top of that layer.**

When a pathfinder option results in more than one shape, the resulting shapes are automatically grouped together. You are going to use the halves individually, so you need to ungroup them.

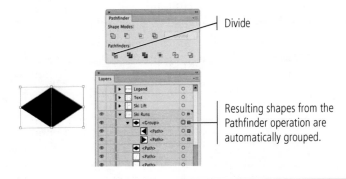

Divide

Resulting shapes from the Pathfinder operation are automatically grouped.

14. With the entire group selected, choose Object>Ungroup.

15. With both objects still selected, transform the selected artwork to 140% proportionally.

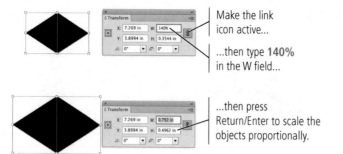

Make the link icon active...

...then type **140%** in the W field...

...then press Return/Enter to scale the objects proportionally.

16. Save the file and continue to the next exercise.

CREATE A NEW PATTERN BRUSH

Now that you have the three objects you need to create the pattern brush, you have to convert those objects to patterns, and then define the pattern brush.

1. With **summit map.ai** open, deselect all objects on the artboard.

2. Using the Selection tool, drag the right-facing triangle shape into the Swatches panel.

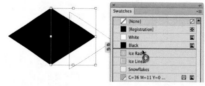

3. In the Swatches panel, double-click the new swatch to highlight the name. Type `Run Start` and press Return/Enter.

4. Delete the right-facing triangle from the artboard.

5. Repeat Steps 2–4 to create a pattern swatch named `Run End` from the left triangle shape, and a swatch named `Run Path` from the diamond shape.

   Make sure you delete the shapes from the artboard after you create the necessary pattern swatches.

6. Use the Show Swatch Kinds menu at the bottom of the panel to show only pattern swatches.

Note:

On some Windows systems, there is a bug that prevents some custom swatches from appearing in the Pattern Brush Options dialog box until you save the file where you created the swatches.

Note:

You can always access the basic brush art by dragging the brush from the Brushes panel onto the artboard.

Note:

If the paths in this project had sharp corners, you would also need to define shapes for both inside and outside corners.

7. **With nothing selected on the artboard, click the New Brush button at the bottom of the Brushes panel.**

8. **In the New Brush dialog box, select the Pattern Brush option and click OK.**

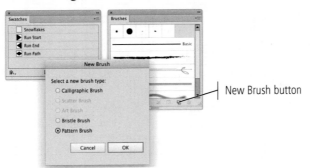

New Brush button

Note:

If anything had been selected when you clicked the New Brush button, Illustrator would have tried to create a new brush based on the current selection.

9. **In the Pattern Brush Options dialog box, name the brush** `Ski Runs`.

10. **Click the Side Tile icon, and then choose Run Path from the list of available pattern swatches.**

Pattern brush tiles must be saved as patterns (as you did in Steps 2–4) before you can access them in the Pattern Brush Options dialog box.

Note:

Pattern brushes can consist of five possible tiles: side, outer corner, inner corner, start, and end. You can define different patterns for any or all of these tiles.

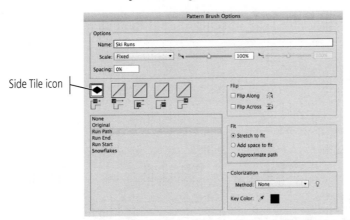

Side Tile icon

Pattern Brush Options

ILLUSTRATOR FOUNDATIONS

As with art brushes, you can control the settings for pattern brushes when you first create them or by double-clicking an existing pattern brush in the Brushes panel.

The **Scale** option adjusts the size of tiles relative to their original size.

The **Spacing** option adjusts the space between tiles in the applied stroke.

The **Tile buttons** allow you to apply different patterns to different parts of the line.

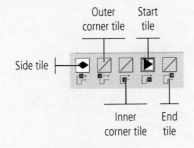

Outer corner tile
Start tile
Side tile
Inner corner tile
End tile

The **Flip Along** and **Flip Across** options reverse the orientation of the art in relation to the path.

The **Fit** options define how the pattern fits on the path. **Stretch to Fit** adjusts the length of the pattern tiles to fit the path. **Add Space to Fit** adds blank space between pattern tiles to maintain proportions in the applied pattern. **Approximate Path** fits tiles to the closest approximate path without changing the tiles.

The **Colorization** methods determine how colors in the paths are affected by colors in the brush stroke artwork.

11. **Click the Start Tile icon, and then click Run Start in the list of patterns.**

12. **Click the End Tile icon, and then click Run End in the list of patterns.**

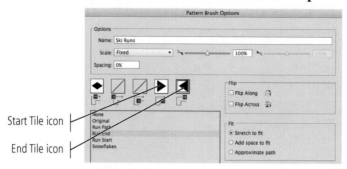

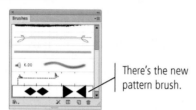

Start Tile icon

End Tile icon

Note:

Art brushes can produce unexpected results on sharp corners and closed paths.

Pattern brushes are the best choices for creating borders on closed paths or for other paths that have sharp corners.

13. **Click OK to create the brush.**

There's the new pattern brush.

14. **Select all four of the paths on the visible layer and click the Ski Runs pattern brush in the Brushes panel.**

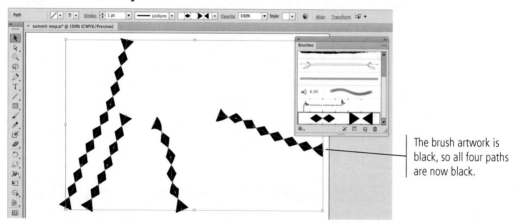

The brush artwork is black, so all four paths are now black.

15. **With all four paths selected, change the stroke weight to 0.5 pt.**

As we explained earlier, changing the stroke size for the applied art brush and changing the stroke width of the path achieves the same result. The 0.5-pt stroke weight means the applied stroke is half the width of the defined brush.

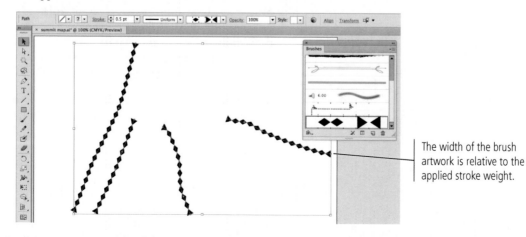

The width of the brush artwork is relative to the applied stroke weight.

16. In the Brushes panel, double-click the Ski Runs brush to open the Pattern Brush Options dialog box.

17. Choose Tints in the Colorization menu, then click OK.

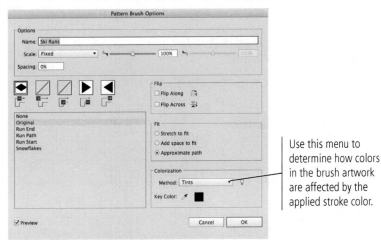

Use this menu to determine how colors in the brush artwork are affected by the applied stroke color.

Note:

Click the Tips button to the right of the menu to see a preview of colorization options.

Note:

The end tile of a pattern brush should always be created with the path end pointing to the right. If the "end" of the end tile points to the left, you could end up with unexpected results such as this:

The Colorization menu controls how colors in an art, scatter, or pattern brush interact with the currently defined stroke color.

- Select None to use only the colors defined in the brush.
- Select Tints to apply the brush stroke in tints of the current stroke color. (Black areas of the brush become the stroke color, other areas become tints of the stroke color, and white remains white.)
- Select Tints and Shades to apply the brush stroke in tints and shades of the stroke color. Black and white areas of the brush remain unaffected; all other areas are painted as a blend from black to white through the stroke color.
- Select Hue Shift to change the defined key color in brush artwork to the defined stroke color when the brush is applied; other colors in the brush artwork are adjusted to be similar to the stroke color. (Black, white, and grays are unaffected). The key color defaults to the most prominent color in the brush art. To change the key color, click the eyedropper in the brush preview to select a different color.

This direction has no effect on the stroke that will be applied in the artwork. If you draw a path from right to left, the end tile of the applied pattern brush will point to the left:

18. In the resulting dialog box, click Apply to Strokes.

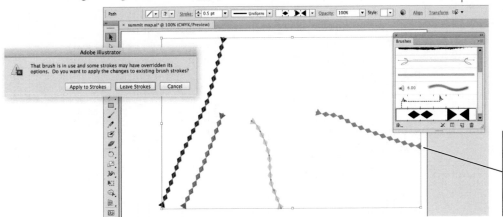

Using the Tint colorization method, black in the brush artwork is reproduced as 100% of the applied stroke color.

19. Save the file and continue to the next exercise.

SAVE CUSTOM BRUSHES

When you create custom brushes, swatches, or other elements, they are only available in the file where you create them. To access those assets in other files, you have to save your own custom libraries.

1. **With summit map.ai open, show the Brushes panel. Open the panel Options menu and choose Select All Unused.**

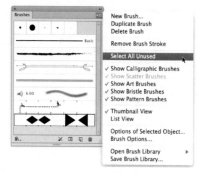

Everything but the Basic brush and the Ski Runs pattern brush should be selected. (Remember, you expanded the appearance of the ski lift paths, so the Ski Lift art brush is not currently applied in the file.)

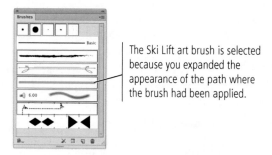

The Ski Lift art brush is selected because you expanded the appearance of the path where the brush had been applied.

Note:

The Basic option is an application default, which effectively removes any applied brush stroke and reverts a path to a simple 1-pt stroke.

2. **Command/Control-click the Ski Lift art brush to deselect it, and then click the panel's Delete button. Click Yes in the dialog box asking if you want to delete the brush selection.**

You are not permanently deleting the brushes from the application; you are only deleting them from the Brushes panel for this file. However, Illustrator still asks you to confirm the deletion.

3. **Open the panel Options menu and choose Save Brush Library.**

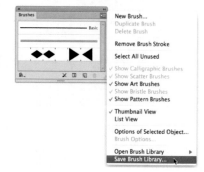

4. **In the resulting dialog box, name the library** `Map Brushes.ai` **and click Save.**

   If you're working on your own computer, the application defaults to a Brushes folder created when the application was installed.

Note:

Brush, symbol, and swatch libraries are saved with the extension ".ai". You can also save swatch libraries in the Adobe Swatch Exchange format (using the extension ".ase") if you want to use a swatch library in another Adobe application such as Photoshop. Keep in mind, however, that swatches containing gradients, patterns, or tints are not "exchangeable" and will not be visible in other applications.

   If you are using a shared computer, you might not be able to save files in the application's default location. If this is the case, navigate to your WIP>Skiing folder to save the Map Brushes.ai file.

5. **Close the Brushes panel.**

6. **Create a new document using the default settings, and then open the Brushes panel.**

7. **Choose Window>Brush Libraries>User Defined>Map Brushes.**

   If you saved the brush library file in your WIP>Skiing folder (in Step 4), choose Other Library from the bottom of the submenu, navigate to your WIP>Skiing folder, and open the `Map Brushes.ai` **file.**

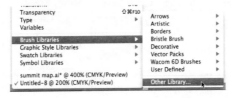

   The Map Brushes panel opens, grouped with the other open brush libraries if there are any. The panel contains only the brushes that were available when you saved the library. (The Basic brush option is not included; it is, however, available in the Brushes panel of any file you open in Illustrator.)

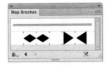

8. **Close the new file without saving, then close the Map Brushes panel.**

9. **Save the** `summit map.ai` **file and continue to the next stage of the project.**

Stage 3 Using Symbols

In many cases, you will need to use multiple copies of a specific graphic in a complex illustration like the one in this project. You can create any element and define it as a **symbol**, which you can then use as many times as necessary in a drawing. All placed **instances** of a symbol are linked dynamically to the saved definition of the symbol; this means that you can change all instances simultaneously by changing the saved definition of the symbol. You can also isolate specific instances of a symbol, which effectively breaks the link to the saved definition of the symbol (and to other instances of the symbol); once the link is broken, changes to the original saved symbol no longer affect the isolated instances.

As with brushes and swatches, symbols are managed in panels. The default Symbols panel (Window>Symbols) has a few randomly selected symbols from various built-in libraries. You can also open other symbol libraries by choosing from the menu at the bottom of the Window menu, or in the Symbol Libraries menu at the bottom of the Symbols panel.

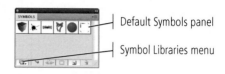

Default Symbols panel

Symbol Libraries menu

If you open a symbol library from the Window menu, the first library opens in its own panel. Successive panels open as separate tabs that are automatically grouped with other open symbol libraries, unless they have been intentionally moved out of the panel group and positioned elsewhere in the workspace. If you open a symbol library using the Symbol Libraries menu at the bottom of the Symbols panel, the new library replaces the active library.

OPEN CUSTOM SYMBOL LIBRARIES

Several elements of this project will benefit from the use of symbols. Many of the symbols for this project have already been created and saved in a custom library, which you can easily load so you don't have to recreate work that has already been completed.

1. **With summit map.ai open, open the Symbols panel (Window>Symbols).**

2. **Click the Symbol Libraries menu button at the bottom of the default Symbols panel.**

3. **Choose Other Library at the bottom of the menu.**

   If you create a custom library on your computer using the default Save location, the library appears in the User Defined submenu of the main Libraries menu. If a custom library was created on another computer, you have to choose Other Library from the menu and navigate to the file that contains the library you want to use.

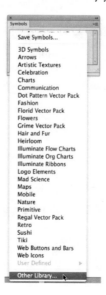

Note:

As with the Brushes panel, your default Symbols panel might have more options than what you see in our screen shots. Again, you will only be using the symbols you create (or import), so the default symbols don't matter in this project.

Note:

The same options are also available for loading swatch libraries and brush libraries that were created on another computer.

4. **Navigate to `map symbols.ai` in your WIP>Skiing folder and click Open.**

The new symbol library appears in its own panel (possibly grouped with other library panels if other symbol libraries are also open).

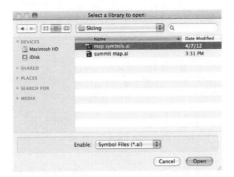

Symbols in loaded libraries are not connected to the current file unless you place an instance of a symbol from the loaded library into the file. When you place a symbol instance from a loaded library, the symbol is added to the default symbol library for the file. (The same is true when working with brush libraries.)

5. **Continue to the next exercise.**

 ## CONTROL SYMBOL INSTANCES

In addition to loading built-in or custom symbol libraries, you can also create new symbols by drawing the art and dragging it into the default Symbols panel. In this exercise, you create a custom symbol to identify the different ski runs on the map — a simple road sign. You need four different signs to label the various runs.

1. **With `summit map.ai` open, show and lock all layers. Create a new layer named `Signs` at the top of the layer stack and make sure it is selected.**

2. **Click and drag the Sign symbol from the Map Symbols panel to the artboard.**

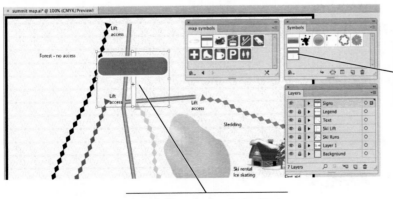

Symbols placed from other libraries are added to the default Symbols panel for the file.

A symbol instance is a single object. You can't directly access the individual shapes that make up the symbol.

Note:

Simply clicking a symbol in an external panel copies that symbol into the file's Symbols panel.

3. **Using the Transform panel, scale the placed instance to 1″ wide (proportionally).**

   When you transform a symbol instance, the Transform/Control panel does not offer the registration point proxy option. The symbol's registration point position, around which transformations will be applied, is defined when you create the symbol.

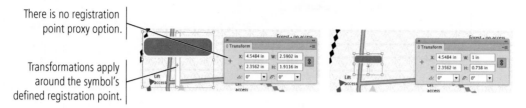

There is no registration point proxy option.

Transformations apply around the symbol's defined registration point.

4. **Using the Selection tool, drag the resized symbol instance to just below the "Lift Access" text near the top of the artboard.**

5. **Clone (Option/Alt-drag) the sign symbol instance three times, and place each clone near the top of each ski run path.**

   Each symbol instance is an object, which means it can be modified — transformed, rotated, stretched, etc. — as you would modify any other object. Transforming a placed instance has no effect on other placed instances of the same symbol.

   Cloning an instance results in an additional instance of the symbol. All instances are linked to the original symbol.

Note:

You can transform the instance as you would any other object, by dragging the bounding box handles. This has no effect on the original symbol, nor on other placed instances of the same symbol.

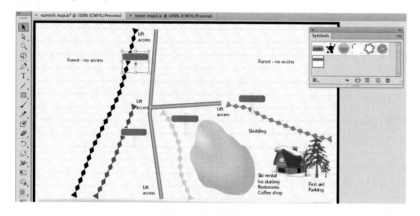

6. **In the Symbols panel, double-click the Sign symbol to enter into Symbol Editing mode.**

   This opens a new artboard, called **Symbol Editing mode**. The symbol artwork is the only visible item on the artboard.

7. **Drag the snowdrift symbol from the Map Symbols panel onto the artboard. Place it over the bottom edge of the signpost.**

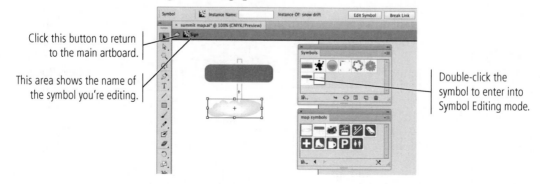

Click this button to return to the main artboard.

This area shows the name of the symbol you're editing.

Double-click the symbol to enter into Symbol Editing mode.

8. **Choose the Type tool in the Tools panel.**

9. **Click away from the sign artwork to create a new type object, then type Snowflake Peak.**

If you see this cursor, clicking will create a new point-type object.

If you see this cursor, clicking will convert the shape to a type container.

10. **Select all of the text and format it as 20-pt ATC Oak Bold, filled with white, with centered alignment.**

11. **Choose the Selection tool, then drag the type object to be centered in the green area of the sign.**

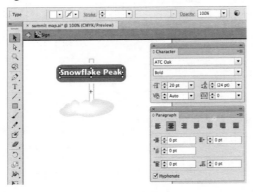

12. **In the top-left corner of the screen, click the left arrow button to exit Symbol Editing mode and return to the main artboard.**

Notice that the new type element has been added to all four placed instances. As we mentioned, the advantage of using symbols is that you can change all linked symbol instances — whether there are 4 or 400 — by making changes only once to the saved symbol definition.

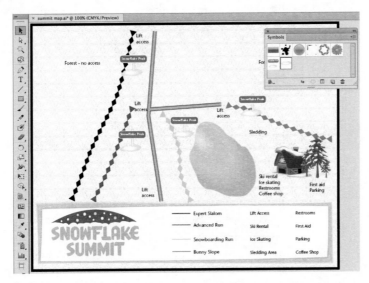

The problem, of course, is that the ski runs are not all named "Snowflake Peak". Although changing the symbol definition allowed you to add, format, and align the type object, you still need to edit it separately on each instance. To change the text on each individual sign, you have to break the link from each instance to the original symbol.

13. **Select all four instances of the Sign symbol and click the Break Link button in the Control panel.**

Once the links are broken, all the elements of the symbol artwork become a group in the main file. Editing the actual symbol will have no effect on instances that are no longer linked to the symbol.

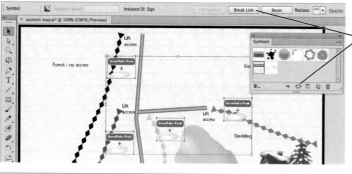

Click either option to break the link to the symbol.

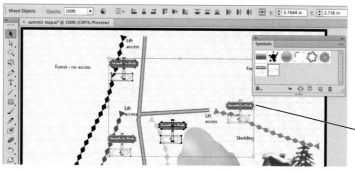

After breaking the link to the symbol, you can now access the individual components of the object.

14. **Change the text of each former symbol instance as follows:**

On the cyan run: Midnight Hill

On the yellow run: SnoSurf Slope

On the pink run: Bunny Hollow

15. **Save the file and continue to the next exercise.**

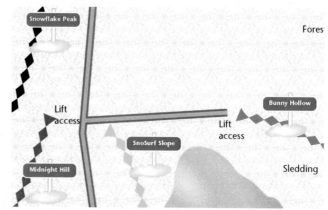

Editing Symbols in Place

You can double-click any placed instance to enter a modified symbol-editing mode, called **editing in place**. Instead of seeing only the symbol artwork, you can see the entire file behind the instance you are editing. Changing an instance in this manner has the same effect as changing the original symbol — all other linked instances reflect the changes when you return to the main artboard.

Double-clicking a placed instance allows you to edit the symbol in the context of the surrounding artwork.

Editing in place shows the symbol at full size, not the scaled dimensions of the placed instance. When you exit Symbol Editing mode, the placed instance returns to its scaled size.

REPLACE SYMBOLS

The next step of this map project involves placing icons around the map to identify different services. The symbols were provided in the supplied library, so this is a relatively simple process of placing symbols in the right place.

1. **With summit map.ai open, lock the Signs layer. Create a new layer named Amenities at the top of the layer stack and make sure it is selected.**

2. **Drag the Lift Access symbol from the Map Symbols panel to the artboard. Place the instance on top of the matching words near the top of the artboard.**

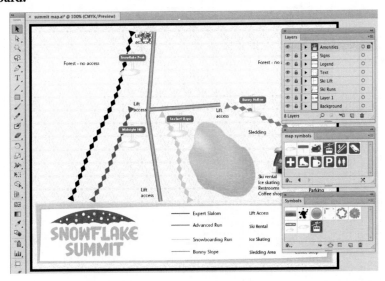

3. **Clone the placed instance three times and place the clones according to the text on the original map.**

4. **Continue dragging symbols from the Map Symbols panel to the artboard, using the text as a guide.**

    Skip the legend for now; you will create that later in this exercise.

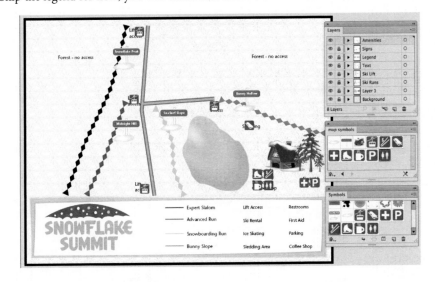

5. **Delete the Text layer from the file.**

6. **Lock the Amenities layer. Unlock the Legend layer and make it active.**

7. **Drag an instance of the Lift Access symbol from the main Symbols panel to the artboard. Place it to the left of the words "Lift Access", centered vertically with the text object.**

8. **Clone the placed instance. Place the clone exactly below the original instance and immediately left of the words "Ski Rental".**

9. **Repeat Step 8 to add two more instances of the symbol, as shown in the following image.**

10. **Shift-click to select all four instance in the legend. Clone the four instances. Place the clones exactly to the right of the original instances so they align with the text in the right column of the legend.**

11. **Select the symbol instance next to the Ski Rental text. Open the Replace With menu in the Control panel and choose the Ski Rental symbol.**

As soon as you select the new symbol, the selected instance changes to the new symbol.

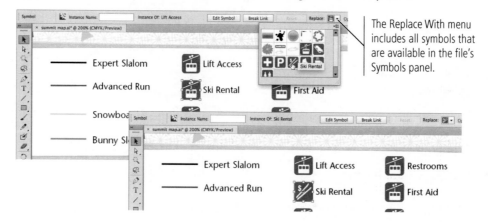

The Replace With menu includes all symbols that are available in the file's Symbols panel.

12. Repeat Step 11 for the remaining symbols in the legend, choosing the correct symbol to match the text.

13. Save the file and continue to the next exercise.

 SPRAY SYMBOLS

The next task is to create the forest around the ski runs. The supplied file already has a perfectly good group of trees near the lodge graphic; you are going to use those trees to create a new symbol, then spray a forest around the map.

1. With **summit map.ai** open, lock the Legend layer and unlock Layer 1.

2. Using the Selection tool, select the trees on the right side of the artboard.

3. Drag the selected group onto the main Symbols panel. In the resulting dialog box, name the symbol Trees, choose the center registration point, and click OK.

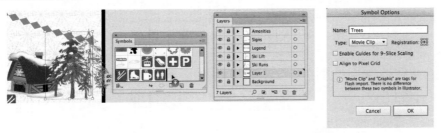

Note:

The Type options are relevant for files that will be exported for Adobe Flash. If your symbols will remain in Illustrator, you can use either the Graphic or Movie Clip option.

When you create a symbol from objects on the artboard, the original objects are automatically converted to an instance of the new symbol.

The selected group is now an instance of the new Trees symbol.

The crosshair identifies the registration point for the symbol instance.

4. Lock Layer 1, then create a new layer named Forest at the top of the layer stack. Make the Forest layer active.

5. Double-click the Symbol Sprayer tool in the Tools panel.

The Symbol Sprayer tool is used to spray multiple symbol instances onto the artboard. Other tools nested under the Symbol Sprayer in the Tools panel can be used to squeeze, spread, pinch, and otherwise modify the sprayed symbol instances.

Double-clicking the tool in the Tools panel opens the Symbolism Tool Options dialog box, where you can change settings that apply when you use the symbolism tools.

Note:

The Symbol Sprayer tool defaults to the last-used size.

Note:

Press the left bracket key ([ ) to decrease or right bracket key ( ]) to increase the size of the tool (and its cursor).

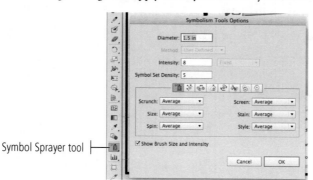

Symbol Sprayer tool

6. In the Symbolism Tools Options dialog box, change the Diameter field to 1.5″ and change the Symbol Set Density to 8. Click OK to apply the change.

Diameter determines the tool's current brush size. Symbol Set Density determines how tightly symbol instances are sprayed; higher values create more instances (spaced closely together) in the symbol set.

7. Click outside of the artboard to the left of the black ski path and drag down, following the ski path as a rough guide.

When you click and drag with the Symbol Sprayer tool, you create a **symbol set** — multiple instances of a single symbol that are treated as a single, cohesive unit.

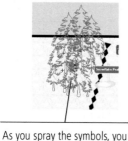

As you spray the symbols, you can see wireframe outlines of the shapes that will be added.

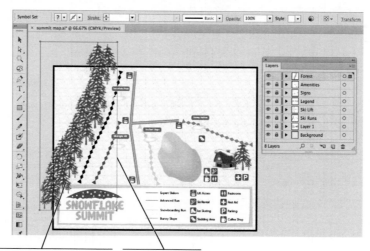

When you release the mouse button, the full-color symbol instances appear on the artboard.

This boundary shows the edge of the symbol set.

8. Without deselecting the symbol set, click again and drag to fill in the entire top-left corner of the artboard.

Each click of the tool adds more instances to the set, but can also affect the position of existing instances in the set. Don't worry if your trees cover other objects on the map, you will fix that problem shortly.

By leaving the set selected, the new instances are added to the existing set.

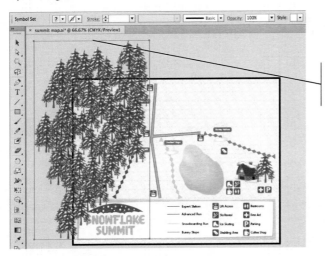

The set expands to include the new instances.

Note:

The slower you drag, the more instances will build up in a single place. We dragged at a moderate pace to place this first set of trees.

If you click and hold the mouse button without dragging, symbol instances pile on top of one another (just as spray paint builds up if you hold the can in one place).

Symbolism Tools Options

ILLUSTRATOR FOUNDATIONS

Double-clicking any of the symbolism tools in the Tools panel opens the Symbolism Tools Options dialog box.

Diameter reflects the tool's current brush size.

Intensity determines the rate of change for modifying instances.

Symbol Set Density creates more tightly packed (higher values) or loosely packed (lower values) instances in the symbol set.

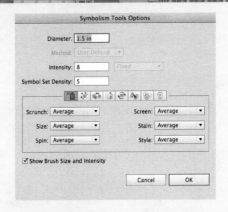

Method determines how the symbol modifier tools (all but the Symbol Sprayer and Symbol Shifter) adjust symbol instances:

- **Average** smoothes out values in symbol instances.
- **User Defined** adjusts instances in relation to the position of the cursor.
- **Random** modifies instances randomly under the cursor.

If the Symbol Sprayer tool is selected in the middle of the dialog box, you can control a variety of options related to how new symbol instances are added to symbol sets; each option has two possible choices:

- **Average** adds new symbols with the average value of existing symbol instances within the brush radius. For example, in an area where the average existing instance is rotated by 10°, new instances will be rotated by 10°.
- **User Defined** applies specific values for each parameter, primarily based on the original symbol size, mouse direction, and current color settings.

If the Symbol Sizer is selected, you have two additional options:

- **Proportional Resizing** maintains a uniform shape for each symbol instance as you resize.
- **Resizing Affects Density** moves symbol instances away from each other when they are scaled up, and moves symbol instances toward each other when they are scaled down.

If the **Show Brush Size and Intensity** option is checked, the cursor reflects the tool diameter.

When using sprayed symbols, many designs call for adjustments to individual components or instances within a symbol set. Without breaking the links between individual instances and the original symbol, you can use a number of tools to modify symbols within a set.

Symbol Sprayer tool — Symbol Styler tool
Symbol Shifter tool — Symbol Screener tool
Symbol Scruncher tool — Symbol Stainer tool
Symbol Sizer tool — Symbol Spinner tool

The **Symbol Shifter** tool pushes instances around the artboard. The tool only affects instances touched by the tool cursor.

The **Symbol Scruncher** tool causes the cursor to act as a magnet; all instances in the set are drawn toward the cursor when you click. Pressing Option/Alt reverses the effect, pushing instances away from the cursor.

The **Symbol Sizer** tool changes the size of instances within a set. Clicking causes instances under the cursor to grow. Option/Alt-clicking causes instances under the cursor to shrink.

The **Symbol Spinner** tool rotates instances under the cursor where you click. Dragging indicates the direction of the rotation.

The **Symbol Stainer** tool changes the hue of instances under the cursor using the defined fill color.

The **Symbol Screener** tool increases the opacity of instances under the cursor. Press Option/Alt to decrease instance opacity.

The **Symbol Styler** tool allows you to apply a graphic style to symbol instances.

9. **Press Command/Control to temporarily access the Selection tool and click away from the symbol set to deselect it.**

   If you don't deselect the active symbol set, clicking again adds more instances to the selected symbol set. In this case, you want to create a second symbol set, so you have to deselect the first set before clicking again with the Symbol Sprayer tool.

   Note:

   Pressing Command/ Control temporarily switches to the Selection tool; when you release the Command/Control key, the Symbol Sprayer tool is again active.

10. **Click the Symbol Sprayer tool above the horizontal ski lift path and drag to create the second forested area.**

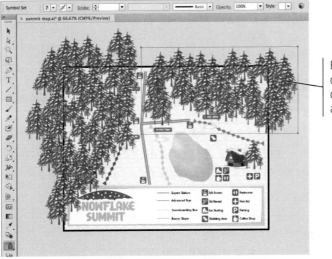

Because you deselected the first set of trees, this group is a separate symbol set.

Note:

Press Option/Alt and drag with the Symbol Sprayer tool to delete symbol instances from a symbol set.

11. **Select the Symbol Shifter tool (nested under the Symbol Sprayer tool).**

12. **Click and drag within the selected set to move all the trees away from the important objects on the map.**

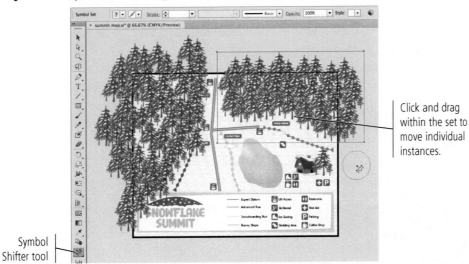

Click and drag within the set to move individual instances.

Symbol Shifter tool

13. **Press Command/Control to temporarily access the Selection tool and click the forest on the left side of the map to select that symbol set.**

14. **Use the Symbol Shifter tool to adjust the position of trees so that no objects on the map are obscured.**

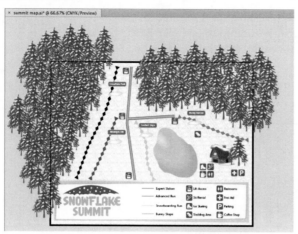

Note:

Although you can't use the Direct Selection tool to access individual instances within a set, you can use the Selection tool to move the entire set all at once.

15. **Save the file and continue to the next exercise.**

 CREATE A CLIPPING MASK

The final step of this project is to save the file so it can be used in other applications. Part of this process requires "finishing off" the edges so that no objects (such as trees) hang past the artwork edges. Rather than manually cutting your artwork, you can square off the design by creating a **clipping mask** to hide the elements you don't want to see.

In this exercise, you are going to perform a few small clean-up tasks, and then create a clipping mask to show only parts of the forest inside the artboard area.

1. **With summit map.ai open, make all layers unlocked and visible.**

2. **Rename Layer 1 as Lodge.**

Remember, it's always a good idea to use indicative names.

3. **Drag the Legend layer to the top of the layer stack.**

Rearranging the layer order makes more logical sense, and prevents the legend from being obscured by the forest.

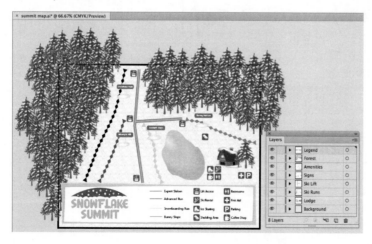

4. **Using the Selection tool, click to select the four lines in the legend. Drag the left-center bounding box handle until the width of the selection is 1.25".**

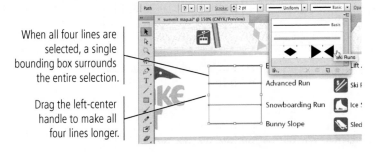

When all four lines are selected, a single bounding box surrounds the entire selection.

Drag the left-center handle to make all four lines longer.

5. **In the Control panel, apply the Ski Runs brush then change the stroke weight to 0.5 pt.**

Use this menu to apply a different brush stroke to the selected paths...

...then change the stroke weight to 0.5 pt to reduce the size of the applied brush strokes.

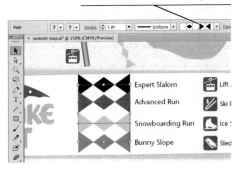
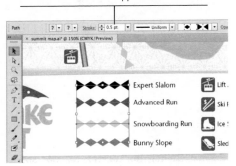

6. **In the Layers panel, click the Forest layer to select it, then press Command/Control and click the Background layer to add it to the selection.**

7. **Open the Layers panel Options menu and choose Collect in New Layer.**

8. **Rename the new layer Clipped Forest, then expand it in the panel.**

This option maintains the layered integrity of your finished artwork by collecting the individual layers into sublayers of the new one — allowing you to treat the finished layers as a single unit by selecting the containing layer.

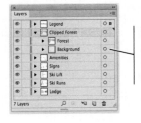

The Collect in New Layer command maintains the original layer names as sublayers in the new layer.

9. **Drag the Background sublayer above the Forest sublayer.**

10. **Click the Selected Art icon for the Clipped Forest layer to select all objects on that layer. Choose Object>Clipping Mask>Make.**

   A **clipping mask** is an object that masks other artwork; only those areas within the clipping mask shape remain visible. This option converts the topmost selected object into a clipping path; other underlying (selected) objects are clipped by the shape of the topmost object.

   Once an object is converted to a clipping mask, the defined fill and stroke attributes are removed. However, you can reapply fill or stroke attributes to any clipping mask shape, just as you would to any other object.

11. **Expand the Background sublayer in the layers panel, then expand the clipping group.**

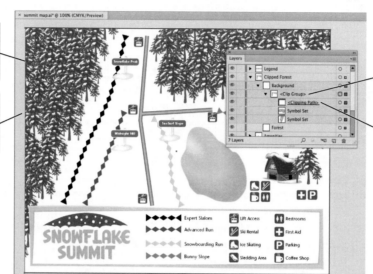

Converting an object to a clipping mask removes the defined stroke and fill values of the shape.

Areas of underlying objects outside of the mask object area are hidden but still present.

All selected objects are now part of a clipping group.

The topmost selected object is converted to a clipping path.

12. **Click the Selected Art icon for only the Clipping Path object.**

13. **Using the Control panel, change the object's fill to the Snowflakes pattern and change the stroke to 6-pt black.**

   The fill attributes of a clipping path object — in this case, the snowflakes pattern — are applied behind the clipped objects.

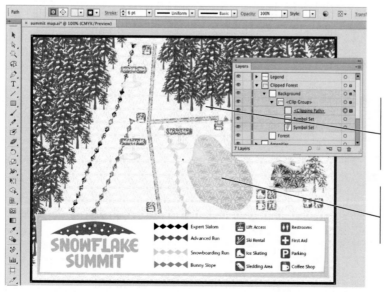

Fill attributes of the clipping path object are applied behind other objects in the clipping group.

Objects on other underlying layers are still obscured by the fill attributes.

Note:

To create a clipping mask, all the objects you want to clip should be part of the same layer as the masking object. If you create a clipping mask for objects on different layers, all affected objects are automatically copied to the layer that contains the mask object (called **flattening**).

Note:

Clipping masks do not permanently affect the artwork. You can remove the mask by selecting the mask shape and choosing Object>Clipping Mask>Release.

14. Drag the Clipped Forest layer to the bottom of the layer stack.

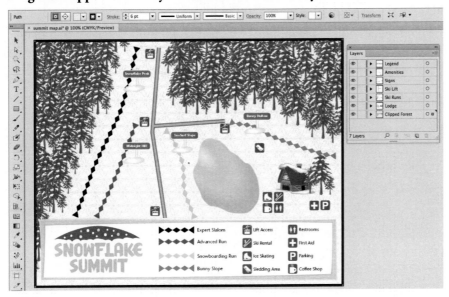

15. Save the file and close it.

1. The _____ panel provides access to colors, patterns, and gradients that have been saved in the active file.

2. _____ brushes scatter copies of an object along a path.

3. _____ brushes apply a brush stroke or object shape across the length of a path.

4. _____ brushes paint a pattern of defined tiles along the length of a path. You can define different tiles for straight edges, inner and outer corners, and the beginning and end of a path.

5. After choosing _____ in the Object menu, you can no longer access a path spine, but you can access the outlines of the resulting shapes.

6. The _____ is used to add multiple copies of a symbol with a single mouse click. When you release the mouse button, added symbol instances are contained within a group.

7. Use the _____ format to export an Illustrator swatch library for use in Photoshop.

8. After clicking the _____ button for a specific symbol instance, editing a symbol's content has no effect on that instance.

9. Double-clicking a symbol instance on the artboard, or double-clicking a symbol in the Symbols panel, enters into _____.

10. A(n) _____ is an object that masks other artwork; only those areas within the _____ shape remain visible.

1. Briefly explain the potential problem caused by using spot colors in gradients.

2. Briefly explain the differences between an art brush and a pattern brush.

3. Briefly explain two advantages of using symbols.

Use what you learned in this project to complete the following freeform exercise.
Carefully read the art director and client comments, then create your own design to meet the needs of the project.
Use the space below to sketch ideas; when finished, write a brief explanation of your reasoning behind your final design.

art director comments

The Los Angeles parks and recreation director has hired you to create an illustrated, user-friendly map of the Griffith Park recreation complex.

❏ Download the park map from the park Web site (http://www.laparks.org/dos/parks/griffithpk/gp_location.htm).

❏ Use drawing techniques to create the basic park layout, including roads, trails, and defined paths.

❏ Create or find symbols to identify the different facilities and services.

❏ Add artwork, images, and color however you prefer to identify the different venues and attractions throughout the park.

client comments

Griffith Park is one of the largest public green spaces in the western United States. The park is home to a number of famous attractions, including the Griffith Observatory, Greek Theater, and the L.A. Zoo. It also offers equestrian trails, bike and hiking trails, and golf courses, as well as swimming, camping, concerts, and a host of other activities.

As you can guess from all of these available activities and attractions, the park is a very large place. We currently have a detailed topographic map from our master plan document, but I'd like something that is more attractive to tourists. I want to create an appealing, colorful, printed brochure that visitors can purchase for a nominal fee at park entrances and facilities, so they can easily find what they're looking for.

project justification

_____

_____

_____

_____

_____

_____

_____

_____

_____

_____

_____

_____

As you completed this map project, you learned a wide range of important new skills — including managing many types of assets (swatches, patterns, and brushes), accessing built-in and custom libraries, and creating your own custom assets. You can apply these skills at any stage of an Illustrator project, saving significant amounts of time and effort.

Some of the planning work for this project was completed by the art director — including creating the icons for different elements of the artwork — and approved by the client in an earlier project meeting. Rather than taking the time to recreate those elements, you streamlined the design process by accessing that artwork as symbols that can be easily updated as necessary.

Add texture to artwork with a custom pattern

Create a custom art brush

Create a custom pattern brush

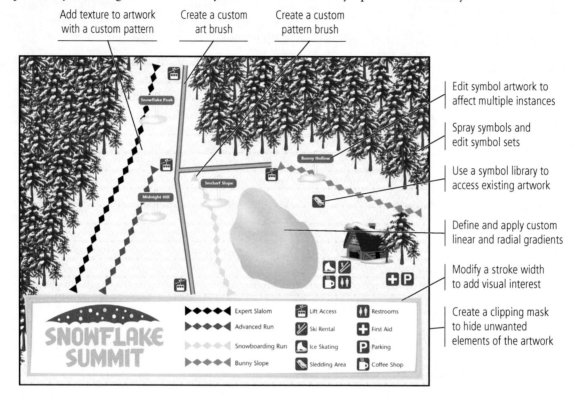

Edit symbol artwork to affect multiple instances

Spray symbols and edit symbol sets

Use a symbol library to access existing artwork

Define and apply custom linear and radial gradients

Modify a stroke width to add visual interest

Create a clipping mask to hide unwanted elements of the artwork

Letterfold Brochure

Your client is a non-profit artists' cooperative in San Francisco that coordinates and hosts special events throughout the year. This year they are launching a new "Arts & Architecture" program, which will be a month-long series of special events all over the city to promote the city's artistic community. You have been hired to create the first brochure to begin advertising the new program.

This project incorporates the following skills:

❏ Creating a template for a letterfold brochure that meets folding production requirements

❏ Placing and managing links to external graphics and images

❏ Importing client-supplied text and controlling the flow of text across multiple frames

❏ Working with styles to automate repetitive text-formatting tasks

❏ Correcting typographic problems such as widows

❏ Formatting tabbed text for better readability

❏ Checking for and correcting spelling errors within the context of a specific layout

❏ Exporting PDF files of specific artboards for print

I really don't have that much input on what the flyer should look like — I am relying on your expert opinion to produce an effective, functional brochure. I have the text, two logos, and several images that I want to include; you can modify those pictures as necessary to better fit the overall project.

A lot of people design folding documents incorrectly. Some people use a six-page layout with each page the size of the final folded job; other people use two pages, each one divided into three equal "columns." In both cases, all panels on the job are the same width — which is wrong.

Paper has inherent thickness; any panel that folds "in" to the other panels needs to be smaller than the other panels. In the case of a folding brochure, the inside panel needs to be 1/16″ smaller than the other panels.

Different types of folding documents also have different facing- or non-facing-page requirements. For a letterfold, the job needs to be set up on two separate "pages" with guides and margins that mirror each other. One page has the front panel, back panel, and the outside of the folding flap; the other page has the three inside panels.

The last item to remember is that the brochure will be a self-mailer; the back panel needs to be left blank, with only the return address in the upper-left corner.

To complete this project, you will:

- ❑ Define folding guides and margins as required for a folding document
- ❑ Create an Illustrator template file so you can access a common layout again later
- ❑ Place images based on the panel position in the final folded piece
- ❑ Import and format client-supplied copy
- ❑ Manage the flow of copy across multiple text frames
- ❑ Define paragraph and character styles to simplify formatting across multiple text elements
- ❑ Control hyphenation and line spacing
- ❑ Format tabs to improve readability
- ❑ Check spelling in a layout
- ❑ Save artboards as PDF files for commercial print output

Stage 1 Creating Documents that Fold

When you design entire pages, you need to be aware of several important measurements. **Trim size** is the size of the flat page (for example, a letter-size piece of paper has a trim size of 8.5 × 11″). When pages are printed on a commercial output device, they are typically combined with other pages (possibly multiple copies of the same page) on a large press sheet. After the ink is dry, the individual pages are cut or trimmed from the press sheets to end up with the final job.

Because commercial printing is a mechanical process, there is inherent variation in the output from one page to another and in the accuracy of any given device (including the cutters that cut apart pages). **Bleed allowance** is the distance objects should extend beyond the trim. Using a bleed ensures that no unwanted white space appears around the edges of the final trimmed output (if there is variation in the cutting process). Most printers require at least a 1/8″ bleed allowance, but you should always check with the output provider who is producing a specific job.

Live area is the space within the trim area where it is safe to place important content. Live area is essentially the opposite of bleed allowance; content within the live area remains untouched during the trimming process.

Folding Document Considerations

There are several common types of folds:

 Letterfolds have two folds and three panels to a side. (These are often incorrectly called "trifold" because they result in three panels.) The panel that folds in should be 1/16″ to 1/8″ narrower than the two outside panels; ask your service provider how much allowance is required for the paper you're using.

 Accordion folds can have as many panels as you prefer. When it has six panels (three on each side), it's often referred to as a **Z-fold** because it looks like the letter Z. Because the panels don't fold into one another, an accordion-fold document has panels of consistent width.

 Double-parallel folds are commonly used for eight-panel rack brochures (such as those often found in a hotel or travel agency). Again, the panels on the inside are narrower than the outside panels. This type of fold uses facing pages because the margins need to line up on the front and back sides of the sheet.

 Barrel folds (also called **roll folds**) are perhaps the most common fold for 14 × 8.5″ brochures. The two outside panels are full size, and each successive panel is narrower than the previous one. You can theoretically have as many panels as you want, but at some point the number of fold-in panels will become unwieldy.

 Gate folds result in a four-panel document; the paper is folded in half, and then each half is folded in half toward the center so the two ends of the paper meet at the center fold. The panels that fold in are narrower than the two outside panels. This type of brochure allows two different spreads: the first revealed when you open the outer panels, and the second revealed when you open the inner flaps.

Note:

Some service providers give their clients folding templates to use for building a layout. You should ask your service provider if these templates are available before you waste time and effort reinventing the wheel.

It's very important to consider the output process when planning a job with documents that are not just a single flat sheet of standard-size paper — documents with multiple pages folded one or more times, or other non-standard page sizes. The mechanics of commercial printing require specific allowances for cutting, folding, and other finishing processes.

There are two basic principles to remember when designing documents that fold. First, folding machines are mechanical devices; paper sometimes shifts as it moves through the machine (most are accurate to about 0.0125"). Second, paper has thickness; thicker paper requires more allowance for the fold. Because of these two principles, any panel that folds into the other panels needs to be smaller than the other panels.

It is also important to realize that the front and back (or "inside" and "outside") of a folding document might require different layouts. If your job requires different-size panels, the position of panels on the front needs to mirror the position of those same panels on the back.

You should note that these issues have little to do with the subjective elements of design. Layout and page geometry are governed by specific variables, including mechanical limitations in the production process. These principles are rules, not suggestions.

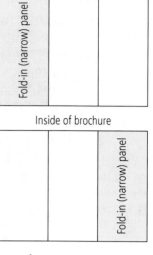

Outside of brochure

Fold-in (narrow) panel

Inside of brochure

Fold-in (narrow) panel

Calculating Panel Size

When working with folding documents, the trim size of a folded document is actually the size of the flat sheet *before* it's folded. If you know the flat trim size of a job, you have to calculate the size of individual panels before you set up the layout.

For example, if you're printing a letterfold brochure on a laser printer that can only print to letter-sized paper, the flat trim size, then, is 11" wide by 8.5" high. The first required calculation is the base size of each panel:

$11" \div 3 = 3.6667"$

But remember, the fold-in panel has to be narrower than the other two panels; you also have to factor the required folding variance into the panel size. Half of the difference is removed from the fold-in panel, and one-fourth of the original variance requirement is added to each outer panel. Assuming a folding variance of 1/8":

Fold-in panel = $3.6667 - 1/16 = 3.6042"$

Outer panel 1 = $3.6667 + 1/32 = 3.698"$

Outer panel 2 = $3.6667 + 1/32 = 3.698"$

You can safely round these values to 3.6" and 3.7", resulting in a panel variance of 0.1", which is enough for most papers that can be run through a desktop laser printer. This seems like a complicated series of calculations, and it is only relevant when printing to a defined flat trim size.

An equally important measurement for folding brochures — and perhaps a more common known factor — is the folded size, or the size of the actual finished product. For example, a rack card or brochure is commonly 4 × 9", which fits into standard display racks (hence the name). If you know the final target size, it is easy to calculate the size of individual panels in the folding document. Using the 4 × 9" rack card with a required 1/8" panel variance as an example:

Outer Panel 1 = 4"

Outer Panel 2 = 4"

Fold-in Panel = $4" - 0.125" = 3.875"$

USE ARTBOARDS TO CREATE THE PANEL LAYOUT STRUCTURE

On the outside of a letterfold brochure, the left panel is the fold-in panel; it is slightly narrower than the other two panels. On the inside of the brochure, the right panel is the fold-in panel. Because the panels for a letterfold brochure are different sizes, the inside of the brochure must be a reflection of the outside. In this exercise, you create a single Illustrator file with multiple artboards to manage both sides of the brochure.

1. **Download A16_RF_Project5.zip from the Student Files Web page.**

2. **Expand the ZIP archive in your WIP folder (Macintosh) or copy the archive contents into your WIP folder (Windows).**

   This results in a folder named **Culture**, which contains the files you need for this project. You should also use this folder to save the files you create in this project.

3. **Open the New Document dialog box and type Rack 4x9 in the Name field.**

4. **Type 6 in the Number of Artboards field.**

   The brochure has 6 panels, and you are going to create each panel as a separate artboard.

5. **Choose the Grid by Row option, change the Spacing field to 0″, and change the Columns field to 3.**

   The arrangement options determine how the multiple artboards appear in the new document. The Grid options place multiple artboards left-to-right, top-to-bottom, based on the defined number of rows. The Arrange options place all artboards in a single row or column.

   By default, the top-left artboard is Artboard 1, and then Artboard 2, and so on. If you select the Change to Right-to-Left Layout option, Artboard 1 automatically appears as the top-right artboard, then Artboard 2, and so on.

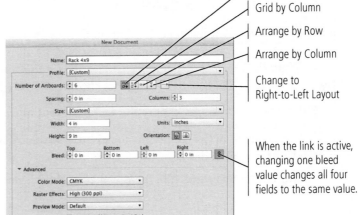

Grid by Row

Grid by Column

Arrange by Row

Arrange by Column

Change to Right-to-Left Layout

When the link is active, changing one bleed value changes all four fields to the same value.

6. **Set the Units to Inches (if necessary), then change the Width to 4″ and the Height to 9″.**

   This is the defined flat size of the folded brochure. Once the file is created, you will use the Artboard tool to change the size of the fold-in panels to meet print requirements.

7. **Change all four bleed fields to 0.**

   With the chain icon active, the bleed fields are constrained; in other words, changing one bleed value changes all four bleed values to the same measurement.

   Although you need bleed allowance for each side of the brochure as a whole, you do not need bleeds for each panel. You will use a different method to create bleed guides later in this stage of the project.

8. **In the Advanced area, choose the CMYK color mode and set the Raster Effects menu to High (300 ppi).**

9. **Click OK to create the file.**

10. **Open the Artboards panel (Window>Artboards).**

Each artboard in the file is listed in the panel, numbered according to its position in the file — left-to-right across the first row and then the second row, as you defined in the New Document dialog box when you created the file.

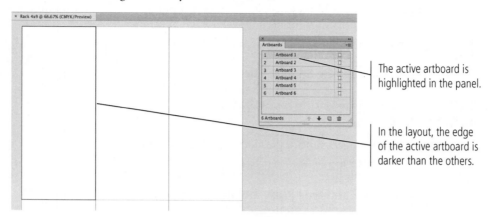

The active artboard is highlighted in the panel.

In the layout, the edge of the active artboard is darker than the others.

11. **Save the file as Rack 4x9.ai in your WIP>Culture folder, and then continue to the next exercise.**

CONTROL ARTBOARD SIZE AND POSITION

As you know, you need one panel on each side of this brochure to be narrower than the other panels. When you create a file, all artboards adopt the size that you define in the New Document dialog box. You can use the Artboard tool and panel to control the size and position of individual artboards within the file.

1. **With Rack 4x9.ai open, choose the Artboard tool in the Tools panel.**

2. **With Artboard 1 active, highlight the existing artboard name in the Control panel and type Outside Fold In.**

Meaningful artboard names are far more useful than the default numbered names.

Note:

Artboard labels only appear in the document window when the Artboard tool is active.

Type the new artboard name in this field.

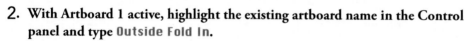

The Control panel shows settings for the active artboard.

Bounding box handles surround the active artboard.

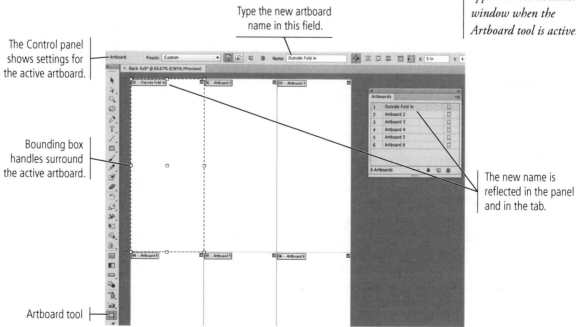

The new name is reflected in the panel and in the tab.

Artboard tool

3. **Choose the right-center registration point in the Control panel.**

4. **Make sure the W and H fields are not linked. Click after the existing W (width) value and type -.125, then press Return/Enter.**

If your Control panel does not show the W and H fields, click the Artboard Options button in the Control panel and use the Artboard Options dialog box to change the artboard width.

Because you know the fold-in panel needs to be 1/8″ smaller than the other panels, it is easy to simply subtract that amount from the original artboard width. By selecting one of the right registration points, you make sure the two panels remain aligned with no space in between the left and center panels.

Unfortunately, Illustrator only shows two decimal places in the size of an artboard. After you subtract 0.125″ from the existing 4″ width, the software rounds the new artboard width to 3.88″ (as you see in the Control or Transform panel). However, the software does store the accurate measurement of 3.875″, as you will see when you create shapes that snap to the artboard edges later in this project.

This is a significant flaw in the software, which you should be aware of in case you need to create an artboard with a specific measurement of more than two decimal places.

Note:

Illustrator recognizes standard mathematical operators in most panel and dialog box fields.

- *Use + to add*
- *Use – to subtract*
- *Use / to divide*
- *Use * to multiply*

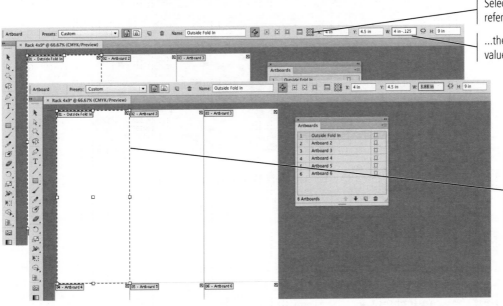

Select the right-center reference point...

...then type after the existing value and press Return/Enter.

The artboard is narrower; the right edge does not move because you selected the right-center reference point as the anchor.

5. **In the Artboards panel, click Artboard 2 to make it active. Use the Control panel to change the artboard name to Outside Center - Mailer.**

As we stated, meaningful names are more useful than generic ones. This name reminds you that this panel needs to contain self-mailer information.

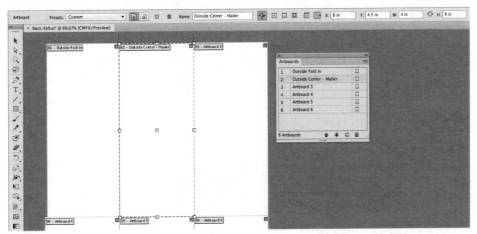

6. **Repeat Step 5 to name the remaining artboards as follows:**

   Artboard 3   Outside Right – Front

   Artboard 4   Inside Left

   Artboard 5   Inside Center

   Artboard 6   Inside Fold In

Note:

As with layers, you can double-click the artboard name in the panel to rename an artboard.

7. **With the Inside Fold In artboard active, select one of the left reference points in the Control panel, and then subtract 0.125″ from the current width.**

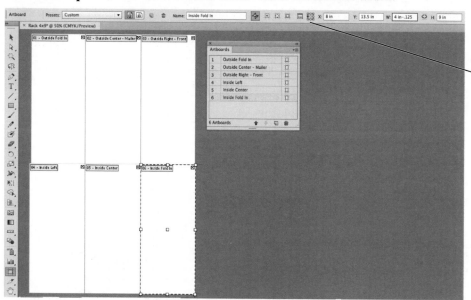

Anchor the left edge of the Inside Fold In artboard before changing its width.

8. **With the Artboard tool active, click the Inside Left artboard in the layout to select it.**

   You don't need to use the Artboards panel to select a particular artboard. Simpy click inside the artboard you want to select.

9. **Click inside the selected artboard area and drag down until the Smart Guides show the left edge aligning to the left edge of the Outside Fold In artboard, with about an inch of space between the two rows.**

   Make sure you click inside the artboard area to move the artboard. If you click too close to the artboard edges, you might accidentally resize the artboard instead.

Use the Smart Guides to align the left edges of the Inside Left artboard and the Outside Fold In artboard.

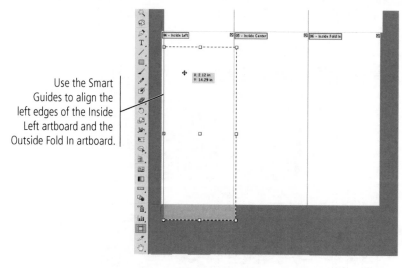

10. **Click the Inside Center artboard and drag until it snaps to the top and right edges of the Inside Left artboard.**

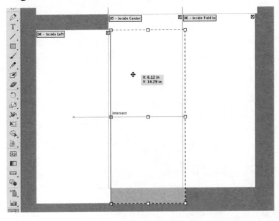

11. **Repeat Step 10 for the Inside Fold In artboard.**

    If you select each artboard in turn, the Y value (in the Control panel) should be the same for each artboard.

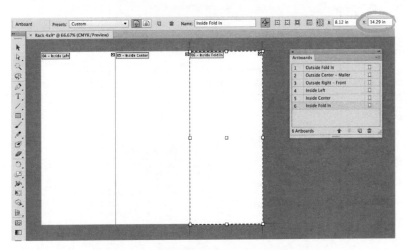

12. **Move the Artboard tool cursor until cursor feedback shows an intersection with the top-left corner of the Outside Fold In artboard.**

13. **Click and drag until cursor feedback shows you are intersecting with the bottom-right corner of the Outside Right - Front artboard.**

    You can always create new artboards by clicking and dragging with the Artboard tool.

Use the cursor feedback to find the top-left corner of the existing artboard.

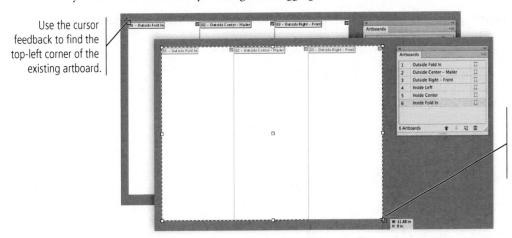

Click and drag to create a new artboard that is the combined size of the three existing artboards.

14. **In the Control panel, change the new artboard name to** `Outside`.

The new artboard is automatically added at the bottom of the list of artboards, numbered according to its top-to-bottom position.

The Control panel shows the artboard's dimensions as 11.88″ wide by 9″ high, which is the same as the height and width of the three panel artboards (4 + 4 + 3.88).

Note:

Remember: The software only shows two decimal places for the artboard dimensions. This Outside artboard is actually 11.875″ wide.

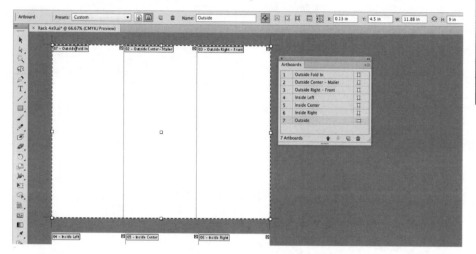

15. **Repeat Steps 12–14 for the lower three artboards, and name the new artboard** `Inside`.

When the layout work is complete, you will use these two composite artboards to output each side of the brochure as a single PDF file.

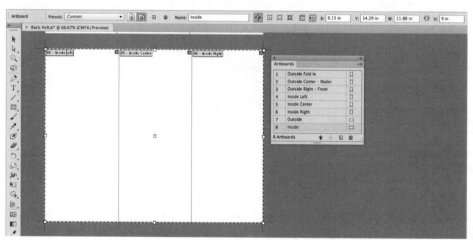

16. **In the Artboards panel, Shift-click to select Artboards 7 and 8 (Outside and Inside).**

17. **Click either selected artboard and drag to the top of the panel.**

You can rearrange the order of artboards by simply dragging in the panel, or selecting a single artboard in the panel and using the Move Up and Move Down buttons at the bottom of the panel.

Moving the artboards up changes the numbers associated with each artboard in the file.

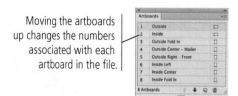

18. **Save the file and continue to the next exercise.**

CREATE MARGIN AND BLEED GUIDES

A few more elements are required in your folding layout to make the actual implementation easier. First, you need to define the bleed area for each side of the brochure (not for each panel); unfortunately, you can't define different bleed settings for individual artboards, so you have to define this area manually. Second, you need to define margin guides for each panel because Illustrator does not include an automatic margin guide option.

1. **With Rack 4x9.ai open and the Outside artboard active, choose the Rectangle tool in the Tools panel and click the Default Fill and Stroke button.**

2. **If rulers are not already visible, choose View>Rulers>Show Rulers (Command/Control-R).**

3. **Using the Smart Guides to snap to the existing artboard edges, create a rectangle that exactly matches the size of the Outside artboard.**

   Remember, the Outside artboard width is the sum of the three individual panel widths: 4 + 4 + 3.875 = 11.875. This should be the width of the rectangle you create.

   As you drag the rectangle, the cursor feedback shows the two-digit decimal places of 11.88″. Remember, this is a flaw in the software — the same flaw that rounded the artboard width to two decimal places. However, when you release the mouse button, the Transform panel shows the accurate three-digit decimal measurement of 11.875″.

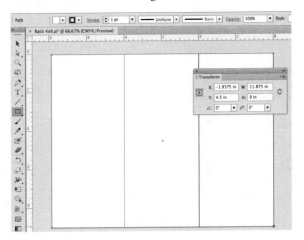

4. **Using the Control or Transform panel, choose the center reference point.**

5. **Break the link between the W and H fields. After the existing W value, type +.25 and then press Return/Enter to apply the change.**

If this icon shows the links together, click it to break the link.

Type after the existing value.

Again, mathematical operators make it easy to add the required 0.125″ bleed to the rectangle. Because you anchored the rectangle at the center reference point, half of the 0.25″ is added to each side of the shape.

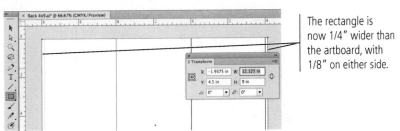

The rectangle is now 1/4″ wider than the artboard, with 1/8″ on either side.

> **Note:**
>
> *Remember, if you have a small monitor or Application frame, the X and Y fields in the Control panel might be condensed into a "Transform" hot-text link that opens the Transform panel, where you can define the guide positions.*

6. **Repeat Step 5 to add 0.25″ to the rectangle height, half on each side.**

You don't need to reselect the reference point because it retains the last-used option.

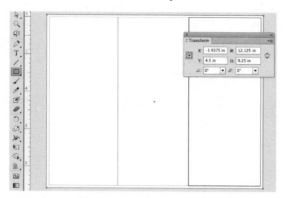

7. **With the resized rectangle selected, choose View>Guides>Make Guides.**

You can use this command to turn any regular object into a nonprinting guide.

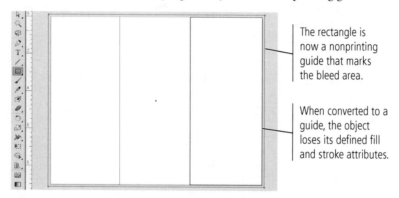

The rectangle is now a nonprinting guide that marks the bleed area.

When converted to a guide, the object loses its defined fill and stroke attributes.

8. **Command/Control-click away from the selected rectangle to deselect it, then release the Command/Control key to return to the Rectangle tool.**

9. **Repeat Steps 3–8 to add a bleed guide around the Inside artboard.**

10. **Using the Artboards panel, make the Outside Fold In artboard active.**

11. **Create a rectangle that aligns with the edges of the active artboard.**

Remember, this is the fold-in panel; its width is 3.875″. The rectangle should exactly match the existing panel width.

12. **With the center reference point active in the Transform or Control panel, use mathematical operators to subtract 0.5″ from the height and width of the rectangle, then convert it to a guide.**

This rectangle defines 0.25″ margins on each side of the panel.

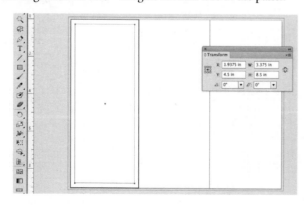

Note:

Press Command/Control-5 to create a guide from any selected object. Add the Shift key to release all guides that have been created from objects.

Note:

Choose View>Guides>Release Guides to convert a guide object into a regular object; the object's original fill and stroke (before you converted it to a guide) are restored. This is an all-or-nothing action. You can't release a single custom guide; you have to release all of them at once.

Note:

View>Guides>Clear Guides removes all guides from the page. If you want to remove only a single guide, you can select it (as long as it's unlocked) and press Delete.

13. **Repeat Steps 10–12 to add 0.25″ margin guides to all panels in the layout.**

The margin-guide rectangles on the full-size panels should be 3.5″ wide by 8.5″ high. On the fold-in panels, the margin-guide rectangles should be 3.375″ wide by 8.5″ high.

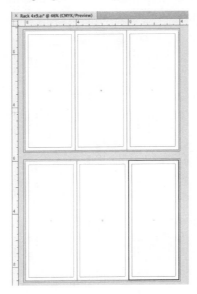

14. **Choose View>Guides, and make sure Lock Guides is checked (active).**

15. **Save the file and continue to the next exercise.**

CREATE FOLDING MARKS

The final step in establishing your folding grid is marking the location of folds. Once you have done so, you should then save your work as a template because this is a common project size and you can reuse the template whenever you need to build a new folding rack brochure.

1. **With Rack 4x9.ai open, choose the Line Segment tool in the Tools panel.**

2. **Control/right-click either ruler. If the bottom option reads "Change to Artboard Rulers" choose that option.**

If you use Global rulers, all measurements relate to the first artboard in the file; using Artboard rulers, all measurements relate to the currently active artboard.

Note:

You can also change from Global to Artboard rulers (and vice versa) in the View>Rulers submenu.

3. **Create a vertical line that is 0.5″ high, anywhere in the pasteboard area above the Outside artboard.**

Use Smart Guides to create the line exactly vertical, or simply press Shift while you drag up or down with the Line Segment tool. (It doesn't matter exactly where you create the line, because you will place it numerically in the next few steps.)

4. **In the Artboards panel, make sure the Outside artboard is active.**

When Artboard rulers are active, the current zero point appears at the top-left corner of the active artboard.

5. **Using the Transform or Control panel, select the top-center reference point. Change the line's X position to 3.875" and Y position to –0.5".**

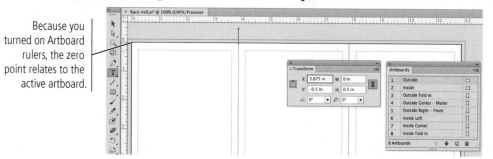

Because you turned on Artboard rulers, the zero point relates to the active artboard.

Note:

The line should appear to blend in with the black line that marks the artboard edges.

6. **In the Artboards panel, click the Ouside Center - Mailer artboard.**

In the Transform and Control panel, you can see that the line's X position is now 0 — because it is exactly aligned with the left edge of the active artboard.

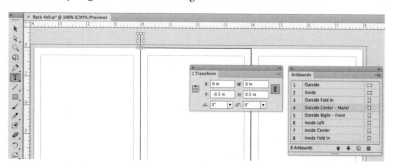

7. **With the line still selected, open the Stroke panel. If you only see the Weight field, open the panel Options menu and choose Show Options.**

8. **In the middle of the Stroke panel, check the Dashed Line option. Type 3 in the first Dash field, press Tab, and type 3 in the first Gap field.**

The dash and gap fields define the specific appearance of dashed lines.

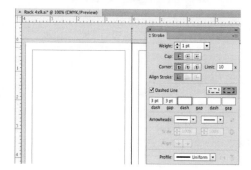

9. **Double-click the Selection tool to open the Move dialog box.**

This opens the Move dialog box, which is an easy way to move or clone the selected object(s) by exact measurements.

10. **Change the Horizontal field to 4, the Vertical field to 0, and click Copy.**

You know the center panel is 4″ wide, so copying the line 4″ to the right places the copy exactly over the panel edge.

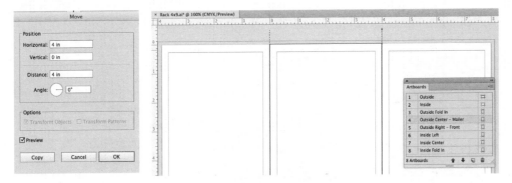

11. **Select both lines above the outside spread, then double-click the Selection tool. Change the Position Horizontal field to 0, the Vertical field to 9.5, and click Copy.**

You are moving the copy by 9.5″ because the marks are 0.5″ and the panels are 9″ high; the total movement places the copied lines immediately below the bottom of the Outside artboard.

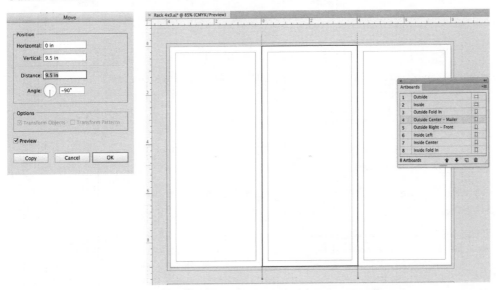

12. **Choose Select>All to select all four folding marks. Press Option/Alt, then click and drag any of the selected marks to clone all four in the same position relative to one another.**

Although the fold marks will occupy a different overall position on the Inside artboard, the center panels are the same width so the relative position of the marks is the same on both "pages" of the brochure. Rather than recreating the marks, you are cloning the existing ones — which you will precisely place in the next few steps.

13. **In the Artboards panel, activate the Inside Center artboard.**

Because you are using Artboard rulers, measurements for the selected objects are now relative to the Inside Center artboard.

14. **Choose the top-left reference point, then change the selection's position to X: 0″, Y: –0.5″.**

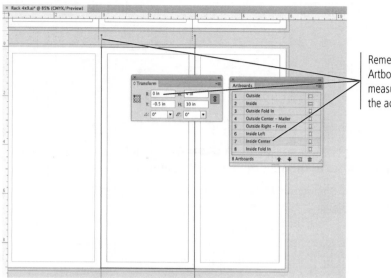

Remember, when Artboard rulers are active, measurements relate to the active artboard.

15. **In the Layers panel, rename the layer Guides and Marks and then lock the layer.**

16. **Choose File>Save As Template. With your WIP>Culture folder selected as the target, click Save.**

Since you have taken the time to properly set up these folding guides, you are saving your work as a template so you can access these same folds whenever you need them.

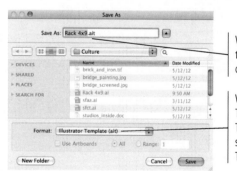

When you save a template, the extension automatically changes to ".ait".

When you use the Save As Template command, Illustrator Template (ait) is automatically selected in the Format/Save As Type menu.

Note:

If you choose the Save As Template option, the resulting dialog box defaults to the application's Templates folder.

17. **Close the file and continue to the next stage of the project.**

Stage 2 Working with Imported Images

Most page-layout jobs incorporate a number of different elements, including images and graphics that exist in external files. Although Illustrator does not include the sophisticated link-management options of a dedicated layout application such as Adobe InDesign, you can place and work with a variety of common image formats. The key to creating a successful job is understanding a job's output requirements so that you use only the types of graphics that are suitable for the project you are building.

PLACE LAYOUT IMAGES

Both sides of the brochure require images that were already created — some in Illustrator and some in Photoshop. When you place external images into a file, you need to understand the concept of file linking so you can create a complete file with all of the information necessary for high-quality, commercial print output.

1. **Choose File>Open. Navigate to Rack 4x9.ait in your WIP>Culture folder and click Open.**

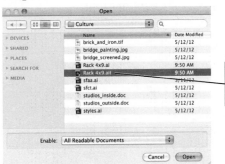

Make sure you choose the template file and not the regular Illustrator file.

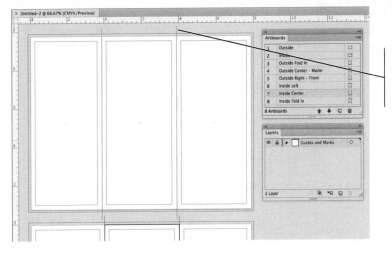#

When you open a template file, you are actually opening a copy of the template with the name "Untitled." This prevents you from accidentally overwriting the original template.

The file created from the template includes all elements in the template.

2. **Add a new layer named Graphics above the existing Guides and Marks layer.**

3. **With the Graphics layer selected, choose File>Place.**

Note:

You could also use the File>New From Template menu command. However, that option defaults to the application's built-in Templates folder (wherever the application is installed).

Note:

You can overwrite a template by manually typing the same file name as the original template when you save the file. You will be asked to confirm that you're sure you want to replace the existing file.

4. Select **bridge_painting.jpg** in the WIP>Culture folder, check the Link option, and click Place.

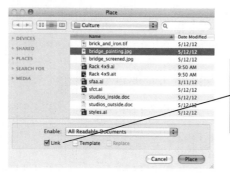

When this box is checked, the placed file will be a link to the actual file; its contents will not be embedded into your document.

5. **Drag the placed image so it fills the Outside Right - Front artboard (including the bleed area that is defined by the custom guide you created).**

The bridge_painting.jpg file is a raster image, which means it has a defined resolution. When you resize a raster image, the number of pixels per inch is stretched or reduced to fit into the new object dimensions. The result of factoring physical size into an image's resolution is called **effective resolution**.

Note:

Placed images are automatically placed in the center of the document window.

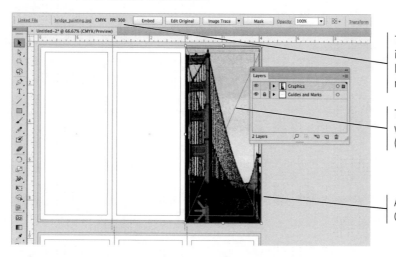

The Control panel shows important information about the linked file, including its name, resolution, and color mode.

The linked file is identified with crossed diagonal (nonprinting) lines.

Align the image to the Outside Right - Front artboard.

6. **Choose File>Place. Select **bridge_screened.jpg** and click Place.**

The Link option remembers the last-used value, so you can simply leave it checked throughout this exercise.

The Link option retains the last-used value, so it is already checked.

7. **Drag the placed image to align with the bleed guides of the Inside artboard.**

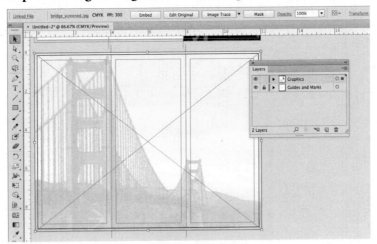

8. **Place the file brick_and_iron.tif into the layout as a linked image, aligned to the bottom-left bleed guides of the Outside artboard.**

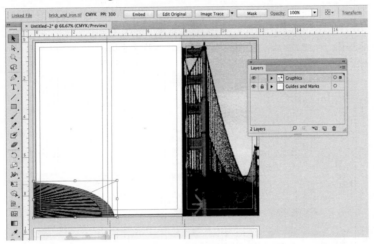

9. **Place the file sfaa.ai into the file as a linked image. In the resulting Place PDF dialog box, choose Art in the Crop To menu and click OK. Align the placed image to the top-left margin guides of the Outside Fold In panel.**

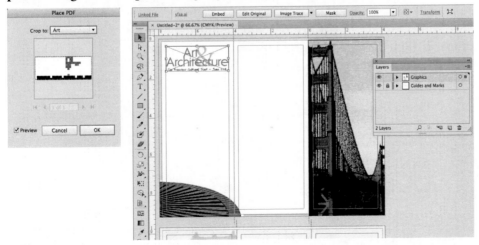

10. **Press Option/Alt, then click and drag the placed logo file to clone it twice.**

11. **Rotate one of the clones 90° counterclockwise, then align it to the top-right margin guide of the Outside Right - Front artboard. Using the Control or Transform panel, anchor the top-right reference point and then scale the image proportionally to 4.95″ high.**

Because the image is rotated, you have to modify the object's height to make it wider.

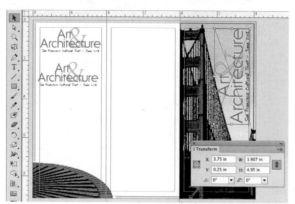

Note:

Remember from Project 1: International Symbols, you can double-click the Rotate tool to access the Rotate dialog box, where you can define a specific rotation for the selected object. As an alternative, you can type the rotation angle in the Rotate field of the Transform panel.

12. **Using the Selection tool, move the other clone from Step 10 to align to the bottom-right margin guide of the Inside Fold In artboard. Press Shift, then click and drag the top-left handle to scale the image to fill the margins of the center and right artboards (as shown here).**

13. **Place the file sfct.ai using the Crop To Art option, then immediately clone the placed image.**

14. **Scale one of the logo copies proportionally to 4.65″ wide, and move it to the Inside Left artboard. Align the logo to the bottom margin guide, and visually align the word "ARTS" to be centered over the left bridge support.**

15. **Rotate the original SFCT logo 90° counterclockwise, and align it to the bottom-left margin guides on the Outside Center - Mailer artboard.**

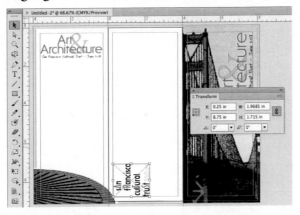

16. **Save the file as a native Illustrator file named culture.ai in your WIP>Culture folder, and then continue to the next exercise.**

 ## MANAGE LINKED AND EMBEDDED FILES

As you have seen, you have the option to either place a link to an external file or embed the external file data directly in your Illustrator file. There are advantages and disadvantages to each method, so you should consider what you need to accomplish before you choose.

When you link to an external file, the external file needs to be available when the Illustrator file is output. If the file is moved or changed in any way after being linked to the Illustrator file, you have to update the linked file before output.

If you embed the external file into the Illustrator file, the physical file data becomes part of the file. This eliminates the potential problem of missing required files, but it can add significantly to the size of your Illustrator file.

1. **With culture.ai open, open the Links panel (Window>Links).**

Every file that has been placed with the Link option is listed in this panel.

2. **Select the first instance of sfct.ai and click the Go To Link button at the bottom of the panel.**

When you click the Go To Link button, the placed file is selected in the layout and centered in the current workspace.

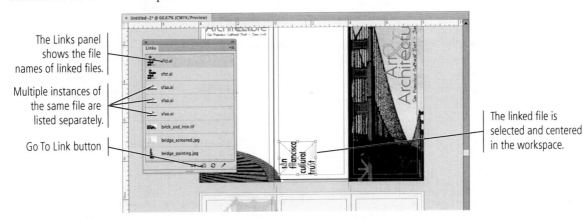

The Links panel shows the file names of linked files.

Multiple instances of the same file are listed separately.

Go To Link button

The linked file is selected and centered in the workspace.

3. **If the selected object is not on the Inside Left artboard, select the second instance of sfct.ai in the Link panel and click the Go To Link button.**

The order of objects in the Links panel depends on which version you moved after cloning the placed file. In our example, the instance on the Inside Left artboard is listed second in the Links panel.

4. **In the Control panel, click the Embed button.**

When you place and embed one Illustrator file into another, it is placed as a group of the objects that make up the placed file. When you embed a previously linked Illustrator file, it is converted to a group of artwork objects, just as if you had placed it without linking.

The selected object is now a group of native artwork objects.

After being embedded, one instance of the Illustrator file is no longer listed in the Links panel.

5. **Using the Selection tool, double-click the group to enter into Isolation mode for the group.**

6. **Using the Direct Selection tool, draw a selection marquee around only the address information.**

Note:

Once you embed an image, you can't un-emded it without re-placing the original image.

You are working in Isolation mode for the group.

Draw a marquee with the Direct Selection tool to select the address information.

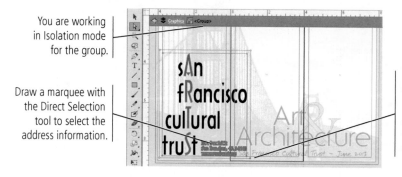

Depending on how you draw the selection, the marquee will select the bottom-right corner of at least one — and probably two — clipping path objects that are part of the placed file.

7. **Press Delete to remove the selected objects.**

When you place a native Illustrator file, the application automatically creates one or more clipping paths around the placed group. Because your selection included the bottom-right corner of the clipping path shapes, you have also deleted that point.

The clipping paths that are created in this type of workflow are almost always unnecessary, but you should be aware of their existence.

Pressing Delete/Backspace removes only the selected point of the clipping path, obscuring the part of the group that is outside the new object shape.

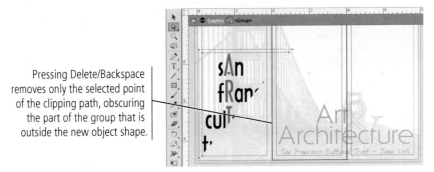

8. **Press Delete to remove the remaining portion of the clipping path objects.**

After you deleted the selected point in Step 6, the remaining points of the clipping-path shape are automatically selected. Pressing Delete in this step removes those points.

9. **In the Edit bar (at the top of the document window), click the arrow button two times to exit Isolation mode.**

10. **Click the SFAA logo on the right side of the layout to select it.**

When you select a placed file in the layout, it is automatically selected in the Links panel.

Note:

You can also double click away from the artwork to exit Isolation mode.

11. **Click the Embed button in the Control panel.**

12. **Repeat Steps 5–9 to enter into the new group and remove the tagline from below the logo. When finished, drag the revised logo down to the bottom margin guide.**

13. Embed the remaining placed Illustrator files into the layout.

Your file now includes two linked JPEG files and one linked TIFF file. All placed Illustrator files have been embedded, so they are now groups on the Graphics layer (which you can confirm if you expand that layer in the panel).

At the end of this project, you are going to export a PDF file that can be output by the commercial printer. PDF consolidates all the necessary pieces — including linked images — into a single piece.

Any archive you create for this file, however, should include all linked images in case you need to make changes at a later date. If the linked files aren't still available, you won't be able to output the file at high quality. Unlike InDesign, which is Adobe's professional page-layout application, Illustrator does not include a packaging utility to automatically gather the required pieces of a file, so you have to create the archive manually.

14. Save the file and continue to the next stage of the project.

Managing Linked Files

ILLUSTRATOR FOUNDATIONS

When you work with linked files, the external files must be available and up-to-date when you output the file to print or PDF. The Links panel uses various icons to help you monitor these files and identify potential problems.

If a file has been **modified**, you can click the Update Link button to show the most current version of the linked file in your Illustrator layout.

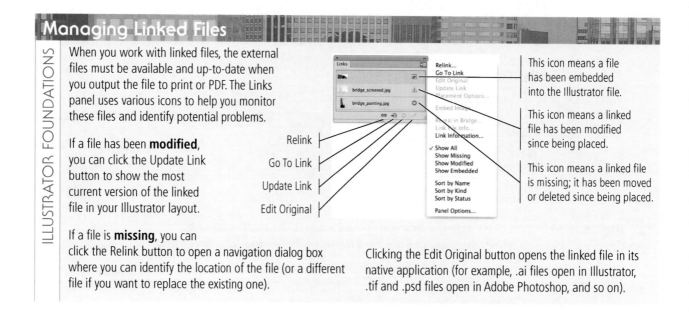

Relink —
Go To Link —
Update Link —
Edit Original —

This icon means a file has been embedded into the Illustrator file.

This icon means a linked file has been modified since being placed.

This icon means a linked file is missing; it has been moved or deleted since being placed.

If a file is **missing**, you can click the Relink button to open a navigation dialog box where you can identify the location of the file (or a different file if you want to replace the existing one).

Clicking the Edit Original button opens the linked file in its native application (for example, .ai files open in Illustrator, .tif and .psd files open in Adobe Photoshop, and so on).

Stage 3 Working with Imported Text

Placing text is one of the most important aspects of page-layout design, whether you create the text directly within the layout or import it from an external file. Some layouts require only a few bits of text, while others include numerous pages. Depending on how much text you have to work with, you might place all the layout text in a single frame; you might cut and paste different pieces of a single story into individual text frames; or you might thread text across multiple frames — maintaining the text as a single story but allowing flexibility in frame size and position. In many cases — including this project — you will use more than one of these methods within a single file.

IMPORT TEXT FOR THE INSIDE PANELS

Illustrator provides a number of tools and options for formatting text, from choosing a font to automatically formatting paragraphs with styles. The first step in this project, however, requires importing the client-supplied text into the brochure layout.

1. **With culture.ai open, make the Inside artboard visible.**

2. **Lock the Graphics layer, then create a new layer named Text at the top of the layer stack.**

3. **With the Text layer active, choose the Type tool in the Tools panel.**

4. **Click and drag to create an area-type object in the top half of the center panel, snapping to the top, left, and right margin guides (as shown here).**

    When you click and drag with the Type tool, you create an area-type object (also simply called a type area, and commonly referred to as a text frame).

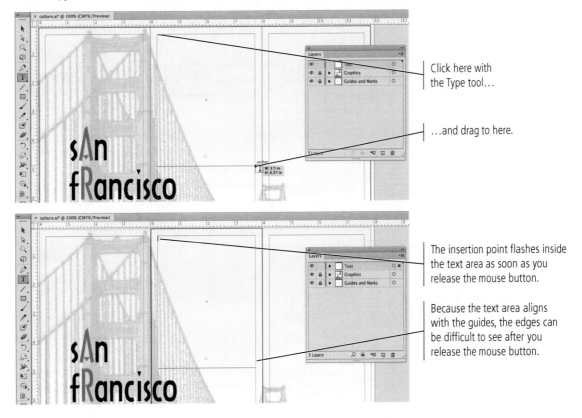

Click here with the Type tool…

…and drag to here.

The insertion point flashes inside the text area as soon as you release the mouse button.

Because the text area aligns with the guides, the edges can be difficult to see after you release the mouse button.

5. **With the insertion point flashing in the new type area, choose File>Place. Navigate to `studios_inside.doc` in the WIP>Culture folder and click Place.**

When you import a Microsoft Word file into Illustrator, the application asks how you want to handle formatting in the file. In addition to the basic text, you can also choose to include special options such as a table of contents, footnotes, and an index.

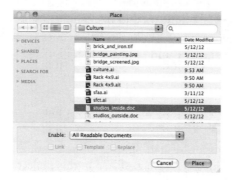

6. **In the Microsoft Word Options dialog box, make sure the Remove Text Formatting option is not checked and click OK.**

If the Remove Text Formatting option is checked, the imported copy will be formatted with the Illustrator default type settings only. Although you will typically reformat most imported text, it's a good idea to import text with formatting so you can review the editorial priority of the copy (i.e., where titles and headings are intended to appear).

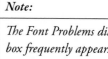

7. **If you see the Font Problems dialog box, click OK.**

For the text to display properly with the formatting that was applied in the Word file, Illustrator needs access to the same fonts that were used in the Word file. If you don't have the same fonts available on your system, you might see a Font Problems dialog box listing the missing fonts. In most cases, you can simply dismiss it because you will replace the original fonts with ones more suited to professional graphic design.

The text from the Word file flows into the type area where the insertion point was flashing. The small red symbol at the bottom of the object is called the **overset text icon**; this icon indicates that the story includes more text than will fit in the available space.

Note:

The Font Problems dialog box frequently appears when you import a Microsoft Word file.

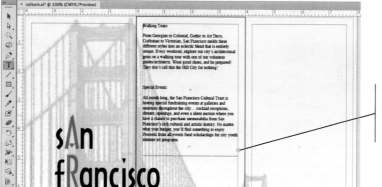

The overset text icon indicates that more text exists, but it does not fit into the current frame.

8. **Save the file and continue to the next exercise.**

Using the Find Font Dialog Box

You can use the Find Font dialog box (Type>Find Font) to replace one font with another throughout a layout. The top half of the dialog box lists every font used in the file; missing fonts are surrounded by chevrons in the list.

The lower half of the dialog box defaults to show the same list as the top half. You can also choose System in the menu to list all active fonts on your computer.

If you click the Change or Change All button, the font selected in the top list will be replaced with the font selected in the bottom list. You can also use the Find button to locate instances of the font selected in the top list without making changes.

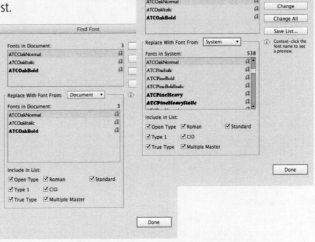

THREAD MULTIPLE TYPE AREAS

When a story includes more text than the current type area can accommodate, you have to decide how to solve the problem. In some cases, when only one or two words are overset, minor changes in formatting will create the additional space you need. If you can edit the text (although graphic designers are typically not permitted to do so), changing a word or two might also help.

When you can't edit the client-supplied text, and when you have a considerable amount of overset text (as in this project), the only solution is to add more space for the leftover text. Here again, you have two alternatives: cut some of the text and paste it into another type area, or link the existing area to one or more additional type areas (called **threading**) so the story can flow through multiple frames.

1. **With culture.ai open, click the overset text icon once with the Selection tool.**

   The overset text icon appears in a small rectangle, which is the **out port** of the selected text frame. By clicking the out port of an area (regardless of whether overset text exists), you can direct the flow of text into another type area.

   When you click an out port with an overset text icon, the cursor changes to the loaded text cursor. You can use that cursor to click any other text frame, or click and drag to create a new frame in the same thread.

Note:

You can use the out ports to link empty frames; when you eventually place text into the frame, it automatically flows from one to another in the chain.

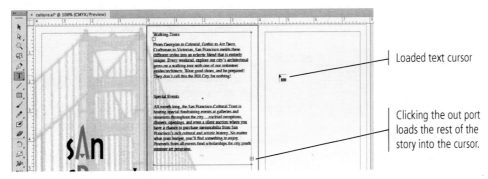

Loaded text cursor

Clicking the out port loads the rest of the story into the cursor.

2. **Using the loaded text cursor, click and drag to create a new type area in the right panel. Snap the edges of the frame to all four margin guides on the panel.**

   When you release the mouse button, the new frame automatically fills with the text that is loaded into the cursor.

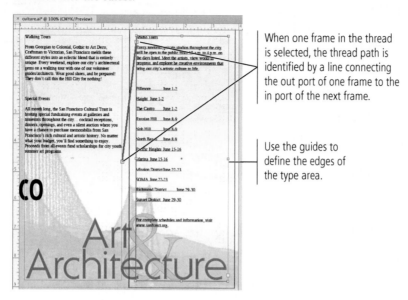

When one frame in the thread is selected, the thread path is identified by a line connecting the out port of one frame to the in port of the next frame.

Use the guides to define the edges of the type area.

3. **Save the file and continue to the next exercise.**

 ## WORK WITH HIDDEN CHARACTERS

Your layout now includes a story that threads across two separate text frames. The only obvious formatting is extra space between paragraphs. You can identify the intended headings (the short paragraphs), but the layout lacks the polish and finesse of a professional design.

1. **With culture.ai open, choose Type>Show Hidden Characters.**

   Hidden characters identify spaces, paragraph returns, and other non-printing characters. It can be helpful to view these hidden characters, especially when you are working with long blocks of text.

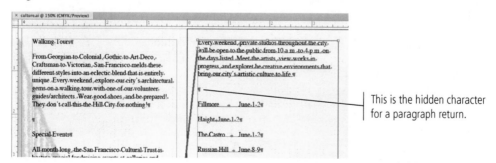

This is the hidden character for a paragraph return.

When you work with client-supplied text, you will frequently find each paragraph separated by two (or more) paragraph returns. This kind of formatting creates the visual effect of space between paragraphs, but it also adds an unnecessary element that needs to be controlled in the story. Because Illustrator's typographic controls allow you to easily change the spacing of paragraphs, these double paragraph returns are unnecessary and should be deleted.

Unfortunately, Illustrator's Find and Replace function is very limited. Unlike InDesign, you can't use the utility to search for a paragraph return character — you have to manually delete the extra paragraph returns.

2. **Using the Type tool, click to place the insertion point in the first empty paragraph in the text, and then press Delete/Backspace.**

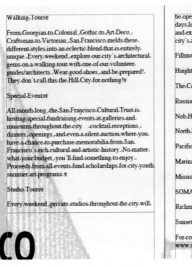

The insertion point is flashing in the empty paragraph.

Pressing Delete/Backspace removes the empty paragraph.

3. **Using the same method, remove all extra empty paragraphs in the story.**

You might need to use the arrow key to move the insertion point into the second frame. Or, you can press Command/Control to select the second frame, then click with the Type tool to place the insertion point in the empty paragraph in that frame.

Note:

In the next exercise, you use paragraph formatting options to control the space between individual paragraphs.

4. **Save the file and continue to the next exercise.**

Using the Find and Replace Dialog Box

Finding and replacing text is a function common to many applications. Illustrator's Find and Replace utility (Edit>Find and Replace) is fairly straightforward, offering the ability to search for and change text in a layout, including a limited number of special characters and options. (The menus associated with the Find and Replace With fields list the special characters that can be identified and replaced.)

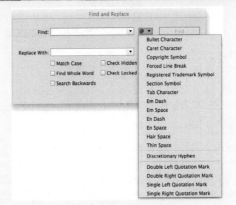

The check boxes below the Replace With field are toggles for specific types of searches:

- When **Match Case** is active, a search only finds text with the same capitalization as the text in the Find field. For example, a search for "Illustrator" does not identify instances of "illustrator" or "ILLUSTRATOR."

- When **Find Whole Word** is active, a search only finds instances where the search text is not part of another word. For example, a search for "old" as a whole word does not include the words "gold" or "embolden."

- When **Search Backwards** is selected, Illustrator searches from the current insertion point to the beginning of the story.

- When **Check Hidden Layers** is active, the search includes text frames on layers that are not visible. In this case, the hidden layer remains visible until you close the Find and Replace dialog box.

- When **Check Locked Layers** is active, the search locates text on locked layers.

DEFINE PARAGRAPH STYLES

When you work with long blocks of text, many of the same formatting options are applied to different text elements throughout the story (such as headings). To simplify the workflow, you can use styles to store and apply multiple formatting options in a single click. Styles also have another powerful benefit: when you change the options applied in a style, any text formatted with that style reflects the newly defined options. In other words, you can change multiple instances of non-contiguous text in a single process, instead of selecting each block and making the same changes repeatedly.

1. **With culture.ai open, click with the Type tool to place the insertion point anywhere in the text and choose Select>All.**

   When you use the Select All command, you select the entire story in all threaded frames.

2. **Open the Paragraph Styles panel (Window>Type>Paragraph Styles).**

   Text imported from a Microsoft Word file is commonly formatted with styles in the native application; those styles are imported into Illustrator when you place the text.

   The Paragraph Styles panel shows that the selected text is formatted with the Body Copy style. The plus sign next to the style name indicates that some formatting is applied other than what is defined by the style. This is a quirk of importing formatted text; although you imported the text and chose to include formatting, Illustrator doesn't recognize something in the style — resulting in the plus sign. This will occur in almost all text you import into Illustrator.

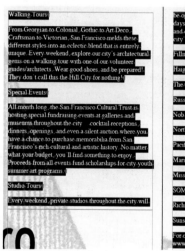
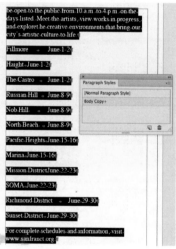

Note:

Not every instance of a plus sign next to a style name is an error, but you should always be sure that what you have is really what you want.

3. **With the text selected, open the Paragraph Styles Options menu and choose Clear Overrides.**

   This is an issue that you should be aware of; if you do not clear the overrides, later changes to the style might not correctly reflect in text formatted with the style. When you work with styles — whether they are imported styles or styles that you create — check the applied styles to see if a plus sign appears where you know it shouldn't.

Note:

You can also click the plus sign in the style name to clear overrides.

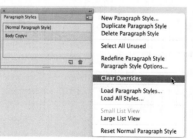

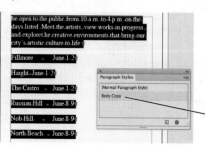

After choosing Clear Overrides, the plus sign is gone.

4. **Command/Control-click away from the text frame to deselect the text (and the containing frames).**

5. **In the Paragraph Styles panel, double-click the Body Copy style item away from the style name.**

   If you double-click the actual style name, you will highlight the name so you can rename it. If you want to edit the style, double-click the style *away* from the style name.

   You can also edit a style by single-clicking it in the panel, and then choosing Paragraph Style Options in the panel Options menu.

6. **In the resulting dialog box, make sure the Preview option is checked.**

   Double-clicking a style opens the Paragraph Style Options dialog box for that style, where you can edit the settings stored in the style.

   Checking the Preview option allows you to immediately see the effect of your changes in the layout before you finalize the changes.

7. **Click Basic Character Formats in the left list to show the related options. Choose ATC Oak Normal in the Font Family menu, change the Size to 12 pt, and change the leading to 15 pt.**

   Different options are available in the right side of the dialog box, depending on what is selected in the list of categories.

   To see the effects of your changes, you have to click away from the active field to apply the new value. You can either tab to another field, or click an empty area of the dialog box to preview the results.

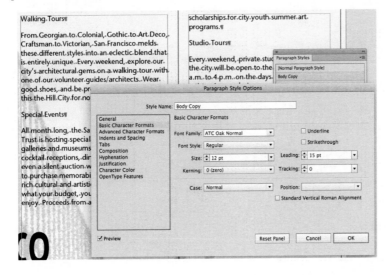

8. **Click Indents and Spacing in the category list. Change the Space Before field to 0 pt and change the Space After field to 10 pt.**

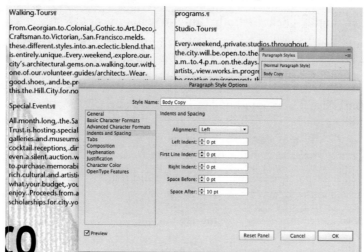

Note:

You do not have to select text to change the definition of a style. In fact, you don't even need to select a text frame for this process to work.

9. **Click OK to finalize the new style definition.**

10. **In the layout, use the Type tool to highlight the first paragraph in the story ("Walking Tours"). Using the Control or Character panel, change the formatting to ATC Oak Bold and change the type size to 13 pt.**

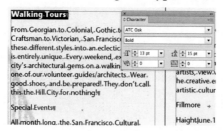

Note:

To open the Character panel, choose Window> Type>Character, or click the Character hot text in the Control panel.

To open the Paragraph panel, choose Window> Type>Paragraph, or click the Paragraph hot text in the Control panel.

11. **Using the Paragraph panel, change the Space After Paragraph field to 3 pt.**

   If you don't see the Space Before Paragraph and Space After Paragraph fields in the Paragraph panel, open the panel Options menu and choose Show Options.

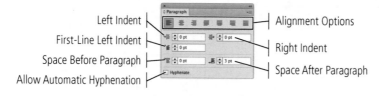

12. **With the same type selected, click the Create New Style button in the Paragraph Styles panel.**

   When you create a new style, it defaults to include all formatting options applied to the currently selected text (or to the location of the insertion point if no characters are selected).

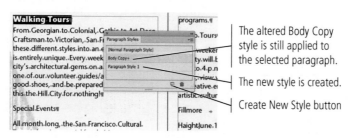

The altered Body Copy style is still applied to the selected paragraph.

The new style is created.

Create New Style button

Note:

Unlike character formatting, paragraph formatting applies to the entire paragraph in which the insertion point is placed. If text is selected, paragraph formatting applies to any paragraph that is entirely or partially selected.

13. **With the heading selected, click Paragraph Style 1 to apply the new style to the selected text.**

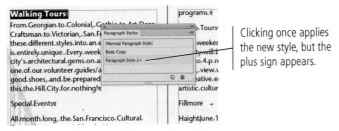

Clicking once applies the new style, but the plus sign appears.

This highlights another anomaly in the application. When you define a style from selected text, you sometimes have to click the new style twice to apply it *and* remove the plus sign from the style name.

14. **With the heading text still selected, click Paragraph Style 1 again to remove the plus sign from the style.**

15. **In the Paragraph Styles panel, double-click the Paragraph Style 1 name. Type Heading, then press Return/Enter to finalize the change.**

16. **Place the insertion point in the second heading (Special Events) and click the Heading style in the Paragraph Styles panel.**

    Applying a paragraph style is as simple as placing the insertion point and clicking a style. You do not need to select the entire paragraph to apply the paragraph style.

17. **Using the same method, apply the Heading style to the Studio Tours heading in the second frame.**

Note:

By default, every Illustrator document includes the [Normal Paragraph Style] option. The formatting applied in this style is the default formatting for new text areas created in the file. You can edit this style to change the default settings for new text areas in the existing file.

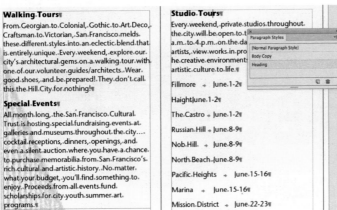

18. **If necessary, use the Selection tool to adjust the height of the first text frame so only the first two sections of copy (Walking Tours and Special Events) appear in that frame, and the entire paragraph after the Special Events heading fits in the frame.**

    Unfortunately, you can't use the Transform panel to change the height of the type area. If you do, you will artificially scale the height of the text within the area to match the new dimensions. This is counter to what you might expect (especially if you are familiar with working in Adobe InDesign). However, you can drag the type area's handles to resize the area. In this case, the text is not scaled; it reflows to fit the new dimensions of the area.

19. Select the first paragraph in the story (Walking Tours). Using the Fill Color menu in the Control panel, change the text color to one of the orange swatches.

We applied this swatch as the text fill color.

Note:

If you don't see the default color swatches, you can access them by opening the Default Swatches>Basic CMYK swatch library.

20. With the same text still selected, open the Paragraph Styles panel Options menu and choose Redefine Paragraph Style.

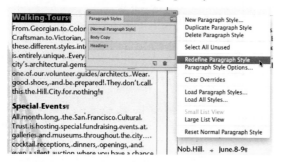

This option changes the selected style formatting to match the formatting of the current text selection (in the document).

Note:

You can delete a style by dragging it to the panel Delete button. If the style had been applied, you would see a warning message, asking you to confirm the deletion. You do not have the opportunity to replace the applied style with another one, as you do in Adobe InDesign.

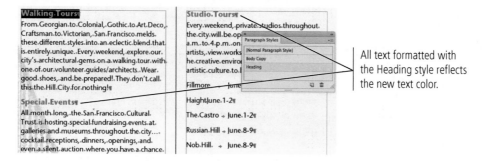

All text formatted with the Heading style reflects the new text color.

21. Save the file and continue to the next exercise

IMPORT STYLES FROM OTHER FILES

Once you create styles, you can apply them to any text in the file, on any artboard. You can also import styles from other Illustrator files so those styles can be used for different projects.

1. With culture.ai open, make sure nothing is selected in the layout and the Paragraph Styles panel is open.

If the insertion point is already flashing in a type object, you can't use the Type tool to create a new type object.

2. Use the Type tool to create an area-type object that fills the empty space on the Outside Fold In artboard (the one on the left).

3. Place the file **studios_outside.doc** into the type area, including formatting. (Click OK if you see the Font Problems dialog box.)

4. Using the Selection tool, drag the bottom-center handle of the type area until all text in the story is visible.

5. Use the Type tool to place the insertion point in the placed text, then choose Select>All. Use the Paragraph Styles panel Options menu to clear the style overrides in the selected text.

When the insertion point is placed, the Select All command selects all text in the active story; text in other (non-threaded) type areas is not selected.

Note:

If the Paragraph Styles panel is closed before you select all the text, the applied style does not appear highlighted when you first open the panel. To work around this bug, open the panel and then select the text that you want to format; the applied style (in this case, Body Copy+) is highlighted so you can use the Clear Overrides option.

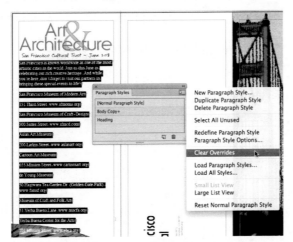

6. Open the Paragraph Styles panel Options menu and choose Load Paragraph Styles.

7. Navigate to the file **styles.ai** (in your WIP>Culture folder) and click Open.

If styles of the same name exist in the open and imported files, Illustrator maintains the definition from the active file. Unlike other applications, Illustrator does not allow you to control the import process for individual styles.

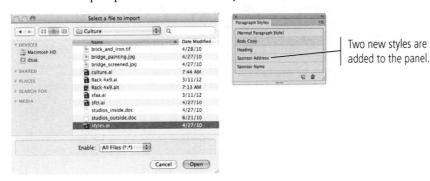

Two new styles are added to the panel.

8. **Select any part of all but the first paragraph, and click the Sponsor Address style.**

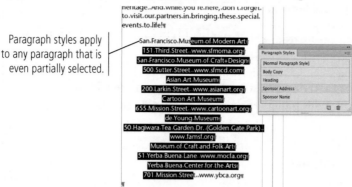

Paragraph styles apply to any paragraph that is even partially selected.

Note:

Paragraph styles relate to entire paragraphs — anything between two paragraph return (¶) characters.

9. **Place the insertion point in the first paragraph you just formatted, and then click the Sponsor Name style to apply it.**

10. **Apply the Sponsor Name style to every other paragraph in the list.**

    Make sure you pay attention to where paragraphs begin and end; don't apply the style to every other *line*.

Note:

You can Option/Alt-click the Create New button in most panels to automatically open the Options dialog box for the asset you are creating.

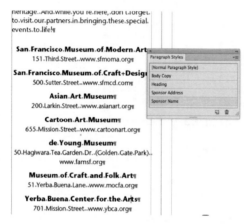

11. **Save the file and continue to the next exercise.**

DEFINE A CHARACTER STYLE

As with paragraph styles, a character style can be used to store and apply multiple character formatting options with a single click. The primary difference is that character styles apply to selected text only, such as italicizing a specific word in a paragraph or adding a few characters in a different font.

1. **With culture.ai open, highlight the web address in the first sponsor listing.**

2. **Using the Control or Character panel, change the font to ATC Oak Italic.**

3. **Open the Character Styles panel (Window>Type>Character Styles).**

4. **Click the Create New Style button at the bottom of the panel.**

   The process of creating a character style is basically the same as creating a paragraph style. The new style is created, but it is not yet applied to the selected text.

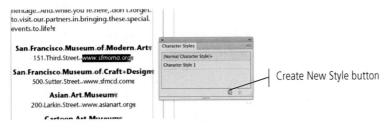

   Create New Style button

5. **Double-click the new style name in the panel. Type Web Address, then press Return/Enter to finalize the new name.**

   Because you double-clicked the style to rename it, the first click of that double-click applied the selected style. Like a paragraph style, new character styles adopt the formatting of the current selection.

6. **Highlight each web address in the list and apply the Web Address character style.**

   Unlike paragraph styles, character styles apply only to selected text.

7. **Save the file and continue to the next stage of the project.**

Stage 4 Fine-Tuning Text

Your text is now in place for both sides of the brochure, but there are still a number of typographic issues that should be addressed so the layout looks professional and well polished, instead of appearing just "good enough." Although some problems will require manual intervention, most of these can be solved using Illustrator's built-in tools and utilities.

APPLY SMART PUNCTUATION

When you import text from an external text file, it is possible that you are importing a number of typographic errors — both typing errors and errors of typography.

From a typography standpoint, some problems such as stright quotes have to do with the way text is encoded in the file you import. Other issues, such as double spaces after a period, are intentionally (but incorrectly) created by the author. In any case, Illustrator includes a utility to find and fix these common issues.

1. **With culture.ai open, make sure nothing is selected in the layout.**

2. **Choose Type>Show Hidden Characters to toggle those characters off.**

3. **Zoom in to the Inside artboard so you can clearly see the text.**

4. **Choose Type>Smart Punctuation.**

   This dialog box makes it very easy to search for and change common characters to their typographically correct equivalents. You can affect selected text only, or you can affect the entire document at once.

   - **ff, fi, ffi Ligatures** converts these combinations to the replacement ligatures.
   - **ff, fl, ffl Ligatures** converts these combinations to the replacement ligatures.
   - **Smart Quotes** converts straight quote marks into true (curly) quotes.
   - **Smart Spaces** eliminates multiple space characters after a period.
   - **En, Em Dashes** converts a double keyboard dash to an en dash and a triple keyboard dash to an em dash.
   - **Ellipses** converts three periods to a single-character ellipsis glyph.
   - **Expert Fractions** converts separate characters used to represent fractions to their single-character equivalents.

5. **In the Replace Punctuation area, check all options but Expert Fractions.**

6. **Choose the Entire Document option, make sure the Report Results box is checked, and then click OK.**

7. **Review the information in the report dialog box, and then click OK.**

8. **Save the file and continue to the next exercise.**

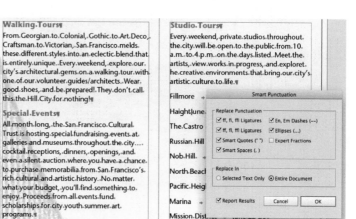

> **Note:**
>
> *Two spaces after a period is a relic from a time when manual typewriters placed every character in the same amount of space (called monospace type). To more clearly identify a new sentence, the typist entered two spaces after typing a period. This convention still survives today, even though most people never use manual typewriters.*

CONTROL HYPHENATION AND JUSTIFICATION

The text on both sides of the brochure shows a problem called a **widow**, which is a very short line at the end of a paragraph (typically one word, or two very short words). Whenever possible, these should be corrected. One way to do so is to adjust the hyphenation and justification settings in a paragraph.

1. **With culture.ai open, use the Type tool to place the insertion point in the paragraph after the Special Events heading.**

2. **Open the Paragraph panel Options menu and choose Hyphenation.**

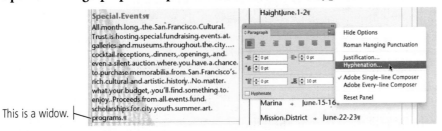

This is a widow.

3. **In the Hyphenation dialog box, activate the Preview check box.**

4. **Check the Hyphenation option to allow automatic hyphenation based on the settings defined in the lower part of the dialog box.**

Allowing hyphenation fixes the widow.

The Hyphenation options allow you to control the way Illustrator applies hyphenation.

- **Words Longer Than _ Letters** defines the minimum number of characters that must exist in a hyphenated word.

- **After First** and **Before Last** defines the minimum number of characters that must appear before or after a hyphen.

- **Hyphen Limit** defines the maximum number of hyphens that can appear on consecutive lines. (Remember, you are defining the *limit*, so zero means there is no limit — allowing unlimited hyphens.)

- **Hyphenation Zone** defines the amount of white space allowed at the end of a line of unjustified text before hyphenation begins.

- If **Hyphenate Capitalized Words** is checked, capitalized words (proper nouns) can be hyphenated.

- The slider allows Illustrator to determine the best spacing. Dragging left allows more hyphens; dragging right reduces the number of hyphens in a paragraph, but might produce less-pleasing results in line spacing.

5. **Click OK to apply the change and return to the layout.**

6. **If the Studio Tours heading moved into the first frame, use the Selection tool to adjust the frame height to force that heading into the second frame.**

Note:

*A **widow** is a very short line — usually one or two words — at the end of a paragraph.*

*An **orphan** is a heading or the first line of a paragraph at the end of a column, or the last line of a paragraph at the beginning of a column.*

Note:

Illustrator does not include automatic orphan control (the "Keep With" options that InDesign users might be familiar with). You have to correct this problem manually by adjusting the frame size.

7. **Navigate to the Outside Fold In artboard and place the insertion point in the first paragraph.**

This short last line can be considered a widow.

8. **Using the Paragraph panel, apply the Justify All Lines alignment option.**

9. **Open the Paragraph panel Options menu and choose Justification.**

This is the Justify All Lines button (from Step 8).

10. **Activate the Preview option, and then change the Minimum Word Spacing field to 70%.**

The Justification dialog box allows you to control the minimum, desired, and maximum spacing that can be applied to create justified paragraph alignment.

- **Word Spacing** defines the space that can be applied between words (where spaces exist in the text). At 100% (the default Desired amount), no additional space is added between words.

- **Letter Spacing** defines the space that can be added between individual letters within a word. All three values default to 0%, which allows no extra space between letters; at 100%, an entire space would be allowed between characters (making the text very difficult to read).

- **Glyph Scaling** determines how much individual character glyphs can be scaled (stretched or compressed) to justify the text. At 100%, the default value for all three settings, characters are not scaled.

- In narrow columns, single words sometimes appear on a line by themselves. If the paragraph is set to full justification, a single word on a line might appear to be too stretched out. You can use the **Single Word Justification** menu to center or left-align these single words instead of leaving them fully justified.

By reducing the Minimum Word Spacing value, the spaces between words in the second line are reduced. Basically, you are telling Illustrator, "Reduce the amount of word spacing down to 70% of the normal spacing that would be applied by pressing the spacebar." This setting results in smaller word spaces throughout the paragraph, and corrects the widow at the end of the paragraph.

Note:

Issues such as paragraph and word spacing are somewhat subjective. Some of your clients will break all other typographic rules to reduce loosely fitted lines, while others will absolutely refuse to allow widows, and still others will disallow hyphenation of any kind.

The specific way you solve problems will be governed by your client's personal typographic preferences.

11. **Click OK to apply the change and return to the layout.**

12. **Save the file and continue to the next exercise.**

FORMAT TABBED TEXT

On the inside of the brochure, the list of dates was created with tab characters separating the locations from the dates. Rather than leaving the list as it is — more or less unformatted and messy — you can adjust tab formatting to present a well-ordered, easy-to-read list.

1. **With culture.ai open, select any part of each list paragraph in the Inside Fold In artboard.**

   Tab positions are technically paragraph formatting attributes, so your changes will apply to any paragraph that is even partially selected.

2. **Open the Tabs panel (Window>Type>Tabs).**

   If the top edge of the active text frame is visible, the Tabs panel will automatically appear at the top of the frame. If the top edge of the frame is not visible, the panel floats randomly in the workspace. Because these two frames are linked, the left side of the Tabs panel appears above the left text frame.

3. **Click the Right-Justified Tab marker at the top of the panel.**

   This defines the type of tab stop you are going to create. If an existing tab marker is already selected on the ruler, clicking a different type of marker changes the type of the selected stop.

4. **Click the ruler in the Tabs panel above the first frame to place a tab stop, and drag to about the middle of the left frame.**

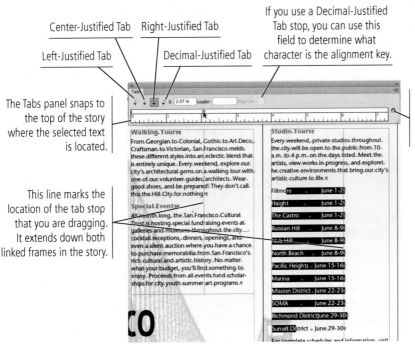

Center-Justified Tab   Right-Justified Tab

Left-Justified Tab   Decimal-Justified Tab

If you use a Decimal-Justified Tab stop, you can use this field to determine what character is the alignment key.

The Tabs panel snaps to the top of the story where the selected text is located.

Click this button to snap the Tabs panel to the top of the active type area (if it is visible in the document window).

This line marks the location of the tab stop that you are dragging. It extends down both linked frames in the story.

5. **Click the existing tab stop and drag right until the line shows the tab located at the right edge of the right frame.**

   Remember, these two frames are slightly different sizes due to the size difference of the artboards. You have to watch the line in the right frame to make sure the tab will be aligned properly.

6. **With the tab stop still selected, type period-space in the Leader field, and then press Return/Enter to apply the change.**

   Whatever you type in the Leader field will occupy the space between tab stops.

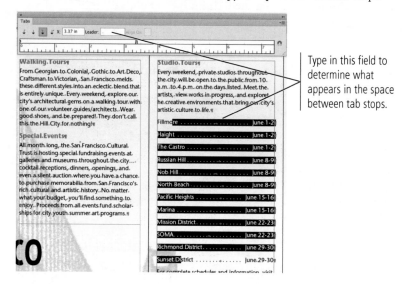

Type in this field to determine what appears in the space between tab stops.

7. **Select any part of all but the last list item, and use the Paragraph panel to change the Space After Paragraph value to 3 pt.**

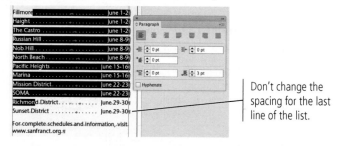

Don't change the spacing for the last line of the list.

8. **Save the file and continue to the next exercise.**

CHECK SPELLING

Misspellings and typos creep into virtually every job, despite numerous rounds of content proofs. These errors can ruin an otherwise perfect job. As with most desktop applications, Illustrator allows you to check the spelling in a document. It's all too common, however, to skip this important step, which could result in spelling and typing errors in the final output.

You might not (and probably won't) create the text for most design jobs, and you aren't technically responsible for the words your client supplies. However, you can be a hero if you find and fix typographical errors before a job goes to press; if you don't, you will almost certainly hear about it after it's too late to fix. You simply can't brush off a problem by saying, "That's not my job" — at least, not if you want to work with that client again.

1. **With culture.ai open, make sure nothing is selected in the layout.**

2. **Choose Edit>Check Spelling.**

Note:

Illustrator checks spelling based on the language defined for the text. You can change the default language in the Hyphenation pane of the Preferences dialog box, or you can assign a specific language to selected text using the Character panel.

3. **In the resulting Check Spelling dialog box, click Start.**

   Illustrator locates the first problem word and highlights it in the layout.

   This error is certainly a typo, but it presents a spell-checking problem: "exploret" is an error, but the second half of the typo ("he") will not be identified as a misspelling. In this case, you have to use the upper field to make the necessary correction to both words.

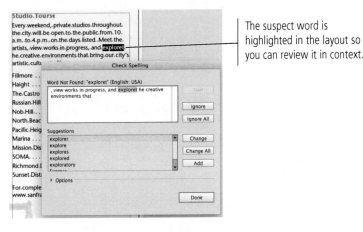

The suspect word is highlighted in the layout so you can review it in context.

4. **In the upper window of the Check Spelling dialog box, change "exploret he" to explore the.**

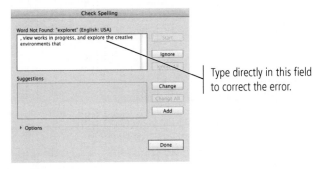

Type directly in this field to correct the error.

5. **Click Change.**

   As soon as you click Change to correct the first error, Illustrator automatically highlights the next suspect word.

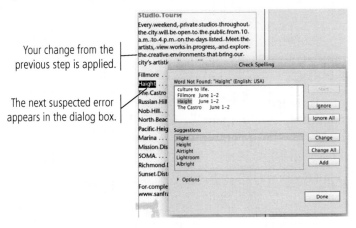

Your change from the previous step is applied.

The next suspected error appears in the dialog box.

Note:

Never simply click Change when you check spelling. Carefully evaluate the suspect word in the context of the layout.

6. **Evaluate the next potential problem, and then click Ignore.**

   "Haight" is a district in the city of San Francisco, and it is spelled correctly.

7. **Continue reviewing any potential problems, making any necessary changes to words that are not place names or Web addresses.**

   Many of the suspected problems in this file are either place names or Web addresses; both are commonly flagged as potential errors, even when they are spelled correctly.

   For the sake of this project, you can assume place names and Web addresses are correct. In a professional environment, those are common sources of typos; always check the accuracy of these words carefully.

   The only other actual spelling error is the word "artisitic" on the Outside artboard.

8. **Click Done to close the Check Spelling dialog box.**

   When Illustrator can't find any more potential problems, the dialog box shows that the Spell Checker utility is complete.

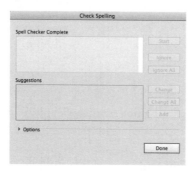

9. **Save the file and continue to the next exercise.**

Check Spelling Options

If you click the Options button at the bottom of the Check Spelling dialog box, you see a number of choices to refine the evaluation.

- The Find section allows the spell checker to identify repeated words (e.g., "the the") and non-capitalized starts of sentences (i.e., lowercase words immediately following a period and space).
- In the Ignore section, you can force Illustrator to skip words that are all uppercase, words with numbers, and Roman numerals.

Click this button to show and hide the Check Spelling options.

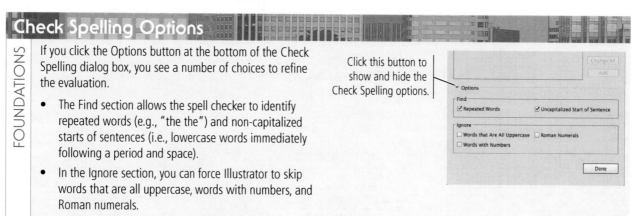

✍ EXPORT A PDF FILE FOR PRINT

The Portable Document Format (PDF) was created by Adobe to facilitate cross-platform transportation of documents, independent of the fonts used, linked files, or even the originating application. The format offers a number of advantages for commercial printing workflows:

- PDF files can contain all of the information needed to successfully output a job.

- Data in a PDF file can be high or low resolution, and it can be compressed to reduce file size.

- PDF files are device-independent, which means you don't need the originating application or the same platform to open and print the file.

- PDF files are also page-independent, which means a PDF document can contain rotated pages and even pages of different sizes.

1. **With culture.ai open, choose File>Save As. Choose Adobe PDF in the Format/Save As Type menu.**

2. **Choose the Range option, type 1-2 in the related field, then click Save.**

   Because you created separate artboards to contain each composite side of the brochure, you can use the Range option to output only those two artboards in the PDF file.

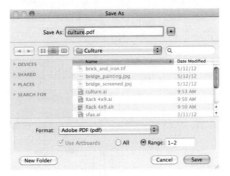

3. **Choose Press Quality in the Adobe PDF Preset menu.**

   The Adobe PDF Preset menu includes six PDF presets (in brackets) that meet common industry output requirements. Other options might also be available if another user created custom presets in Illustrator or another Creative Suite application.

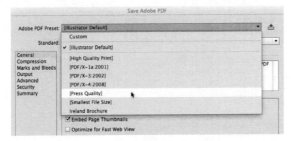

   Because there are so many ways to create a PDF — and not all of them are optimized for commercial printing — the potential benefits of the file format are often negated. The PDF/X specification was created to help solve some of the problems associated with bad PDF files entering the prepress workflow. PDF/X is a subset of PDF, specifically designed to ensure that files have the information necessary for and available to the digital prepress output process. Ask your output provider whether you should apply a PDF/X standard to your files, and if so, which version to use.

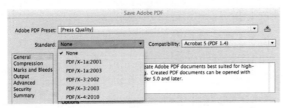

   The Compatibility menu determines which version of the PDF format you will create. This is particularly important if your layout uses transparency. PDF 1.3 does not support transparency, so the file will require flattening. If you save the file to be compatible with PDF 1.4 or later, the transparency information will be maintained in the PDF file; it will have to be flattened later in the output process (after it leaves your desk).

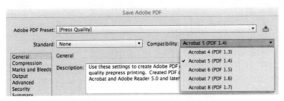

4. Review the Compression options.

The Compression options determine what — and how much — data will be included in the PDF file. This set of options is one of the most important when creating PDFs, since too-low resolution results in bad-quality printing, and too-high resolution results in extremely long download times.

Before you choose compression settings, you need to consider your final goal. If you're creating a file for commercial printing, resolution is more important than file size. If your goal is a PDF for posting on the Web for general consumption, file size is equally important as (if not more than) image quality.

You can define a specific compression scheme for color, grayscale, and monochrome images. Different options are available, depending on the image type:

- ZIP compression is lossless, which means all file data is maintained in the compressed file.

- JPEG compression options are lossy, which means data is discarded to create a smaller file. When you use one of the JPEG options, you can also define an Image Quality option (from Low to Maximum).

If you don't compress the file, your PDF file might be extremely large. For a commercial printing workflow, large file size is preferable to poor image quality. If you don't have to submit the PDF file via modem transmission, large file size is not an issue. If you must compress the file, ask your service provider what settings they prefer you to use.

Note:

Since you chose the High Quality Print preset, these options default to settings that will produce the best results for most commercial printing applications.

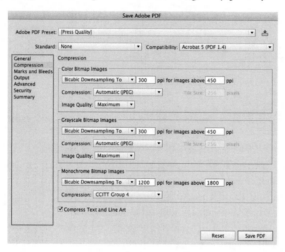

5. In the Marks and Bleeds options, check the Trim Marks option, and change the Offset field to 0.125″.

Most printers prefer trim marks to appear outside of the bleed area, which is 0.125″ for this project; this requires a 0.125″ offset.

Note:

The Output options relate to color management and PDF/X settings. Ask your output provider if you need to change anything for those options.

6. **In the Bleeds section, make sure the four fields are not linked. Change the Top and Bottom values to 0.5″, and change the Left and Right values to 0.125″.**

Because you did not define a specific bleed setting for the artboards in this file, the Use Document Bleed Settings option won't work.

You have to manually define the area on each side to include in the exported file. You're including more space on the top and bottom so the folding marks will be visible in the resulting PDF file.

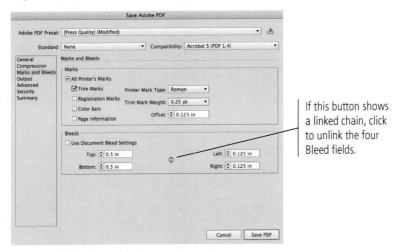

If this button shows a linked chain, click to unlink the four Bleed fields.

7. **Click Save PDF. When the process is finished, review the resulting PDF file.**

8. **Close the PDF file and return to Illustrator, then close the culture.ai file.**

1. _____ is the size of a flat page, before folding, and after it has been cut from a press sheet.

2. _____ is the area where it is safe to place important content.

3. _____ is the amount you must extend objects beyond the actual artboard edge for them to safely appear at the cut edge of the final job.

4. For a folding document, panels that fold in need to be at least _____ smaller than outside panels.

5. The _____ command can be used to convert any object into a nonprinting guide.

6. Using _____ rulers, measurements relate to the first artboard in the file.

7. Using _____ rulers, measurements relate to the currently active artboard.

8. The _____ icon indicates that more text exists in the story, but does not fit into the current text area or chain.

9. You can use the _____ dialog box to change all instances of a selected font in the active file.

10. You can choose the _____ command to show visible, nonprinting indicators of spaces and paragraph return characters.

1. Briefly explain how the mechanics of printing affect the layout for folding documents.

2. Briefly explain two advantages of using styles for text formatting.

3. Briefly explain the difference between linked and embedded files.

Use what you learned in this project to complete the following freeform exercise.
Carefully read the art director and client comments, then create your own design to meet the needs of the project.
Use the space below to sketch ideas; when finished, write a brief explanation of your reasoning behind your final design.

Your client was very pleased with your work, and has recommended your agency to a colleague at the local chamber of commerce. Your new client, Outdoor Adventures, specializes in "extreme tourism" — rock climbing, white water rafting, and similar activities.

To complete this project, you should:

❑ Create a letterfold brochure to present the client's information in an aesthetically pleasing layout.

❑ Reserve the middle panel of the brochure's outside for mailing information, including only the client's logo and return address.

❑ Use any or all of the client's supplied images to support the text. All files are in the **AI6_PB_Project5.zip** archive on the Student Files Web page.

Our company caters to what we call the "extreme tourist." We put together tour packages for people who like to experience and challenge nature. Some of our most popular tours take people up Mount Whitney, rafting down the Colorado River, and even hiking through the Alaskan ice fields.

Our business is doing very well with people who live on the West Coast, but we would like to extend our reach to the entire United States. We've purchased mailing lists from magazines that have a similar audience as our clients, and we want to create a brochure that we can mail to approximately 10,000 potential new clients.

We've given you the text for the brochure — there isn't much of it, because the images tell a more dramatic story of what we do. We've given you a number of images from our previous tours, and you can use as many of them as you think are necessary. If you want to use any other images, just make sure they follow the general theme of "outdoor adventures."

To begin the letterfold layout, you built technically accurate folding guides for each side of the brochure. To speed up the process for the next time you need to build one of these common letterfold jobs, you saved your initial work as a template.

Completing this project also required extensive work with imported text, specifically importing styles from a Microsoft Word file and controlling the flow of text from one frame to another. You also worked with several advanced text-formatting options, including paragraph and character styles and typographic fine-tuning.

Templates and styles are designed to let you do the majority of work once and then apply it as many times as necessary; many different projects can benefit from these tools, and you will use them extensively throughout your career as a graphic designer.

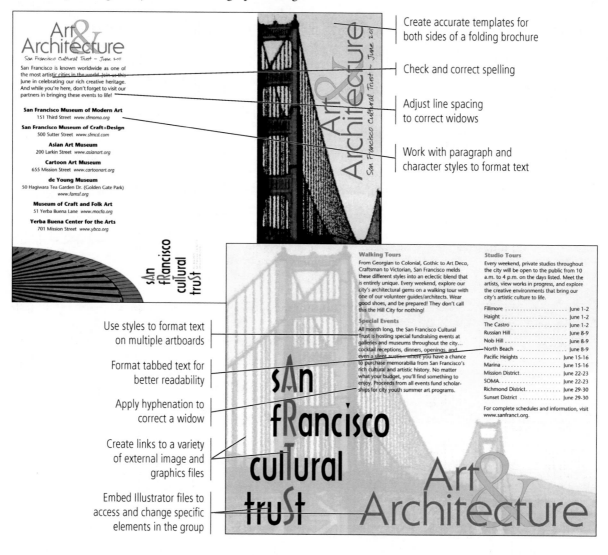

Create accurate templates for both sides of a folding brochure

Check and correct spelling

Adjust line spacing to correct widows

Work with paragraph and character styles to format text

Use styles to format text on multiple artboards

Format tabbed text for better readability

Apply hyphenation to correct a widow

Create links to a variety of external image and graphics files

Embed Illustrator files to access and change specific elements in the group

Cereal Box

Your client, a food manufacturer, is redesigning the packaging for its primary product — a cereal targeted at the health-conscious consumer. The client hired you to build the new package. You will incorporate elements from the old design as you develop an attractive, modern packaging concept.

This project incorporates the following skills:

❏ Sampling colors to create custom swatches

❏ Placing a variety of external files in the appropriate locations to meet package design requirements

❏ Creating type on an irregular path

❏ Controlling object blending modes and opacity

❏ Using warp and 3D effects to add depth to artwork

❏ Understanding and defining raster effect settings

❏ Expanding appearance attributes

❏ Flattening transparent effects and attributes

❏ Previewing 3D artwork

client comments

Our current package was designed about 20 years ago; it's little more than a white box with a bowl of cereal and our brightly colored logo on the front. We've conducted some focus group studies with our primary target market: women aged 25–50 with an expressed interest in eating well and living a healthy lifestyle. We've found this group prefers a less stark appearance — they find less empty white space and softer colors more appealing than a stark white background.

The new package should use the old logo, but we'd like it to be softer than it is in the basic file. It's vivid pink, which was popular in the 1980s when the old package was designed. We also want to add some color to the entire box to avoid the "sea of white space" syndrome.

We were recently endorsed by the Association for a Healthy America; the organization sent their endorsement logo, which should be included on the box. We also want to incorporate the "recycled" logo in some subtle way; using recycled materials wasn't a big deal in the '80s, but it is now.

art director comments

We have a template from the printer with the package structure already laid out, based on the existing die that's used to cut the flat box from the press sheet. There's no need to reinvent the wheel, so use this template to build the new cereal box artwork.

With the growing focus on breast cancer research and overall health awareness, pink has adopted a new symbolic meaning in American culture. Because the client is targeting the health-conscious female consumer, pink should play a prominent part in the design. Complement and contrast the pink with one or two other colors for various elements; the best bet is to simply pick some colors from the main image for the box cover.

The Food and Drug Administration requires food manufacturers to include product weight and nutrition information on every food package that will be sold in U.S. stores. Other elements are purely decorative, but all six sides of the box should work together to create a cohesive design.

project objectives

To complete this project, you will:

- [ ] Create the package file from a template
- [ ] Sample colors to create custom swatches
- [ ] Place a variety of external files in the appropriate locations to meet package design requirements
- [ ] Create type on an irregular path
- [ ] Change object blending modes and opacity
- [ ] Apply raster effects to vector objects and placed images
- [ ] Apply effects to pieces of a group
- [ ] Create warp and 3D effects
- [ ] Define raster effect settings
- [ ] Expand appearance attributes
- [ ] Preview and control transparency flattening
- [ ] Flatten transparency in a PDF file
- [ ] Preview a 3D representation of the completed box artwork

Stage 1 Building the File Structure

When you work on a package design, it's important to realize that many types of packages have a standard size and shape. If you look around your local grocery store, you'll see that similar products typically have similar packages. Although there is something to be said for standing out in a crowd, packaging design is often governed by the space allowed on store shelves — which means you probably won't have any choice regarding the size and shape of the package.

You also need to understand that packages are typically designed and printed as a flat layout, using a template to indicate edges and folds; they are then die-cut, folded, and glued. The next time you finish a box of cereal, tear it apart along the glue flaps to see how the package was designed. Because these types of packages are common sizes, printers often have existing templates you can use.

CREATE THE PACKAGE FILE FROM A TEMPLATE

The printer for this package has provided you with a template file that includes the die-cut layout and folding guides. You will use this file as the basis for the entire project.

1. Download **A16_RF_Project6.zip** from the Student Files Web page.

2. Expand the ZIP archive in your WIP folder (Macintosh) or copy the archive contents into your WIP folder (Windows).

   This results in a folder named **Cereal**, which contains the files you need for this project. You should also use this folder to save the files you create in this project.

3. Create a new file by opening the **cereal_box.ait** template file from your WIP>Cereal folder. Resize the view so you can see the entire artboard.

   The file has three layers: one has guides indicating the location of the folds, one has guides that define margin areas for each panel, and one has the die lines for the box shape.

4. Add four new layers, placing them in the following stacking order:

   Back
   Jumpstart Side
   Front
   Nutrition Side

   The image below includes a different-colored overlay on the area of each panel; these overlays are not included in template file you opened to create this project.

Note:

There are many ways to organize artwork. Placing each panel's elements on a separate layer makes this type of complex artwork easier to manage.

Note:

Even though the panel layers are above the guide layers, guides always appear in front of artwork.

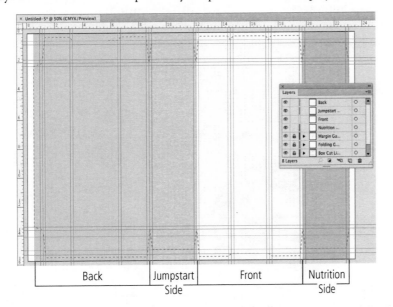

5. **Drag the Box Cut Line layer to the top of the layer stack.**

Be careful how you drag the layer to reposition it. If you accidentally move the layer to the wrong place in the stack, or move it to be a sublayer of another layer, simply drag it again to the top of the layer stack.

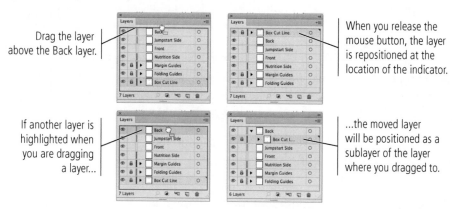

Drag the layer above the Back layer.

When you release the mouse button, the layer is repositioned at the location of the indicator.

If another layer is highlighted when you are dragging a layer...

...the moved layer will be positioned as a sublayer of the layer where you dragged to.

The Box Cut Line layer shows the location of the cut lines. Although it will not be printed, this layer needs to be visible while you create the basic package.

6. **Save the new file as a native Illustrator file named heartsmart.ai in your WIP>Cereal folder, then continue to the next exercise.**

SAMPLE COLORS AND CREATE CUSTOM SWATCHES

Now that you have set up the basic box document and layers, the next step is to place the image that will fill the front cover. You can then select colors directly from the image, enabling you to create a cohesive package design.

1. **With heartsmart.ai open, lock all but the Front layer and hide the Margin Guides layer. Select the Front layer as the active one.**

2. **Choose File>Place. Navigate to the file box front.jpg in the WIP>Cereal folder. Make sure the Link and Template options are not checked, and then click Place.**

Remember from Project 5: Letterfold Brochure, to embed an image when you place it, make sure the Link option is not checked in the Place dialog box.

3. **Position the placed image so its bottom-left corner aligns with the bottom-left corner of the front panel area (as shown in the following image).**

4. **Display the Swatches and Color panels, and then choose the Eyedropper tool in the Tools panel.**

5. **Click the Eyedropper tool in the dark purple area at the left side of the image.**

   Clicking with the Eyedropper tool changes the color in the Color panel; this method is called **sampling** color.

This file includes only four color swatches: Registration, White, Black, and CMYK Green.

Sampled color values appear in the Color panel.

We clicked here to sample the purple color.

Eyedropper tool

Note:

If you don't see the color sliders in the Color panel, choose Show Options in the panel's Options menu.

6. **Open the Color panel Options menu and choose Create New Swatch.**

   This option defines a new color swatch based on the current ink percentages.

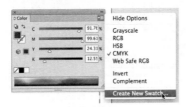

7. **In the resulting New Swatch dialog box, activate the Global check box, and then click OK to accept the default swatch name and color values.**

   The sampled color is added as a saved swatch, so you can access exactly the same color again later.

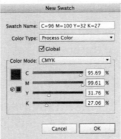

8. **Use the Eyedropper tool again to sample the light gold color in the image background, and then add the sampled color as a second global swatch.**

We sampled the light gold color in this area.

9. **Add a third global swatch by sampling the light pink color in the leaf veins below the cereal bowl.**

You might need to zoom in to sample the color in the thin line of the leaf vein.

Note:

If your Color and Swatches panels are docked, drag them out of the dock so you can use them both at once.

We sampled this leaf vein.

Note:

You could also simply click the New Swatch button in the Swatches panel to create a custom color swatch.

10. **Add a fourth global swatch by sampling the dark pink color in the leaves below the cereal bowl.**

We sampled this area of the leaf.

All four swatches are global swatches.

11. **Save the file and continue to the next exercise.**

 ## CREATE THE BACKGROUND SHAPES

You are now ready to draw the basic background shapes for the design. Remember, the die-cut lines identify the outside edges of the box shape. The Folding Guides layer shows the location of the various folds; these guides also identify the edges of the four panels in the job. In this exercise, you use the folding guides and the die-cut template shape to create solid-colored background shapes for most of the box surface.

1. **With heartsmart.ai open, unlock and select the Back layer.**

2. **Choose the Rectangle tool from the Tools panel. Set the fill color to the light pink swatch, and set the stroke to None.**

3. **Draw a rectangle that fills the top-flap area of the back panel, extending beyond the cut-line edges by at least 1/8″.**

Like any other job where ink is supposed to print all the way to the trim edge, packaging design also requires bleed allowance. Rather than trying to meticulously match the die-cut shape, a rectangle does the job far more easily.

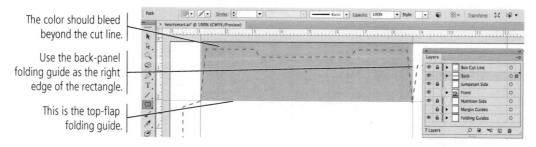

The color should bleed beyond the cut line.

Use the back-panel folding guide as the right edge of the rectangle.

This is the top-flap folding guide.

4. **Draw another rectangle that fills the back panel area, including the bottom flap. Make sure the bottom edge bleeds past the bottom cut line.**

5. **Change this rectangle's fill color to the light gold swatch.**

6. **Show the Margin Guides layer. Use the Selection tool to move the left edge of the gold rectangle to the margin guide on the outside glue flap.**

   The box will be glued together along this flap. The back panel color should extend past the folding guide so there will be no white space where the side meets the back panel.

Note:

Because the Box Cut Line layer is above the Back layer, you can still see the cut line when the filled rectangles are in place.

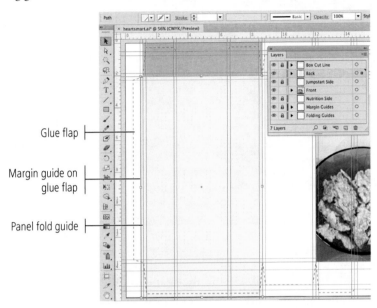

Glue flap

Margin guide on glue flap

Panel fold guide

7. **Unlock and select the Jumpstart Side layer.**

8. **Use the Rectangle tool to draw a shape of the entire side panel. Bleed the rectangle past the top cut line and extend the rectangle to the margin guide on the bottom flap. Fill the rectangle with the light pink swatch.**

   The white space remaining on the bottom flap will be used by the printer to add registration marks and color swatches for checking color on press.

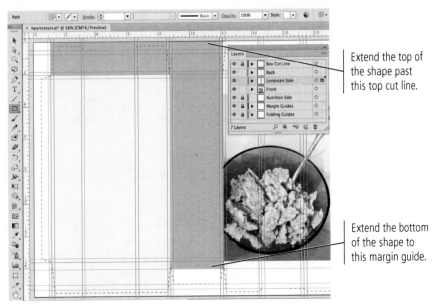

Extend the top of the shape past this top cut line.

Extend the bottom of the shape to this margin guide.

9. Select the Front layer (which should already be unlocked).

10. Draw the top flap shape with a light pink fill, and extend its bottom edge into the front panel area. Leave a small gap (approximately 1/8″) between the pink shape and the placed image.

11. Draw the bottom flap shape with a light gold fill.

This is the shape from Step 10.

This is the shape from Step 11.

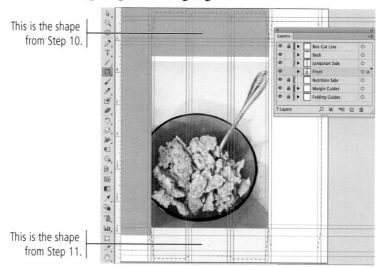

Note:

When creating the background shapes, you might find it helpful to show the margin guides only when necessary.

12. Unlock and select the Nutrition Side layer.

13. Draw the side panel shape with a light pink fill. Extend the shape to the same margin guide on the bottom flap as the other side panel. Extend the right edge of the shape at least 1/8″ past the right cut line.

14. Hide the Margin Guides and Folding Guides layers and review the layout.

15. **If necessary, adjust the objects so the only gap between background elements is the white line on the front panel.**

   At this point, zooming in is very helpful to check for small gaps that are not easily visible at small view percentages.

16. **Make sure each object appears on the correct layer.**

   If you placed an element on the wrong layer, simply drag the Selected Art icon in the Layers panel to the correct layer. Just make sure the layers involved are unlocked.

17. **Save the file and continue to the next stage of the project.**

Stage 2 Understanding Package Requirements

The nature of a specific package determines what standard elements you must include in the design. In this case, a cereal box generally requires nutritional information, the package weight (in both ounces and grams), the "best by" date, and a UPC bar code label. Additionally, HeartSmart cereal is being recommended by the Association for a Healthy America; this type of product endorsement should be displayed prominently on the package.

This package design has four basic panels, and each panel combines many elements. Most of these elements have already been created; you are going to use Illustrator to combine or **composite** the various elements into a single, unified layout. (You have already placed the primary image on the front panel, which was necessary to sample the colors you used to build the rest of the layout.)

The most logical way to proceed is to place or create the rest of the basic design elements. You can then decide what, if anything, still needs to be done to create an attractive, finished package design.

PLACE THE NUTRITION PANEL CONTENT

When you design a complex project such as this package, it helps to decide on a logical approach to accomplish the task. Rather than jumping around in the layout, it makes more sense to work on one panel at a time.

You are going to start with the nutrition panel on the right side of the page, and then work your way across to the back panel. (You could just as easily work from left to right; but for this project, we decided to start with the simplest panel.)

1. **With heartsmart.ai open, make sure the Nutrition Side layer is active. Lock all other layers, and show both guide layers.**

2. **Choose File>Place. Place the file nutrition.ai from the WIP>Cereal folder into your cereal box layout. Make sure the file is embedded (not linked), and base the placement on the Crop To Art option.**

As you know, when you place a native Illustrator file into another Illustrator file, it is contained by a bounding box that marks the outermost edges of the selected Crop To area. All objects in the placed file are grouped together so you can treat the placed graphic as a single object.

3. **Center the placed nutrition information in the panel area (between the margin guides), and align its top edge with the top of the cereal bowl image.**

When you place another file into an Illustrator file, it is automatically centered in the workspace; the placed file might not be visible until you move it into place. Although you can't see the actual file, you can still click within the visible bounding box of the placed file and drag to move it into place.

If you have difficulty working with placed files behind the locked layers, try zooming in to the correct area before placing; the placed artwork will still be centered in the workspace, but by zooming you center the approximate area in the workspace so the placed file will be centered in roughly the correct position.

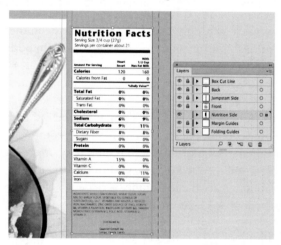

Note:

The Nutrition Facts text has been converted to outlines to ensure that the type will look exactly the same no matter where it is printed.

4. **Place (embed) the file afha.ai into the layout, using the Crop To Art option.**

5. **Position the placed endorsement graphic below the nutrition information. Center the graphic between the panel's vertical margin guides, and position the bottom edge at the bottom margin guide.**

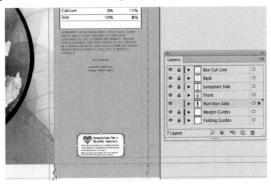

6. **Save the file and continue to the next exercise.**

PLACE THE FRONT PANEL CONTENT

1. **With heartsmart.ai open, lock the Nutrition Side layer. Unlock and select the Front layer.**

2. **Place (embed) bar code.eps into the layout, positioning it on the right side of the bottom flap. Move the bar code so the bottom corner is 1/8″ from the right edge of the front flap, and align the bottom edge with the bottom edge of the side flap.**

Note:

UPC (Universal Product Code) barcodes are specially created files that contain information about the item's name, price, and so on. These files are created by specialist bar-code companies, based on specific requirements; you can't draw a series of lines and call it a bar code.

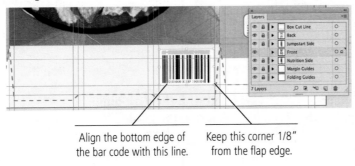

Align the bottom edge of the bar code with this line.

Keep this corner 1/8″ from the flap edge.

3. **Using the Type tool, click near the bottom of the front panel area to create a point-type object, and then type:**

   NET WT
   20 OZ (567 g)

4. **Format the text as 12-pt ATC Maple Medium with centered paragraph alignment. Change the text color to the custom purple swatch you created earlier.**

5. **Place the type object in the bottom-right corner of the box front area (inside the margin guides).**

Note:

If you have not already done so for previous projects, you need to install the ATC fonts to complete the rest of this project as described. As explained in the Getting Started section of this book, those fonts are available on the Resource Files Web site where you downloaded the files for this project.

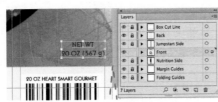

6. Place (embed) **hs logo.ai** into the layout, based on the Crop To Art option, and positioned in the top center of the front panel area. Align the left edge of the file with the left margin guide of the front panel area.

The crossbar of the "t" in "Heart" should overlap the line of empty white space, as shown below.

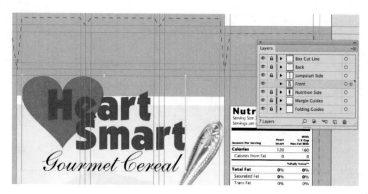

7. In the top-left section of the top flap, click and drag with the Type tool to create an area-type object. Type BETTER IF USED BY in the new type area, then format the text as black 11-pt ATC Maple Medium with centered paragraph alignment.

8. Resize the type area width to fit the top-left flap, as marked by the guides (and shown in the following image).

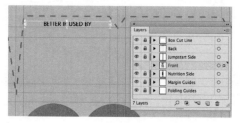

9. Directly below the type object, draw a rectangle filled with the dark pink custom swatch, positioned within the rectangle created by the guides.

The sell-by date is typically stamped onto pre-printed boxes during the packaging process because every day's production has a different date. This area provides a defined space for stamping the date.

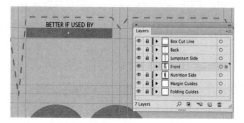

10. Save the file and continue to the next exercise.

PLACE THE JUMPSTART PANEL CONTENT

1. With **heartsmart.ai** open, lock the Front layer. Unlock and select the Jumpstart Side layer.

2. Using the Type tool, click and drag to create an area-type object that fills the Jumpstart Side panel (snapping to the margin guides).

   Be sure the cursor is near the panel margin guide before you click and drag with the Type tool. If you click too close to the edge of the existing pink rectangle, clicking with the Type tool will convert the existing shape into an area-type object. Use the shape of the cursor as a guide for when you can click to create a new type area.

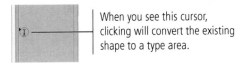
When you see this cursor, clicking will convert the existing shape to a type area.

If the cursor is far enough away from the edges of existing shapes, you can click and drag to create a new type object.

   (To work around this potential problem, you can also click and drag to create a small type area in the middle of the panel, and then use the Selection tool to resize the type area to fit in the panel's margin guides.)

3. With the insertion point flashing in the new type area, place the file **side copy.doc** into the new type area. Accept the default Microsoft Word options, and click OK if you receive a Font Problems warning.

   This text has been formatted in the original word-processing file using ATC fonts.

Note:

Remember from Project 5: Letterfold Brochure, you can check the Remove Text Formatting option when you import a Microsoft Word document. If you check that option, however, any formatting applied in the text file will not be maintained when the text is placed in Illustrator. This means you won't be able to see what the author (usually, the client) intended for various text elements.

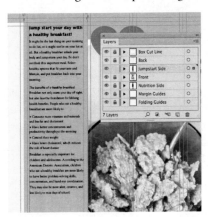

4. If necessary, use the Selection tool to adjust the type area to exactly fit inside the panel's margin guides.

5. Select the entire first paragraph ("Jump start your day...") and change its color to the custom purple swatch.

6. Select the entire third paragraph ("The benefits of...") and change its color to the custom purple swatch.

Change both of these paragraphs to the custom purple swatch.

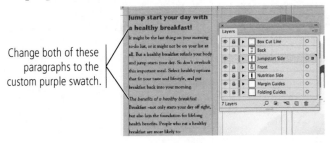

7. **Open the Glyphs panel (Type>Glyphs).**

8. **In the first bulleted paragraph, select and delete the bullet character.**

9. **Search through the glyphs of various fonts to find a bullet that fits the overall product message (natural, healthy, heart-smart). When you find a glyph you like, double-click it to place that glyph at the location of the insertion point.**

   We used a leafy heart ornament from the Minion Pro font, but you can use whatever glyph from whatever font you prefer.

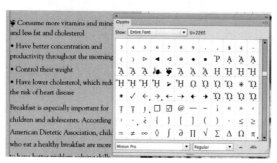

10. **Change the color of the placed glyph to the custom purple swatch.**

11. **Copy the custom glyph, and then paste it to replace the remaining three bullets.**

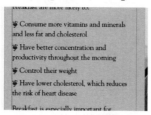

The Glyphs Panel in Depth

The Glyphs panel (Type>Glyphs) provides access to every glyph in a font, including basic characters, extended ASCII and OpenType character sets, and even pictographic characters in Unicode fonts.

Using the Glyphs panel is simple: make sure the insertion point is flashing where you want a character to appear, and then double-click the character you want to place. You can view the character set for any font by changing the menu at the bottom of the panel. By default, the panel shows the entire font, but you can show only specific character sets using the Show menu.

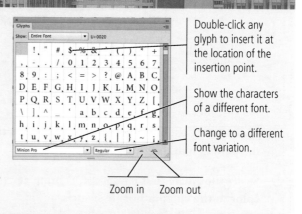

Double-click any glyph to insert it at the location of the insertion point.

Show the characters of a different font.

Change to a different font variation.

Zoom in   Zoom out

ASCII is a text-based code that defines characters with a numeric value between 001 and 256. The standard alphabet and punctuation characters are mapped from 001 to 128. Extended ASCII characters are those with ASCII numbers higher than 128; these include symbols (copyright symbols, etc.) and some special formatting characters (en dashes, accent marks, etc.).

OpenType fonts offer the ability to store more than 65,000 glyphs (characters) in a single font — far beyond what you could access with a keyboard (even including combinations of the different modifier keys). The large glyph storage capacity means that a single OpenType font can replace separate "Expert" fonts that contain variations of fonts.

Unicode fonts include two-bit characters common in some foreign language typesetting (e.g., Cyrillic, Japanese, and other non-Roman or pictographic fonts).

12. **Select any part of the four bulleted paragraphs. Using the Paragraphs panel, change the left indent to 12 pt and the first-line left indent to -12 pt.**

    This type of negative first-line indent is called a **hanging indent**.

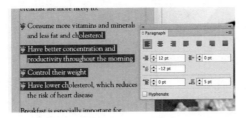

13. **Command/Control-click away from the text area to deselect it.**

14. **Place (embed) the file js figure.ai, based on the Crop To Art option. Using the Selection tool, position the placed logo at the top of the panel area, aligned to the panel's top and right margin guides.**

15. **With the placed artwork selected, choose Object>Text Wrap>Make.**

    Applying a **text wrap** to an object forces surrounding text to flow around that object instead of directly in front of or behind it.

Note:

You can modify the text wrap size by choosing Object>Text Wrap>Text Wrap Options.

16. **Using the Type tool, select the entire first paragraph and change the type size to 15 pt.**

    This fits the text onto four lines to the left of the placed artwork.

17. **Save the file and continue to the next exercise.**

1. With **heartsmart.ai** open, lock the Jumpstart Side layer. Unlock and select the Back layer.

2. Place (embed) the file **recycle.eps** onto the bottom flap of the back panel. Position it as shown in the following image.

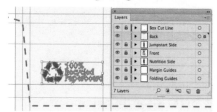

3. Create a type area below the middle of the top flap on the back panel. Type TO CLOSE, PUSH TAB UNDER HERE.

4. Format the text as 11-pt ATC Maple Medium with centered paragraph alignment.

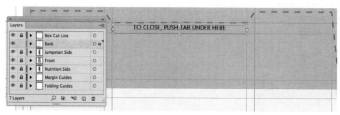

5. Choose the Selection tool and click away from the type object to deselect it.

6. Choose File>Place. Navigate to the file **flake heart.psd** and click Place. In the resulting dialog box, check the Show Preview option.

The resulting Photoshop Import Options dialog box allows you to control how Photoshop elements are translated into Illustrator:

- Use the **Layer Comp** menu to import a specific layer comp saved in the Photoshop file.

- If you link to the file instead of placing it (in the Place dialog box), you can use the **When Updating Link** menu to control what happens if you update the linked image.

- **Convert Layers to Objects** converts Photoshop layers to Illustrator objects. This option preserves type layers as editable type objects in Illustrator; it also preserves masks, blending modes, transparency, and slice information. (Adjustment layers and layer effects are flattened into the placed objects.)

- **Flatten Layers to a Single Image** combines all Photoshop layers into a single layer. The appearance of the image is preserved, but you can't edit the layers.

- **Import Hidden Layers** can be checked to include layers that are not visible in the Photoshop file.

- **Import Slices** is only available if the Photoshop file includes slices for Web layouts. If this option is checked, the slices will be maintained in the imported file.

Note:

*Learn more about Adobe Photoshop in the companion book of this series, **Adobe Photoshop CS6: The Professional Portfolio**.*

7. **Choose the Flatten Layers to a Single Image option and click OK.**

   This image has only one layer, which you will not edit, so this option has the same result as converting Photoshop layers to Illustrator objects.

8. **Position the placed image in the center of the back panel area. Leave about 2″ between the panel's top folding guide and the top of the placed image.**

9. **Using the Type tool, create an area-type object in the area below the placed heart image, using the sides of the heart to define the approximate width of the area. Place the top edge of the area about 1/2″ from the bottom of the heart graphic.**

10. **Place the file back copy.doc into the area, using the default Microsoft Word import options.**

11. **Using the Selection tool, extend the bottom edge of the type area until all of the text is visible.**

12. **Select all placed text and change the text color to the custom purple swatch.**

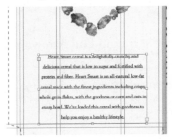

13. **Unlock the Jumpstart Side layer.**

   The Smart Punctuation utility, which you will apply in the next step, does not work on locked layers.

14. **Open the Smart Punctuation dialog box (Type>Smart Punctuation). Check all Replace options except Expert Fractions, and choose the Entire Document option. Click OK, read the results dialog box, and click OK to continue to the next step.**

Make sure the Entire Document option is selected.

15. **Save the file and continue to the next exercise.**

USE A LINE TO CREATE A TRIANGLE

The text on the top flap of the back panel explains where to push the tab, but arrows would be helpful. You could draw these shapes manually, but Illustrator's built-in stroke end treatments can easily be used to create the necessary shapes.

1. **With heartsmart.ai open and the Back panel selected, create a short, vertical line to the right of the text on the top flap. Change the line's stroke to 2-pt black.**

   Don't worry about the exact length of the line. You are only using the line to create an arrowhead shape; you will eventually delete the line, leaving only the arrowhead.

2. **In the Stroke panel, open the End Arrowhead menu and choose Arrow 7.**

   You can apply different end treatments to the start and end of the line using the options on the left and right (respectively). If you drew your line from top to bottom, the resulting arrow points down because the right menu defines the line's end treatment.

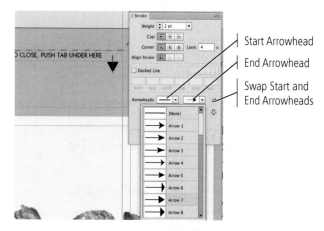

3. **If your arrow is pointing down, click the Swap Start and End Arrowheads button on the right side of the Stroke panel.**

   This button provides an easy way to reverse the direction of a line.

4. **Change the scale of the applied arrowhead to 75%.**

   The Scale menus change the size of the end treatment relative to the stroke weight. If you change the stroke weight, the end treatments will change according to the new weight.

5. **If the arrowhead obscures the line you just drew, click the left Align option in the Arrowheads section of the Stroke panel.**

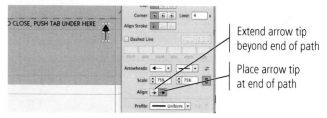

6. **With the line selected, choose Object>Path>Outline Stroke.**

   This command converts a stroke to a filled path. The end treatment is also converted to a filled shape, which is grouped with the line shape.

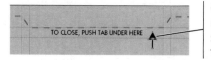

7. Click away from the group to deselect it.

8. Using the Direct Selection tool, select only the rectangle part of the group and delete it.

9. Select the remaining triangle and apply a 1-pt white stroke to the shape.

10. Clone the triangle, and place the copies on either side of the text.

11. Save the file and continue to the next exercise.

 ## CREATE TYPE ON A PATH

Instead of simply flowing text into a type object, you can create unique typographic effects by flowing text onto a path. A text path can be any shape you can create in Illustrator, whether it's a simple shape created with one of the basic shape tools, a straight line drawn with the Line Segment tool, or a complex graphic drawn with the Pen tool.

1. With **heartsmart.ai** open, select the Back layer and lock all other layers.

2. Deselect everything in the layout.

3. Select the Pen tool. Change the fill to None and the stroke to 1-pt black.

4. Draw a curve above the top of the flake heart, as shown in the following image.

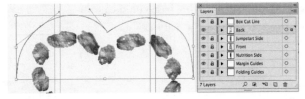

5. Select the Type tool in the Tools panel, and then click near the left side of the path you just drew.

   Clicking an existing path with the Type tool converts the path to a type path. You could select the Type on a Path tool (nested under the Type tool), but it's not necessary because when the Type tool cursor is near an existing path, it automatically switches to the Type on a Path tool cursor.

   When the Type tool cursor is near an existing path, it switches to the Type on a Path tool cursor.

   The 1-pt black stroke attribute is automatically removed when you convert the stroke to a type path.

   After converting the path to a type path, the insertion point flashes on the path.

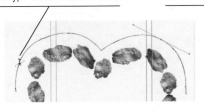

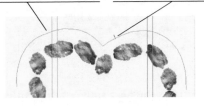

6. **With the insertion point flashing along the path, type** A healthy start for your heart!.

7. **Select all the text on the path (Select>All) and format it as 36-pt ATC Laurel Book with centered alignment. Change the text color to the purple swatch.**

   Depending on where you clicked, some of the message might not be visible after you change the formatting; the location where you clicked defined the starting point for text along the path. You will adjust the text position on the path in the next two steps.

   The text is centered between the location where you clicked with the Type tool and the end point of the path.

8. **Choose the Direct Selection tool in the Tools panel.**

   When the insertion point is placed in type on a path (or type on a path is selected), switching to the Direct Selection tool reveals the start and end points of the type path. Modifying those points is the same basic concept as changing the left and right indents for text in a regular type area.

This is the start bar for the text (basically, the left indent for the type path).

This is the center point of the type path, based on the current start and end points.

This is the end bar for the text (basically, the right indent for the type path).

   You can also click a type path with the Selection tool, or click the type on the path with the Direct Selection tool, to reveal the start and end points of the type.

9. **Click the start bar and drag to the left end of the path.**

   If you change the start or end point, the center point also changes, based on the new amount of available space. The text is now centered, based on the entire path.

Note:

Make sure you click the start bar and not the white square that represents the in port of the text path.

Moving the start bar to the beginning of the path repositions the center point as well.

10. **If necessary, reposition the path's start bar so the space between "start" and "for" is positioned at the dip in the path.**

   This might be necessary, depending on the shape of your type path; if the "t" in start and the "f" in for are too close together where the path dips, use an extra space to move the letters away from the dip.

11. **Save the file and continue to the next stage of the project.**

You can control the appearance of type on a path by choosing Type>Type on a Path>Type on a Path Options. You can apply one of five effects, change the alignment of the text to the path, flip the text to the other side of the path, and adjust the character spacing around curves (higher Spacing values remove more space around sharp curves).

The **Align options** determine which part of the text (baseline, ascender, descender, or center) aligns to which part of the path (top, bottom, or center).

The **Flip** check box turns type onto the other side of the path; this option is useful for putting text inside shapes.

The **3D Ribbon** effect maintains horizontal edges of type while rotating vertical edges to be perpendicular to the path.

The **Rainbow** (default) effect keeps each character's baseline parallel to the path.

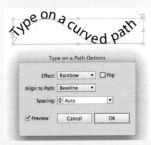

The **Stair Step** effect aligns the left edge of each character's baseline to the path without rotating any characters.

The **Skew** effect maintains the vertical edges of type while skewing the horizontal edges around the path.

The **Gravity** effect aligns the center of each character's baseline to the path, keeping vertical edges in line with the path's center.

Stage 3 Working with Effects

Illustrator includes a number of effects for enhancing objects in a layout. Effects in Illustrator are live and non-destructive, which means they can be edited or removed from an object without destroying the original object.

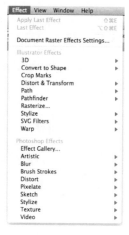

When you work with effects, you should be aware that many of these options eventually result in rasterized elements, even when you apply them to vector objects. For example, a drop shadow (in the Stylize submenu) creates a soft-edge shadow object that blends from the shadow color to fully transparent. To achieve this effect on output, the shadow has to be rasterized into pixels that reproduce the visual effect.

The Drop Shadow, Inner Glow, Outer Glow, and Feather options in the Stylize submenu all utilize some form of graded transparency, and they all result in objects that reproduce as pixels (rasters) instead of vectors. In this stage of the project, you use effects and transparency controls to add visual interest to different elements of your artwork. In Stage 4 of this project, you will learn how to control transparent objects that need to be rasterized before they can be successfully output.

 ## APPLY AN EFFECT TO PART OF A GROUP

As you know, all elements of placed graphics are grouped together in the file where they are placed. Any groupings from the original file are also maintained, often resulting in a complex series of multiple nested groups — which can make it difficult to access specific elements to make changes or apply effects.

1. **With heartsmart.ai open, unlock all the content layers.**

2. **Using the Selection tool, click the placed graphic on the Jumpstart Side panel to select it.**

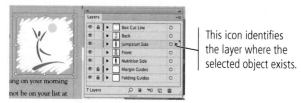

This icon identifies the layer where the selected object exists.

3. **In the Layers panel, click the arrow to the left of the Jumpstart Side layer.**

   Clicking this arrow shows the objects contained on the layer (called sublayers). You can further expand groups so you can show — and select — the individual elements in a group.

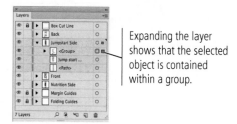

Expanding the layer shows that the selected object is contained within a group.

4. **Open the Layers panel Options menu and choose Panel Options. In the resulting dialog box, choose Large in the Row Size section, and then click OK.**

Enlarging the panel rows makes it easier to see what is contained on each layer and sublayer.

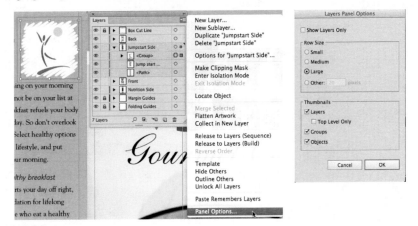

5. **Click the arrow to expand the group that contains the selected object.**

6. **Continue expanding groups until a group thumbnail shows the dancing man figure (with the grass and sun).**

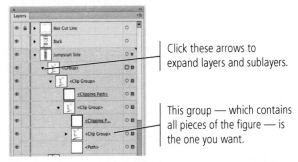

Click these arrows to expand layers and sublayers.

This group — which contains all pieces of the figure — is the one you want.

7. **Click the Target icon next to the small figure group to isolate it.**

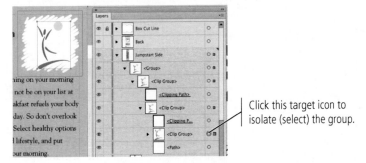

Click this target icon to isolate (select) the group.

8. **Choose Effect>[Illustrator Effects] Stylize>Drop Shadow.**

Make sure you choose the option in the Ilustrator Effects section and not the Photoshop Effects section.

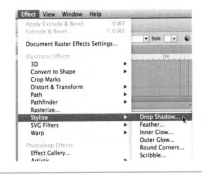

9. **Activate the Preview check box, then change the drop shadow settings to the following:**

Mode:	Multiply
Opacity:	75%
X Offset:	0.02″
Y Offset:	0.02″
Blur:	0.04″
Color:	Black

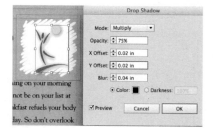

Note:

Effects dialog boxes remember the last-used settings.

10. **Click OK to apply the drop shadow.**

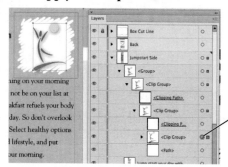

The solid target indicates that an effect has altered the appearance of the sublayer.

Note:

Illustrator remembers the last-used effect, and the specific settings you used to apply that effect. The top of the Effect menu includes the option to apply the last-used effect without opening the related dialog box, or to open the dialog box for the last-used effect.

11. **Open the Appearance panel (Window>Appearance).**

The drop shadow is treated as an appearance attribute. You can edit the applied settings by clicking the effect hot text in the Appearance panel. You can remove the effect by dragging it to the Appearance panel's Delete button.

Click the hot text to open the dialog box and change the settings of the applied effect.

Note:

Refer to Project 3: Identity Package for more about the Appearance panel.

12. **Collapse the expanded Jumpstart Side layer in the Layers panel, save the file, and then continue to the next exercise.**

Technical Issues Concerning Transparency

Because object opacity, blending modes, and some effects relate to transparency, you should understand what transparency is and how it affects your output. Transparency is the degree to which light passes through an object so objects in the background are visible. In terms of page layout, transparency means being able to "see through" objects in front of the stacking order to objects in back of the stacking order.

Because of the way printing works, applying transparency in print graphic design is a bit of a contradiction. Commercial printing is, by definition, accomplished by overlapping a mixture of (usually) four semi-transparent inks in different percentages to reproduce a range of colors (the printable gamut). In that sense, all print graphic design requires transparency.

But design transparency refers to the objects on the page. The trouble is, when a halftone dot is printed, it's either there or it's not. There is no "50% opaque" setting on a printing press. This means that a transformation needs to take place behind the scenes, translating what we create on screen into what a printing press produces.

When transparent objects are output, overlapping areas of transparent elements are actually divided into individual elements (where necessary) to produce the best possible results. Ink values in the overlap areas are calculated by the application, based on the capabilities of the mechanical printing process; the software converts our digital designs into the elements that are necessary to print.

In Stage 4 of this project, you learn how to preview and control the output process for transparent objects.

ILLUSTRATOR FOUNDATIONS

APPLY RASTER EFFECTS TO DESIGN ELEMENTS

Transparency and blending modes can help unify various elements of a design. Other effects — specifically glows, drop shadows, and similar styles — combine graded transparency and blending modes to add depth to otherwise flat artwork.

1. **With heartsmart.ai open, select the placed heart image on the back panel.**

2. **Choose Effect>[Illlustrator Effects] Stylize>Outer Glow.**

   As with the Drop Shadow effect, this option is in the Illustrator Effects Stylize menu, not the Photoshop Effects Stylize menu.

   The Outer Glow effect adds a transparent effect behind the selected object. The Mode menu, color swatch, and Opacity menu determine the appearance of the glow effect. The Blur field defines the width of the apparent effect (how far the glow extends from the edges of the object).

3. **Check the Preview box, and then click the color swatch to the right of the Mode menu.**

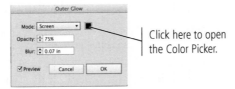

   Click here to open the Color Picker.

4. **In the resulting Color Picker dialog box, click the Color Swatches button to show the swatches saved in the current file.**

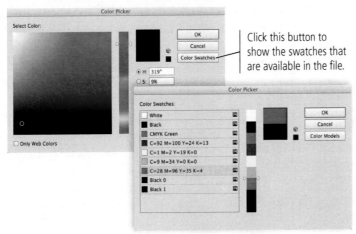

   Click this button to show the swatches that are available in the file.

5. **Choose the dark pink custom swatch and click OK.**

6. **In the Outer Glow dialog box, choose Multiply in the Mode menu, set the opacity to 75%, and change the Blur field to 0.05".**

The Multiply blending mode combines the base color (the light gold background) with the glow color (the dark pink at 75% opacity).

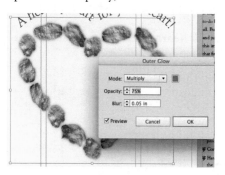

Note:

You can use any color for the glow, but using an existing swatch helps unify the design.

7. **Click OK to apply the glow effect.**

8. **Save the file and continue to the next exercise.**

Understanding Blending Modes

ILLUSTRATOR FOUNDATIONS

Blending modes control how colors in an object interact with colors in underlying objects. Objects are set to Normal by default, which simply overlays the top object's color onto underlying objects (i.e., the "base"). If the top object is entirely opaque — a solid color you can't see through — it is unaffected by underlying objects.

- **Darken** returns the darker of the blend or base color. Base pixels that are lighter than the blend color are replaced; base pixels that are darker than the blend color remain unchanged.

- **Multiply** multiplies (hence the name) the base color by the blend color, resulting in a darker color. Multiplying any color with black produces black; multiplying any color with white leaves the color unchanged.

- **Color Burn** darkens the base color by increasing the contrast. Blend colors darker than 50% significantly darken the base color by increasing saturation and reducing brightness; blending with white has no effect.

- **Lighten** returns whichever is the lighter color (base or blend). Base pixels that are darker than the blend color are replaced; base pixels that are lighter than the blend color remain unchanged.

- **Screen** is basically the inverse of Multiply, always returning a lighter color. Screening with black has no effect; screening with white produces white.

- **Color Dodge** brightens the base color. Blend colors lighter than 50% significantly increase brightness; blending with black has no effect.

- **Overlay** multiplies or screens the blend color to preserve the original lightness or darkness of the base color.

- **Soft Light** darkens or lightens base colors, depending on the blend color. Blend colors lighter than 50% lighten the base color (as if dodged); blend colors darker than 50% darken the base color (as if burned).

- **Hard Light** combines the Multiply and Screen modes. Blend colors darker than 50% are multiplied, and blend colors lighter than 50% are screened.

- **Difference*** inverts base color values according to the brightness value in the blend layer. Lower brightness values in the blend layer have less effect on the result; blending with black has no effect.

- **Exclusion*** is very similar to Difference, except that mid-tone values in the base color are completely desaturated.

- **Hue*** results in a color with the luminance and saturation of the base color and the hue of the blend color.

- **Saturation*** results in a color with the luminance and hue of the base color and saturation of the blend color.

- **Color*** results in a color with the luminance of the base color and the hue and saturation of the blend color.

- **Luminosity*** results in a color with the hue and saturation of the base color and the luminance of the blend color (basically the opposite of the Color mode).

To prevent problems in the output process, avoid applying Difference, Exclusion, Hue, Saturation, Color, and Luminosity blending modes to objects with spot colors.

CHANGE OBJECT BLENDING MODES AND OPACITY

The effects and transparency controls in Illustrator allow you to add dimension and depth to virtually any design element. You can change the transparency of any object, apply different blending modes so objects blend smoothly into underlying objects, and apply creative effects (such as drop shadows) that incorporate transparency.

1. **With heartsmart.ai open, select the recycle logo at the bottom of the back panel and open the Transparency panel (Window>Transparency).**

2. **Choose Color Burn in the Blending Mode menu.**

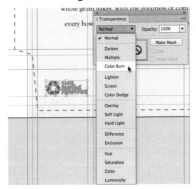

After changing the blending mode, the logo is a blend of the original purple logo color and the gold color of the background object.

3. **Using the Direct Selection tool, select the heart shape in the logotype on the front panel.**

4. **In the Transparency panel, change the Opacity value to 50%.**

   The Opacity value determines how much of the underlying colors show through the affected object. If an object is 75% opaque, 25% of the underlying colors are visible.

Use the slider to try different levels, or type a specific value in the field.

5. **Select the entire logo with the Selection tool.**

6. **Clone the logo. Use the Transform panel to scale the clone to 45% proportionally, and then position the resized version in the empty space of the nutrition panel (between the nutrition information and the AHA logo).**

7. In the Layers panel, drag the Selected Art icon to the Nutrition Side layer.

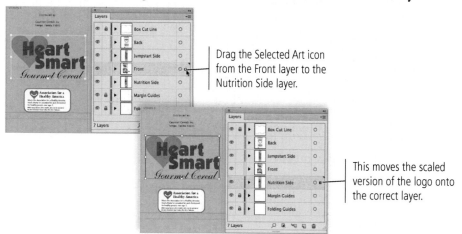

Drag the Selected Art icon from the Front layer to the Nutrition Side layer.

This moves the scaled version of the logo onto the correct layer.

Understanding Transparency Panel Options

Three options at the bottom of the Transparency panel allow you to control transparency settings relative to grouped objects. (If you don't see these check boxes, choose Show Options in the panel Options menu.) If **Isolate Blending** is checked for the entire group, blending changes only apply to other objects in the same group. The group effectively knocks out the underlying shapes.

The Hard Light blending mode is applied to the purple letters in the grouped logo.

When Isolate Blending is checked for the entire group, the blending mode does not affect the underlying gold object.

If **Knockout Group** is checked, transparency settings for elements within the group do not apply to other elements in the same group. The transparent effects are only applied to objects under the entire group. In this case, elements within the group knock out other objects in the same group.

The opacity of the purple letters has been reduced to 50%.

When Knockout Group is checked, the opacity only affects underlying objects that are not part of the grouped logo.

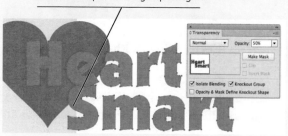

If **Opacity and Mask Define Knockout Shape** is checked (at the bottom of the panel), the mask object's opacity creates a knockout effect. Where the mask is 100% opaque, the knockout effect is strong; in areas of lower opacity, the knockout effect is weaker.

ILLUSTRATOR FOUNDATIONS

An opacity mask defines the transparency of selected artwork. In Illustrator, you can create an opacity mask by selecting two or more shapes and clicking the Make Mask button in the Transparency panel. The topmost selected object (or group) becomes the masking object; underlying objects in the selection are the masked artwork.

The best way to explain the concept of opacity masks is through example. The first image shows two separate objects: the top object (the word "GOLD" converted to outlines) and the gradient-filled rectangle.

When you define an opacity mask, shades in the masking object (in this example, the word "GOLD") determine the degree of transparency in the masked artwork (the gold gradient).

- Where the mask is white, the masked object is 100% visible;
- Shades of gray in the mask allow some of the underlying object to be visible; and
- Black areas of the mask completely obscure underlying areas.

Masked artwork thumbnail   Mask thumbnail

When the **Clip** option is checked, the masking object also determines which parts of the masked artwork are visible. Any areas outside the mask object are not visible. In this image, we turned off the Clip option to allow the gradient-filled rectangle to be visible beyond the edges of the masking lettershapes.

When the **Invert Mask** option is checked, tones in the masking object are reversed (black becomes white and white becomes black). Transparency of the masked artwork is also effectively reversed.

By default, the masking object and masked artwork are linked, which means you can't move one without the other. If you click the Link icon between the masked artwork and the mask thumbnails, you can move the two elements independently.

Turn off the Link option to move either object independently of the other.

8. Clone the resized logo. Move the second clone to the Jumpstart Side layer, and position it in the layout at the bottom of that panel.

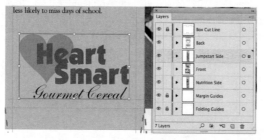

9. Clone the resized logo again. Move the new clone to the Back layer, rotate the artwork 180°, place it in the center of the top flap on the back panel, and scale it proportionally to fit in the flap area.

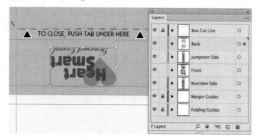

10. Save the file and continue to the next exercise.

 ## WARP DESIGN ELEMENTS

The final piece of the design is a banner across the bottom that announces a promotional premium (in this case, a recipe booklet). Rather than simply creating a flat banner, you're going to use effects to create a two-piece, three-dimensional banner that appears to wave across the box.

1. With **heartsmart.ai** open, lock everything but the Front layer. Select the Front layer as the active one.

2. Create a rectangle near the bottom of the front panel area that is 5.5″ wide and 1″ high. Fill the rectangle with the dark pink custom swatch and set the stroke to None.

3. Using the Add Anchor Point tool, add an anchor point to the right edge of the rectangle, halfway between the corners. Use the Direct Selection tool to drag the point left, creating the basic banner shape.

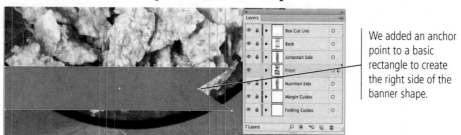

We added an anchor point to a basic rectangle to create the right side of the banner shape.

4. Using the Type tool, click to create a point-type object near the center of the banner shape.

5. Type Yummy! Cereal Recipes, and then format the text as 28-pt ATC Maple Ultra with 125% vertical scaling and a white fill.

6. Position the text relative to the banner shape (as shown in the following image).

7. Select the text and the banner, and group them (Object>Group). With the group selected, choose Effect>Warp>Arc.

8. In the resulting Warp Options dialog box, activate the Preview check box.

The icon for each warp style suggests the result that will be created.

The Bend value determines how much warping will be applied.

Distortion values change the horizontal and vertical perspectives.

9. Choose Arch in the Style menu.

As the Arch icon suggests, the object's left and right edges are unaffected by an Arch warp.

Note:

You can choose from any of the 15 styles in the Style menu (these are the same as the options listed in the Effect>Warp submenu).

10. Change the Bend value to –25 and click OK to apply the warp.

The warp effect is also treated as an appearance attribute. When the warped object is selected, you can see the original object shape.

The bounding box and paths reflect the actual objects without the applied appearance attributes.

11. Create another rectangle that's 2″ wide by 1″ high, filled with the dark pink custom swatch, positioned on the right side of the front panel area.

12. **Using the same method from the first banner shape, add a point to the left edge of the shape, and then drag it right to create the second banner shape.**

13. **Use the Type tool to add a point-type object with the words** Free Inside **formatted as 20-pt ATC Maple Ultra with a white fill and a vertical scale of 125%. Group the second banner with its text.**

Note:

Similar warp options are available by choosing Object>Envelope Distort>Make with Warp.

14. **Apply a warp effect using the Rise style and a 50% Bend value.**

15. **If necessary, move the second banner up or down until you are satisfied with its position relative to the first banner.**

16. **Save the file and continue to the next exercise.**

 ## CREATE A 3D EFFECT

3D effects allow you to create three-dimensional objects from two-dimensional artwork. You can simulate depth by changing an object's rotation along three different axes, or use extrusion settings to basically "pull" (extrude) an object in three directions. You can also control the appearance of 3D objects with lighting, shading, and other properties.

1. **With heartsmart.ai open, select the first banner group you created in the previous exercise.**

2. **Choose Effect>3D>Extrude & Bevel and activate the Preview option.**

   In the 3D Extrude & Bevel Options dialog box, the cube/preview shows the approximate position of the original object (the blue surface) in relation to the object created by the settings in this dialog box.

Note:

The X Axis value rotates an object around an invisible horizontal line.

The Y Axis value rotates an object around an invisible vertical line.

The Z Axis value rotates an object around an invisible line that moves from the front of an object to the back.

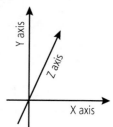

3. **Click the preview icon and drag it around.**

   As you drag the preview cube, the values in the three fields change, based on how and where you drag. In the layout, the selected group also changes because the Preview option is active.

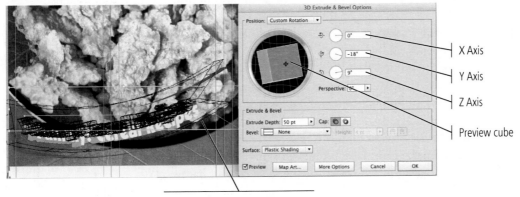

While you move the preview icon, the object appears as a wire frame (the basis of 3D artwork).

4. **When you're done experimenting with the preview, specify the following values:**

   X Axis = 14°   **Y Axis = 0°**   **Z Axis = 0°**
   Extrude Depth = 50 pt

> **Note:**
>
> *The surface of the object only appears after the wires are calculated internally.*

5. **Click OK to apply the effect.**

6. **Select the small banner group and choose Effect>Apply Extrude & Bevel.**

   The top menu option shows the last-used effect. If you use this menu command, the effect will be applied with the last-used settings. You will not see the effect's dialog box.

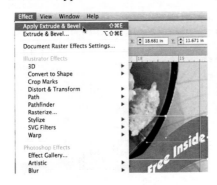

> **Note:**
>
> *Remember: Choosing the same option more than once in the Effect menu actually applies a second instance of that effect to the selected object. Use the Appearance panel to modify the settings of an applied effect.*

7. **Adjust the two banners across the bottom of the box until you are satisfied with their positions.**

8. **Save the file and continue to the next stage of the project.**

Stage 4 Preparing Artwork for Output

For all intents and purposes, the box artwork is now finished. You have placed and formatted the client's text, composited a number of external graphics and images, created several design elements directly from within Illustrator, and enhanced many of the layout objects using built-in transparency controls and effects.

Whenever you design a file, it's important to consider the ultimate goal of the project — in other words, how the job will be output, and what needs to happen to ensure that what you see on your screen is what you receive in the printed job.

The best practice is to leave transparent elements intact as long as possible — ideally, all the way through final output. However, some applications and devices do not have the ability to directly interpret information about transparency.

Although some output devices can accurately translate transparent elements to printed elements, older equipment might have problems rendering transparency. You should not assume that your output provider has the most current hardware or software.

Similarly, if the file you're creating will be placed into another layout — for example, an ad that is placed into a magazine or newspaper layout — you also need to consider the capabilities of the software being used to create the larger project. Older versions of layout software might not be able to interpret transparent elements correctly.

For transparent elements to output properly in these workflows, the transparent elements must be converted or **flattened** into information that can be rendered.

The following exercises explain the concept of flattening so you will understand what to do if your file needs to work with older equipment that does not support transparent design elements.

DEFINE RASTER EFFECT SETTINGS

Flattening means dividing transparent elements into the necessary vector and raster objects to properly output the file. In some cases, flattening results in the creation of new rasterized objects (for example, where transparent text overlaps a raster image).

This is white text with the Screen blending mode applied.

Flattening creates a second raster image with the pixels altered to create the same apparent effect as the screened text. The vector outlines of the original type object mask the new raster element.

Some effects, such as drop shadows, create entirely new raster elements where none existed previously.

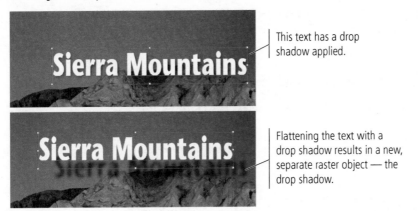

This text has a drop shadow applied.

Flattening the text with a drop shadow results in a new, separate raster object — the drop shadow.

If you are going to create raster objects — either manually or allowing Illustrator to manage the process — you need to be able to control the resolution of those elements. For high-quality print jobs, you should use at least 300 pixels per inch.

1. **With heartsmart.ai open, choose Effect>Document Raster Effects Settings.**

2. **Review the settings in the resulting dialog box.**

These settings are already optimized for high-quality output, applied in the printer's original document template. However, it's always a good idea to check the settings before you apply them.

The **Color Model** menu determines the mode that will be used for new rasterized objects (CMYK, Grayscale, or Bitmap for a document in CMYK mode; an RGB option replaces CMYK if the file uses the RGB color mode).

The **Resolution** options include three basic settings (72 ppi for low-resolution screen display, 150 ppi for medium-resolution desktop printers, or 300 ppi for high-resolution PostScript output). If necessary, you can also assign a custom resolution value in the Other field.

The **Background** options determine how unfilled areas of the file will be handled when placed into another file. If White is selected, underlying objects will not be visible through empty areas of the file.

In the **Options** area:

- **Anti-alias** helps to create smooth transitions, reducing stair-stepping around the edges of rasterized objects.

- **Create Clipping Mask** creates a vector mask that makes the background of the rasterized image appear transparent.

- **Add _ Around Object** creates a specific-sized border around a rasterized image. If you use the White Background option, this area will be filled with white.

- **Preserve Spot Colors** allows spot-color objects to be maintained as spot colors instead of being converted to CYMK.

3. **Click OK to close the dialog box.**

4. **Continue to the next exercise.**

Note:

Note the warning at the bottom of the dialog box that says, "Changing these settings may affect the appearance of currently applied raster effects."

EXPAND APPEARANCE ATTRIBUTES

When you output a file, the RIP processes the PostScript stream to create the print. Extremely complex designs can take a long time to output (depending on the processing capability of the output device) and can even "jam the RIP" — crash the device and cause an output error. To prevent output problems associated with overly complex designs, you might want to expand appearance attributes after the design has been finalized.

1. **With heartsmart.ai open, use the Selection tool to select the right banner shape. Display the Appearance panel.**

   At this point, you can still change or delete any attribute of any object. After expanding effects, the file will output faster, but you won't be able to change the effect settings.

The bounding box and paths show the original objects' shapes.

Two effects have been applied to this object: Warp (Rise) and 3D Extrude & Bevel. Opacity values are those determined by the default settings for the effects you applied.

2. **Choose Object>Expand Appearance.**

The paths show the new objects created by expanding the effects.

The effects are no longer editable.

3. **Using the same process, expand the appearance of the left banner.**

4. **Choose File>Save As. Save the file as heartsmart expanded.ai in your WIP>Cereal folder and continue to the next exercise.**

   We recommend saving the expanded version as a separate file so you can make changes to the original file if necessary.

 PREVIEW TRANSPARENCY FLATTENING

If you are designing with transparency, it's a good idea to know exactly what elements will be affected when the file is flattened for output. Illustrator provides a Flattener Preview panel that you can use to review the file for potential problems.

1. **With heartsmart expanded.ai open, choose Window>Flattener Preview.**

2. **If nothing appears in the white space of the panel, click the Refresh button.**

Drag this corner to make the panel larger, and then click Refresh to enlarge the preview image.

3. **In the Highlight menu, choose All Affected Objects.**

The red areas in the preview show all objects that are somehow affected by transparency in the file; all of these objects will somehow be affected by flattening.

You can use the Flattener Preview to highlight different kinds of areas, enabling you to determine which flattener settings are best for the entire file or for a specific object.

- **None (Color Preview)** displays the normal layout.

- **Rasterized Complex Regions** highlights areas that will be rasterized based on the Raster/Vector Balance defined in the applied preset.

- **Transparent Objects** highlights objects with opacity of less than 100%, blending modes, transparency effects (such as drop shadows), and/or feathering applied.

- **All Affected Objects** highlights all objects affected by transparency, including the transparent objects and the objects overlapped by transparent objects. All of these objects will be affected by flattening.

- **Affected Linked EPS Files** highlights all EPS files linked in the file but not embedded.

- **Expanded Patterns** highlights patterns that will be expanded by flattening. (Pattern effects must be expanded if they are affected by transparency; this takes place automatically when you output the file.)

- **Outlined Strokes** highlights all strokes that will be converted to filled objects when flattened. (For example, a 5-pt stroke with the Screen blending mode will be converted to a 5-pt-high rectangle filled with the underlying object when the file is flattened.)

4. **In the Highlight menu, choose Transparent Objects.**

The highlighted areas reduce to only the objects where transparency is applied.

5. **Choose Show Options in the panel Options menu, and then click Refresh.**

The options show the specific settings that will be used to flatten the artwork, based by default on a flattener preset.

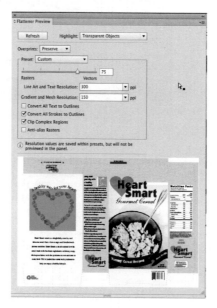

6. **Close the Flattener Preview panel, and then continue to the next exercise.**

Understanding Flattener Presets

Illustrator includes four default flattener presets, which are appropriate for many typical jobs. You can also create your own flattener presets by choosing Edit>Transparency Flattener Presets and clicking New in the resulting dialog box. In addition, you can use the Transparency Flattener Presets dialog box to load flattener presets created on another machine — such as one your service provider created for their specific output device and/or workflow.

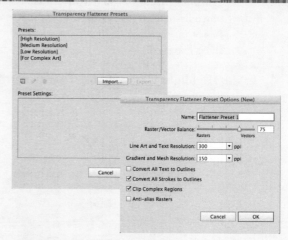

- The preset **Name** will be listed in the related output menus. You should use names that suggest the preset's use, such as "PDF for XL Printing Company." (Using meaningful names is a good idea for any asset that can have a name — from color swatches to output presets.)

- **Raster/Vector Balance** determines how much vector information will be preserved when artwork is flattened, from 0 (all information will be flattened as rasters) to 100 (maintains all vector information).

- **Line Art and Text Resolution** defines the resulting resolution of vector elements that will be rasterized, up to 9600 ppi. For good results with commercial printing, this option should be at least 600–1200 ppi (ask your output provider what settings they prefer you to use).

- **Gradient and Mesh Resolution** defines the resolution for gradients that will be rasterized, up to 1200 ppi. This option is typically set to 300 ppi for most commercial printing applications.

- **Convert All Text to Outlines** converts all type to outline shapes; the text will not be editable or selectable in a PDF file.

- **Convert All Strokes to Outlines** converts all strokes to filled paths.

- **Clip Complex Regions** forces boundaries between vector objects and rasterized artwork to fall along object paths, reducing potential problems that can result when only part of an object is rasterized.

- **Anti-Alias Rasters** helps to create smoother edges in the raster images that are created from vector graphics.

FLATTEN TRANSPARENCY FOR SELECTED OBJECTS

Although flattening is typically managed for you when you output a file, you can flatten selected objects manually at any point in the process. Like expanding an object's appearance, flattening is a permanent action — you can no longer edit any effect or setting that caused the transparency. This process should only be done at the very end of a project; again, we recommend maintaining your original file and saving a new version with the manually flattened artwork.

1. **With heartsmart expanded.ai open, unlock all of the content layers, and then select the heart image on the back panel.**

2. **Choose Object>Flatten Transparency and activate the Preview option.**

3. **Choose the High Resolution option in the Preset menu, and check the Preserve Alpha Transparency option.**

   To produce the outer glow effect applied to this object, the color blends outward to become fully transparent at the edges. In other words, the pixels toward the outer edge of the effect are more transparent than the pixels at the inner edge of the effect. This type of effect requires a mechanism to describe the degree of transparency for each pixel. Alpha transparency is a type of mask that defines the degree of transparency for each pixel in the resulting raster objects.

Note:

If Preserve Alpha Transparency is not checked, the flattened artwork will have a white background; the effect will not blend into the background color.

When Preview is checked, two bounding boxes are visible — the original image and the result of flattening the outer glow effect.

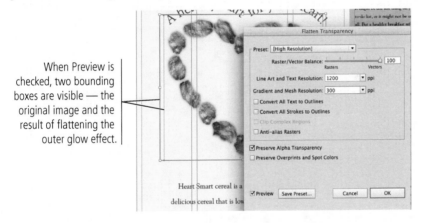

4. **Click OK to flatten the transparency of the selected object.**

5. **In the Layers panel, expand the Back layer, then expand the group containing the cereal heart. Click the eye icon to hide the top object in the group.**

   Flattening the object created a new raster object to reproduce the Outer Glow effect.

6. **Show the cereal object again.**

7. **Save the file and continue to the next exercise.**

EXPORT A PDF FILE FOR PROOFING

Although packaging such as this box is commonly printed directly from the Illustrator file, you should still create a proof that your client can review either on screen or printed. The PDF format is ideal for this use because the client doesn't need Illustrator to open or print the proof file.

1. **With heartsmart expanded.ai open, choose File>Save As.**

2. **Navigate to your WIP>Cereal folder as the destination and choose Adobe PDF in the Format/Save As Type menu.**

3. **Click Save.**

4. **Choose High Quality Print in the Adobe PDF Preset menu.**

   The Adobe PDF Preset menu includes six PDF presets that meet common industry output requirements.

5. **Choose Acrobat 4 (PDF 1.3) in the Compatibility menu.**

   The Compatibility menu determines which version of the PDF format you will create. Not all clients will have the latest versions of technology, so you should consider saving all proof-quality PDFs to be compatible with the earliest version of PDF possible.

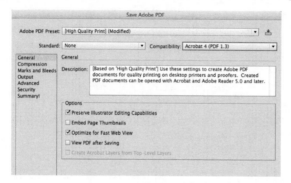

6. **Click Advanced in the list of options.**

   PDF 1.3 does not support transparency, so the file will require flattening. If you save the file to be compatible with PDF 1.4 or later, the transparency information will be maintained in the PDF file; it will have to be flattened later in the process.

7. **Choose High Resolution in the Preset menu.**

   Even though this PDF is for proofing purposes, high-resolution produces better results. If file size is not a concern, it's a good idea to use the high-resolution flattener even for proofs.

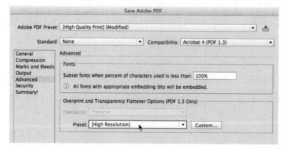

8. **Click Save PDF to output the file.**

9. **Close the PDF file, then continue to the final stage of the project.**

Stage 5 Previewing the Box Design in 3D

In Stage 3, you used the 3D Extrude & Bevel feature to add depth to the banners on the front of the box. This effect can also be used to create a box shape and preview your flat box artwork in three dimensions, which is especially useful for showing a client how the art will look when the final piece is printed and folded.

CREATE SYMBOLS FOR BOX PANELS

For this process to work, you first have to do a bit of set-up work. The artwork for each panel has to be saved as a symbol before it can be applied to the 3D box shape. This means you have to do some cutting and clean up work so you have the exact shapes you need before you create the 3D box preview.

1. Open **heartsmart expanded.ai** from your WIP>Cereal folder.
   Immediately save the file as a new Illustrator file named **box preview.ai**.

2. Lock the Box Cut Line, Margin Guides, and Folding Guides layers.
   Hide all layers but the Jumpstart Side, Folding Guides, and Box Cut Line layers.
   Unlock and select the Jumpstart Side layer.

3. Select the pink background shape, and use the Selection tool to drag the background shape edges to match the folding guides for the side panel.

4. Select and group all objects on the Jumpstart Side layer.

5. Open the Symbols panel (Window>Symbols) and float it away from the panel dock.

6. Drag the group of objects from the artboard into the Symbols panel. In the resulting dialog box, name the symbol **Jumpstart Panel** and click OK.

7. **Choose Large List View in the Symbols panel Options menu.**

The Large List view allows you to see both the thumbnail and name of the available symbols.

8. **Repeat the process for the Front layer, Back layer, and Nutrition Side layer, hiding and locking other layers as necessary. If an element only exists on a flap, delete it. Name the symbols Front Panel, Back Panel, and Nutrition Panel, respectively.**

9. **Save the file and continue to the next exercise.**

 ## MAP THE ART TO A 3D BOX

Now that you have symbols for each side of the box, you have to create a shape that you can turn into a three-dimensional box. This shape needs to be the correct size for the existing artwork, so you will again use the panel folding guides to build the shape.

1. **With box preview.ai open, delete the content layers, the Margin Guides layer, and the Box Cut Line layer.**

2. **Create a new layer named Box Rendering at the top of the layer stack, and select it as the active layer.**

3. **Using the Rectangle tool with the light gold fill and no stroke, draw a shape that fills the front panel area (excluding the flaps).**

4. **Using the Measure tool (nested under the Eyedropper tool), drag a horizontal line to measure the width of the Nutrition Side panel.**

Click and drag with the measure tool to find the width of the panel area.

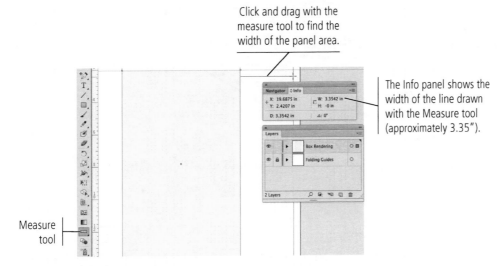

The Info panel shows the width of the line drawn with the Measure tool (approximately 3.35″).

Measure tool

5. **Hide the Folding Guides layer.**

6. **Select the rectangle from Step 3 and choose Effect>3D>Extrude & Bevel. Make sure the Preview option is unchecked.**

An active preview slows down the application because it re-renders the artwork after every change.

7. **Define the following parameters, and then check the Preview option to review the results:**

X axis	–3°	Perspective	50°
Y axis	32°	Extrude Depth	Width of the side panel
Z axis	–1°		(from Step 4)

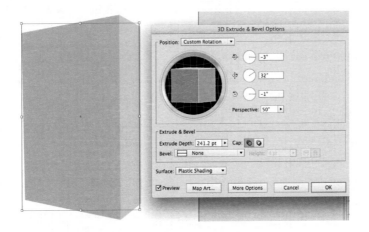

Note:

When you type the panel width in the Extrude Depth field, make sure you type the correct measurement increment (″). The dialog box automatically makes the correct conversion to points.

8. **Uncheck the Preview box, and then click the Map Art button.**

When the Map Art dialog box is open, the object in the layout displays as a 3D wireframe preview even when the Preview option is unchecked. The red line around the preview shows which side (surface) of the shape is being mapped.

9. Choose Front Panel in the Symbol menu.

The picture of the front of the box is placed on the page, but you need to adjust it so it exactly fits the page outline; otherwise, there will be gray areas when you render the picture.

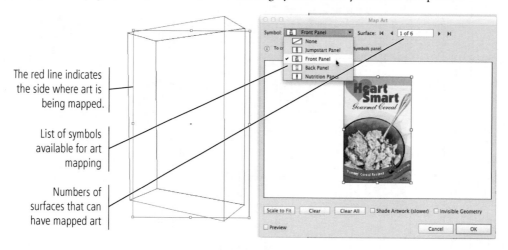

The red line indicates the side where art is being mapped.

List of symbols available for art mapping

Numbers of surfaces that can have mapped art

10. Check the Preview option in the Map Art dialog box.

Illustrator renders a preview of the symbol on the 3D box shape (this might take a few minutes to complete).

Note that the negative-space stripe on the box front, which appears white against the white artboard, is now gray because the 3D box shape is gray. To solve this problem, you will edit the symbol (after you exit the 3D Extrude &

Bevel Options dialog box) to create an actual white stripe in the symbol art.

11. Click the Preview check box to turn off the preview.

Rendering 3D artwork takes time, and must be redone every time you make a change in the dialog box. It's a better idea to turn off the preview while you're making changes, and then turn it on only when you want to review your progress.

12. Click the right Surface arrow until you are looking at Surface 3, and then choose Nutrition Panel in the Symbol menu.

The thumbnail is placed in the wrong orientation, so you need to rotate it. You can click an object in the Map Art preview and drag to move the symbol artwork, or you can use the bounding box handles to resize or rotate the symbol until it fits the gray surface shape.

13. **Click the symbol artwork in the preview and drag down so you can see the top bounding box handles.**

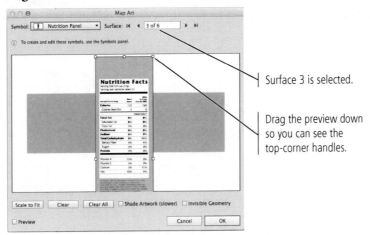

Surface 3 is selected.

Drag the preview down so you can see the top-corner handles.

14. **Place the cursor near one of the top corner handles, press Shift, and drag around to rotate the artwork 90° counterclockwise.**

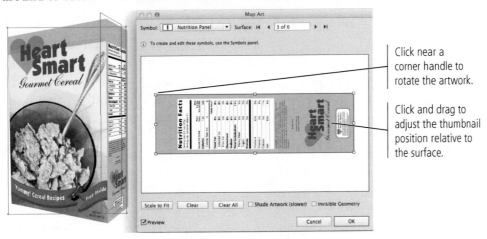

Click near a corner handle to rotate the artwork.

Click and drag to adjust the thumbnail position relative to the surface.

15. **Drag the rotated art in the preview until it aligns with the gray surface shape, then check the Preview box and review the results.**

16. **Click OK to close the Map Art dialog box, and then click OK again to finalize the 3D box preview.**

17. **In the Symbols panel, double-click the Front Panel symbol to enter Symbol Editing Mode.**

18. **In the area of the empty white space, draw a white-filled rectangle the same width as the symbol artwork and send it to the back of the stacking order.**

Note:

Once art has been mapped, you can view the 3D virtual effect from different angles by changing the settings in the 3D Extrude & Bevel Options dialog box.

19. **Click the arrow button in the top-left corner of the document window to exit Symbol Editing mode.**

20. **Save the file and close it.**

1. You can use the _____ tool to sample colors from placed images.

2. Unchecking the _____ option when placing images results in an embedded file.

3. The _____ can be used to review all the available characters in a font.

4. Checking the _____ option when you place a native Photoshop file results in a single object on a single layer in the Illustrator file.

5. The _____ determines the left-indent position of type on a path.

6. You can use the _____ panel to review and edit applied effects.

7. Applying a _____ to an object forces surrounding text to flow around that object instead of directly in front of or behind it.

8. The _____ is the specific method used to blend the color of one object into the colors of underlying objects.

9. _____ refers to the degree to which light passes through an object.

10. A(n) _____ can be used to restrict opacity to selected objects; colors in the topmost object determine which areas of the underlying object are visible.

1. Briefly explain how the concept of a die cut relates to package design in Illustrator.

2. Briefly explain the concept of sublayers, including at least one example of their potential benefit.

3. Briefly explain how transparency settings relate to Illustrator files created for commercial printing.

Use what you learned in this project to complete the following freeform exercise.
Carefully read the art director and client comments, then create your own design to meet the needs of the project.
Use the space below to sketch ideas; when finished, write a brief explanation of your reasoning behind your final design.

art director comments

Your agency has been hired to develop packaging for a new video game called *Eye of Horus*, which is an adventure game set in Egypt when the pyramids were being built.

To complete this project, you should:

❏ Disassemble (flatten) an existing game box and measure the different elements. Create a die-cut template in Illustrator using those measurements.

❏ Design box artwork for the new video game, using images or creating illustrations that support the general theme of the product.

❏ Incorporate the product name on all sides of the box.

client comments

The new game is a typical action-adventure game with a historical context. The goal is to the navigate a labyrinth inside one of the pyramids to find the Pharaoh's treasure without being captured by the various beasties that protect the hidden chamber.

One side panel needs to list system requirements for the game. We know it will work on both Mac and Windows, but we're still trying to work out the bugs on the latest system releases so we haven't finalized that information yet. For now, use placeholder bullets that say something like 'requirement listing'. That way we can see the formatting even though the actual text isn't ready yet. We'll also have to incorporate the Apple and Windows logos, so leave space for those logos on the same panel.

The back of the box will incorporate some screen captures, which we'll provide as soon as the development is finalized. For now, just leave placeholders to mark the space where those will be placed.

Finally, make sure you build a space on either the back or one side of the box for a bar code.

project justification

_____

_____

_____

_____

_____

_____

_____

_____

_____

_____

_____

_____

_____

The large artboard size and layer controls, coupled with the extensive set of creative tools, make Illustrator ideally suited to meet the complex needs of packaging design. You can design sophisticated artwork that can be wrapped or folded into virtually any shape to package virtually any product.

This project combined the technical requirements of packaging design — specifically using a custom die-cut template supplied by the output provider — with the artistic capabilities necessary to create the final design for a standard-size cereal box. You composited a number of existing elements and created others, then used a number of features to modify artwork — adding interest and depth to unify the different pieces into a single, cohesive design.

Create artwork to fit a printer-supplied die-cut template

Place external elements as necessary for package design

Create type on a custom path

Use transparency to unify artwork components

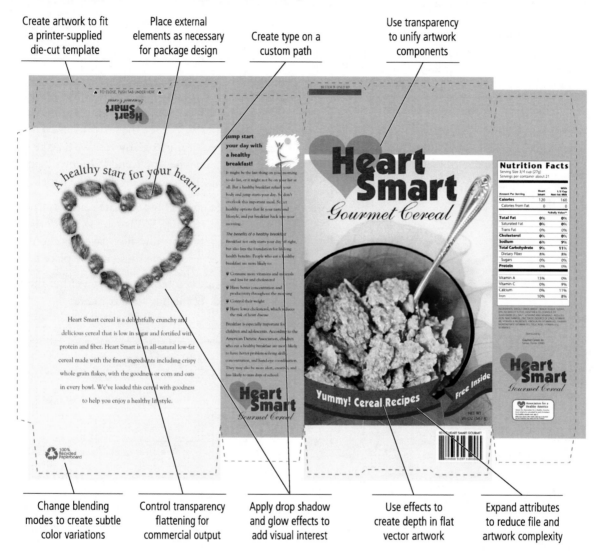

Change blending modes to create subtle color variations

Control transparency flattening for commercial output

Apply drop shadow and glow effects to add visual interest

Use effects to create depth in flat vector artwork

Expand attributes to reduce file and artwork complexity

Consumer Infographics

As the illustrator for a magazine publisher, it's your job to create interesting graphics for articles in a variety of magazines. Next month's feature article is about trends in alternate fuel costs for consumer automobiles. You need to create several graphs and one illustration to accompany the article.

This project incorporates the following skills:

❑ Creating graphs to present data in a visual format

❑ Editing graph data to change the appearance of a graph

❑ Importing data from an external file

❑ Managing fills, legends, and labels to make graphs more visually appealing

❑ Defining a perspective grid

❑ Putting objects into the correct perspective

client comments

The feature article in next month's personal finance magazine looks at alternative-fuel vehicles, and whether people are really getting their money's worth when they buy a hybrid, CNG, or other non-gasoline car.

We need three different graphs:

- Historical gasoline pricing data from the government energy administration
- Average monthly spending per vehicle (from a long-term survey)
- Number of cars per household (from the same survey)

Since this is a general-interest consumer magazine, and not a cut-and-dry financial report, I'd like something more than just a set of plain graphs. I'd like you to put the graphs into some kind of context or overall illustration to make the presentation more interesting.

Finally, we went some kind of illustration showing the three highest and lowest average gasoline prices by state. I don't want just a boring table of numbers.

art director comments

Before you start creating the graphs, you should evaluate the kinds of data you have. That way, you can determine which type of graph will best suit the data. Illustrator's graphing tools support many graph types, but you probably won't need more than a few. Bars and pies are the most common types, but the others have important uses too.

You might want to look at some other consumer and personal financial magazines to see how different kinds of graphs and charts are typically used — and how they are incorporated into illustrations to make the data appear more attractive and interesting.

I sketched a "gas station sign" idea that I think will be a good container for the final illustration. I already put it into an Illustrator file and created the swatches I want you to use in the artwork.

project objectives

To complete this project, you will:

- ❏ Create line, bar, and pie graphs to present different types of data
- ❏ Edit live graph data to change the segment breakdown in a graph
- ❏ Import data from an external file to create a graph
- ❏ Edit fills, legends, and labels to create aesthetically pleasing, technically accurate graphs
- ❏ Create a perspective grid for complex, three-dimensional artwork
- ❏ Draw new objects on different perspective planes
- ❏ Move and transform perspective objects
- ❏ Create type objects in perspective
- ❏ Place existing artwork and symbols in perspective

Stage 1   Creating Charts and Graphs

The first stage of this project revolves around one of the more powerful but least-used functions in Illustrator — the ability to generate graphics based on data. Information graphics (referred to as "infographics") are illustrations that deliver information; bar graphs, pie charts, and area charts are all examples of information provided in a visual format that makes it easier to understand.

Successfully designing infographics requires knowing which kind of chart best shows which type of information. Once you know what kind of chart you need, Illustrator provides the tools to generate the chart.

Distinguishing Types of Graphs

Column graphs compare values across several categories using vertical columns.

Bar graphs compare values over several categories using horizontal bars.

Line graphs plot a series of points across the graph, connecting those points with a line. These graphs show a progressive change in values, such as different prices over time.

Stacked column graphs divide each column into segments to show the relationship between pieces of the total value.

Stacked bar graphs are horizontal versions of stacked column graphs.

Area graphs are modified line graphs; the space below the line is filled to emphasize the plotted values.

Scatter graphs plot multiple data points along the horizontal and vertical axes. These graphs are used to show trends or clusters in the data points.

Pie graphs show categorical values as percentages of the whole.

Radar graphs compare sets of values in a circular format. These graphs are useful for displaying cyclical data such as annual sales by month.

ILLUSTRATOR FOUNDATIONS

CREATE A LINE GRAPH

The first graph for this project is based on historical data of gasoline prices, compiled by the United States Energy Information Administration (www.eia.doe.gov). Because this data tracks a change in value over time, a line graph is the best way to represent this information visually.

1. Download **A16_RF_Project7.zip** from the Student Files Web page.

2. Expand the ZIP archive in your WIP folder (Macintosh) or copy the archive contents into your WIP folder (Windows).

   This results in a folder named **Fuel**, which contains the files you need for this project. You should also use this folder to save the files you create in this project.

3. Open the file **billboard.ait** from your WIP>Fuel folder.

   You will use this artwork as the "frame" for each of the graphs you build in this project.

4. In the Tools panel, choose the Line Graph tool (it might be nested under one of the other graph tools).

   When you choose a specific graph tool, it becomes the default tool in the Tools panel. Depending on what was previously done in your version of the application, your default graph tool might be different than ours.

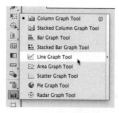

5. Click and drag inside the sign area on the billboard artwork, leaving approximately 0.25″ between the area you drag and the sign frame.

   The size you define here represents the size of the graph shape only; it does not include the legend or axis labels. If you know the amount of space available for the entire graph (including labels and legend), you should define a smaller graph size so the labels and legend fit within the available space.

Note:

If you click once with a graph tool, a dialog box opens where you can define the height and width of the new graph (just as when you single-click with one of the basic drawing tools).

Note:

You cannot resize a graph object by dragging bounding box handles or using the Transform panel. You can, however, use the Scale dialog box (Object> Transform>Scale).

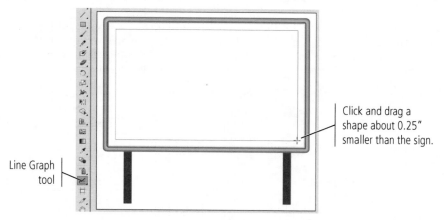

Line Graph tool

Click and drag a shape about 0.25″ smaller than the sign.

When you create a new graph, a spreadsheet-like window opens. This is the Illustrator Data panel, where you enter the data that will make up your graph. You can simply type in the various data cells, but many graphing projects will involve importing data from an external file — as you do in this project.

6. **In the Data panel, click the Import Data button.**
Navigate to the file `prices.txt` **in the WIP>Fuel folder and click Open.**

This data was originally a Microsoft Excel file, but it was exported as a tab-delimited text-only file. You cannot directly import an Excel file into Illustrator; if you try, you will see either an error message or incomprehensible data that is useless for making a graph.

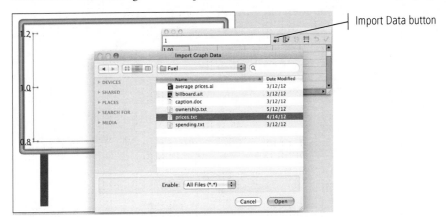

Import Data button

7. **Click the Apply button in the Data panel.**

As you can see, there is clearly a problem in the resulting graph. The imported data has two columns of numbers, but the first column actually shows the years associated with the data in the second column. By default, Illustrator's Data panel treats all numbers as parts of the data. In cases like this — when you want certain numbers to be treated as regular text rather than actual data — you have to enclose those numbers within quotes in the Data panel.

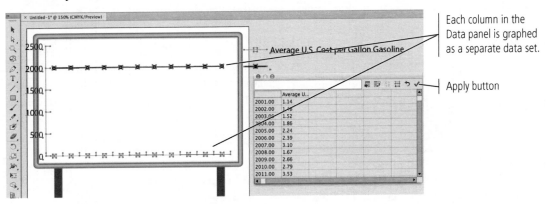

Each column in the Data panel is graphed as a separate data set.

Apply button

8. **Click the 2001.00 cell in the Data panel to select it.**

9. **In the text field at the top of the panel, add quote characters on both sides of the number.**

You can't use the arrow keys on your keyboard to move the insertion point within the Data panel text field. You have to click in the appropriate location to add a new character.

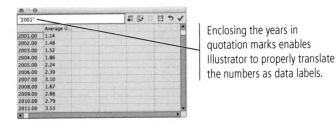

Enclosing the years in quotation marks enables Illustrator to properly translate the numbers as data labels.

Note:

Unlike traditional spreadsheet applications, you can't drag data cells to a new location in the panel. You can, however, cut cells and paste them into a new position if you need to add new data in between existing data.

10. Press Return/Enter to highlight the next cell down, and then add quote characters around the 2002 text.

Pressing Tab moves to the next cell in the row. Pressing Return/Enter moves to the next cell down in the column. You can also use the arrow keys to move through the cells.

11. Repeat this process for all years in the table, then click the Apply button at the top of the Data panel.

Unfortunately, there is no way to speed up this process. You simply have to type the quotes for each year in the data.

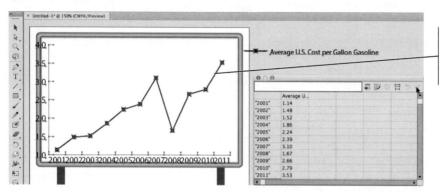

Because the first column is now treated as labels, the graph has only one data set.

Note:

Pressing the Enter key on your numeric keypad has the same effect as clicking the Apply button.

12. Click the Cell Style button at the top of the Data panel. In the resulting dialog box, change the Number of Decimals field to 3 and then click OK.

By default, the Illustrator Data panel shows the first two decimal points in the imported data. The Number of Decimals option changes the number of digits that are visible after the decimal point. If the data does not include as many decimals as you allow, Illustrator adds 0s at the end of the existing values.

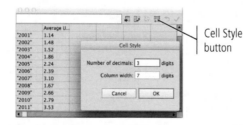

Cell Style button

Note:

The Column Width field can be changed to make longer data points visible in the Data panel cells.

13. Click the Data panel Close button to close the panel. When asked if you want to save changes to the data, click Save/Yes.

Adding the extra decimal is technically a change, even though you won't see a significant change in the actual graph.

Panel Close button

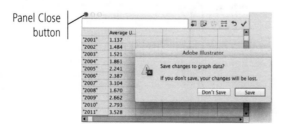

14. Save the file as price_graph.ai in your WIP>Fuel folder and then continue to the next exercise.

FORMAT GRAPH ELEMENTS

When you create a graph in Illustrator, all of the elements within the graph are grouped together in a special graph object. As a general rule, you should maintain a graph object as a graph object as long as possible in case you need to change some aspect of the graph data — which happens far more often than you might expect. The special nature of a graph object makes changing the individual elements a bit tricky, but you can change the formatting of various pieces within the graph as long as you understand how to access them.

1. **With price_graph.ai open, click any part of the graph object with the Selection tool.**

2. **In the Character panel, change the character formatting to 8-pt ATC Oak Normal with 90% horizontal scale.**

   Type objects in a graph object are originally formatted with Illustrator's default type settings. When a graph object is selected, changes to type formatting options apply to all type elements within the graph object.

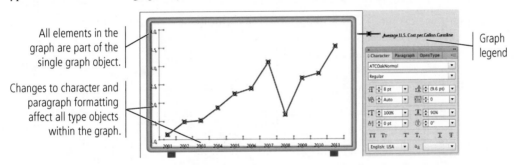

All elements in the graph are part of the single graph object.

Changes to character and paragraph formatting affect all type objects within the graph.

Graph legend

3. **With the entire graph object selected, use the arrow keys to nudge the graph object until it is centered in the sign area.**

   You can't drag bounding box handles to resize a graph. If you need to resize a graph object, you must choose Object>Transform>Scale and resize the entire graph to a percentage of its original size.

4. **Click away from the graph object to deselect it.**

5. **Choose the Direct Selection tool, then click the legend type object to select only that object.**

   The Direct Selection tool is the key to changing individual elements within a graph. You can't double-click to "enter into" the graph, as you can with a regular group.

6. **Change the formatting of the selected object to 12-pt ATC Oak Bold Italic.**

7. **Using the Direct Selection tool, drag the legend type object to the top-right corner of the sign area.**

When the first row of your data defines labels for each column, the graph automatically includes a legend with a small block of the wedge color and the related label. You can change the type or position of the legend, or you can remove it completely by editing the graph type settings.

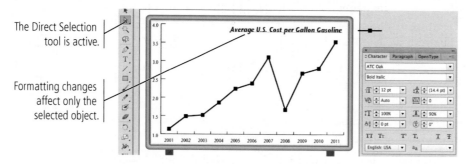

The Direct Selection tool is active.

Formatting changes affect only the selected object.

8. **Draw a marquee with the Direct Selection tool to select both parts of the legend icon, and move it entirely outside the artboard area.**

In this case, there is only one column of values, so the textual label clearly corresponds to the single line of data points; the icon symbols are unnecessary. You can't delete the legend icon objects because they are technically part of the graph. Anything entirely outside the artboard area is excluded when an Illustrator file is placed into another file; this technique effectively removes the legend icon without breaking apart the graph.

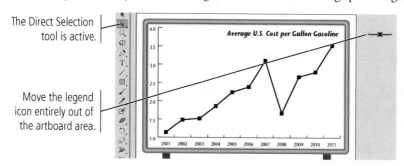

The Direct Selection tool is active.

Move the legend icon entirely out of the artboard area.

9. **Using the Direct Selection tool, draw a marquee to select any part of each line and square that represents a data point in the graph.**

10. **Use the Fill Color and Stroke Color swatches in the Control panel to change both attributes to the darkest available green swatch in the panel.**

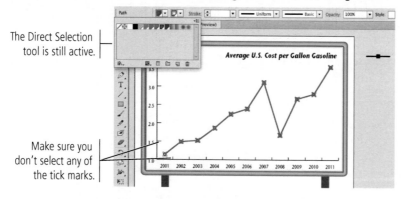

The Direct Selection tool is still active.

Make sure you don't select any of the tick marks.

11. **Save the file and continue to the next exercise.**

CHANGE GRAPH OPTIONS

When you create a graph, the content of the graph is defined by the default settings for the type of graph you are creating. You can change a number of parameters, including the axis values and legends.

1. **With price_graph.ai open, click any part of the graph object with the Selection tool.**

2. **Control/right-click the graph object and choose Type in the contextual menu.**

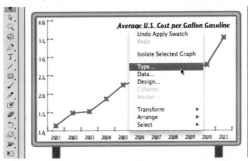

Note:

You can access the same graph-editing options in the Object>Graph submenu.

3. **Open the Graph Options menu and choose Value Axis.**

This dialog box has different options, depending on the type of graph you are creating. The value axis (in this case, the vertical axis on the left) is the one that marks the range of values that are depicted in the data; the current axis labels are automatically generated based on the data in the table. This graph shows prices in dollars, so you are going to change the axis labels to more accurately reflect those prices.

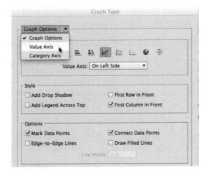

4. **Choose Full Width in the Tick Marks Length menu.**

By default, tick marks are short lines on the inside of the graph area. You can choose Full Width to extend the tick marks across the full width of the graph, or you can choose None to turn off the value axis divisions.

5. **In the Add Labels area, type $ in the Prefix field and type 0 [zero] in the Suffix field.**

The prefix will be added before the existing axis labels; the suffix will be added at the end of the existing axis labels.

6. **Click OK to apply the changes to the graph.**

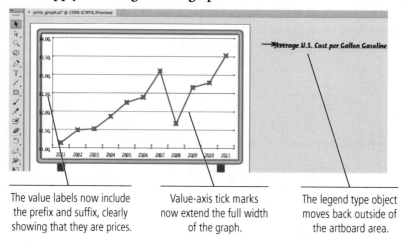

The value labels now include the prefix and suffix, clearly showing that they are prices.	Value-axis tick marks now extend the full width of the graph.	The legend type object moves back outside of the artboard area.

7. **Use the arrow keys to nudge the graph so the full axis labels fit inside the sign area.**

    When you change the graph options, strange and unpredictable things can sometimes occur. In this case, the legend label moves back close to its original position. Always review your graph carefully when you edit these graph options.

8. **Deselect everything in the file, then use the Direct Selection tool to select and drag the legend type object back into place at the upper-right of the sign area.**

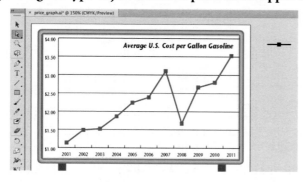

9. **Save the file and close it, then continue to the next exercise.**

CREATE A BAR GRAPH

The second required graph is based on data from a long-term survey that asked 500 people to track the amount of money spent on fuel for each automobile in their household. The submitted values were averaged and sorted based on the type of fuel used. Because this data shows a comparison of values for different categories, a bar graph will accurately represent the data.

Orientation is the only real difference between a bar graph and a column graph; bar graphs represent each data set as a horizontal bar, while column graphs use vertical columns. Because the billboard you're using as a background is horizontally oriented, a bar graph is more appropriate for this project.

1. **Open billboard.ait from the WIP>Fuel folder, and choose the Bar Graph tool in the Tools panel.**

2. **Click and drag inside the sign area on the billboard artwork, leaving approximately 0.25" inside the edges of the sign frame.**

For this graph, you are going to move the category labels inside the bars that represent each category. You don't need to leave room outside the graph for the labels.

3. **Click the Import Data button in the Data panel. Navigate to spending.txt in your WIP>Fuel folder and click Open.**

Bar Graph tool

4. **Click the Apply button in the Data panel to generate the graph, then close the Data panel.**

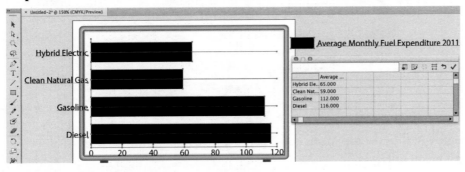

5. **With the graph object selected, change the type formatting to 8-pt ATC Oak Normal.**

6. **Nudge the graph object as necessary until it fits inside the sign area (excluding the category labels on the left).**

7. **Control/right-click the graph object with the Selection tool and choose Type in the contextual menu.**

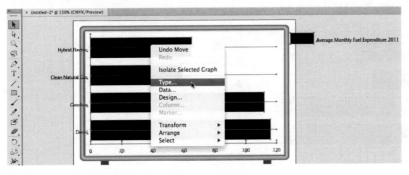

8. **Choose Value Axis in the Graph Options menu.**

9. **Check the Override Calculated Values box. Type 25 in the Min field, type 125 in the Max field, and type 4 in the Divisions field.**

For bar graphs, Illustrator uses a range beginning with 0 and extending in increments as necessary to show all of the defined data. You can use the Min and Max fields to define the values of a specific axis, such as always extending to 100 instead of ending at 70 or some other lower value.

The Divisions field determines how many labels are added to the value axis (the horizontal axis for this bar graph); the number of labels will always be one more than the number of divisions you define.

10. **Choose None in the Tick Marks Length menu.**

11. **Type $ in the Prefix field.**

The value axis in this chart represents numbers of dollars; it is appropriate to reflect those units in the axis labels. In this case, it is not necessary to add a suffix for these large sums of money (e.g., $50 is sufficient; $50.00 would be unnecessary).

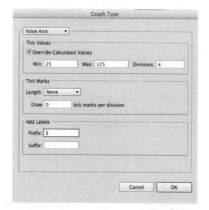

Note:

If you are including divisions in your graph, you can add subdivisions using the Draw _ Tick Marks Per Division option.

Note:

Unfortunately, the Graph Type dialog box does not include a Preview check box. You can't see the results of your choices until you click OK. As long as the graph object remains a graph object, you can always make changes.

12. **Choose Category Axis in the top menu and change the corresponding Tick Marks Length menu to None.**

By default, categories are separated by tick marks (just as values are). In the case of a bar graph, however, tick marks are usually unnecessary.

13. **Click OK to close the Graph Type dialog box and apply your changes.**

14. **Save the file as spending_graph.ai in your WIP>Fuel folder and continue to the next exercise.**

EDIT GRAPH DATA

As long as you maintain a graph object without ungrouping it, you can edit both the parameters and the data that make up the graph. Any changes in the data are automatically reflected in the graph object on the artboard.

1. **With spending_graph.ai open, select the graph object with the Selection tool. Control/right-click the graph object and choose Data in the contextual menu.**

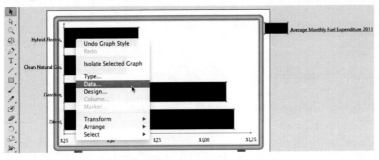

2. **Click the cell below the Diesel cell and type Flex Fuel.**

3. **Press Tab to highlight the cell to the right, and type 79.**

4. **Click the Apply button in the Data panel.**

    The graph automatically changes to include the new data. The height of existing bars changes to accommodate the new fifth category in the defined space of the graph.

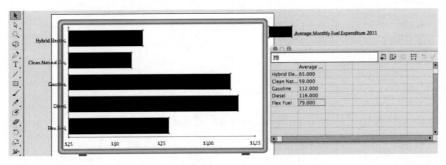

5. **Close the Data panel.**

6. **Using the Direct Selection tool, click away from the graph object to deselect it, then Shift-click to select only the five bars in the graph.**

7. **Using the Gradient panel, change the bars' fill to the Green Gradient swatch that is saved in the file. Rotate the gradient until you are satisfied with the appearance of the graph.**

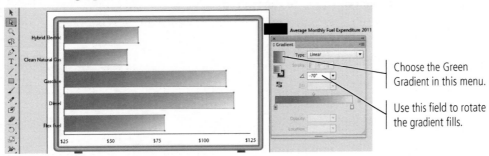

Choose the Green Gradient in this menu.

Use this field to rotate the gradient fills.

8. Select only the category-label type objects. Change the objects to left paragraph alignment and change the font to 10-pt ATC Oak Bold.

9. Drag the label objects right until they are entirely inside the graph bars.

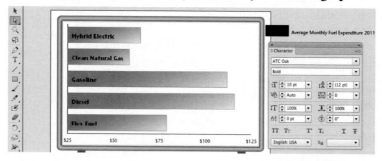

10. Select only the legend type object. Change it to 12-pt ATC Oak Bold Italic with right paragraph alignment.

11. Use the Type tool to place the insertion point after the word "Fuel" and press Shift-Return/Enter to add a line break.

12. Use the Direct Selection tool to select and drag the type object into position in the top-right corner of the sign.

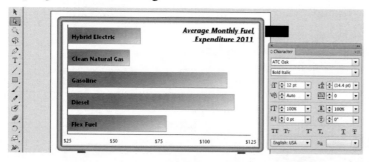

13. Select only the legend icon, and then drag it entirely off of the artboard.

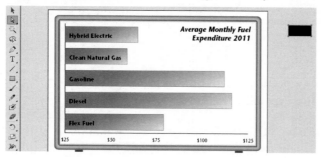

14. Save the file and close it, then continue to the next exercise.

CREATE A PIE GRAPH

The final required graph is based on data from a random survey of 500 people, who were asked the following question:

How many vehicles does your household own for personal use?

Each person gave a single response to the question, so the combined percentages of responses will equal 100%. A pie graph is the best way to show values as percentages of the whole.

1. **Open the file billboard.ait from the WIP>Fuel folder, and choose the Pie Graph tool in the Tools panel.**

2. **Click and drag inside the sign area on the billboard artwork, leaving approximately 0.25″ inside the edges of the sign frame.**

   Regardless of the shape you draw, pie graphs are always circles.

3. **Click the Import Data button in the Data panel. Navigate to ownership.txt in your WIP>Fuel folder and click Open.**

Note:

Pie graphs always present numbers as percentages of the whole. If data is provided as actual numbers instead of percentages, Illustrator calculates the necessary percentages based on the entered data.

Pie Graph tool

4. **Click the Apply button in the Data panel.**

5. **Close the Data panel, then choose the Selection tool in the Tools panel.**

6. **Control/right-click the graph and choose Type in the contextual menu.**

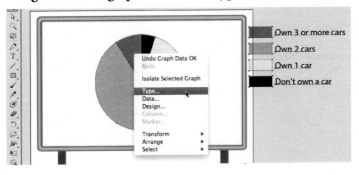

Note:

You can create more than one pie graph by entering additional sets of values in subsequent rows of the Data panel.

7. **In the Options area of the Graph Type dialog box, choose Legends in Wedges in the Legend menu.**

   You can use the Legend menu to remove the legend completely, create a standard stacked legend (the default), or place the legend labels inside the associated wedges.

Note:

If you check Add Legend Across Top when the Standard Legend option is selected, the legend appears as a row above the graph.

8. **Click OK to return to the document.**

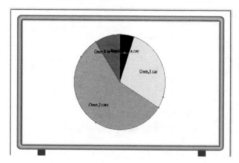

9. **With the graph selected, change the text formatting to 9-pt ATC Oak Normal.**

10. **Click away from the object to deselect it, and then use the Direct Selection tool to move the top two legend objects out of the wedges (as shown here).**

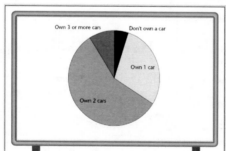

11. **Save the file as ownership_graph.ai in your WIP>Fuel folder and then continue to the next exercise.**

EDIT PIE GRAPH ELEMENTS

Pie graphs are very common, but they present several unique formatting challenges and opportunities. In this exercise, you manipulate the graph legend to add information, and then apply gradients to the wedges to add visual interest.

1. **With `ownership_graph.ai` open, select the graph with the Selection tool.**

2. **Control/right-click the graph and choose Data from the contextual menu.**

3. **Select the first label field in the Data panel, then place the insertion point at the end of the existing text (Don't own a car) in the field at the top of the panel.**

4. **Type |5%, then click the Apply button.**

   The pipe character (Shift-Backslash) is used to create a new line in the graph label.

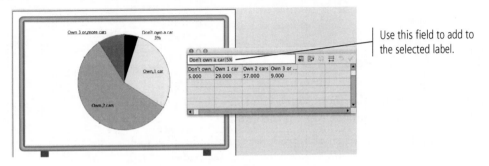

   Use this field to add to the selected label.

5. **Using the same method, add the appropriate values to each label in the Data panel, then close the Data panel.**

   The point of infographics is to make data easy to view and understand; the labels now reflect the actual data that was used to create the graph wedges.

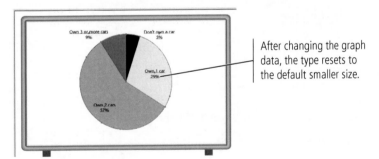

   After changing the graph data, the type resets to the default smaller size.

6. **With the graph selected, change the type size back to 9 pt. If necessary, adjust the label placement using the Direct Selection tool.**

   Legend type is automatically scaled to some smaller size to fit the graph whenever you reapply the data.

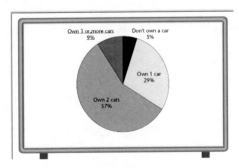

7. **Click away from the graph object to deselect it, then use the Direct Selection tool to select only the Own 1 Car wedge.**

8. **In the Control panel, open the Fill panel and choose the Green Radial swatch.**

   Radial gradients are automatically applied from the center of the object, as determined by the outermost edges of the selected shape. For a gradient to be centered in the entire graph area instead of just the wedge shape, you have to use the Gradient tool to reposition the gradient center.

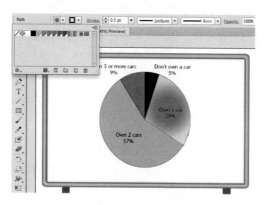

Note:

If a pie graph wedge is 75% or more of the graph area, a radial gradient will be correctly centered in the graph area because the outermost edges of the wedge are the same as the outermost edges of the graph.

9. **Choose the Gradient tool in the Tools panel. Click the center point of the graph, and then drag to the outside edge of the graph.**

   As you learned in Project 2: Balloon Festival Artwork, selecting the Gradient tool activates the Gradient Annotator, which allows you to control the gradient's angle, position, and colors.

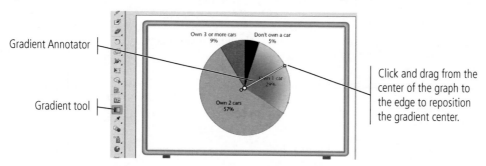

Gradient Annotator

Gradient tool

Click and drag from the center of the graph to the edge to reposition the gradient center.

10. **Repeat Steps 7–9 to apply the green gradient to each wedge in the graph.**

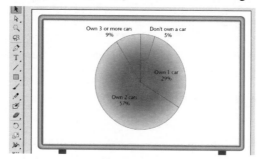

11. **Using the Direct Selection tool, click the Don't Own a Car wedge, and then Shift-click the wedge legend to add it to the selection.**

12. Drag the two selected objects up away from the other wedges of the graph.

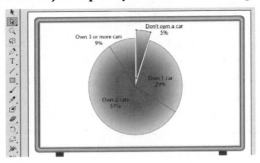

13. Repeat Steps 11–12 to move all four wedges apart from one another.

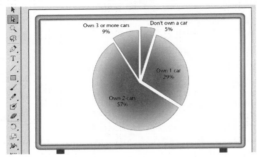

14. Click the graph with the Selection tool to select the entire object, and drag it to the right side of the sign area.

15. Place **caption.doc** into the file (File>Place), preserving the text formatting in the placed file.

16. Position and resize the resulting type area into the left side of the sign area.

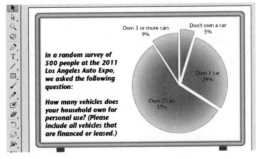

17. Save the file and close it, then continue to the next stage of the project.

Stage 2 Drawing in Perspective

The second half of the word "infographics" means adding visual elements that make data more attractive and accessible. The graphs from the first half of this project use a "road sign" background to present data in a visual manner that makes sense with the magazine article they illustrate.

Infographics can be as basic as graphs and charts, or as complex as any art you can conceive. In the second half of this project, you will create a sign like you would see at a gas station posting fuel costs. Each side of the sign will display the three highest or lowest average fuel prices (by state) from the previous month. You are also going to include a "station sign" graphic that includes the magazine name, and text showing what type of data is being shown.

DEFINE THE PERSPECTIVE GRID

In this series of exercises, you will create artwork based on a pencil sketch. As you will see in the sketch, you are drawing a sign similar to one that you might really see when you drive down the road. Objects in the real world have depth — which means the sign you are drawing should reflect that same level of dimension.

To recreate this effect using two-dimensional drawing tools, you need to understand the basic artistic principle of perspective. The concept of perspective means that all lines on the same surface (or plane) eventually appear to meet at a single point in the distance, called the **vanishing point**. Lines move closer together as they approach the vanishing point, creating the illusion of depth.

Illustrator CS6 includes a Perspective Grid tool that makes it very easy to define the perspective planes that will guide your drawing.

1. **Open the file average prices.ai from your WIP>Fuel folder.**

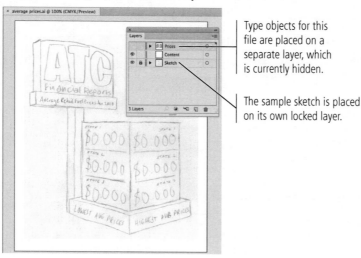

Type objects for this file are placed on a separate layer, which is currently hidden.

The sample sketch is placed on its own locked layer.

2. **Choose the Perspective Grid tool in the Tools panel.**

   When you first choose this tool, the default two-point perspective grid appears in the file. You can change the grid to one-point or three-point perspective by choosing the appropriate option in the View>Perspective Grid menu.

Note:

Press Shift-P to access the Perspective Grid tool.

3. If you can't see all handles of the perspective grid, zoom out slightly.

In two-point perspective, there are two vanishing points — left and right — and three planes — left, right, and ground. Illustrator's perspective grid shows the left plane in blue, the right plane in orange, and the ground plane in green.

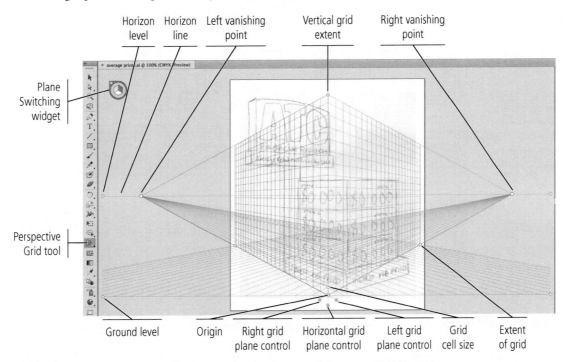

If you have never worked with perspective drawing, the grid might seem intimidating at first. However, once you understand the various elements, you will see how this grid makes it very easy to draw in correct perspective. To begin, you should also understand several basic terms related to dimensional drawing:

- A **plane** is a flat surface (even if it is only theoretical).
- A **vanishing point** is the location where all lines on a plane appear to converge.
- The **horizon line** is the height of the theoretical viewer's eye level.
- The **origin** is the zero point for perspective objects. For objects on the horizontal plane, the origin point is X: 0, Y: 0. For objects on the left or right plane, the origin point is X: 0.

Note:

You can change the position of the Plane Switching widget by double-clicking the Perspective Grid tool to open the Perspective Grid Options dialog box.

4. With the Perspective Grid tool active, click either Ground Level handle and drag until the origin aligns with the corner in the sketch (as shown here).

You can use the Ground Level handles to move the grid without affecting the perspective.

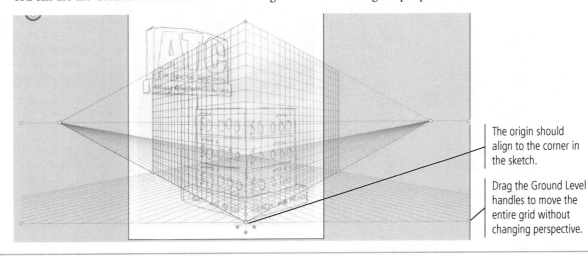

The origin should align to the corner in the sketch.

Drag the Ground Level handles to move the entire grid without changing perspective.

5. **Click either Horizon Level handle and drag up until the horizon line matches the top edge of the front sign in the sketch.**

   Changing the horizon line changes the height of both vanishing points. All three perspective planes are affected by the change.

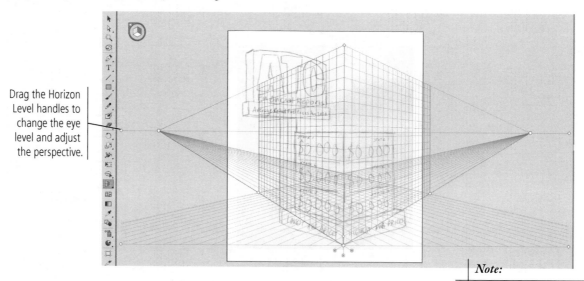

Drag the Horizon Level handles to change the eye level and adjust the perspective.

6. **Zoom out to show more area around the perspective grid.**

7. **Click the Right Vanishing Point handle and drag right until the bottom line of the orange grid aligns with the bottom line in the sketch.**

   Keep in mind that you're working from a sketch, which is probably not exact. The ultimate goal is to create accurate perspective artwork, using the sketch as a *rough* guide.

Note:

Click and drag the Grid Plane control handles to move the vertical planes without moving the vanishing point.

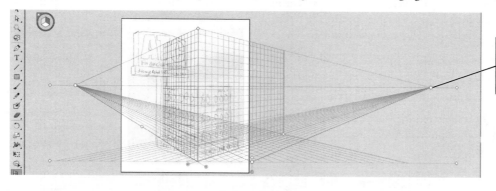

Drag a vanishing point to change the perspective of the related plane.

8. **Click the Left Vanishing Point handle and drag left until the bottom line of the blue grid aligns with the bottom line in the sketch.**

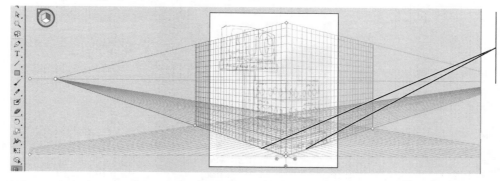

The bottom edges of the plane grids should align to the bottom lines in the sketch.

If you choose View>Perspective Grid>Lock Station Point, both vanishing points move when you drag either. They are effectively locked in position relative to each other. The origin point becomes a pivot, around which the vanishing points rotate.

9. **Click the Extent of Grid handle for the right plane, and drag left until the rightmost orange gridline aligns with the right edge of the sign.**

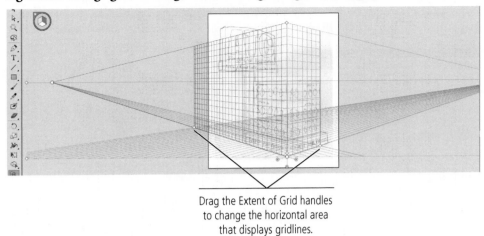

Drag the Extent of Grid handles to change the horizontal area that displays gridlines.

10. **Click the Extent of Grid handle for the left plane, and drag right until the leftmost blue gridline aligns with the left edge of the sign.**

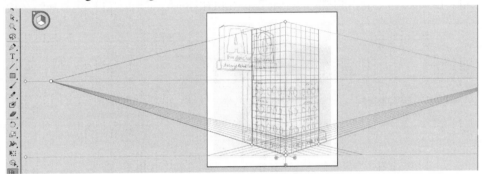

11. **Click the Vertical Grid Extent handle and drag down until the top edge of the grid aligns with the top edge of the sketched sign.**

It is important to realize that the perspective grid is only a visual guide; the extent of the grid planes does not limit the location of the planes. Each plane is theoretically infinite.

Drag the Vertical Grid Extent handle to change the vertical area that displays gridlines.

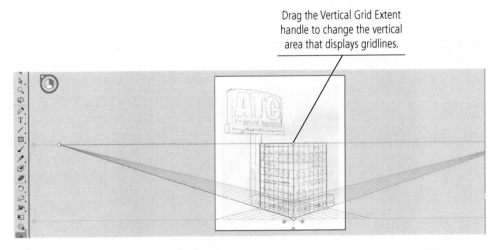

12. **Zoom into the front sign in the sketch and review the grid.**

13. **Click the Grid Cell Size handle and drag up until the first row of the grid appears to match the height of the sign's platform.**

The grid cell size is the same for all planes on the grid. Although you are basing the grid size on the right plane, all three grids change to reflect the new grid size.

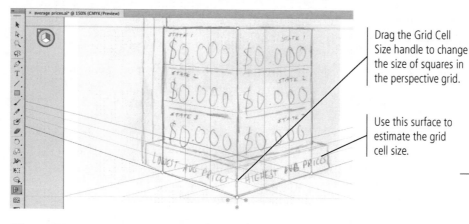

Drag the Grid Cell Size handle to change the size of squares in the perspective grid.

Use this surface to estimate the grid cell size.

Note:

The origin snaps to the horizontal (ground) plane grid. When you change the grid size, the origin point moves.

14. **Choose View>Perspective Grid>Define Grid.**

You can use this dialog box to define very specific, numeric grid settings, which can be useful for precise technical illustration.

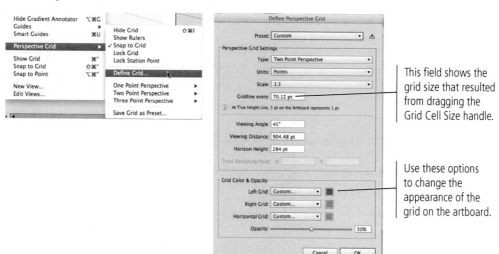

This field shows the grid size that resulted from dragging the Grid Cell Size handle.

Use these options to change the appearance of the grid on the artboard.

15. **Change the Gridline Every field to 50 pt and reduce the grid Opacity to 30%, then click OK to apply your changes.**

Reducing the grid opacity makes it easier to see what you're building.

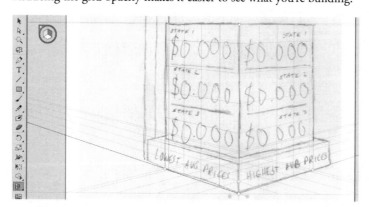

Note:

If you choose View>Perspective Grid>Show Rulers, the Y position of gridlines appears near the edge of each vertical perspective plane.

16. **Save the file as** `prices_feb.ai` **in your WIP>Fuel folder and then continue to the next exercise.**

ILLUSTRATOR FOUNDATIONS

Illustrator supports one-, two-, and three-point perspective grids, all of which can be accessed in the View>Perspective Grid submenus.

Only one perspective grid can exist in a single file, regardless of the number of artboards in the file. If you choose a different preset from one of the submenus, you replace any grid that already exists in your file.

If you have established a grid that you think you might need again, you can save it as a preset by choosing View>Perspective Grid>Save Grid As Preset. The resulting dialog box has most of the same options as the Define Perspective Grid dialog box, but you can type a name in the top field for easier recognition. Your saved grid presets will then be available in the View>Perspective Grid submenus.

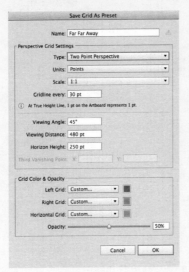

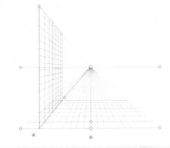

Default one-point perspective grid.

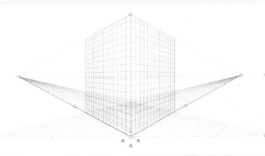

Default two-point perspective grid.

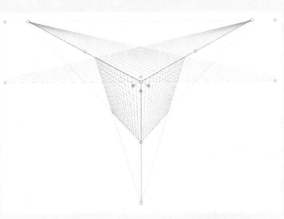

Default three-point perspective grid.

DRAW IN PERSPECTIVE

Once you have defined a perspective grid, creating objects in perspective is a fairly simple process. The most important issue is determining which plane you should draw on, and making sure that plane is active when you draw.

1. With **prices_feb.ai** open, choose the Rectangle tool in the Tools panel and reset the default fill and stroke attributes.

2. In the Layers panel, make the Content layer active.

3. In the Plane Switching widget, click the Right Grid proxy to make it the active plane.

4. Using the Rectangle tool, click near the corner of the sketch, then drag right to create a shape that represents the right-front edge of the sign platform.

   Although you are drawing with the basic Rectangle tool, the new shape automatically adopts the perspective defined by the active plane in the grid.

Click the Right Grid proxy in the widget to change the active plane.

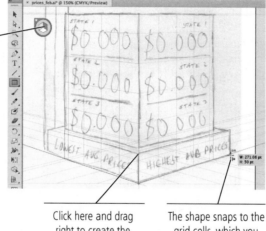 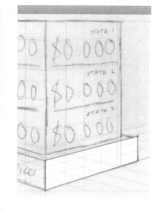

Click here and drag right to create the rectangle in perspective.

The shape snaps to the grid cells, which you defined as 50-pt high.

5. **Click the Left Grid proxy in the Plane Switching widget.**

6. **Starting at the top-right corner, draw another rectangle representing the left-front edge of the platform.**

   Smart guides work in perspective drawing mode just as they do in regular drawings. You can snap to existing objects to align edges and corners when you draw new objects. However, the perspective grid also acts magnetic by default, so it might be difficult to snap to exactly the right location.

Click the Left Grid proxy in the widget to change the active plane.

Click here and drag left to create the rectangle in perspective.

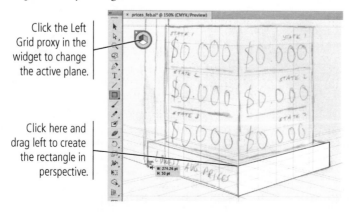

Note:

It might be helpful to turn off the snapping behavior by choosing View>Perspective Guide>Snap to Guide.

Note:

Click the background area in the Plane Switching widget to select No Active Grid if you want to draw objects that aren't attached to the perspective grid.

7. **Click the Horizontal Grid proxy in the Plane Switching widget.**

8. **Using the Rectangle tool with the default fill and stroke attributes, draw another rectangle representing the top surface of the platform.**

   Start at the left corner and drag to the right corner, snapping to the existing points to create the top surface of the sign platform.

   Click the Horizontal Grid proxy to change the active plane.

   Click here and drag to create the rectangle in perspective.

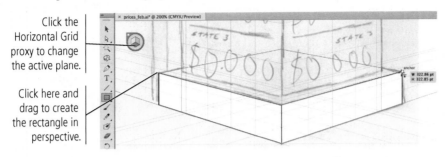

9. **Deselect the active shape, then zoom into the outside corner where the top surface meets the front right surface.**

10. **Use the Layers panel to hide the Sketch layer, and then choose View>Perspective Grid>Hide Grid.**

    As you can see, our example shows the corners are not precisely aligned.

Note:

Press Shift-V to access the Perspective Selection tool.

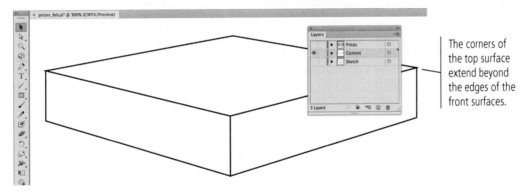

The corners of the top surface extend beyond the edges of the front surfaces.

11. **Using the Selection tool, select the top-surface shape. In the Stroke panel, click the Bevel Join corner shape.**

    To move or resize a perspective object within the perspective grid, you have to use the Perspective Selection tool (nested under the Perspective Grid tool). This is a very important distinction, and one that is easy to forget. If you move or resize a perspective object with the regular Selection tool, the object's perspective is not maintained in the transformation.

    In this case, you are only changing a property of the object — not changing the object's actual dimensions — so you do not need to use the Perspective Selection tool.

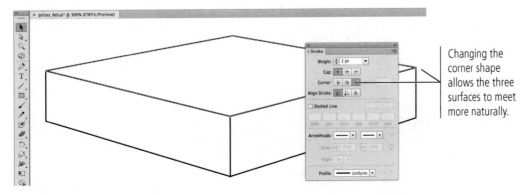

Changing the corner shape allows the three surfaces to meet more naturally.

12. **Using any method you prefer, fill the top surface with the Green 1 swatch, fill the right-front surface with the Green 2 swatch, and fill the left-front surface with the Green 3 swatch.**

Note:

A perspective drawing object is still a drawing object. You can use the Control panel, Swatches panel, or Color panel to change the fill and stroke colors of the selected shape.

Fill and stroke options are available in the Control panel even when a drawing object is selected with the Perspective Selection tool.

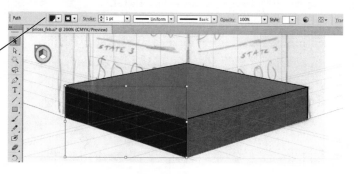

13. **Click the Perspective Grid tool in the Tools panel.**

When you choose the Perspective Grid tool, the grid automatically reappears. You can also choose View>Perspective Grid>Show Grid.

14. **Show the Sketch layer, then save the file and continue to the next exercise.**

MOVING OBJECTS IN PERSPECTIVE

One of the most powerful advantages of drawing in Illustrator's perspective grid is the fact that it is mostly non-destructive. Perspective objects can be moved around on their planes, and even moved to different planes, without degrading their quality.

1. **With `prices_feb.ai` open, choose the Perspective Selection tool (nested under the Perspective Grid tool).**

Remember: To move or resize a perspective object within the perspective grid, you have to use the Perspective Selection tool.

Note:

The perspective grid does not need to be visible to transform objects in perspective; in fact, it is sometimes easier to make fine changes when the grid is not visible.

2. **Press Option/Alt-Shift, then click the rectangle on the right-front face of the platform and drag up until the top edge aligns with the top edge of the sketched sign.**

The same keyboard shortcuts for transforming objects work for transforming objects in perspective. Press Shift to constrain an object's movement to 45° angles (including exactly horizontal or vertical). Press Option/Alt to clone the object that you are dragging.

As you move the clone, you can see how the object adopts the appropriate shape based on the active perspective plane.

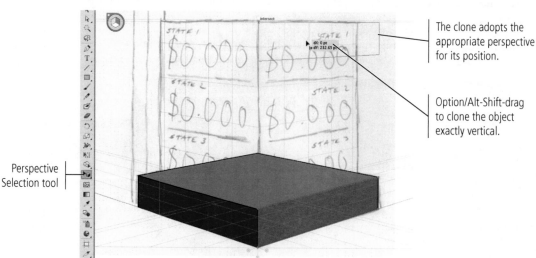

Perspective Selection tool

The clone adopts the appropriate perspective for its position.

Option/Alt-Shift-drag to clone the object exactly vertical.

3. **Using the Perspective Selection tool, click the bottom-center handle of the rectangle, and drag down until it meets the top edge of the first shape.**

Remember, to resize an object in perspective, you have to use the Perspective Selection tool and not the regular Selection tool.

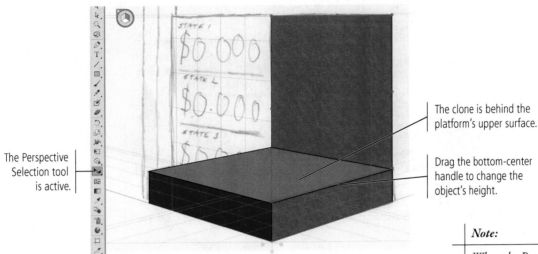

The Perspective Selection tool is active.

The clone is behind the platform's upper surface.

Drag the bottom-center handle to change the object's height.

4. **Choose Object>Arrange>Bring To Front to move the second rectangle above the top edge of the platform.**

Object stacking order in perspective drawing follows the same rules as in regular drawing. New objects are automatically created at the top of the stacking order on the active layer. When you clone an object, the new clone is stacked immediately above the object you cloned.

5. **Change the object's fill color to white.**

6. **Press and hold the 5 key, then click the white rectangle and drag left.**

Pressing the 5 key while dragging an object moves the object perpendicular to the plane where the object sits. In other words, the object moves nearer or farther away without changing its horizontal (X) position on that plane.

Note:

When the Perspective Selection tool is active, arrows in the cursor icon remind you which plane is active.

Left Grid

Right Grid

Horizontal Grid

No Grid

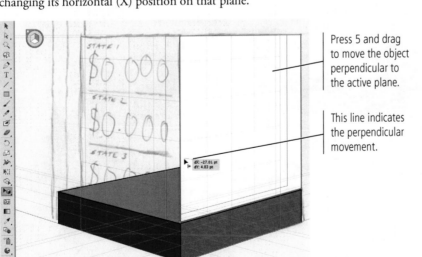

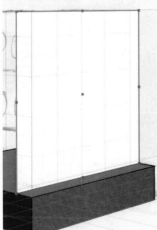

Press 5 and drag to move the object perpendicular to the active plane.

This line indicates the perpendicular movement.

7. **Using the Perspective Selection tool, drag the left-center handle until the left edge aligns with the left edge of the lower shape.**

The sketch appears to view the exact corner of the sign, so the corners of the two surfaces should appear to align.

8. **Drag the right-center handle left to bring the sign edge in from the platform edge.**

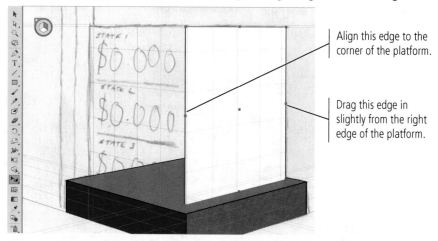

Align this edge to the corner of the platform.

Drag this edge in slightly from the right edge of the platform.

Note:

Using the Perspective Selection tool, you can only select and group multiple objects if they exist on the same plane.

Using the regular Selection tool, you can select and group objects on different perspective planes. If you do, selecting an object in the group with the Perspective Selection tool only affects the object you click; you can't move or transform objects on different planes at the same time.

9. **Press Option/Alt, then click and drag the rectangle to clone it to the left. While still holding the Option/Alt key, press 1 to move the clone to the left perspective plane.**

   You can move an object to a different plane by pressing the appropriate shortcut key while you drag the object:

   - Left plane: 1
   - Horizontal (ground) plane: 2
   - Right plane: 3
   - No plane: 4

   These keyboard shortcuts relate only to the main numbers on the keyboard; the numeric keypad numbers do not work for switching planes.

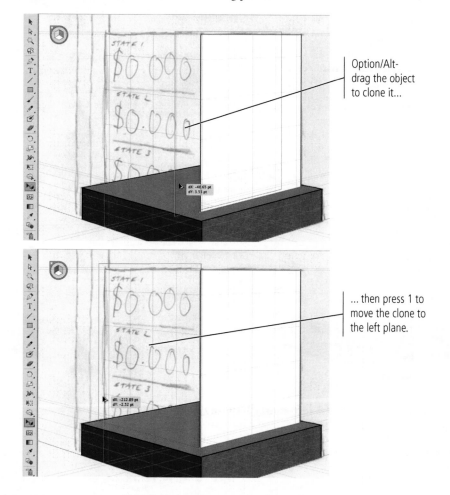

Option/Alt-drag the object to clone it...

... then press 1 to move the clone to the left plane.

10. **Using the Perspective Selection tool, resize the object to the appropriate shape by dragging the object handles.**

If necessary, turn off the Snap to Grid feature to resize the object appropriately.

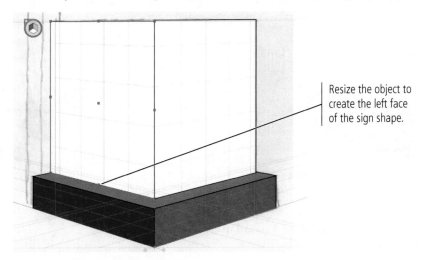

Resize the object to create the left face of the sign shape.

11. **Save the file and continue to the next exercise.**

WORK WITH TYPE IN PERSPECTIVE

Most drawing objects can be created or placed in perspective, with a few exceptions (notably graph objects). Both point-type and area-type objects can be applied to a perspective grid. The text remains editable unless you release the object from the perspective grid.

1. **With prices_feb.ai open, make sure the Content layer is active.**

2. **Choose the Type tool in the Tools panel. Click anywhere in the file to create a new point-type object, and type LOWEST AVERAGE PRICES.**

3. **In the Character or Control panel, choose ATC Oak Normal as the font and change the size to 22 pt.**

Type objects are created unattached to any plane.

4. **Choose the Perspective Selection tool, and choose the Left Grid proxy in the Plane Switching widget.**

5. **Click the type object and drag until it appears in front of the left-face side of the sign platform.**

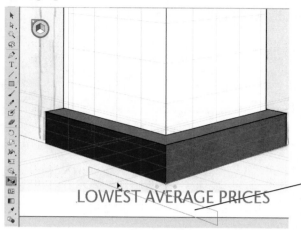 

Start dragging with the Perspective Selection tool to place the type object onto the active plane.

6. **Click the right-center handle of the type object and drag left until the type fits entirely inside the platform face.**

7. **With the type object selected, click the Edit Text button in the Control panel.**

When a perspective type object is selected, you have to enter into the text to change the color of the text. Unlike other objects, you can't change the fill or stroke attributes of a perspective type object without first entering into Edit Text mode.

8. **With the text highlighted in Edit Text mode, use the Control panel to change the fill color to white.**

 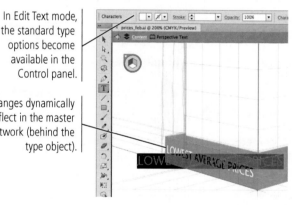

Edit Text button

In Edit Text mode, the standard type options become available in the Control panel.

Changes dynamically reflect in the master artwork (behind the type object).

9. **Click the arrow button at the top of the document window two times to exit Edit Text mode.**

Note:

You can also double-click the type object to enter the Edit Text mode.

10. **Using the Perspective Selection tool, Option/Alt-click the type object and drag right to clone it. While still dragging the clone, press 3 to move the clone to the right plane.**

11. **With the cloned type object selected, click the Edit Text button in the Control panel.**

12. **Select the word LOWEST and type HIGHEST.**

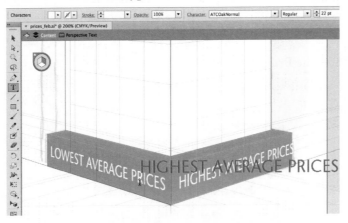

13. **Click the arrow button at the top of the document window two times to exit Edit Text mode.**

14. **Using the Perspective Selection tool, click and drag the side center handles until the type fits entirely inside the platform face.**

15. **Save the file and continue to the final exercise.**

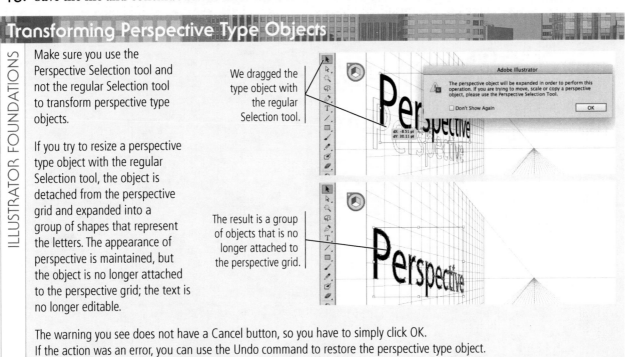

Transforming Perspective Type Objects

Make sure you use the Perspective Selection tool and not the regular Selection tool to transform perspective type objects.

If you try to resize a perspective type object with the regular Selection tool, the object is detached from the perspective grid and expanded into a group of shapes that represent the letters. The appearance of perspective is maintained, but the object is no longer attached to the perspective grid; the text is no longer editable.

We dragged the type object with the regular Selection tool.

The result is a group of objects that is no longer attached to the perspective grid.

The warning you see does not have a Cancel button, so you have to simply click OK. If the action was an error, you can use the Undo command to restore the perspective type object.

ATTACH OBJECTS TO THE PERSPECTIVE GRID

Adding existing flat artwork to the perspective grid is a fairly simple process. The important issue in this case is recognizing that flat artwork placed into perspective often (but not always) needs some additional work to add the depth that is inherent in dimensional artwork.

1. **With `prices_feb.ai` open, show the Prices layer.**

   These two area-type objects represent characters on a sign; they do not need additional elements of depth to appear accurate.

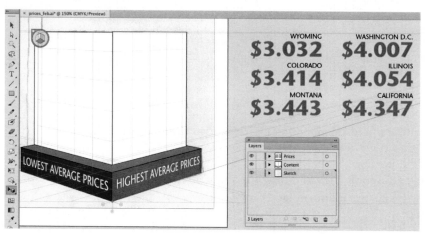

Note:

The average gasoline prices in this file are from www.gasbuddy.com, which posts current gasoline pricing information for locales all around the United States. If you want to update your exercise file depending on when you complete this project, find the current prices and edit the type objects on the Prices layer.

2. **Choose the Perspective Selection tool, and choose the Left Grid proxy in the Plane Switching widget.**

3. **Click the left type object (with the Wyoming price), and drag it into position on the left face of the sign. Resize the type object to fill the sign face.**

4. **Still using the Perspective Selection tool, click the right type object (with the Washington D.C. price) and begin dragging. Press 3 to switch to the right plane, and position the second type object on the right face of the sign. Resize the type object to fill the sign face.**

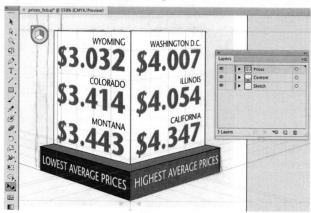

5. **Create a new layer named Station Sign immediately above the Sketch layer.**

   Like object stacking order, layer stacking order is the same in perspective drawing as it is in regular drawing. The same perspective grid applies to all layers.

6. **With the Station Sign layer selected, open the Symbols panel (Window>Symbols). Click the Station Sign symbol in the panel and drag it onto the artboard.**

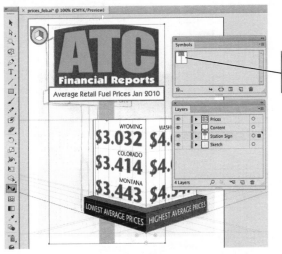

Drag an instance of this symbol onto the Station Sign layer.

Note:

If you completed Project 4: Ski Resort Map, you should understand the concept of symbols. Editing the actual symbol changes any placed instance of that symbol, including those that are placed in perspective.

7. **Click the Right Grid proxy in the Plane Switching widget.**

8. **Use the Perspective Selection tool to drag the symbol instance into perspective, with the bottom-left corner of the signpost at the origin point of the grid.**

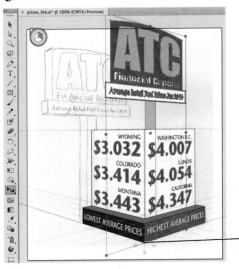

Align the left corner of the signpost with the corner of the grid.

9. **Press 5, then click the symbol instance and drag left to move the station sign perpendicular to the plane, until it appears behind the price sign.**

   You should realize that the Illustrator perspective grid is precise; when you place the sign into perspective, you can see how <u>imperfect</u> the original sketch was.

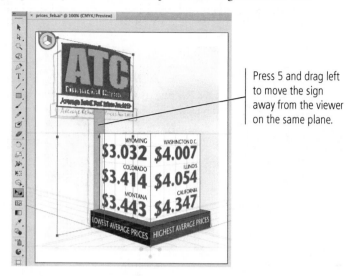

Press 5 and drag left to move the sign away from the viewer on the same plane.

10. **Select the Left Grid proxy in the Plane Switching widget.**

    Unlike the type objects, the sign needs a few additional elements to create the appearance of depth. Remember, one of the most important issues of drawing in perspective is placing objects on the correct plane. Because the sign faces the right plane, you need to add depth to the sign along the left plane.

11. **Using the Rectangle tool, draw three new shapes to create the left faces of the station sign and its post. Fill the shape on the post's left side with 70% black, and fill the two shapes on the sign's left side with the Green 3 swatch.**

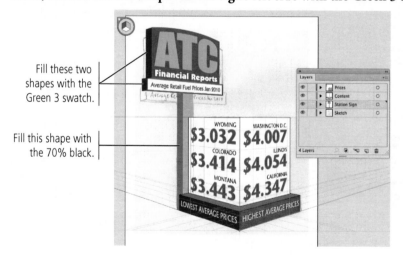

Fill these two shapes with the Green 3 swatch.

Fill this shape with the 70% black.

12. **Double-click the symbol instance on the artboard. Read the resulting message, and then click OK.**

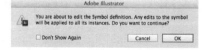

    You need to edit the type in the sign to reflect the correct date (Feb 2012). Rather than editing a perspective type object, you need to edit the type object inside of the symbol.

ILLUSTRATOR FOUNDATIONS

Attaching Objects to the Perspective Grid

If you create a regular drawing object that is not attached to a perspective plane, you can attach it to a specific plane by selecting it with the Perspective Selection tool and choosing Perspective>Attach to Active Plane in the object's contextual menu (or choosing Object>Perspective>Attach to Active Plane). The object's shape is maintained, but the bounding box changes to reflect its new perspective boundaries.

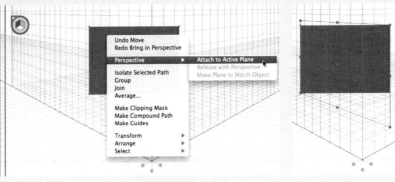

Releasing Objects from the Perspective Grid

To convert an object from a perspective object to a regular object, you can choose Perspective>Release with Perspective in the object's contextual menu (or choose Object>Perspective>Release with Perspective). The selected shape becomes a regular drawing object; the apparent perspective is maintained, but the object is no longer attached to a plane. The object's bounding box reveals the outermost edges of the flat artwork.

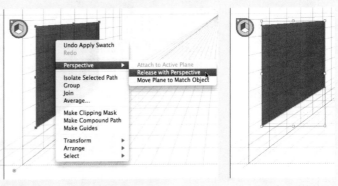

Moving the Plane to Match Perspective

If you have moved objects perpendicularly away from the active plane, you can adjust the grid plane to meet the position of the selected object by choosing Perspective>Move Plane to Match Object in the object's contextual menu (or choosing Object>Perspective>Move Plane to Match Object). The active plane snaps to the face of the selected object, which makes it easier to create or place new objects along the same plane as the existing object.

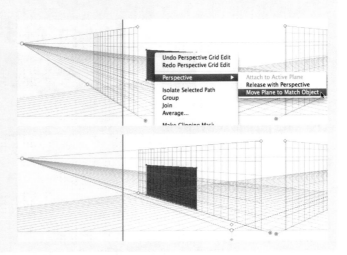

13. **Using the Type tool, select the words "Jan 2010" on the sign and type** Feb 2012.

Click the arrow to exit Symbol Editing mode.

14. **Click the arrow button at the top of the document window to exit Symbol Editing mode.**

The edited text appears in the placed symbol instance.

15. **Delete the Sketch layer, then choose View>Perspective Grid>Hide Grid.**

16. **Save the file and close it.**

Project Review

fill in the blank

1. A _____ graph shows values as percentages of the whole.

2. A _____ graph plots values as a series of connected points, showing progressive change in value.

3. You must use _____ to enter numbers as text in the Data panel.

4. You must use the _____ to select one segment of a graph without ungrouping the entire graph.

5. You can click the _____ button in the Data panel to increase the number of decimals that are included in each data cell.

6. The _____ is the height of the theoretical viewer's eye level.

7. The _____ is the spot where multiple lines on the same perspective converge.

8. The _____ tool is used to define the position of various attributes of the perspective grid.

9. The _____ is used to determine which perspective plane is active.

10. The _____ tool is used to move or resize objects in perspective.

short answer

1. Briefly explain what is meant by the term "infographics."

2. Briefly explain the concept of two-point perspective.

3. Briefly explain the difference between the Selection tool and the Perspective Selection tool.

Use what you learned in this project to complete the following freeform exercise.
Carefully read the art director and client comments, then create your own design to meet the needs of the project.
Use the space below to sketch ideas; when finished, write a brief explanation of your reasoning behind your final design.

art director comments

The main theme for next month's magazine is "Living Green." The main articles all focus on some aspect of environmental conservation, such as renewable energy, recycling strategies, and landfill reduction. Your job is to create information graphics for data that will accompany the cover story.

To complete this project, you should:

❏ Download the **AI6_PB_Project7.zip** archive from the Student Files Web page.

❏ Use the supplied data to create three information graphics that present the data in some visually interesting way.

❏ Create illustrations for each set of data that support the overall theme of the article.

client comments

The main focus of next month's cover story is the growing energy shortage in some areas of the country, and different methods that are being explored to supply affordable electricity to an ever-growing number of people in large metropolitan areas such as New York City and Los Angeles.

The author has compiled three different sets of data about renewable energy — wind power, water power, and so on — that will support the ideas and facts in the article. We need some type of illustrated graph for each of these data sets.

We want our readers to see the graphs even if they only flip through and skim the article. Create a compelling illustration for each one so they are more than just graphs. However, keep in mind that the data is the most important element — it needs to be clear and understandable.

Use a consistent color scheme in all three graphs; green should play a prominent role because people naturally associate that color with environmentalism and natural resources.

project justification

_____

_____

_____

_____

_____

_____

_____

_____

_____

_____

_____

_____

_____

_____

Information graphics like the ones you created in this project are frequently used in newspapers, magazines, and presentations to visually represent complex statistics or other numerical data. Information graphics range from simple pie charts and line graphs to elaborate full-color images.

When you create this type of illustration, keep in mind that "information" is the first word in information graphics. Also notice that this category of illustration work is not called "information decorating" — the information or data being presented is always the priority. Although aesthetic appeal is a primary concern of most graphic designers, the integrity of the information is the most important aspect of creating information graphics.

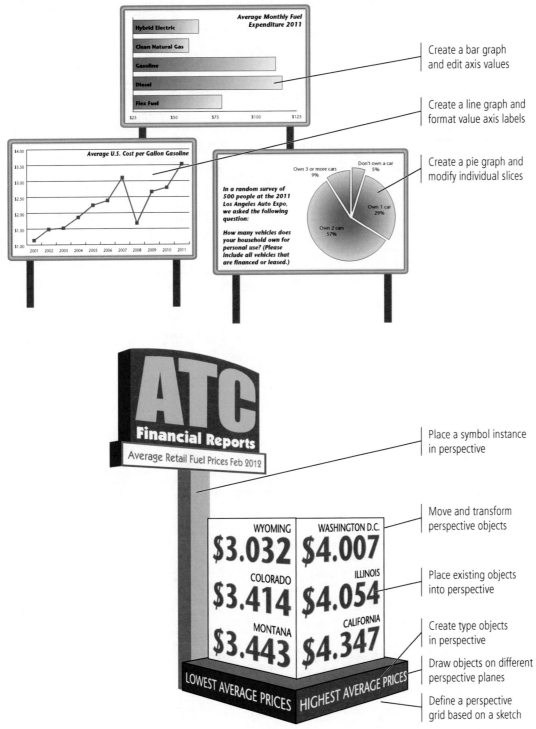

Create a bar graph and edit axis values

Create a line graph and format value axis labels

Create a pie graph and modify individual slices

Place a symbol instance in perspective

Move and transform perspective objects

Place existing objects into perspective

Create type objects in perspective

Draw objects on different perspective planes

Define a perspective grid based on a sketch

Web Site Interface

As an in-house designer for a multimedia services company, your job is to create the pieces that are required for the company's new Web site home page. The basic site structure has already been designed; you need to make changes that were requested by the marketing manager, and then slice the page into pieces that can be reassembled in a Web-design application.

This project incorporates the following skills:

❏ Using Image Trace to create complex vector artwork from a photograph

❏ Using Live Color to make universal and individual changes to the colors in a group

❏ Slicing a page into pieces and defining settings for individual slices

❏ Saving images in appropriate formats for display on the Web

client comments

We're very happy with the overall look of the site, and the retro icons for the six service rollovers are great! Since the Tampa image is predominantly red, though, we want to change the blue to red in all the current design elements.

For the home page, we want the main area — where the Tampa photo is now — to include six rollovers that screen back the Tampa image and show one of the main branches of our service business.

We were also thinking that the skyline would look good as a "paint-by-numbers" kind of drawing rather than a basic photo. That will go better with the overall feel of the icons.

art director comments

Instead of taking days to manually create an illustration from the skyline photo, you can use Illustrator's Image Trace function to accomplish the same goal. Experiment with the different settings — specifically, the number of colors — until you get the look we need. You can create color groups to make it easier to adjust the colors in the site.

In addition to the rollovers in the main page area, the navigation buttons in the blue bar also need to be rollovers. Use some kind of subtle effect to create the second state (what the buttons look like on rollover).

Before you slice up the page, keep in mind that the six icons in the main area and the navigation buttons are rollovers. You're going to have to export the file twice to create all the necessary bits and pieces.

While you're making the necessary changes and cutting apart the pieces, I'll have the Dreamweaver developer start working on the Web site framework that will reassemble the slices you create.

project objectives

To complete this project, you will:

❏ Use Image Trace to create a complex vector illustration

❏ Create color groups to manage the color swatches in the file

❏ Adjust global color attributes in all selected artwork

❏ Adjust individual colors in a group to change all objects where the color is applied

❏ Define a graphic style to easily apply multiple effects to objects

❏ Create slices from existing page guides

❏ Define individual slice settings

❏ Optimize image settings and export slices

Using Image Trace and Live Color

As you learned in the previous projects of this book, you can use Illustrator to create virtually any type of illustration — from a basic vector drawing to a complex photo illustration to a folding-brochure layout. You can also use Illustrator to build and cut apart the pieces that make up a Web site (as you will do in this project), even defining specific styles for navigational buttons and multiple states of rollover areas. Those pieces can then be correctly reassembled in a professional Web-design application such as Adobe Dreamweaver to create a fully functional Web site.

In the first stage of this project, you are going to use built-in tools to create a complex illustration, then you will use color groups and Live Color to adjust global and specific colors to unify the overall site design.

 USE IMAGE TRACE TO CREATE A COMPLEX IMAGE

If you have completed the other projects in this book, you should have a solid foundation for creating basic and complex vector graphics, whether based on a sketch, based on a photograph, or from scratch. Another option — Image Trace — makes it very easy to create vector graphics directly from an image, using a variety of options to determine how realistic the resulting illustration will be.

1. Download **AI6_RF_Project8.zip** from the Student Files Web page.

2. **Expand the ZIP archive in your WIP folder (Macintosh) or copy the archive contents into your WIP folder (Windows).**

   This results in a folder named **Consulting**, which contains the files you need for this project. You should also use this folder to save the files you create in this project.

   Make sure you save files for this project using the exact names we define in the steps. If you use different file names — including misspellings or different capitalization — the HTML code will not be able to locate the necessary files.

3. **Open the file dh site.ai from the WIP>Consulting folder.**

4. **Open the Layers panel and review the contents of the layers in the file.**

This layer contains the icons and semi-transparent overlay for the six different category rollovers.

This layer contains all persistent objects, such as the top banner, the navigation bar, and the bar at the bottom of the page.

This layer contains an image that fills the primary area on the site home page.

5. **Hide all but the Tampa layer, and then use the Selection tool to select the image on the visible layer.**

The selected object is a 72-ppi RGB photo.

Click to apply the Image Trace function to the selected image.

Open this menu to choose a specific Image Trace preset.

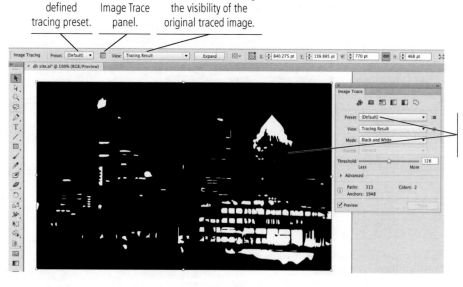

Note:

In the Layers panel, Option/Alt-clicking the Eye icon for a layer hides all other layers in the file.

6. **In the Control panel, click the Image Trace button.**

By clicking this button, Illustrator automatically traces the image using the default black-and-white preset.

The result is a special type of object called a **image tracing object** (which you can see in the Control panel). As long as you don't expand the tracing object, you can change the settings to produce different results from the same picture.

Note:

You can also apply the default Image Trace settings by choosing Object>Image Trace>Make.

7. **Open the Image Trace panel (Window>Image Trace).**

When you trace an image, the original photo is hidden, and the illustrated version appears in its place.

Choose a defined tracing preset.

Open the Image Trace panel.

Use this menu to change the visibility of the original traced image.

The default Image Trace is a black-and-white illustration.

8. **Open the Preset menu and choose Low Fidelity Photo.**

   Illustrator includes a number of Image Trace presets that you can apply to any image. These can be accessed in the Image Trace panel or Control panel when a tracing object is selected.

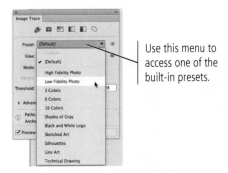

Use this menu to access one of the built-in presets.

When the Preview option is checked at the bottom of the panel, every change requires Illustrator to reprocess the image to generate the correct curves. Because this is a rather large image, processing each change could take considerable processing power and time (depending on your computer).

9. **At the bottom of the panel, uncheck the Preview option.**

   Rather than waiting to preview each change, it's a better idea to activate the preview after defining your initial choices; you can then toggle the preview on and off as necessary to reduce the time you spend sitting and waiting.

10. **Click the arrow to the left of the Advanced heading to expand the panel.**

11. **Change the Paths option to 75%.**

    This controls how tightly the tracing conforms to the original image; a higher number means more tightly fitting paths.

12. **Change the Corners option to 25%.**

    This controls how corners in the original image are represented in the tracing; a higher number results in more corners instead of rounded paths.

    Click here to show or hide the advanced options.

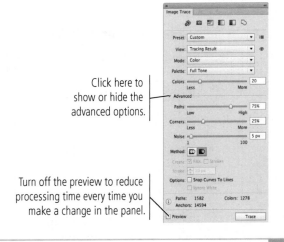

13. **Change the Noise option to 5 px.**

    This controls the smallest-size area that is ignored in the tracing result; higher values mean fewer small spots of color in the tracing.

    Turn off the preview to reduce processing time every time you make a change in the panel.

14. Check the Preview option at the bottom of the panel to review the results of your choices.

The change is subtle, but you should notice slightly more accurate path shapes (Step 11), more rounded corners on the buildings (Step 12), and fewer small areas that represent the building windows (Step 13).

15. Open the View menu and choose Tracing Result with Outlines.

By default, vector outlines that make up the image-tracing object are not visible in the document. Without expanding the image tracing object, these preview options allow you to view the resulting paths based on your current Image Trace settings.

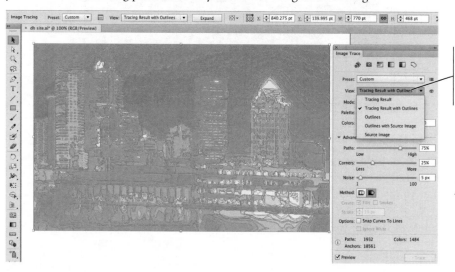

When Tracing Result with Outlines is selected, you can see the vector paths that will make up the resulting illustration.

Note:

To access the individual anchors and paths, you have to expand the image-tracing object.

16. Choose Tracing Result in the View menu.

This turns off the path outlines and restores the illustration to full opacity.

17. Click the Eye icon to the right of the View button and hold down the mouse button.

This button provides a quick method for reviewing the original image, while still experimenting with the Image Trace options.

Click and hold this button to show the original image that is used to make the Image Trace.

18. Choose Limited in the Palette menu, then change the Colors option to 8.

By allowing only a small number of colors, you force Illustrator to create larger objects of solid colors — ultimately resulting in more of a "paint-by-numbers" effect.

When you use a Limited palette, you can define the specific number of colors to allow in the illustration.

As long as you don't expand the tracing object, you can change the settings that generate the illustration. Generating and regenerating the tracing result might take a minute, depending on your settings and computer capabilities; be patient.

19. Save the file and then continue to the next exercise.

Note:

Increase the number of possible colors to create a more realistic result (and a more complex illustration).

Image Trace Options

With so many options and sliders, the Image Trace panel might seem intimidating at first. As with any tool, it's easier to get the desired results if you understand the options.

Buttons at the top of the panel apply specific color modes to the illustration: (from left) Auto Color, High Color, Low Color, Grayscale, Black and White, or Outline.

- **Preset** includes a number of built-in groups of settings that produce specific results, such as Sketched Art or Technical Drawing.
- **View** changes what is visible in the document. You can show the tracing result with or without outlines, the source image with or without outlines, or only the source image.
- **Mode** defines the color mode (color, grayscale, or black and white) of the resulting illustration.
- **Palette**, which is available when the Mode is set to Color, defines the specific colors that can be used; the default Full Tone option allows Illustrator to use an unlimited palette to create the illustration.
- **Threshold**, which is only available when the Mode is set to Black and White, defines the maximum tonal value that will remain white before an area is filled with black.
- **Colors.** When Full Tone or Automatic is selected in the Palette menu, this option defines the accuracy of illustration colors as a percentage; higher values result in a larger number of colors being used.

  When the Limited palette is selected, this option defines the specific number of colors Illustrator can use to trace the image. More colors create more depth, but also increase the complexity and number of points in the illustration.
- **Paths** adjusts how closely traced paths will follow the pixels of the original image.
- **Corners** defines the minimum angle that can be traced as a sharp corner instead of a smooth curve.
- **Noise** adjusts the smallest color area (in pixels) that can be drawn as a path.
- **Method** determines whether shapes in the illustration are created as abutting (left) or overlapping (right).
- When you use the Black and White color mode, you can use the **Create** options to define whether the illustration is created as fills, strokes, or a combination of both.
  - **Fills** results in solid-filled paths.
  - **Strokes** results in paths with an applied stroke color and weight. The Stroke Width field defines the maximum stroke weight that can be applied before a stroke will be recreated as a fill object.
- **Snap Curves to Lines** replaces slightly curved lines with straight lines.
- **Ignore White** does not create shapes to represent white areas in the image.

USE A COLOR GROUP TO CHANGE MULTIPLE SWATCHES

Color groups are useful for organizing color swatches into logical and manageable collections. You can make changes that affect all colors within a group; this takes the concept of global color swatches one step further. In this exercise, you create a group from the tracing object swatches so you can make changes that affect the entire illustration.

1. **With dh site.ai open, select the image-tracing object.**

2. **Click the Expand button in the Control panel.**

   Once expanded, you can no longer use the Image Trace panel to change the object. You can, however, use the regular Illustrator toolset to edit the anchors, paths, and colors that make up the resulting illustration.

After expanding the tracing object, the selection is now a regular group.

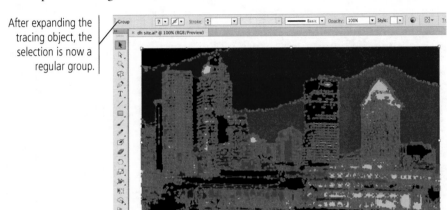

3. **With the resulting group selected, click the New Color Group button at the bottom of the Swatches panel.**

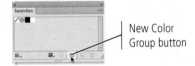

New Color Group button

4. **In the resulting dialog box, type Tampa Colors in the Name field. Choose the Create From Selected Artwork radio button, check the Convert Process to Global option, and turn off the Include Swatches for Tints option.**

5. **Click OK to create the new color group.**

   By checking the Selected Artwork option, every color used in the selection is added as a separate swatch in the group; the group contains the eight colors that you allowed when you defined the Image Trace settings. Each is a global swatch, which means editing the swatch will affect the appearance of any object where that swatch is applied.

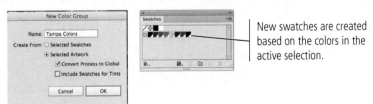

New swatches are created based on the colors in the active selection.

6. **With the artwork still selected, click the color group folder icon to select the entire group.**

   If you click a swatch instead of the group folder, you will change the fill/stroke attribute (whichever is active) of the selected objects.

7. **Click the Edit or Apply Color Group button at the bottom of the Swatches panel.**

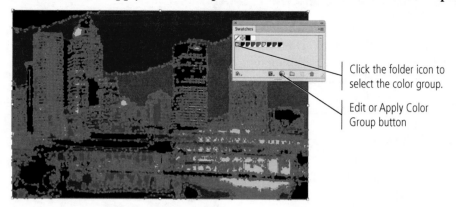

Click the folder icon to select the color group.

Edit or Apply Color Group button

8. **Change the Recolor Artwork dialog box to Edit mode, and make sure the Recolor Art option is checked in the bottom-left corner.**

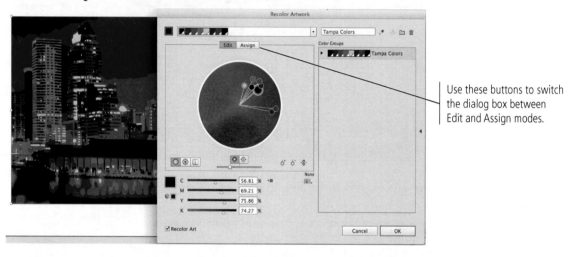

Use these buttons to switch the dialog box between Edit and Assign modes.

9. **Make sure the Link Harmony Colors button is active. Drag the Brightness slider (below the color wheel) right to lighten all colors in the image.**

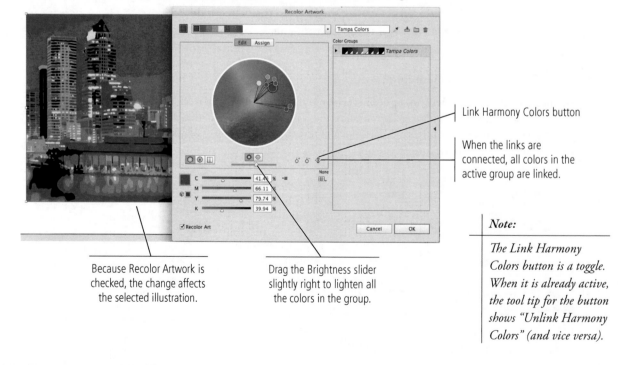

Link Harmony Colors button

When the links are connected, all colors in the active group are linked.

Because Recolor Artwork is checked, the change affects the selected illustration.

Drag the Brightness slider slightly right to lighten all the colors in the group.

Note:

The Link Harmony Colors button is a toggle. When it is already active, the tool tip for the button shows "Unlink Harmony Colors" (and vice versa).

10. **Click OK to apply the change. Click Yes when asked if you want to save the changes to the color group.**

11. **Save the file and continue to the next exercise.**

USE A COLOR GROUP TO MANAGE FILE COLORS

In addition to managing universal changes to all swatches in a group, color groups can also be useful for simplifying a design and managing the individual colors included in specific areas of a file. In this exercise, you use a color group to combine similar colors into tints of a single color swatch.

1. **With dh site.ai open, lock the Tampa layer, and then show the Background and Rollovers layers.**

2. **Choose Select>All to select all artwork on the two unlocked layers.**

3. **With the artwork selected, click the New Color Group button at the bottom of the Swatches panel.**

4. **In the resulting dialog box, type Site Colors in the Name field. Choose the Create From Selected Artwork radio button, and make sure both check boxes are selected.**

5. **Click OK to create the new color group.**

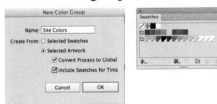

6. **With the artwork still selected, click the Site Colors color group folder to select the entire group, and then click the Edit or Apply Color Group button.**

   This group currently contains 13 colors, but most of the colors are tints of black. It will be easier to manage the group if you combine the different gray swatches into tints of a single black swatch. You also have two very similar shades of gold, which might be combined to produce a more unified piece of artwork.

Note:

Unchecking the Include Swatches for Tints option does not solve this problem because the artwork was not created with tints of a swatch.

7. **If necessary, change the Recolor Artwork dialog box to Assign mode.**

8. **In the list of colors, click each gold color and review the color contents at the bottom of the dialog box.**

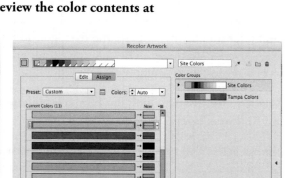

These values show that the two gold colors are virtually the same.

9. **Drag the second gold bar onto the first one to combine both colors into a single swatch.**

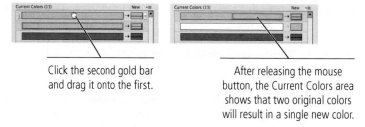

Click the second gold bar and drag it onto the first.

After releasing the mouse button, the Current Colors area shows that two original colors will result in a single new color.

10. **Click the fifth color in the list of current colors and drag it into the fourth row.**

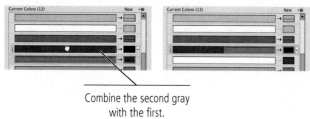

Combine the second gray with the first.

11. Repeat Step 10 to combine all gray shades (including the whites and the black swatch at the bottom of the list) into the first gray color.

When you get to the lower swatches in the Current Colors list, the one you're dragging to will have scrolled out of the window. You can click a Current Color swatch and drag to the top of the window to scroll up to the swatch you need to target.

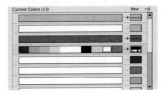

12. Click OK to return to the document.

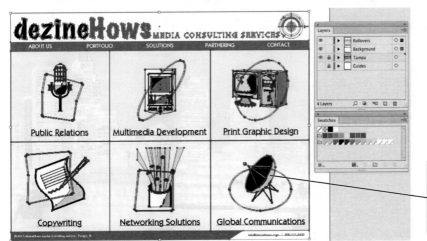

Consolidating the Site Colors swatches has no visible effect on the selected artwork. Shades are created as tints of the single black swatch.

13. Open the Swatches panel Options menu and choose Select All Unused.

14. Delete the selected swatches from the file.

15. With the artwork still selected on the artboard, reselect the Site Colors group and click the Edit or Apply Color Group button at the bottom of the Swatches panel.

16. **Display the Recolor Artwork dialog box in Edit mode, and then show the Smooth Color Wheel. Below the color wheel, click the Unlink Harmony Colors button to disconnect the color spokes from one another.**

17. **Select the blue color spoke. In the bottom area of the dialog box, display the color sliders in RGB mode and then define the spoke to be R=196 G=35 B=22.**

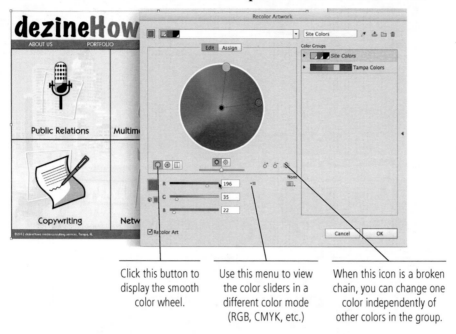

Click this button to display the smooth color wheel.

Use this menu to view the color sliders in a different color mode (RGB, CMYK, etc.)

When this icon is a broken chain, you can change one color independently of other colors in the group.

18. **Click OK to change the color group, and click Yes when asked if you want to save changes to the current group.**

19. **Save the file and continue to the next exercise.**

 ## WORK WITH LIVE PAINT GROUPS

A Live Paint Group is a special type of Illustrator group. Using the Live Paint Bucket tool, you can navigate through various swatches in a color group and apply those colors to different areas of the selected group. The advantage to this type of group is that fills are not necessarily defined by object edges. Rather, Illustrator identifies overlapping areas and allows you to treat the separate areas as distinct objects, even though they are part of the same vector shape.

1. **With dh site.ai open, deselect everything in the file and then click the microphone artwork with the Selection tool to select that group.**

2. **Choose the Live Paint Bucket tool (nested under the Shape Builder tool), and then click the Site Colors group icon in the Swatches panel to select that group.**

The Live Paint Bucket tool includes three sample swatches from the active color group. The center swatch is the active swatch.

Live Paint Bucket tool

Note:

If no color group is selected, the Live Paint Bucket tool shows the default ungrouped swatches.

3. **Press the Right Arrow key until the red swatch appears selected in the tool cursor.**

The Left and Right Arrow keys navigate between the swatches in the active group.

4. **Click the black area at the base of the microphone to change the fill color of that object.**

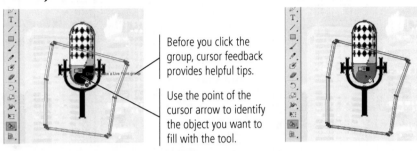

Before you click the group, cursor feedback provides helpful tips.

Use the point of the cursor arrow to identify the object you want to fill with the tool.

5. **Press Command/Control, then click the Multimedia icon artwork to select it.**

Remember, pressing Command/Control temporarily switches to the last-used selection tool (Selection or Direct Selection) — in this case the actual Selection tool.

Using this method allows you to quickly select a different icon; when you release the Command/Control key, the Live Paint Bucket tool is still active and the Site Colors group is still selected.

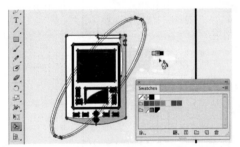

6. **Zoom in to the active selection so you can clearly see the black area in the top-left corner of the PDA screen.**

7. **Click the top-left section of the black area, as shown in the following image.**

The Live Paint Bucket tool identifies divisions in the selected artwork, even though they are not technically divisions.

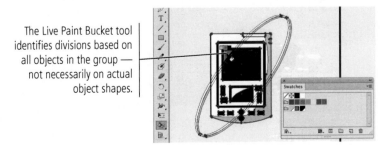

The Live Paint Bucket tool identifies divisions based on all objects in the group — not necessarily on actual object shapes.

8. **Using the Direct Selection tool, click away from the active group to deselect it, and then click only the object you filled with the red swatch.**

9. **Click the selected object and drag right.**

    Moving objects in a Live Paint group is different than moving individual objects in a regular group. Illustrator recognizes the original placement of the fill color, almost as if there is an underlay of the fill color, and the "filled" object is revealing that area of the color. Moving the individual object changes which part of the color "underlay" is visible.

After you move the object, a different area of the red fill is visible.

Note:

Use the Live Paint Selection tool to select pieces of a Live Paint group.

10. **Choose Edit>Undo Move to reposition the object that you moved in Step 9.**

11. **Select the entire group again. Use the Live Paint Bucket tool to fill the other pieces of the reflection object with the red swatch.**

12. **Use the same techniques to change at least one element in each graphic to the red swatch.**

Note:

When working with the Live Paint Bucket tool, press Shift to paint the stroke of an object instead of the fill.

13. **Save the file and continue to the next stage of the project.**

Stage 2 Creating Web Site Graphics

It is common practice to create the look and feel of a Web site in Illustrator, and then hand off the pieces for a programmer to assemble in a Web-design application such as Adobe Dreamweaver. In the second half of this project, you complete a number of tasks to create the necessary pieces for the final Web site, including the different states (versions) of areas that change appearance when the user's mouse rolls over those areas.

EXAMINE THE PIXEL GRID

When you use the Save for Web command, vector objects will be converted to raster files so they display properly on screen. As you learned at the beginning of this book, raster objects are composed of pixels. Illustrator includes a number of tools for making sure you achieve the best possible quality in the output raster files.

1. **With dh site.ai open, zoom in to the top-left corner of the artwork. Make sure you are viewing the file at 600% or higher.**

2. **Choose View>Pixel Preview.**

   This option shows the pixel grid that will be used when the artwork is exported and converted to raster images. The grid represents 72-ppi resolution, so each square in the grid is 1/72 of an inch.

   Objects are obviously bitmapped because you are viewing at such a high view percentage. However, you can see how the edges of shapes are defined by the position of pixels in the grid. This is an accurate representation of the pixel content that will exist in the final exported images.

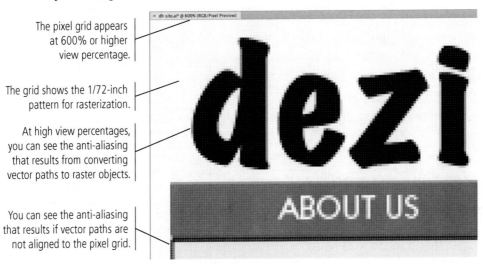

The pixel grid appears at 600% or higher view percentage.

The grid shows the 1/72-inch pattern for rasterization.

At high view percentages, you can see the anti-aliasing that results from converting vector paths to raster objects.

You can see the anti-aliasing that results if vector paths are not aligned to the pixel grid.

3. **Make the Selection tool active, and then choose Select>All.**

4. **Open the Transform panel and make sure all panel options are visible.**

   If you don't see the Align to Pixel Grid check box, choose Show Options in the panel Options menu.

5. **Click the Align to Pixel Grid box to activate that option.**

   When objects align to the pixel grid, straight lines reproduce more sharply because they no longer require anti-aliasing to fill the pixel grid. The shift in position is very, very slight — but it can make a significant difference in the sharpness of exported raster images and small type objects.

After aligning to the pixel grid, this line is no longer anti-aliased. It will be much sharper when rasterized.

Note:

When you create a new file, you can check the Align New Objects to Pixel Grid option in the New Document dialog box to automatically create new objects in alignment with the pixel grid.

6. **Choose View>Fit Artboard In Window, and choose View>Pixel Preview to turn off this option.**

7. **Save the file and continue to the next exercise.**

COMPOUND EFFECTS TO CREATE A GRAPHIC STYLE

The five type objects in the red bar will become navigation buttons; you will slice these elements and define targets for them in a later exercise. It is common practice to change the appearance of navigation buttons when the mouse rolls over them (called a **mouseover** or **rollover**).

   Because of the way Illustrator manages page slicing, you need to be able to easily apply and remove the altered appearance from mouseover type objects — a process that is easily accomplished by using graphic styles.

1. **With dh site.ai open, deselect everything on the artboard.**

2. **Use the Selection tool to select the About Us type object in the red bar.**

3. **Choose Effect>Stylize>Drop Shadow.**

4. **Apply a small drop shadow using the following settings, then click OK to finalize the effect.**

Note:

Illustrator includes several built-in style libraries, which you can access from the Window>Graphic Style Libraries menu, or by clicking the Graphic Styles Libraries Menu button at the bottom of the Graphic Styles panel.

Mode:	Multiply
Opacity:	85%
X Offset:	0
Y Offset:	4 pt
Blur:	1 pt
Color:	Black

5. **Choose Effect>Stylize>Drop Shadow again. When you see the warning message, click Apply New Effect.**

You can apply multiple effects to a single object, including multiple instances of the same effect.

6. **Apply a second drop shadow effect using the following settings:**

Mode:	Screen
Opacity:	30%
X Offset:	0
Y Offset:	–4 pt
Blur:	1 pt
Color:	Use the gold swatch from the Tampa Colors group.

To use one of the existing swatches as the shadow color, click the color swatch in the Drop Shadow dialog box to open the Color Picker. Then, click the Color Swatches button to show the existing swatches in the file. Select the gold swatch, then click OK.

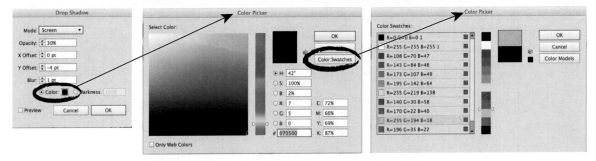

7. **Open the Graphic Styles panel (Window>Graphic Styles).**

Graphic styles are managed in much the same way as the swatches and other libraries you used in Project 4: Ski Resort Map.

8. **With the shadowed type object selected, click the New Graphic Style button at the bottom of the Graphic Styles panel.**

9. **With the new style selected in the panel, choose Graphic Style Options from the panel Options menu.**

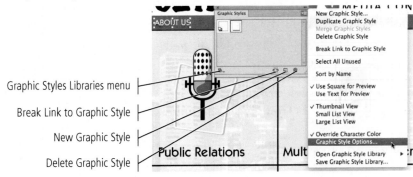

Graphic Styles Libraries menu

Break Link to Graphic Style

New Graphic Style

Delete Graphic Style

10. **Name the new style** Text Over State **and click OK.**

This graphic style contains all effects and attributes applied in the first type object (the one that was selected when you created the style). You can now use the named-style button to apply multiple saved effects to other objects with a single click. You will use this style later to create the "over" states of the navigation buttons.

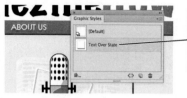

You can choose one of the List views (in the panel Options menu) to show the style names.

11. **With the About Us text element selected, open the Appearance panel Options menu and choose Reduce to Basic Appearance.**

If you clicked the Clear Appearance button at the bottom of the panel, the type object would revert to the default appearance of black fill with no stroke. In this instance, you want to retain the same basic fill color but remove the drop shadows, so you need to use the Reduce to Basic Appearance option.

Note:

Illustrator includes a number of built-in styles, which can be accessed in the Window>Graphic Style Libraries submenu. These libraries function in the same manner as the swatch libraries you used in Project 4: Ski Resort Map.

12. **Save the file and continue to the next exercise.**

 ## CREATE SLICES FROM SELECTIONS

The next step is to divide the file into **slices** (pieces) that can work properly on a Web page; you will then define hyperlink destinations for the main links. For most Web pages you design, each element that needs to link to a different location should become a slice, as should any element that requires unique output options (such as file format).

Illustrator includes three primary options for creating slices: based on guides, based on a selection, and based on a manually defined area.

1. **With** dh site.ai **open, make sure nothing is selected in the file.**
Hide the Rollovers layer and make the Guides layer visible and unlocked.

2. Select the Guides layer, then choose Object>Slice>Create from Guides.

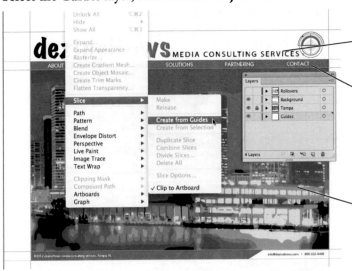

This heading banner will provide a link to the dezineHows home page.

Each button needs to link to a different HTML page.

This area will include the six rollovers, each of which navigates to a different page in the dezineHows site.

Because the original designer used guides to carefully align the different elements of this file, the guides are a perfect choice for beginning to slice the page.

Note:

If you choose Create from Selection, whatever is selected on the artboard will become a custom slice.

Each slice is identified by a small number and icon in the top-left corner.

User-defined slices are identified by darker indicators.

Automatic slices are screened back.

Understanding User and Automatic Slices

Although some slices can be created based on page guides or specific object boundaries, other slices will be easier to manage by simply drawing them manually. The Slice tool allows you to create user slices for any area of the page.

When you define user slices, automatic slices are added as necessary to support the ones you define. Those automatic slices will be named with sequential numbers based on the page name when you export the page. If you want to define a custom file name, link, or other option for a slice, you have to create a user slice instead of an automatic slice.

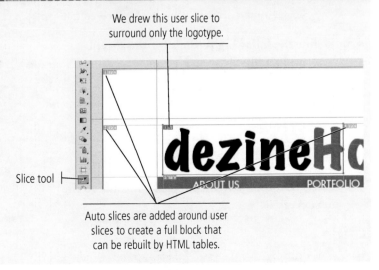

We drew this user slice to surround only the logotype.

Slice tool

Auto slices are added around user slices to create a full block that can be rebuilt by HTML tables.

3. **Choose the Slice Selection tool (nested under the Slice tool in the Tools panel). Click away from the artwork to deselect all slices, and then click the company logo to select only that slice.**

4. **With Slice 03 selected, choose Object>Slice>Slice Options.**

Note:

You can toggle slice numbers and icons on and off by choosing View>Show/Hide Slices.

Selected slice —

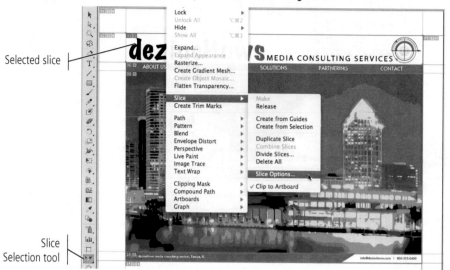

Slice
Selection tool —

For every slice, you can define a number of settings:

- **Name** is the file name that will be used when you save the page or slice for the Web.

- **URL** is the page or file that opens if a user clicks the slice. (Slices don't have to be links; if you don't want a slice to link to something, simply leave the URL field blank.)

- **Target** is the location where the URL opens when you click the slice. Although there are other options available in full-scale HTML development applications such as Dreamweaver, you will primarily use "_self" to open the link in the same window or "_blank" to open the link in a new window. (This field is grayed out until you define a URL.)

- **Message** text appears in the browser's status bar. If you don't type a specific message, the URL link will display.

- **Alt** text appears in place of an image when image display is disabled in the browser, or when a Web page is being read by screen-reader software for a visually impaired user.

- **Background** defines a color to place behind transparent areas of a specific slice.

5. **Define the following settings for the slice:**

   Name: dh_logo

   URL: index.html

   Target: _self

   Message and Alt text:
           dezineHows Media Consulting Services

6. **Click OK, then save the file and continue to the next exercise.**

DIVIDE SLICES

Two areas of the page need to be divided into equal areas: the navigation bar and the main page area. Rather than trying to manually create these slices, you are going to divide the existing slices into equal pieces.

1. **With dh site.ai open, use the Slice Selection tool to click the navigation bar slice.**

2. **Choose Object>Slice>Divide Slices.**

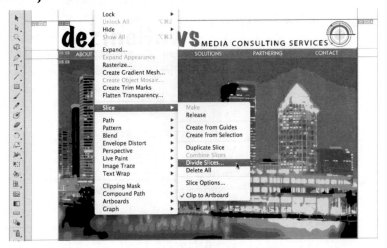

3. **Activate the Preview option in the Divide Slice dialog box and uncheck the Divide Horizontally option.**

   This bar includes five buttons that are distributed horizontally, which means you need to add vertical slices to separate the buttons.

4. **In the Divide Vertically section, type 5 in the Slices Across field.**

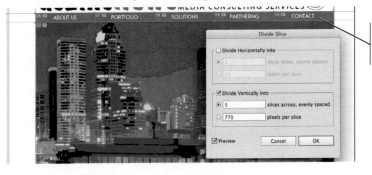

With the Preview option selected, you can see the five slices that will be created.

5. **Click OK to create the new slices.**

6. **Click away from the selected slices to deselect them.**

   You can change the options for only one slice at a time.

7. **Using the Slice Selection tool, click the first button slice, and then choose Object>Slice>Slice Options.**

8. **Define the following options for the slice.**

> Name: about_btn
>
> URL: about.html
>
> Target: _self
>
> Alt: Link to About Us page

9. **Click OK to apply the slice options.**

10. **Using the same method, change the options for the remaining buttons.**

Portfolio button

> Name: portfolio_btn
>
> URL: portfolio.html
>
> Target: _self
>
> Alt: Link to Portfolio page

Solutions button

> Name: solutions_btn
>
> URL: solutions.html
>
> Target: _self
>
> Alt: Link to Custom Solutions page

Partnering button

> Name: partners_btn
>
> URL: partners.html
>
> Target: _self
>
> Alt: Link to Partnering page

Contact button

> Name: contact_btn
>
> URL: mailto:info@dezinehows.com
>
> Alt: Email dezineHows

Note:

Make sure you use the exact names shown here, or the links in existing HTML files will not work properly.

Note:

The mailto: protocol is the proper code format for creating an email link. Do not add a space between the colon and the email address.

11. **Using the Slice Selection tool, select the Tampa illustration slice and choose Object>Slice>Divide Slices.**

12. **With the Preview option active, check the Divide Horizontally option.**

    This area includes three icons across and two down, which means you need to divide this slice in both directions.

13. **Change the Divide Horizontally option to 2, change the Divide Vertically option to 3, and then click OK.**

Note:

You can also create slices of a specific size using the Pixels Per Slice option.

14. **Click away from the slices to deselect them.**

15. **Show the Rollovers layer, and use the following information to individually select and define slice options for the six new slices.**

Public Relations

Name: pr_btn

URL: pr.html

Target: _self

Alt: Link to PR page

Multimedia Development

Name: multimedia_btn

URL: multimedia.html

Target: _self

Alt: Link to Multimedia Development page

Print Graphic Design

Name: print_btn

URL: print.html

Target: _self

Alt: Link to Print Design page

Copywriting

Name: writing_btn

URL: copywriting.html

Target: _self

Alt: Link to Copywriting page

Networking Solutions

Name: networks_btn

URL: networking.html

Target: _self

Alt: Link to Networking Solutions page

Global Communications

Name: communications_btn

URL: communications.html

Target: _self

Alt: Link to Global Communications page

16. **Select the bottom slice and define the following options.**

Name: copyright_bar

URL: mailto:info@dezinehows.com

Alt: Copyright 2012, dezineHows Media Consulting Services

17. **Hide the Rollovers layer, save the file, and continue to the next exercise.**

OPTIMIZE IMAGE SETTINGS AND EXPORT SLICES

After all content has been placed and the slices have been defined, you can safely export the necessary image files for the Web. When you use Illustrator's Save for Web function, only visible content will be included in the resulting slices. Because the Rollovers layer is currently hidden and your navigation buttons are reduced to their basic appearance, the first export process will create all the basic images (the default states of the rollovers).

Note:

You need to export the page twice to produce all the necessary image files (the basic slices and the rollover slices).

1. **With dh site.ai open, make sure nothing is selected in the file and then choose File>Save for Web.**

   The Save for Web dialog box defaults to show the optimized version of the image. You can use the tabs at the top of the preview to show the original image or split the window into two panes (each pane can have different settings for experimentation).

2. **Using the Slice Selection tool, click the top-left illustration slice (Slice 12) in the main page area.**

   The large space around the page objects is the result of Illustrator's auto-slicing, based on the defined artboard area. These slices will be removed in the Web-design application when the final pages are assembled.

   Illustrator defaults to export slices using the GIF format, which is appropriate for vector art with areas of flat color (such as this logo).

Note:

The tools in the Save for Web dialog box serve the same purpose as the related tools in the main interface.

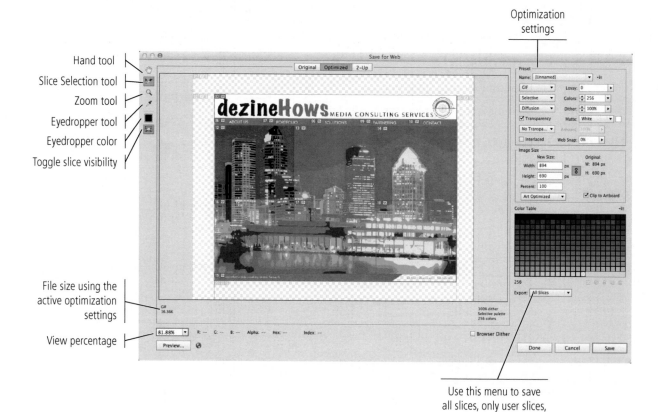

Optimization settings

Hand tool
Slice Selection tool
Zoom tool
Eyedropper tool
Eyedropper color
Toggle slice visibility

File size using the active optimization settings

View percentage

Use this menu to save all slices, only user slices, or only selected slices.

When optimizing files for the Web, the format you use affects the display of the colors in the exported file; it also dictates compression and transparency capabilities. The Save for Web dialog box allows you to save images or slices in a number of formats (JPEG, GIF, PNG-8, or PNG-24), and define options specific to the format you choose.

JPEG

JPEG is the format of choice for continuous-tone images (such as photos) since it can store up to 24-bit color. The JPEG format compresses information using lossy compression, which means information is lost in the resulting file. It is not well suited for text or graphics, since its compression method introduces a blurring effect to the graphics.

You can choose a predefined compression level (Low, Medium, High, Very High, or Maximum) or define a specific quality percentage. These choices refer to the quality of the resulting image, not the amount of compression applied; the higher quality you want, the less compression you should apply.

- The **Optimized** check box creates an enhanced JPEG with a slightly smaller file size. Some older browsers don't support this feature.
- The **Progressive** option allows the image to appear in stages as more data downloads; this option is only available if the Optimized check box is selected.
- The **Blur** option applies a Gaussian blur to the exported image, which allows higher compression without destroying the image.
- The **ICC Profile** preserves the profile of the image in the exported file.
- The **Matte** option defines a color for any pixels that were transparent in the original image. The JPEG format does not support transparency.

PNG-8 and PNG-24

PNG is another format used for Web graphics and images. Two versions of the format — PNG-8 and PNG-24 — support 8-bit and 24-bit color respectively. For the PNG-8 format, the options are the same as for the GIF format, except that PNG-8 files cannot be compressed. PNG-24 can support continuous-tone color as well as transparency.

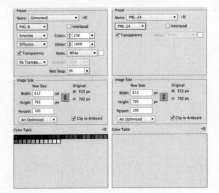

GIF

GIF is an 8-bit format typically used for graphics and artwork that don't have a large range of color. It is ideally suited for files with large areas of solid color, but it is ill suited for continuous-tone images that have subtle color variations.

When you save a file in the GIF format, all the colors are mapped to a color table (called **indexed color**). Indexed color is an 8-bit color model in which the specific 256 values are based on the colors in the image. You can remap the indexed colors using a number of options:

- **Perceptual** gives priority to colors to which the human eye is more sensitive.
- **Selective** is similar to Perceptual, but favors broad areas of color. This usually produces the best results.
- **Adaptive** samples colors appearing most commonly in the image.
- **Restrictive (Web)** uses a standard 216-color Web-safe color table. This option can result in drastic color shift.

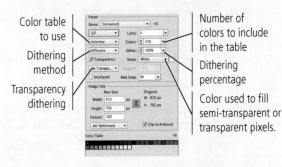

The **Lossy** option reduces file size by selectively discarding data; higher settings result in more data being discarded.

The **Dithering Method** option applies **dithering**, which blends two available colors to simulate additional colors. A higher dithering percentage creates the appearance of more colors and more detail, but can also increase the file size.

The **Transparency** and **Matte** options determine how transparent pixels are treated. If Transparency is checked, semi-transparent pixels blend into the defined Matte color.

The **Transparency Dithering** option allows you to dither transparency in a similar manner as dithering colors.

The **Interlace** option allows the image to display in stages as more data downloads (similar to progressive JPEG files).

The **Web Snap** option specifies a tolerance level for shifting colors to the closest Web palette equivalents.

3. **Choose JPEG in the Format menu, and choose Medium in the Compression Quality menu.**

Because this image is based on a photograph and does not require transparency, the JPEG format might be a better choice than the default GIF format.

Define Medium quality/compression.

Optimized preview of the selected slice

File size

4. **Change all six of the Tampa slices to the JPEG format with Medium compression quality.**

5. **Double-click the copyright slice at the bottom to open the Slice Options dialog box.**

6. **At the bottom of the dialog box, open the Background Color menu and choose White from the menu. Click OK to apply the change.**

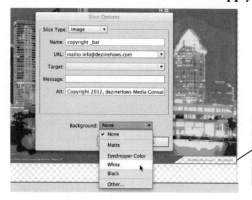

You need to change the background color of this slice so the page background doesn't show through the area.

7. **In the options for that slice, uncheck the Transparency option.**

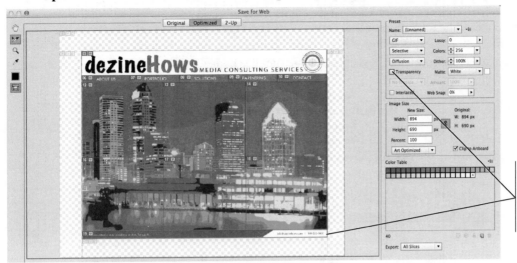

When Transparency is turned off for this slice, the background area is white (as you defined in Step 6).

8. **Click the Save button. Navigate to your WIP>Consulting>site_files folder as the target location, then click Save.**

> **Note:**
>
> *Clicking Done in the Save for Web dialog box closes the dialog box and saves your slice optimization settings. Clicking Cancel closes the dialog box without saving your choices.*

9. **On your desktop, review the contents of your WIP>Consulting>site_files folder.**

The Save for Web function automatically creates an **images** folder, where all the slices are placed. The file names you defined are used for all of the user-defined slices. Auto-slices are named based on the original file name and the number of the slice; a hyphen replaces the space in the original file name.

> **Note:**
>
> *Illustrator automatically replaces spaces in file names with hyphens.*

10. **Save the Illustrator file and continue to the next exercise.**

Using the Save for Web dialog box saves your image slices, but does not save your work in the native Illustrator file. You have to save the Illustrator file separately after the HTML and images have been exported.

CREATE THE ROLLOVER IMAGES

The final step is to create the rollover images, which will be combined in the final HTML files by the Dreamweaver developer. The artwork is already complete, so you simply have to make the correct elements visible, change the slice names, and save the additional images into your WIP folder.

1. With **dh site.ai** open, show the Rollovers layer.

2. Using the Selection tool, select all five type objects in the horizontal navigation bar and apply the Text Over State graphic style.

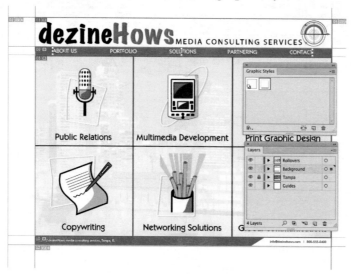

3. Choose File>Save for Web.

4. Using the Slice Selection tool in the Save for Web dialog box, double-click the About Us slice to open the Slice Options dialog box for that slice.

5. In the Name field, change the letters "btn" to **over**. Click OK to make the change.

6. Repeat Steps 4–5 for all of the remaining slices in the navigation bar, and for the six slices that make up the Tampa illustration in the main page area.

7. **Click Save. If necessary, navigate to the WIP>Consulting>site_files folder.**

8. **Click Save. When you see the Replace Files dialog box, click Replace.**

This dialog box shows that some slices already exist in the location where you are saving the files; these are the slices you created when you exported the first time. Because these slices haven't changed, you can safely overwrite the original slices with the new versions.

9. **On your desktop, review the contents of your WIP>Consulting>site_files folder.**

You now have all the necessary pieces to hand off to the Web designer.

10. **Save the Illustrator file and close it.**

fill in the blank

1. Choosing the _____ option in the Control panel Preview menu reveals the vector objects that result from the Image Trace function.

2. You can check the _____ option in the Recolor Artwork dialog box to reflect color changes in selected objects.

3. If the _____ option in the Recolor Artwork dialog box is active, you can make universal changes (such as brightness) to all colors in a group.

4. The _____ tool can be used to apply color swatches from selected groups based on overlapping areas rather than entire vector objects.

5. Choosing the _____ option in the Appearance panel removes applied effects and resets an object to only its fill and stroke.

6. Use the _____ protocol at the beginning of a link target to create a link that opens a pre-addressed email message.

7. When defining slice settings, the _____ option defines the file that should open when a user clicks that slice.

8. The _____ tool is used to manually cut apart a page into smaller pieces for Web delivery.

9. When setting image optimization settings in the Save For Web dialog box, the _____ format allows lossy compression and does not support transparency; it is best used for photos.

10. The _____ format supports transparency but not a large number of colors; it is best used for artwork or graphics with large areas of solid color.

short answer

1. Briefly explain the differences between the JPEG, GIF, and PNG formats for exporting Web images.

2. Briefly explain two advantages of designing a Web site interface in Illustrator.

3. Briefly explain two disadvantages of designing a Web site interface in Illustrator.

Portfolio Builder Project

Use what you learned in this project to complete the following freeform exercise.
Carefully read the art director and client comments, then create your own design to meet the needs of the project.
Use the space below to sketch ideas; when finished, write a brief explanation of your reasoning behind your final design.

art director comments

Every professional designer needs a portfolio of their work. If you have completed the projects in this book, you should now have a number of different examples to show off your skills using Illustrator CS6.

The eight projects in this book were specifically designed to include a broad range of *types* of projects; your portfolio should use the same principle.

client comments

For this project, you are your own client. Using the following suggestions, gather your best work and create printed and digital versions of your portfolio:

❏ Include as many different types of work as possible.

❏ Print clean copies of each finished piece that you want to include.

❏ For each example in your portfolio, write a brief (one- or two-paragraph) synopsis of the project. Explain the purpose of the piece, as well as your role in the creative and production process.

❏ Design a personal promotion brochure — create a layout that highlights your technical skills and reflects your personal style.

❏ Create a PDF version of your portfolio so you can send your portfolio via email, post it on job sites, and keep it with you on a flash drive at all times — you never know when you might meet a potential employer.

project justification

The Image Trace and Live Color options extend Illustrator's basic drawing tools, allowing you to create complex vector graphics with a degree of detail that would be extremely difficult to create otherwise. The paint-by-numbers effect that you created from the Tampa photo would require significant time and skill to create from scratch. Consolidating color swatches into groups provides an easy way to make color changes to existing artwork, whether it was created by Image Trace or using conventional drawing tools.

Although many developers use dedicated Web-design software like Adobe Dreamweaver to build sophisticated Web sites, the images for those sites have to come from somewhere. It is not uncommon for a designer to build the "look and feel" of a site in Illustrator, then slice and export the pieces so the developer can reassemble them in the Web-design application.

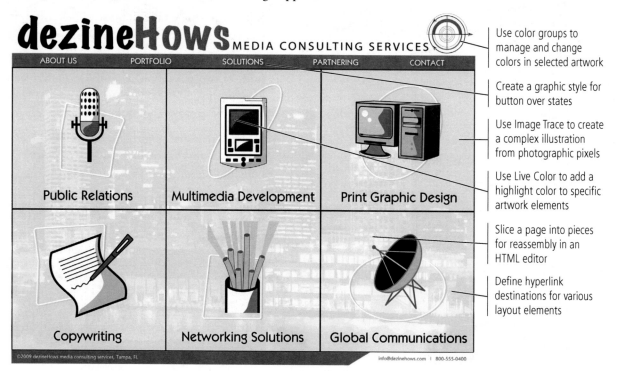

Use color groups to manage and change colors in selected artwork

Create a graphic style for button over states

Use Image Trace to create a complex illustration from photographic pixels

Use Live Color to add a highlight color to specific artwork elements

Slice a page into pieces for reassembly in an HTML editor

Define hyperlink destinations for various layout elements

Index